To the High, Mighty, and most Hopeful Prince, Charles Philip Arthur George, Prince of Wales, the second joy and hope of our times, the Eldest Son and Heir apparent to our dread Sovereign Queen Elizabeth's most puissant Majesty, his Highness's most unworthy servant dedicates all his labours, and wishes all felicity.

CW01501879

The Rhetoric of Exemplarity
in Early Modern England

The Rhetoric of Exemplarity in Early Modern England

MICHAEL ULLYOT

OXFORD
UNIVERSITY PRESS

UNIVERSITY PRESS

Great Clarendon Street, Oxford, OX2 6DP,
United Kingdom

Oxford University Press is a department of the University of Oxford.
It furthers the University's objective of excellence in research, scholarship,
and education by publishing worldwide. Oxford is a registered trade mark of
Oxford University Press in the UK and in certain other countries

© Michael Ullyot 2022

The moral rights of the author have been asserted

First Edition published in 2022

Impression: 1

Published in the United States of America by Oxford University Press
198 Madison Avenue, New York, NY 10016, United States of America

British Library Cataloguing in Publication Data
Data available

Library of Congress Control Number: 2021946347

ISBN 978–0–19–284933–5

DOI: 10.1093/oso/9780192849335.001.0001

Printed and bound by
CPI Group (UK) Ltd, Croydon, CR0 4YY

'[T]he sea of examples hath no bottome.'

Sir Walter Ralegh, *History of the World* (1614)

Acknowledgements

My reading of Thomas Heywood's *Fvnerall Elegie* (1613) at the Huntington Library laid the imaginative groundplot of this book in 2000. Since then I have incurred an embarrassment of advice and support: above all from Noreen Humble, author of *Xenophon of Athens: A Socratic on Sparta* (Cambridge University Press, 2021); but also from Bill Sherman and Patricia Parker at the Folger Shakespeare Library; from Gavin Alexander, Christopher Burlinson, Lauren Kassell, Aysha Pollnitz, Richard Serjeantson, and Andrew Taylor at the University of Cambridge; from my doctoral supervisor David Galbraith at the University of Toronto, along with Rob Carson, Alexandra Gillespie, Elizabeth D. Harvey, Sandy Johnston, Ian Lancashire, David Lawrence, Nancy Lindheim, Randall McLeod, Scott Schofield, Paul Stevens, and Andrew Wallace; from Elizabeth Hanson at Queen's University, Kingston; from my postdoctoral supervisor David Norbrook, then Merton Professor of English Literature at the University of Oxford, along with Katherine Duncan-Jones, Laurie Maguire, Richard McCabe, the late Kevin Sharpe, and Bart van Es; from Catharine MacLeod at the National Portrait Gallery; from Peter Mack and Teresa Grant Taylor at the University of Warwick; from Robert Yorke at the College of Arms; and from my research assistants Jasmine Elliot, Sarah Hertz, Sarah Hill, Kirsten Inglis, Jess Nicol, and Kate O'Neill at the University of Calgary. Thanks to Lorna Hutson and Robert Stagg, a Plumer Visiting Fellowship at the Centre for Early Modern Studies and Saint Anne's College, Oxford, afforded me time to complete the manuscript. At the press Ellie Collins, Karen Raith, and two marvellous anonymous readers offered timely, judicious advice. For sharing unpublished research I am grateful to Peter W. M. Blayney (on *Basilicon Doron*); to James Doelman (on Henry's elegies); and to David Gunby (on John Webster's *A Monvmental Colvmne*).

Along with the Huntington and Folger libraries, the institutions and schemes that funded this research include: the Department of English at the University of Toronto; the Centre for Reformation and Renaissance Studies at the University of Victoria College, Toronto; the Ontario Graduate Scholarship Program; the Social Sciences and Humanities Research Council of Canada; the Department of English and Comparative Literature at Columbia University; the Renaissance Society of America; the Faculty of English and Linacre College at the University of Oxford; and the Faculty of Humanities, Faculty of Arts, Department of English, and University Research Grants Committee at the University of Calgary.

I am grateful to the following for permission to reprint excerpts from previously published work herein: 'Spenser and the Matter of Poetry' from *Spenser Studies: A Renaissance Poetry Annual* 27 (2012), 77–96 in Chapter 2; 'James's Reception and Henry's Receptivity: Reading *Basilicon Doron* after 1603,' from *Prince Henry Revived: Image and Exemplarity in Early Modern England*, ed. Timothy V. Wilks (London: Paul Holberton, 2007), 65–84, in Chapter 3; 'The Life Abridged: Exemplarity, Biography, and the Problem of Metonymy' from *The Journal of the Northern Renaissance* 3:1 (2011), 58-81, in Chapter 5; and 'Early Modern Biography, New Historicism, and the Rhetoric of Anecdotes' from *Clio: A Journal of Literature, History, and the Philosophy of History* 40:3 (2011), 307–329 in the Conclusion.

Colleagues and friends who shaped this book with insights, advice, and support are the late Jim Carscallen, Simon Cauchi, Crystal Chokshi, Andrew Escobedo, Harper Dafforn, Stefania Forlini, Hugh Gazzard, Faye Halpern, Paul Hammer, Heather Hirschfeld, David Scott Kastan, Scott Lucas, Margaret MacMillan, Brian Nance, Michelle O'Callaghan, Anne Lake Prescott, Elizabeth Sauer, Monica Sommerville, Malcolm Smuts, Chloe Wheatley, Jerry Wayne Wilkinson, Tim Wilks, and Janet Wilson. To my parents, G. Les E. Ullyot and Suzanne Ullyot, I owe my first bookshelf and every opportunity since to expand it. To my daughters, Sabine and Leah, here's one more book for your own shelves.

Contents

List of Figures

A Word on Typography

The lion's share of my evidence in this study is from early printed books. Quotations faithfully reproduce their variable typographic conventions of emphasis, capitalization, punctuation, and orthographical substitution—including i/j, u/v, vv/w, and italics or roman type.

Introduction

Historicizing Exemplarity

Literary criticism is exemplary rhetoric. Critics try to persuade readers of their characterizations of texts through exemplary excerpts. They only succeed if those excerpts are really exemplary, not aberrations from the surrounding texts' features—if they exhibit in a condensed form qualities of texts that are praiseworthy or blameworthy.[1] Defending or accusing texts is the critic's aim, making them a judicial rhetorician in Aristotle's three-part division of rhetoric.[2]

I use judicial rhetoric in this study of occasional texts from the late sixteenth and early seventeenth centuries. The texts themselves use deliberative rhetoric to exhort or dissuade their readers. Judicial rhetoric is oriented toward the past, deliberative rhetoric toward the future; usually deliberative rhetoric idealizes exemplary subjects to impart moral lessons, to encourage its object (the reader) to imitate or avoid the subject's behaviour. All of the texts in this study use biographical and experiential anecdotes—exemplars—from varied sources: classical and biblical, distant and recent, fabulated and factual. Whatever their origin or nature, exemplars serve what Harry Berger calls rhetoric's transactional function. Exemplarity is the trope that transacts deliberative rhetoric's persuasion to imitate or avoid.[3]

My rhetoric, if it succeeds, will persuade you that ethical imitation is untenable. Exemplarity's objects are bound to fail because they are contingent, whereas

---

[1] John D. Lyons, *Exemplum: The Rhetoric of Example in Early Modern France and Italy* (Princeton: Princeton University Press, 1989), 3–4. '[T]he critical text, to the extent that it claims some status as theoretical statement, fabricates examples as part of its own validation. The more literary criticism aspires to exceed paraphrase, the more it generates examples. Paraphrase would tell us simply what the object text says. Criticism attempts to locate the text within various larger descriptive categories, whether these be tropological patterns, literary schools or styles, socio-historical movements, ideologies, generative poetic models, philosophical doctrines, or other categories. When the literary text is studied in view of achieving such broader description, the critical text will subsume the literary text as example' (4).

[2] Aristotle's three branches of rhetoric are deliberative, seeking to encourage or dissuade; judicial, to accuse or defend; and epideictic, to praise or blame (Richard Lanham, *A Handlist of Rhetorical Terms* (Berkeley-Los Angeles: University of California Press, 1991), 164–5).

[3] Berger writes, 'the tropological division consisted of the art of adapting linguistic expression . . . to the social and dialectal organization of speech'; whereas '[t]he transactional division consists in mastering the strategies of linguistic communication, the relations of senders to receivers' ('Narrative as Rhetoric in *the Faerie Queene*.' *English Literary Renaissance* 21, no. 1 (1991): 5, 6).

The Rhetoric of Exemplarity in Early Modern England. Michael Ullyot, Oxford University Press. © Michael Ullyot 2022. DOI: 10.1093/oso/9780192849335.003.0001

exemplarity's subjects are idealized. The reader of an occasional text operates in a historical moment, with a fallible body, amid circumstances that militate against imitating some incongruous exemplar. Don Quixote fails to imitate Amadis of Gaul largely because his Golden Age La Mancha is distant from Amadis's fourteenth-century conditions. Cervantes's mock knight illustrates an incongruity that rhetoricians of exemplarity try to mitigate. They adapt examples like Amadis to the conditions of their reception by distilling their virtues of courage and service. Otherwise positive exemplarity is recurrently a story of objects failing to replicate subjects' performances of such virtues.

Three decades ago, John D. Lyons and Timothy Hampton established two foci for scholars of early modern exemplarity: on positive, aspirational examples rather than negative, cautionary ones; and on the uses of this rhetoric in fictional, devotional, and theatrical genres like epic, homily, tragedy, *roman*, scripture, and exegesis.[4] Since then, François Rigolot has focused on essays,[5] and critics of English literary exemplarity have focused on persuasion, historiography, and nationhood in Shakespearean drama,[6] or vernacular uses of rhetoric in Spenser and Sidney.[7] Aside from sermons, most occasional genres have been peripheral to scholarship on this rhetoric. And yet as rhetoric, exemplarity is always occasional—always contingent on the moment of its delivery and reception, when objects imitate or avoid subjects.[8]

I historicize this rhetoric to illustrate my thesis that avoiding cautionary examples is far easier than imitating aspirational ones. More bluntly, it is the only kind of exemplarity that works in practice. An unacknowledged tension at the core of exemplary rhetoric is the incommensurability of its subjects and its objects. Consider Hampton's authoritative definition of its operation: 'a contingent past activity is raised to a momentary universality that makes

---

[4] See Lyons, *Exemplum*; Timothy Hampton, *Writing from History: The Rhetoric of Exemplarity in Renaissance Literature* (Ithaca: Cornell University Press, 1990); and Hampton, 'Examples, Stories, and Subjects in *Don Quixote* and the *Heptameron*.' *Journal of the History of Ideas* 59, no. 4 (1998): 597–611. For theoretical studies in later rhetoric see Alexander Gelley, ed. *Unruly Examples: On the Rhetoric of Exemplarity* (Stanford: Stanford University Press, 1995).

[5] Francois Rigolot, 'The Renaissance Crisis of Exemplarity.' *Journal of the History of Ideas* 59, no. 4 (1998): 557–63; and 'Problematizing Renaissance Exemplarity: The Inward Turn of Dialogue from Petrarch to Montaigne.' In *Printed Voices: The Renaissance Culture of Dialogue*, ed. Dorothea Heitsch (Toronto: University of Toronto Press, 2004), 3–24.

[6] Joel B. Altman, *The Improbability of Othello: Rhetorical Anthropology and Shakespearean Selfhood* (Chicago: University of Chicago Press, 2010); Peter Mack, *Reading and Rhetoric in Montaigne and Shakespeare* (London: Bloomsbury Academic, 2010); and Maria Del Sapio Garbero, ed. *Identity, Otherness and Empire in Shakespeare's Rome* (Farnham: Ashgate, 2009).

[7] Jenny C. Mann, *Outlaw Rhetoric: Figuring Vernacular Eloquence in Shakespeare's England* (Ithaca: Cornell University Press, 2012).

[8] A rare counter-example is Alison K. Frazier's study of exemplarity in Italian Renaissance life-writing, specifically *vitae* of philosophers, princes, and saints in the history of moral philosophy ('Biography as a Genre of Moral Philosophy.' In *Rethinking Virtue, Reforming Society: New Directions in Renaissance Ethics, c.1350–c.1650*, ed. David A. Lines and Sabrina Ebbersmeyer (Turnhout: Brepols, 2013), 215–40).

discernible its value for the present' while deliberately concealing the activity's contingencies.[9] Exemplarity relies on ahistorical treatments of its subjects, on the belief that narrating them in digestible and emotive parcels is the pathway to persuasion. But exemplarity's objects are always historical, operating in real or fictional conditions removed from exemplarity's subjects.[10] If their 'value for the present' is a cautionary lesson, so much the better. If it is a positive exhortation, however, aspirations to follow their example are doubtful. Occasional texts, whose objects explicitly inhabit moments in history, exacerbate exemplary rhetoric's endemic problem of incommensurate subjects.

Literary criticism also describes incommensurate subjects, distant texts whose complexity is irreducible to exemplary summary. But its prevailing rhetorical aim is judicial, so at worst it will mislead judgements, not actions. It never aims to be the final word on its texts, rather leaving its readings and judgements open to contestation. Criticism is contingent on ready evidence from known sources, so it is provisional when methodologically self-aware. It is susceptible to emergent counter-evidence or the subtler qualifications of alternate evidence. Its judgements are valuable when they serve as points of departure. Accordingly, in this study of exemplary rhetoric in late Elizabethan and Jacobean occasional texts I aim to provoke readers to respond with judgements that qualify my own.

Exemplarity in Occasional Texts

Two occasional poems addressed to Henry, Prince of Wales (1594–1612) before and after his death illustrate the dichotomy between deliberative predictions and judicial descriptions. The first seeks to provoke the Prince's self-awareness of his future legacy and representations, which is often an implicit subtext of positive exemplarity. The poet George Chapman had in 1598 dedicated both *Seaven Bookes of the Iliades* and *Achilles Shield* to Robert Devereux, second Earl of Essex (1565–1601), before Essex's disgrace and execution led Chapman to dedicate his *Homer Prince of Poets... in twelve Bookes of his Iliads* (1609) to Prince Henry, followed by the complete *Iliads of Homer Prince of Poets* (1611). This time, Chapman hoped for better luck with his choice of patron.[11] Henry was heir to King James I, and all signs pointed to his auspicious future.

---

[9] Hampton, *Writing from History*, 11.

[10] For a similarly historicist study how of medieval hagiography 'inevitably registers the differences between the sacred past and the devotional present, even as it assumes a coherent religious tradition linking them,' see Catherine Sanok, *Her Life Historical: Exemplarity and Female Saints' Lives in Late Medieval England* (Philadelphia: University of Pennsylvania Press, 2007), p. x.

[11] These hopes, too, were false. 'No poet was ever so unlucky in his choice of patrons' (Rolf Soellner, 'Chapman's Caesar and Pompey and the Fortunes of Prince Henry.' *Medieval and Renaissance Drama in England* 2 (1985): 138).

Chapman's dedicatory poem focuses less on Homer's *Iliad* than on its most famous reader, Alexander the Great, and on his admiration for Achilles. This admiration began when Alexander read Homer, where he found

> *him* reviv'd
> For whose life Alexander would have given
> One of his kingdomes: who (as sent from heaven,
> And thinking well that so divine a creature
> Would never more enrich the race of Nature)
> Kept as his Crowne his workes, and thought them still
> His Angels, in all power to rule his will;
> And would affirme that Homers poesie
> Did more advance his Asian victorie
> Than all his Armies.

Chapman gives little credit to Alexander's armies, and all to his reading. Chapman uses Alexander to bid for continued patronage, urging Henry to cultivate poets capable of offering him a similarly permanent memorial:

> O! tis wondrous much
> (Though nothing prisde) that the right vertuous touch
> Of a well-written soule to vertue moves.
> Nor have we soules to purpose if their loves
> Of fitting objects be not so inflam'd.[12]

This 'vertuous touch' of the reader's soul by 'a well written soule' insinuates Chapman's poetry into a causal relationship with Henry's anticipated virtues. (In Chapman's words, Achilles similarly mourns Patroclus as 'A virtuous soule.'[13]) If Henry follows Alexander and allows this text 'to rule his will,' Achilles' 'divine' example will inspire his own worldly conquests.

Alexander is Chapman's ideal exemplar for his dedication's twin purposes: both to praise Henry's heroism by comparing him to a great hero, and to secure Henry's patronage by suggesting that heroic acts deserve fitting representations. 'Who, but for Homer, would ever have heard of Achilles?' as Keith Thomas asks. 'What better way, therefore, of ensuring lasting fame than by becoming the patron of a poet? Or so the poets claimed.'[14] Henry may or may not be like Alexander, in

---

[12] George Chapman, *The Iliad, Chapman's Homer*, Bollingen Series XLI, ed. Allardyce Nicoll (Princeton: Princeton University Press, 1956), 3–4, ll. 20–9, 29–33.

[13] Chapman, *Iliad*, 454, 23.8.

[14] Keith Thomas, *The Ends of Life: Roads to Fulfilment in Early Modern England* (Oxford: Oxford University Press, 2009), 253. 'The desire to be posthumously remembered was a basic motive for literary patronage. Few books were published without a dedicatory eulogy of their sponsor; and the creation of fame was a primary object of the literary endeavour' (253).

the heroic sense. But he can certainly be like Alexander in the self-conscious sense, the aspirational reader feeling biographical envy. This envy reflects well on Chapman, who offers Henry both the model of heroism and the promise of fame, should Henry patronize the right poets. Rhetoric can provoke actions, but actions can provoke rhetoric in turn.

I call this mutually reinforcing process the exemplary cycle: patrons' actions and writers' rhetoric, spurring new actions worthy of new rhetoric, in a sort of recursive perpetual-motion machine. Like any cycle, its beginning is indeterminate—but let us say that the process starts with a rhetorician's effort to influence an object, and continues or ends with the object either following or ignoring that influence. Any number of reasons could determine why a reader like Henry might follow or ignore the influence of a rhetorician like Chapman, but for exemplarity to succeed (i.e. to dissuade or encourage behaviour), it must operate in both its object (Henry) and its rhetorician (Chapman). That is because the rhetoric of exemplarity has a bifold structure: it is both a rhetorician's effort to influence, and a reader's receptivity to being influenced. (This mutual dependency informs the three types of decorum on which exemplarity depends, which I define below.)

Yet receptivity to influence is inert if the reader is unable to act on that influence. The exemplary cycle rotates through alternating actions, rhetoric, and new actions only if the audience is capable of acting. But Henry died within a year of Chapman's dedication. William Drummond wrote him an elegy, *Teares on the death of Meliades* (1612), lamenting Henry's loss in terms that indirectly respond to Chapman's lost Homeric biography:

> A booke had beene of thy illustrous deedes.
> So to their nephewes aged Syres had told
> The high exploits perform'd by thee of olde;
> Townes raz'd, and rais'd, victorious, vanquish'd bands,
> Fierce Tyrants flying, foyl'd, kild by thy hands.
> And in deare Arras, Virgins faire had wrought
> The Bayes and Trophees to thy countrie brought:
> While some great *Homer* imping wings to fame,
> Deafe *Nilus* dwellers had made heare thy name.[15]

Citing the virgins and poets who might have recounted these 'illustrous deedes,' Drummond concedes that his elegy is a poor substitute for the Homeric epics that Henry's life ought to have inspired. Drummond uses a lost narrative as the index

---

[15] *Death of Meliades* (1613), sig. A2v. Cicero compares the deafening roar of the Nile (or 'dull-making cataract of Nilus,' in Philip Sidney's phrase) to man's deafness to the music of the spheres (Sidney, *A Defence of Poetry* (1595). In *English Renaissance Literary Criticism*, ed. Brian Vickers. (Oxford: Clarendon Press, 1999), 390 n. 230).

of a lost life, using the subjunctive tense ('had beene,' 'had wrought,' 'had made') to weigh the loss of Henry's unwritten biography.

Henry's death bespeaks the necessity of historicizing exemplary rhetoric. It is necessary because all rhetoric is localized in the time and place of its delivery and reception. It is particularly necessary for positive exemplarity because repeating past successes while avoiding past failures is doubly difficult. Consider Chapman's rhetoric. It typifies positive exemplarity's ethical injunctions: be like this 'fitting object' Alexander in this respect, and you (Henry) will implicitly earn a biography fit for Achilles, while you avoid Alexander's envy of Achilles. Not only was Henry incapable of fulfilling this advice, he was incapable of fulfilling any advice whatsoever. His death undermined Chapman's prescriptive, positive rhetoric and earned Drummond's descriptive, negative rhetoric.

Prescriptive rhetoric takes risks that descriptive rhetoric avoids. I make that distinction because both are characteristic of occasional texts, but have different orientations: prescriptive rhetoric tries to persuade readers to do something, while descriptive rhetoric tries to persuade them to believe something about what has already been done.[16] Prescriptive rhetoric is predictive, descriptive rhetoric retrospective. While both address their audiences, descriptive rhetoric focuses more squarely on its occasion. Both Chapman's dedication and Drummond's elegy, in this case, are occasional texts—a category that includes any text that transparently addresses an historical and rhetorical moment.

My definition of occasional texts is broader than O. B. Hardison's, which distinguishes them from more transcendent genres like epics because they are explicitly 'begotten by a real and contemporary event.' An epic romance like Edmund Spenser's *Faerie Queene*, according to Hardison's formula, centres on idealized experiences in ahistorical settings 'removed from everyday life.'[17] An occasional poem like Spenser's *Epithalamion* may use mythological allusions to link its subject to similarly ineffable events, but its subject remains the event of the poet's marriage. Hardison's definition is inadequate to the prescriptive rhetoric of a dedication like Chapman's, which directly addresses a specific reader to provoke a specific interpretation. It is, in Hardison's terms, 'begotten' by an occasion in time, the public presentation of a book to a potential reader and patron. Rather than the categorical term 'occasional text,' however, it is more useful to describe a given text's historicity as a mode that some texts adopt more or less overtly.

---

[16] Within this dichotomy, deliberative rhetoric is prescriptive, while both judicial and epideictic rhetoric are descriptive.

[17] O. B. Hardison, *The Enduring Monument: A Study of the Idea of Praise in Renaissance Literary Theory and Practice* (Chapel Hill: University of North Carolina Press, 1962), 108. This landmark study of early modern eulogy divides epics from occasional texts along a spectrum from the transcendent to the quotidian. The term 'epic romance' owes to Colin Burrow, *Epic Romance: Homer to Milton* (Oxford: Clarendon Press, 1993); see my introduction to Ch. 2 for a definition. On more expansive definitions of 'occasion' after the seventeenth century, beyond public events to mental experiences, see John Carroll Dolan, *Poetic Occasion from Milton to Wordsworth* (Basingstoke: Palgrave Macmillan, 2000).

To rephrase George Orwell: all texts are occasional, but some are more occasional than others.

Among the more explicitly occasional texts are elegies, epithalamia, and panegyrics: predicated on descriptions of events, but with rhetorical aims to induce praise, blame, or other judgements through selective emphases. Their authors often overlay descriptions of an event with allusions, citations, metaphors, similes, and other figurations of its valent meanings, positive or negative.[18] This is a tension within the occasional mode: its author takes an event as their subject, and must reflect it back to itself—so those who experienced it will recognize what they experienced. But the author must also represent its more momentous origins, precedents, and effects. Both Spenser's *Astrophel* elegy for Philip Sidney, for instance, and Arthur Gorges's *The Olympian Catastrophe* for Henry attribute their deaths to supernatural causes. They overlay the bare facts of events with fictions positing them as more momentous than contemporaneous witnesses could recognize.

Texts in this occasional mode, including Chapman's dedication, are an ideal object for studies of exemplarity. By reflecting the historicity of their origins and their reception, and by contrasting with other records of their subjects and their readers, occasional texts reveal just how rhetorical exemplarity is—how different from lived experience, for example. Historicizing exemplarity reveals whether its rhetoric is solid or hollow. In cases of positive exhortation like Chapman's use of Alexander, Henry's experience suggests how difficult it is to replicate past successes. His failure to meet Chapman's expectations suggests that there is something about Henry or his exemplar Alexander that is unsuited to the other, something indecorous in the very comparison. If it is uncharitable to describe Henry's death as a lapse of decorum, an unsuitable response, then might we feel better describing Chapman's choice of Alexander as inadvertently and circumstantially indecorous? I pose the question because exemplarity, like all rhetoric, is predicated on decorum—but as deliberative rhetoric that induces or dissuades conduct based on examples, exemplarity depends on both of decorum's aesthetic and ethical meanings. My task now is to account for those two meanings, to apply them to the exemplary cycle of rhetoric and actions, and to address how lapses of decorum propagate through my argument that positive exemplarity is incommensurable with experience.

Varieties of Decorum

In a classic definition of decorum, J. F. D'Alton assigns it the aesthetic and ethical meanings that I adopt. Decorum's meaning was

---

[18] See Jacques Lezra, *Unspeakable Subjects: The Genealogy of the Event in Early Modern Europe* (Stanford: Stanford University Press, 1997).

primarily an aesthetic one, rooted in man's sense of the order and harmony that constitute the beauty of the visible Universe, but the concept soon came to be applied to the sphere of human conduct, and...was made the norm to guide men in the various duties of their lives.[19]

Hanna H. Gray similarly uses both stylistic and ethical terms to define decorum:

the idea of always speaking appropriately, of suiting style and manner to subject, aim, and audience is treated as the exact analogue of behaving with decorum, of choosing the actions and responses which are best in harmony with and most appropriate to individual character and principles on the one hand, the nature of circumstances on the other.[20]

Ethical exemplarity provokes behavioural change, of the sort that extends beyond ornamental, extrinsic style; because the change must originate from within, I substitute 'ethical' for D'Alton and Gray's terms related to conduct and behaviour. I am more preoccupied in this study with rhetoric's effects on inward morals than on aesthetic appearances, because ethical exemplarity succeeds only by altering its objects' morals. Accordingly, I use 'ethical' to describe rhetoricians' principles and motives, and 'moral' to describe individuals' inner motives and impulses.

Returning to Berger's terms, exemplarity is transactional rather than merely tropological; the rhetorician describes subjects that motivate the object to alter their behaviour in ways that are more ethical than stylistic. Outward conduct is easier to historicize than inward motives, however, so my argument is as concerned with ethics as it is with aesthetics. It is equally concerned with the decorum that governs those social rules that signal class divisions. Both rhetoricians and their objects follow social rules, informed by their surroundings. As Cicero and Aristotle define decorum in implicitly social terms, their early modern admirers— all men acutely aware of class distinctions—used the concept to reinforce the values of a dominant social class.[21] Those orators who could imitate the habits,

---

[19] J. F. D'Alton, *Roman Literary Theory and Criticism: A Study in Tendencies* (London: Longman, 1931), 115.

[20] Hanna H. Gray, 'Renaissance Humanism: The Pursuit of Eloquence.' *Journal of the History of Ideas* 24 (1963): 506.

[21] Wayne A. Rebhorn interprets the treatises of Thomas Wilson (1560), George Puttenham (1589), and Antoine Furetiere (1658) as defining decorum in terms of class exclusion: 'the contrast between good, decorous rhetoric and its contrary...[is] an opposition between the symbolic center of the country, including the capital and the court, and the provinces' ('Outlandish Fears: Defining Decorum in Renaissance Rhetoric.' *Intertexts* 4, no. 1 (2000): 3–24). Derek Attridge identifies Puttenham's tendency to elevate 'the language of a tiny minority of English speakers' (*Peculiar Language: Literature as Difference from the Renaissance to James Joyce* (London: Methuen, 1988), 34).

words, and manners of that class were deemed most authoritative, even if such distinctions are arbitrary.

Decorum is an intrinsically vague concept. At its core it exists to distinguish art from nature. Art is that which resembles other art, and occurs not naturally but imitatively. Poetic language, for instance, is so because it resembles other poetic language, and because it differs from natural language. Derek Attridge thus argues that decorum is a concept that resists concrete or absolute definitions in order to reify its own exclusivity, much as higher social classes do:

> [I]f art—whether the art of poetry or the art of courtly conduct—were reconcil-
> able to rule, it would be available to all who were willing to make the effort. As the
> existence of poetry, like the power of the court, is predicated upon exclusiveness,
> such a conclusion is unthinkable.[22]

Decorum's irreducibility to rules precludes the uninitiated from enacting it; if you have to ask the price of admission, as it were, you can't afford it. It 'is best seen not as a rule, but as an imperative; it is not prescriptive but animative.'[23] That makes decorum intensely difficult to teach, because it is easier to recognize than to define: 'The rule of decorum cannot be theorized because it is always already the application of a rule,' Victoria Kahn writes.[24] Even George Puttenham, the Elizabethan rhetorician who wrote a lost treatise on decorum, calls it 'easier to conceive than to express.'[25]

Nonetheless there are many useful, if relativistic, definitions of decorum. It was so fundamental a concept for Roman rhetoricians that they translated the Greek *propon* ('appropriateness') as this word that governed a near-universal range of domains: not only grammar and rhetoric, but also arithmetic, geometry, music, astrology, and natural science, as Colleen Ruth Rosenfeld argues. Each had its particular method and means of apprehending and expressing knowledge.[26] Decorum's universality is rooted in 'the Platonic and Aristotelian view that virtue cannot be attained without practical sagacity or prudence—the ability to discern

---

[22] Attridge, *Peculiar Language*, 36.

[23] Julian Lamb, 'A Defense of Puttenham's *Arte of English Poesy*.' *English Literary Renaissance* 39, no. 1 (2009): 35. Attridge echoes this claim: 'decorum is precisely that aspect of the poet's art which is not reducible to a rule' (*Peculiar Language*, 30).

[24] Victoria Kahn, 'Humanism and the Resistance to Theory.' In *Literary Theory/Renaissance Texts*, ed. Patricia A. Parker and David Quint (Baltimore: Johns Hopkins University Press, 1986), 377, cit. Lamb, 'Defense of Puttenham,' 27.

[25] George Puttenham, *The Art of English Poesy*, ed. Frank Whigham and Wayne A. Rebhorn. (Ithaca: Cornell University Press, 2007), 347. Lamb argues that Puttenham's difficulty contributes to his belief in the pedagogical benefit of examples over precepts ('Defense of Puttenham,' 27).

[26] Colleen Ruth Rosenfeld, *Indecorous Thinking: Figures of Speech in Early Modern Poetics* (New York: Fordham University Press, 2018), 6–7. She is paraphrasing Ramus's *Arguments in Rhetoric against Quintilian* (1549).

what is right in the given circumstances'.[27] Those who could not do so were plainly inept.

That descriptor, *ineptus*, is Cicero's in *De oratore*, for the orator whose speech is not fit (or *aptus*, from the verb *apere*, 'to fit two things together') for the occasion and for their audience.[28] Cicero's Crassus uses different terms for decorum, from 'aptitude' to 'congruity,' before arriving at the rhetorical definition of speaking 'gracefully.'[29] Similarly in *The Art of English Poesy* (1589), Puttenham uses manifold terms for decorum that testify to 'its elusiveness as a stable concept.'[30] He summarizes these terms as a 'lovely conformity, or proportion, or convenience between the sense and the sensible.'[31] Puttenham devotes a chapter to decorum in his guide to literary language, because it was the criterion on which early modern readers judged nearly every feature of a literary text: its diction, its images and symbols, its subject and genres, and its uses of high, middle, or low styles.[32]

I described these definitions of decorum as relativistic, yet it is difficult to imagine an absolute definition of an idea predicated on the mutual fitness of words or actions and expectations.[33] Fitting words to their circumstances is the shorthand definition of rhetorical decorum that Jean Luis Vives uses to define it as rhetoric's prevailing concern: 'the business of suiting one's words to the circumstances in which one speaks, and of paying attention to the audience, the time and place, the nature of the subject, and one's own character.'[34] Yet the term 'rhetorical decorum' is too broad; to grasp how exemplary rhetoricians and their audiences uphold or violate decorum, we must be more granular.

At least three subspecies of decorum govern the rhetoric and interpretation of exemplars. I will now define the three varieties that pertain to my argument—taxonomic, generic, and receptive—before I outline my chapters on texts that

---

[27] T. McAlindon, *Shakespeare and Decorum* (London: Macmillan, 1973), 8. Aristotle and Cicero define decorum in broad terms as practical judgement, by which one adapts behaviours to particular circumstances (Victoria Kahn, *Rhetoric, Prudence, and Skepticism in the Renaissance* (Ithaca: Cornell University Press, 1985), 35, 30).

[28] Rebhorn, 'Defining Decorum,' n.p.

[29] Rebecca Helfer, 'Remembering Sidney, Remembering Spenser: The Art of Memory and *the Ruines of Time.*' *Spenser Studies: A Renaissance Poetry Annual* 22 (2007): 139.

[30] Those terms include 'decency, discretion, seemliness, comeliness, agreeableness, seasonableness, well-temperedness, aptness, fittingness, good grace, conformity, proportion, and conveniency' (Attridge, *Peculiar Language*, 29).

[31] Puttenham, *English Poesy*, 348. '[T]he Elizabethans—preferring native or native-sounding words—variously referred to [decorum] as comeliness, seemliness, fitness, decency, meetness, propriety, grace' (McAlindon, *Shakespeare and Decorum*, 6–7). Puttenham's terms are themselves decorous, suggesting 'a harmony between thought and word, between word and deed,' and between eloquence and virtue (McAlindon, *Shakespeare and Decorum*, 6).

[32] Rosemond Tuve, *Elizabethan and Metaphysical Imagery: Renaissance Poetic and Twentieth-Century Critics* (Chicago: University of Chicago Press, 1947), 192–247. Metaphysical poets' unorthodox imagery was thus viewed as rebelliously indecorous (226–30).

[33] My word choice echoes McAlindon's: 'Fitness of this kind underlines the relativistic character of decorum and brings to mind Quintilian's remark that propriety demands above all else "a wide adaptability"' (*Shakespeare and Decorum*, 9).

[34] The source, *De ratione dicendi* (On Rhetoric), is paraphrased in Rebhorn, 'Defining Decorum,' n.p.

uphold or violate them. By taxonomic decorum I mean the rhetorician's choice and description of a subject suited to an object, conducive both to the object's circumstances and to their desired interpretation. Generic decorum is the rhetorician's choice of a genre to suit their subject, object, and occasion—such as an epithalamion for a wedding, or an elegy for a funeral. (Taxonomic and generic decorum govern Chapters 2 and 3, in which writers choose and describe exemplars to induce responses from their readers.) Finally, I define receptive decorum as the suitability of the object's deliberate, active reception of exemplary subjects, either by imitating positive ones or by avoiding negative ones. (Receptive decorum and its lapses are the subject of Chapters 4 and 5, in which readers fail to meet rhetoricians' expectations.) The term 'receptive' is from Alexander Gelley's description of exemplary rhetoric's 'outward reach to an agency of reception' with a pragmatic 'goal of ethical transformation.'[35] I include 'active' in my definition of receptive decorum because it is not merely interpretive. It begins with interpretation, or the object's judgement of the exemplar's narrative (or generic) decorum, but then it extends to the object's deliberate, consequent acts of imitation or avoidance.

Exemplarity follows an ethical impetus, to provoke actions that imitate or avoid its models; but it is predicated on and propelled by a two-stage rhetorical impetus, first to choose models and then to convey them in efficacious language. Its success or failure depends on the mutual suitability of abstract entities (subjects) to their concrete circumstances (objects), of exemplars to audiences. But exemplarity depends equally on the audience's response. It is, as I have already claimed, both an intention to influence and a receptivity to being influenced. To succeed, therefore, exemplarity must meet all three varieties of decorum: taxonomic, generic, and receptive. I now address each variety in turn, to expand my brief definitions with examples.

Taxonomic and generic decorum together govern the rhetorician's selection and description of an exemplar. Often the two are entangled in each other; for instance, many examples are freighted with inescapable meanings and fates, like Niobe with suffering or Solomon with wisdom. Exemplars' ethical imports are manipulable, but only to a point; a rhetorician who cites them must negotiate with meanings reinforced by their preceding citations. Similarly, exemplars frequently also arrive with generic preconditions; it would be difficult to tell a happy story about Niobe, Hecuba, or other icons of suffering, just as a tale of woe befalling Bacchus or Pantagruel would jar with their associations with merriment. However, the fact that such stories are imaginable testifies to the division of narrative characteristics from generic conventions—a division that we can easily recognize in more multivalent characters with more varied ethical associations:

---

[35] Gelley, *Unruly Examples*, 3. He briskly cites its classical and medieval origins before progressing to exemplarity's postmodern recapitulation as (paraphrasing Walter Benjamin) the 'situated praxis' of narratives 'embedded in a life process' (6).

Troilus with both joy and pain, for instance, or Griselde with both forbearance and reconciliation.[36] A gratifying story of Troilus that ends in his consummation with Cressida is generically different from Rosalind's account of his ignominious death in Shakespeare's *As You Like It*: 'Men have died from time to time, and worms have eaten them, but not for love.'[37] Her moral that Orlando ought not to exaggerate his love-sickness rests on a tension between taxonomic decorum (Troilus as emblem of lovelorn suffering) and generic decorum (Troilus meeting his fate not from heartache, but from 'a Grecian club').

Taxonomic decorum mitigates the fallacy—or the paradox, if you prefer—of exemplary rhetoric, the notion that a resemblance between a subject and an object makes its ethic more compelling. For instance, Spenser uses genealogical links between his characters and his readers to suggest their ethical congruity. Whenever a writer says words to the effect that a reader ought to imitate their ancestors, there is taxonomic decorum: because you are descended from them, the writer tells the reader, you should imitate them in the particular ways that I suggest, however diluted or remote their influence may be. When Robert Fletcher dedicates *The Nine English Worthies* (1606) to Prince Henry, for instance, he posits the eight kings named Henry as a domestic version of the Nine Worthies, should the Prince of Wales complement them. A moment's consideration would tell any reader that such a claim is more imaginative than substantive, yet the resemblance among men who share a common Christian name requires a willing suspension of disbelief. A far more extensive example of this exemplary heuristic is John Foxe's *Book of Martyrs* (*Acts and Monuments*), whose martyrs' Protestant faith is essential to their ethos of sympathy and admiration among readers who share their religious convictions and sense of persecution. So taxonomic decorum is the first necessary criterion when choosing an exemplary subject, even if their connection to an object is tenuous and accidental.

As decorum eludes easy definition, it is often more visible in the breach than the observance.[38] A lapse of taxonomic decorum is an inappropriate example, offered at the wrong moment or to the wrong object—like John Hayward dedicating his *First Part of the Life and Raigne of King Henrie the IIII* (1599), which describes Richard II's deposition, to Robert Devereux, second Earl of Essex on the eve of his rebellion. This lapse earned Hayward unwanted attention and imprisonment, a sign that history told with polemical, prescriptive, or other exemplary intent could

[36] Examples are not genres but modes: 'Exemplarity shapes a general context of expression and address in many genres' (Elizabeth Allen, *False Fables and Exemplary Truth in Later Middle English Literature* (New York: Palgrave Macmillan, 2005), 3). Using Northrop Frye's definition of mode in *Anatomy of Criticism: Four Essays* (Princeton: Princeton University Press, 1957), Allen defines exemplarity as an intensified mimetic mode, in which objects imitate subjects (161).

[37] William Shakespeare, *As You Like it*, The Arden Shakespeare, 3rd Series, ed. Juliet Dusinberre. (London: Thomson Learning, 2006), 4.1.97–9.

[38] Rosenfeld argues that early modern theories of indecorum focus on three discrete forms: deformities, vanities, and affectations (*Indecorous Thinking*, 7).

violate taxonomic decorum.[39] It also reveals that such lapses largely depend on circumstances beyond the rhetorician's control—for had Essex's revolt succeeded, we would congratulate Hayward for his taxonomic decorum.[40]

A rhetorician's choice of genre may or may not arise from their choice of exemplars, as my Troilus example illustrates. Indeed, the order of these choices depends on the occasion. Generic decorum is more than dirge-in-funeral conventional thinking. Genre entails a capacious set of text-features like tone, setting, character, and circumstances that a rhetorician selectively adopts.[41] Below the level of the text lies a sequence of events and incidents. These more localized moments can adopt various modes, like satirical or pastoral, independent of their surrounding genre. Rhetoricians will represent either extended or localized narratives depending on their desired effects and circumstances, but for the sake of simplicity I include genres and modes under the umbrella term generic decorum.

Authors of occasional texts throughout this study use generic decorum to negotiate between events and rhetoric: from the dedications of Chapter 3, to the elegies and sermons of Chapter 4, to the biographies of Chapter 5. But the interplay of subject, audience, and occasion is complex and can be contradictory, as Chapter 2 on Spenser will show. For instance, Spenser aims in some poems of his *Complaints* volume (1591) to resist occasions that he considers uninspiring, because he aims to provoke his aristocratic readers both to patronize and to inspire more heroic poems. Spenser deliberately violates generic decorum—pointing to differences between what exemplary subjects do and what a given object deserves—to pressure his objects to alter their actions. We have already seen how Drummond laments Henry's death as a lost heroic story: 'A booke had beene of thy illustrous deedes.' Comparable lamentations recur when Henry's elegists contrast their lost aspirations for his heroic genres with the elegies that his death necessitates.[42]

Historical contingencies—Essex's rebellion, Henry's death—complicate taxonomic and generic decorum; yet receptive decorum suffers most from this affliction. All three are subject more to external, unpredictable events than to

---

[39] For a more extensive discussion of this dedication and Henry's response see 'The Education of a Stuart Prince' in Ch. 3. Censorship in this period, as Cyndia Susan Clegg has shown, testifies to the dangerous power of words (*Press Censorship in Elizabethan England* (Cambridge; New York: Cambridge University Press, 1997); *Press Censorship in Jacobean England* (Cambridge; New York: Cambridge University Press, 2001); *Press Censorship in Caroline England* (Cambridge; New York: Cambridge University Press, 2008)). See also John D. Staines, 'Elizabeth, Mercilla, and the Rhetoric of Propaganda in Spenser's *Faerie Queene.' Journal of Medieval and Early Modern Studies* 31, no. 2 (2001): 283–312; and Annabel Patterson, *Censorship and Interpretation: The Conditions of Writing and Reading in Early Modern England* (Madison: University of Wisconsin Press, 1984).

[40] Two books that address Essex's rebellion, trial, and execution in the context of the Elizabethan succession crisis are Alexandra Gajda, *The Earl of Essex and Late Elizabethan Political Culture* (Oxford: Oxford University Press, 2012) and Janet Dickinson, *Court Politics and the Earl of Essex, 1589–1601* (London: Pickering & Chatto, 2012). On Essex's as 'the last honour revolt' of a medieval tradition, see Mervyn James, *Society, Politics and Culture: Studies in Early Modern England* (1986), 416–65.

[41] See 'Generic Decorum' in Ch. 2.   [42] See 'Lamentations' in Ch. 4.

any rhetoricians' purposeful designs, but receptive decorum is utterly beyond a rhetorician's control. Receptive decorum is, again, the way that an object imitates or avoids an exemplary subject, whether intentionally or not. It is a narrative judgement, not a moral one; it rests entirely on what happens next in time.

Consider a 1594 dedication to Essex. The writer identified only as O. B. prefaces his dialogue on a well-lived life, *Qvestions of Profitable and Pleasant Concernings*, with conventional tropes of 'former worthies' exemplifying 'the perfection of vertues absolute in themselues, deliuered... ouer vnto their posteritie,' namely to Essex himself. This dialogue between two men, Huddle and Dunstable, concerns unnamed worthies whose reputations for 'notable deedes and exploites' are threatened by a range of vices that O. B. seeks to cure. O. B. incites Essex to avoid these vices first by invoking the second Earl's father, Walter Devereux, in his dedication; and then by citing the second Earl's inherited virtues and the world's 'vndoubted hope, [that] you will alwaies hold greene and lasting in the increase of them, without suffering any rottennesse or corruption of vices at any time to approach you.'[43] It is tempting to read these words through the lens of Essex's 1601 rebellion—which we could view as his fall from virtue to vice. But Paul Hammer describes Essex's motive for the rebellion as a principled and virtuous stand against the court factions surrounding Elizabeth.[44] In O. B.'s terms, it is the rottenness and corruption of Essex's circumstances, not of his virtue, that undoes him. Whether or not his actions violate the receptive decorum of O. B.'s worthies like Walter Devereux, Essex's resulting trial and execution make him a cautionary tale. Debating the injustice of his breach of receptive decorum will not alter it.

Nor is Essex's violation of receptive decorum unique. The deaths of Philip Sidney and of Prince Henry at the respective ages of 35 and 18 disappointed observers and admirers who bemoaned their lost potential. Both were young, vigorous men who died in their prime, violating expectations for their futures. Some of these expectations owed to the longer lives of their exemplars, but they owed more acutely to their abrupt deaths: Sidney after an injury in battle, and Henry (it is thought) of typhoid fever. Both deaths violated receptive decorum simply because they made Sidney and Henry inadequate to their exemplars' models. This seems unfair, because it is; receptive decorum imposes a near-impossible standard. That neither Essex nor Henry died heroically, and that even Sidney was lamented for dying young, reveals a difficult truth about positive exemplarity. It is magisterially indifferent to its objects' limitations. Rhetoricians of positive exemplarity try to make their objects' contingent lives and experiences

---

[43] O. B., *Profitable and Pleasant Concernings* (1594), sigs. A2r, C2r, A2v.

[44] Paul E. Hammer, *The Polarisation of Elizabethan Politics: The Political Career of Robert Devereux, 2nd Earl of Essex, 1585–1597* (Cambridge: Cambridge University Press, 1999), esp. 20–2 on Essex's conspicuous cultivation of exemplary virtues (e.g. resisting idleness or sycophancy); and 333–8 on his misplaced faith that Elizabeth would reciprocate by advancing him.

resemble their subjects' more purposeful narratives; but those subjects are unattainable, idealized models of ethical conduct that their objects can imitate but never replicate. The discontinuities between past subjects and present objects underscore this study's prevailing argument: that positive exemplarity is ever susceptible to failure, and only negative exemplarity can succeed.

My categorical argument will not proceed merely from a series of spectacular lapses, but from conditions of the culture in which they occurred. In Chapter 1 I expand on the Protestant and humanist habits informing early modern exemplarity; but I characterize early modern English culture more broadly as belated and vulnerable, a pale imitation of ancient (Greek and Roman) standards. I mean 'vulnerable' in both the humanist and the human sense. It is Thomas Greene's term for the belated humanist text's susceptibility to the charge that it compares poorly to its sources. Vulnerability is the condition of translations and imitations that are inadequate responses to ancient standards.[45] It is also the condition of exemplarity's present objects, always susceptible to unflattering comparisons with past subjects. Sidney and Henry's blameless deaths, and Essex's rebellion and execution, are lapses of receptive decorum—but they are also different forms of narrative decline from precedents. When I historicize their receptions and their lapses, it reveals that they are as vulnerable to a sense of belatedness as contemporary translations are. Michel Jeanneret is one of many who describes a growing realization in humanist Europe that, with each new discovery and transmission of classical knowledge and experience, this heritage grew increasingly irretrievable: 'At the same time as the classical world was coming to light, it was also getting further away, getting lost.'[46] The classical past thus served as the impossible standard by which to judge any cultural or textual derivatives. That included exemplarity's objects, when they tried to imitate rather than avoid its models.

But all was not dispiriting negativity and caution. Exemplarity's objects could never reproduce the past, because humanists (as Jeanneret argues) had shown it to be irretrievably foreign; but they could adapt and imitate those elements that were reproducible. Readers like Michel de Montaigne opted for liberal modifications of their classical heritage. In his essay 'De l'experience,' he asserts that all exemplars 'limp' between their origins and their objects: '*tout exemple cloche, et la relation qui se tire de l'experience est tousjours defaillante et imparfaicte; on joinct toutesfois*

---

[45] Thomas Greene, 'Erasmus's "Festina Lente": Vulnerabilities of the Humanist Text.' In *Mimesis: From Mirror to Method, Augustine to Descartes*, ed. John D. Lyons and Stephen G. Nichols Jr. (Hanover: University Press of New England, 1982), 132–48. See also Jane Tylus, *Writing and Vulnerability in the Late Renaissance* (Stanford: Stanford University Press, 1993).

[46] Michel Jeanneret, 'The Vagaries of Exemplarity: Distortion or Dismissal?' *Journal of the History of Ideas* 59, no. 4 (1998): 566. 'Recognizing and acknowledging the phenomenon of irreversible development—whether good or bad—counts as one of the most important intellectual acquisitions of the Renaissance,' Jeanneret writes, in contrast with medieval precedents: 'The Middle Ages had been able to maintain the illusion of continuity and ... had seen itself reflected in it as in a mirror' ('Vagaries,' 566). See also Anthony Grafton, *Commerce with the Classics: Ancient Books and Renaissance Readers* (Ann Arbor: University of Michigan Press, 1997).

les comparaisons par quelque coin' [every example limps and any correspondence which we draw from experience is always feeble and imperfect; we can neverthe-less find some corner or other by which to link our comparisons]. As he adds, *'Toutes choses se tiennent par quelque similitude'* [All things are connected by some similarity], though not without our finding that similarity.[47] Montaigne's 'limping' exemplars are 'feeble and imperfect' not on account of their impotence, but merely their distance from their origins. Jeanneret's encouraging counterpoint to his dispiriting characterization of humanist gloom is Montaigne's refusal to see the past as lost or the present as irretrievably belated. Endorsing Montaigne's 'dynamic and irreverential reading,' Jeanneret declares a need for 'critical and rejuvenating' rather than pedantic and profitless readings.[48] Exemplarity's objects might as well view their subjects as unattainable, due to the rigours of receptive decorum.

This study focuses on the early modern English biographers and subjects who ignored Montaigne's advice and took their reading too seriously. I examine the culture of rhetoric and expectations that fuelled self-consciousness about their legacies, and the disparities between early modern biographical writing and the lives it describes.[49] Biographical writing is a mode that obtains in a wide range of texts, beyond straightforward 'biographies'—a word that was not coined until 1660.[50] But I also discuss writing that was expressly biographical, particularly when it undertook to distil exemplary lessons or illustrative anecdotes from lived experience. I chart how exemplars shifted from a flexible source of *copia*, in Erasmus's formulation, to concrete and historically inflected narratives of imme-diate import; from a technique of informing and influencing readers to an instrument of personal ambition for high-born male readers. I focus on these readers because they were in a position to perform public actions complementary

---

[47] Original from Michel de Montaigne, *The Complete Essays of Montaigne*, tr. Donald A. Frame (Stanford: Stanford University Press, 1958), 522; translation from Michel de Montaigne, *The Complete Essays,* tr. M. A. Screech (London: Penguin, 1991), 1213.

[48] Jeanneret, 'Vagaries,' 576–7. 'Montaigne is the example, par excellence, of an amateur who venerates but mistreats the classics,' Jeanneret adds, translating the following statement from his *Essais*: 'I do not study books, I dip into them: as for anything I do retain from them, I am no longer aware that it belongs to somebody else: it is quite simply the material from which my judgement has profited and the arguments and ideas in which it has been steeped: I straightaway forget the author, the source, the wording and other particulars' (576, 577).

[49] I exclude autobiographies from the category of 'biographical writing' because of their relative lack of exemplary rhetoric. For studies of autobiography in this period see Michelle M. Dowd and Julie A. Eckerle, 'Recent Studies in Early Modern English Life Writing.' *English Literary Renaissance* 40, no. 1 (2010): 132–162; subsequent studies include Adam Smyth, *Autobiography in Early Modern England* (Cambridge: Cambridge University Press, 2010) and Kathleen Lynch, *Protestant Autobiography in the Seventeenth-Century Anglophone World* (Oxford: Oxford University Press, 2012).

[50] Yet biographies appear in a range of forms in the sixteenth and early seventeenth centuries, as Kevin Sharpe and Steven N. Zwicker claim in *Writing Lives: Biography and Textuality, Identity and Representation in Early Modern England* (Oxford: Oxford University Press, 2008). For a thorough overview of the theory and practice of seventeenth-century biography, see Allan Pritchard, *English Biography in the Seventeenth Century: A Critical Survey* (Toronto: University of Toronto Press, 2005).

to their births. Such men tended to be remembered, argues Keith Thomas, whereas women tended to be praised for their self-effacement—'for modesty, regarded as a necessary female virtue, implied a deliberate avoidance of fame or public attention.'[51] As patrons, moreover, these men were most often addressed by rhetoricians, offering both precedents and promises of exemplary reputations.

As I have said, exemplarity operates in a cycle: imitations for the sake of future imitability, readings for the sake of being read, and a self-conscious duty both to the past and to the future. Rhetoricians described exemplarity as such, promising readers—especially potential patrons—that if they imitated past examples and cultivated sympathetic biographers, they could become future examples. This study's five chapters chart the exemplary cycle through one revolution, from representations to experience to renewed representations. My task now is to introduce the readers and texts that propagate this cycle through time.

Overview

This study's three parts each comprise two chapters. The first part is a theoretical overview of the terms of my discussion. It includes the present Introduction, which advocates for historicizing ethical exemplarity in poetic (fictional) and extra-literary occasional texts of the late sixteenth and early seventeenth centuries; and Chapter 1, which begins this historicizing by situating exemplary rhetoric in the era's Protestant memorials and humanist pedagogy. The former precipitated a shift from stylistic to behavioural examples, and provoked controversies among writers like John Donne, Ben Jonson, and William Shakespeare about misinterpreting the legacies of the dead;[52] while the latter emphasized the pragmatic application of knowledge to conduct, and encouraged writers like Sidney and Spenser to focus on poetry's doctrinal and other rhetorical functions.[53]

The study's second part concerns the taxonomic, generic, and receptive forms of decorum that negotiate between rhetoric's exemplars and its readers. In Chapter 2, I find in Spenser's *Faerie Queene* his response to the problem of what one ought to read, and how. Spenser's answer is history, deployed and distorted to teach high-born readers how to be worthy of future historiography. The chapter concerns Spenser's two ambivalent responses to Sidney's repudiation of history in *The Defence of Poesy* (see 'Taxonomic Decorum' in Chapter 2). Spenser asserts that a 'Poet historical' can reshape historical events to rhetorical ends. First, his

---

[51] Thomas, *Ends of Life*, 254. Michael MacKeon argues that, in the eighteenth century, 'biographical exemplarity underwent a revolution that replaced the illustrious by the domestic example'—whereas before, only the lives of illustrious (public) men and women could teach patterns of virtue (*The Secret History of Domesticity: Public, Private, and the Division of Knowledge* (Baltimore: Johns Hopkins University Press, 2005), 338).

[52] See 'Virtuous Lies' in Ch. 1.   [53] See 'Sidney's Subjunctives' in Ch. 1.

representations of invented readers or tellers of history in *The Faerie Queene* suggest that they can use their power of exemplary persuasion for good or ill effects on his characters Arthur, Britomart, and Paridell. Spenser uses their genealogies to compel these readers to action, just as he seeks to do with his poem's readers at Elizabeth's court, including the Queen herself (see 'The Ends of History' in Chapter 2). Chapter 2 then surpasses Spenser's invented circumstances in this epic romance to consider how his *Astrophel* and his *Complaints* resist their actual circumstances; I call them anti-occasional poems because they resist these circumstances and posit better ones (see 'Generic Decorum' in Chapter 2). In *Astrophel*, Spenser laments Sidney's death by allegorizing its supernatural causes. In the *Complaints*, he laments two causes of poor poetry: the lack of adequate historical subjects and of material support for poets. Spenser's ambivalence toward circumstantial occasions as a poetic subject reflects a prevailing sense among writers throughout this study: that their rhetoric must compensate for their readers' inadequacies.

Sidney was the prevailing exemplar of public and private virtues for a generation—both for his life, in which he cultivated both arts and arms long before his literary achievements were recognized; and for his death, after an injury in a religious war in the Low Countries, that made him an instant model of militant Protestant virtue. It was among the most honourable ways to die in a time when military prowess was associated with every form of virtue.[54] Sidney left his admirers with a prevailing sense of lost potential, so they sought others who could take up his example of learning, of courtly sophistication, of religious and patriotic militancy.[55] The first was Essex, a fellow member of the Earl of Leicester's circle. Like Sidney, Essex exhibited prowess in tilts, tournaments, masques, and other acts of performative chivalry; and he similarly earned a reputation for successfully prosecuting the Protestant cause in overseas campaigns. Essex also deliberately cultivated comparisons with Sidney. But his series of public disagreements with Elizabeth culminated in his ill-conceived rebellion in February 1601, for which he was tried and executed. His disenchanted sympathizers retreated into decorous silence for a few years, only to find a new object of their intentions in the fractious climate of the fledgling Stuart dynasty after 1603: Henry, Prince of Wales. There was an intense competition for the attention of King James's heir, as multiple writers argued in manuscript and print about how his future militancy might correct his father's apparent pacifism. But when Henry violated receptive decorum by dying young in November 1612, this whole prospective enterprise collapsed into an outpouring of elegies lamenting his foreclosed future.

---

[54]   Thomas, *Ends of Life*, 54.

[55]   In *Writing After Sidney: The Literary Response to Sir Philip Sidney, 1586–1640* (Oxford: Clarendon Press, 2006), Gavin Alexander posits the rhetoric of incompletion or *aposiopesis* as a technique of urging readers to fulfil Sidney's literary and exemplary legacies.

All three men—Sidney, Essex, and Henry—were subjected to expectations and addresses because they were born of the right families, and willingly performed public roles that attracted others' attention and intentions. In this study my goals are critical, not biographical; yet my aim is to see each man as the object of other people's exemplary rhetoric while he lived, and their subject after he died. That means I pay witness to each man as he appeared in public, and as public records register those perceptions.[56] Sidney left a longer trail of private writings to discern how he imagined himself, complementing his public image—but for Essex and Henry I dig into archives to study their own writings. The imbalance of public and private evidence for all three men means that I cannot infer their internal views and desires from others' perspectives, so as I say those rhetorical efforts are my primary object of study. The limitations of the archival record, and the possibility that new knowledge will emerge from undiscovered or neglected documents, are conditions befalling scholars of any period. In my case they also determine both my subject of public rhetoric and my methods of addressing it through fragments of evidence that are themselves exemplary—suggestive, I mean, of other evidence that they represent metonymically.

The writers who promulgated public perceptions of Sidney, Essex, and Henry fuelled the exemplary cycle, my focus in Chapter 3. It takes up the Sidney legend from Spenser and contrasts his disillusionment with the eagerness with which elegists and writers of dedications compared Sidney to Essex after 1586. The chapter begins with comparative readings of Sidney's exemplary qualities in these texts, and situates them in the pedagogical theories and habits of using examples to teach civic virtues and vices (see 'Sidney's Virtues' in Chapter 3). It extends my account of the exemplary cycle to the dedicatory epistles for Essex and Henry, from 1577 to 1612, to see how they not only forecast these men's future actions but also suggestively offer to write them. The exemplary cycle is most overt in moments like Chapman's praise of Henry as the ideal reader of his 1611 translation of Homer's *Iliad* comparing him to Alexander the Great, also discussed above (see 'Exemplarity and Occasional Texts'). Alexander's envy of Achilles for having Homer to write his biography illustrates positive exemplarity's untenable premise, that reading carefully and choosing the right biographer has a greater effect on your legacy than do your actions (see 'Words and Actions' in Chapter 3). I close the chapter with a series of dedications, panegyrics, civic pageants, and other texts praising Henry as an 'abridgement' or epitome of his reading. Chapter 3 also focuses on the Prince's interest in historical exemplars, and his tendency to conceive and forecast his own legacy in like terms (see 'The Education of a Stuart Prince' in Chapter 3).

[56] For an introduction to the division of inward self-knowledge from outward self-presentations in this period, see Katharine Eisaman Maus, *Inwardness and Theatre in the English Renaissance* (Chicago: University of Chicago Press, 1995), 1–34.

My lattermost two chapters focus on lapses of receptive decorum—and find evidence in them that positive models are notoriously difficult to reanimate. (I describe this in 'Generic Decorum' in Chapter 2 by focusing on Spenser's response to Sidney, but I see it more extensively in the addresses to and depictions of Essex and Henry.) Essex and Henry's impatience with circumstantial limits on their ambitions caused their premature deaths for discrete reasons. Chapter 4 centres on the sermons, elegies, and epitaphs written for Henry between 1598 and 1614, while Chapter 5 is about his posthumous biographies and memoirs. My comparatively heavy emphasis on Henry owes to the awkwardness of praising Essex after 1601. The penultimate chapter begins my discussion of what happens when positive expectations devolve into negative experience, particularly when there is an imperative to describe that experience. The imperative owes to its immediacy, the rhetorical condition that the authors of previous, speculative representations were glad to avoid. After Essex's disgrace and execution most found it wise to avoid the subject; but Henry's unexpected and guiltless death at the age of 18 confronted writers with his human frailty—a quality that most writers had ignored or denied for years. They mask their discomfort with words of consolation and eulogy in the writings for Henry's family and household, but Henry's frailty is there, most pointedly in sermons and epitaphs.

Like Essex, Henry's failure to realize his ambitions and expectations repudiated the efficacy both of rhetoric, and (more pointedly) of positive ethical examples. It became more difficult—though not impossible, as I will show—to cite or recount a life while ignoring irrefutable and inconvenient truths, like the Prince's inability to be more than a cautionary example. When rhetoricians aim to exhort audiences, they often distort their subject's features. But when they aim to warn audiences, the truth is essential to their efficacy. Chapter 4 opens with Henry's death in November 1612.[57] It reveals Chapman's poor timing, and his renegotiation of Henry's exemplarity in his *Epicede or Funerall Song*. Henry's inability to imitate positive ethical examples is by no means the end of this rhetoric, but the beginning of new adaptations, rationalizations, and attempts to fit his experience to alternate models. Like Spenser's *Astrophel* and Gorges's *Olympian Catastrophe*, Chapman's elegy praises and exonerates Henry by attributing his death to supernatural forces, offering an allegorical explanation for inexplicable events.[58]

Elegies are reluctant genres because they resist their occasions. Indeed, most elegies for Henry have eulogistic and consolatory purposes, as my comprehensive survey reveals.[59] But the immediacy of Henry's death prompted others to confront his cautionary legacy, and in epitaphs and sermons these writers (Drummond, George Wither, Daniel Price, and others) distilled both the positive and negative lessons of his experience. If they used allegory, unlike Chapman it was to relate his

---

[57] See 'Decline and Fall' in Ch. 4.   [58] See 'Attributions' in Ch. 4.
[59] See 'Lamentations' in Ch. 4.

death to precedents and forces antithetical to human ambition.[60] Their willingness to represent the circumstances that provoked them stems from their authors' morals, but also from the untenable position of praising one who died despite previous praise.

Henry's fatal illness demonstrated the limits both of his past exemplary aspirations and of the rhetoric that encouraged them. It revealed that the heroic and inspirational comparisons made throughout his life had been not only imperfect but delusive, encouraging a well-intentioned but destructive self-consciousness that Henry could not sustain. It also evidenced the rhetorical flexibility of Henry's own exemplarity. When writers and orators (poets, biographers, and preachers) linked his death to classical, historical, biblical, and other precedents that signalled the cautionary lesson of his experience, Henry became a symbol of frailty and mutability. The failure of his ambitions fostered a more pervasive disillusionment with positive ethical exemplars.

In the fifth chapter, we witness how biographers and memoirists in the years after Henry's death tried to identify both his positive and his negative legacies. The consolatory song of John Cooper (alias Giovanni Coprario) for Henry's successor, Charles, struck a balance between those two legacies: 'follow yet thy Brothers fame, | But not his fate.'[61] But inheritances are not so selective. Henry's biographies are anecdotal in form; like most exemplary lives, they are designed to provoke imitation.[62] They address Charles as the reanimating reader and recipient only of his brother's desirable qualities.[63] This selective inheritance is typical of exemplary biography, which Hampton (again) describes as 'a multitude of discrete metonymically related segments or moments.' The word 'metonymically' means that some parts represent other parts; but I argue that positive ethical exemplarity has a metonymy problem, made visible by focusing on the occasional texts that have been neglected in previous studies of exemplary rhetoric. Moments in an exemplar's biography cannot stand for other, contrary moments when they commix success with failure, exhortation with caution. This problem arises because Henry's death fulfils the second meaning of 'abridgement'—not only a condensation or encapsulation but also a premature conclusion.[64] After 1612, rhetoricians continued to make incautiously exuberant comparisons between the living and the dead, but among biographers there was perhaps a shift toward restraint— or rather toward compiling shorter biographies associated with a common institution (e.g. a university) or other characteristics.[65]

My argument also has implications for the archival methods that literary critics like me use to study early modern English texts. A critic is susceptible to archival

---

[60] See 'Warnings' in Ch. 4. [61] John Coperario, *Songs of Mourning* (1613), sig. C2r.
[62] See 'Papirus Cursor' in Ch. 5. [63] See 'The Book of Henry' in Ch. 5.
[64] See 'The Education of a Stuart Prince' in Ch. 3.
[65] Pritchard shows that brief and anthologized lives are the dominant form of the late seventeenth century (*English Biography*, 12, 22, 145–6).

disruptions and discoveries, just as a rhetorician of exemplarity is to shifting historical circumstances. As my Conclusion asks, to what degree are our citations of textual evidence exemplary, even when our texts consist of assiduously cross-referenced and seemingly representative archival materials? The problem of metonymy—this reliance on parts to represent other parts—that besets rhetoricians of exemplarity also obtains in the new historicist critical techniques that have prevailed in early modern studies for four decades, originating in cultural anthropology.[66] Both the biographer and the new historicist use anecdotes to make arguments about things in the past but also to advertise their archival resourcefulness, their privileged access to a truth that is 'real,' yet dependent on them to reveal it.[67] Anecdotes are brief and sententious narratives that preface historically inflected literary criticism. They serve arguments by epitomizing the phenomena that critics are poised to describe.[68] My conclusion identifies the critical anecdote's inherent unreliability, and traces its history past the eighteenth century to its origins in the early modern rhetoric of exemplarity.

To return to my opening claim of this Introduction: criticism is judicial rhetoric that seeks to propagate judgements about past things. My rhetorical goal in what follows is to convince you that exemplarity was a prevailing habit of mind among late Elizabethan and early Jacobean public figures and the rhetoricians surrounding them—and moreover, that poets after Sidney's *Defence* and Spenser's *Faerie Queene* recognized their power, even though events undermined their ambitions. As I proceed through motivated readings of literary and other texts, you will recognize the rhetorical turns and selective evidence that constitute interpretive work in this discipline. Recognize them in order to take up the same methods in response and correction—ever humbled by the recognition that archives have the means to undermine a critic's every effort to master them through storytelling.

---

[66] See Catherine Gallagher and Stephen Greenblatt, *Practicing New Historicism* (Chicago: University of Chicago Press, 2000); Sarah Maza, 'Stephen Greenblatt, New Historicism, and Cultural History, or, What We Talk about When we Talk about Interdisciplinarity.' *Modern Intellectual History* 1, no. 2 (2004): 249–65; and H. Aram Veeser, 'The New Historicism.' In *The New Historicism Reader*, ed. H. Aram Veeser (New York: Routledge, 1994), pp. ix–xvi.

[67] Stephen Greenblatt, 'The Touch of the Real.' *Representations* 59 (1997): 14–29.

[68] Michael Ullyot, 'The Rhetoric of Anecdotes in New Historicism.' *Clio: A Journal of Literature, History, and the Philosophy of History* 40, no. 3 (2011): 307–29; Joel Fineman, 'The History of the Anecdote: Fiction and Fiction.' In *The New Historicism*, ed. H. Aram Veeser (New York: Routledge, 1994), 49–76. For the anecdote in historiography, see Annabel Patterson, 'Foul, his Wife, the Mayor, and Foul's Mare: The Power of Anecdote in Tudor Historiography.' In *The Historical Imagination in Early Modern Britain: History, Rhetoric, and Fiction, 1500–1800*, ed. Donald R. Kelley and David Harris Sacks (Cambridge: Cambridge University Press, 1997), 159–78; and her more expansive *Reading Holinshed's Chronicles* (Chicago: University of Chicago Press, 1994).

1

Virtuous Action

The provisional definitions of exemplarity offered thus far have served to rationalize my method of historicizing this rhetoric. Witnessing its effects in the late sixteenth and early seventeenth centuries further depends on a definition rooted in Protestant and humanist practices, and their effects on rhetoric. My task now is to give exemplarity a more historicized definition, and to recognize its contributions both to a rhetorical rationale for poetry and to anxieties of posthumous misinterpretation.

I will begin by defining the terms describing exemplary rhetoric etymologically, to show how its ethical (i.e. not stylistic) facets relate to its Greek and Latin forebears—namely the *paradeigma* and *exemplum*. Then I will locate the mid-sixteenth-century origins of later Protestant encomia and eulogies that identified admirable qualities of the dead as imitable. This practice oriented exemplary virtues outward, from the sphere of private devotion to public doctrine. It is also the main difference between medieval and early modern exemplarity. This reorientation served the aims of humanist pedagogy, which focused on the student's reactivation of ethical virtues, reviving the *paradeigmata*'s emphases on conduct over style. The pedagogue's methods of double translation and imitative performance encouraged self-conscious reanimations for the sake, at least partially, of future descriptions. Such pragmatic humanism also contributed to some of the fractious and 'politic' critiques of Queen Elizabeth's and then King James's policies, which motivated some followers of Sidney, Essex, and Henry in turn.

Most of this chapter focuses on the ideologies informing the exemplary rhetoric surrounding these three men; the rhetoric itself I treat in Chapters 3 to 5. The latter half of this chapter turns from Protestant doctrines and humanist indoctrination to poetry's 'doctrinable' aspect, as both Sidney and Spenser term its rhetorical function: 'feigning notable images of virtues, vices, or what else, with that delightful teaching' that defines a poet's task in exemplary and Horatian terms.[1] Sidney's definition of the 'right poet' refutes Plato's charge that poets are liars, permitting them the 'learned discretion' to overrule 'what is, hath been, or shall be' in favour of 'what may be and should be.'[2] The chapter closes by taking up Spenser's 'Poet historical' in *The Faerie Queene*, who seeks to activate abstract

---

[1] Sidney, *Defence*, 347.
[2] Sidney, *Defence*, 346. Sidney's division of poets from historians owes to Aristotle's *Poetics*.

The Rhetoric of Exemplarity in Early Modern England. Michael Ullyot, Oxford University Press. © Michael Ullyot 2022.
DOI: 10.1093/oso/9780192849335.003.0002

virtues in the narrative time of romance—in order to provoke readers in the real time of late Elizabethan history to do the same.[3]

Virtuous Lies

Exemplarity is a concept that combines the stylistic and ethical purposes of an example derived from the Greek *paradeigma* and the Latin *exemplum*, along with the latter's Old French and Middle English cognate *exemplaire*. All three words have rhetorical weight: an example is cited for its effect on an implied object, either to follow or to eschew. Aristotle identifies *paradeigma*, or the historical example, as one of two essential techniques of logical persuasion. (The other is the *enthymeme*, a rhetorical syllogism or tacit, omitted premise.[4]) He categorically asserts that 'all speakers produce logical persuasion by means of paradigms or enthymemes and by nothing other than these.'[5] Desiderius Erasmus is less categorical in *De Copia* (1512): 'A most effective means of making what we are saying convincing and of generating copia [or abundance] at the same time is to be found in illustrative examples, for which the Greek word is *paradeigmata*.'[6] Erasmus makes 'illustrative examples' an essential persuasive method, by which the orator or writer resourcefully displays compellingly numerous instances of some claim. François Rigolot's definition of the *exemplum*—'an illustrative anecdote with a moral point'—echoes Erasmus's definition of the *paradeigma* but with a different result, moral conduct rather than stylistic abundance.[7] The division of stylistic from ethical aims is murkier than I suggest. Style is also a rhetorical object— Berger, again, describes such rhetoric as tropological, to distinguish it from transactional whose object is ethical conduct—but the aim of exemplarity in the texts I am critiquing here is more often ethical conduct.[8] Ethical conduct is more prevalent in the late sixteenth and early seventeenth centuries than it had been in

---

[3] See 'Generic Decorum' in Chapter 2.

[4] Aristotle offers this example of an *enthymeme*: 'to show that Dorieus has won a contest with a crown it is enough to have said that he won the Olympic games, and there is no need to add that the Olympic games have a crown as the prize; for everybody knows that' (*On Rhetoric: A Theory of Civic Discourse*, tr. George A. Kennedy (New York: Oxford University Press, 1991), 42). Kennedy glosses this passage: 'Aristotle regards rhetoric, and thus the *enthymeme*, as addressed to an audience that cannot be assumed to follow intricate logical argument or will be impatient with premises that seem unnecessary steps in the argument' (*On Rhetoric*, 42 n. 60). Walter J. Ong writes that Aristotle broadens Boethius's meaning of *enthymeme* from a scientific syllogism with an unelaborated premise to an internalized 'argument' governing 'decisions regarding human actions'; it is 'something unexpressed, unarticulated,...something within one's soul, mind, heart, feelings, hence something not uttered or "outered" and to this extent not a fully conscious argument, legitimate though it may be' (*Rhetoric, Romance, and Technology: Studies in the Interaction of Expression and Culture* (Ithaca: Cornell University Press, 1971), 12).

[5] Aristotle, *On Rhetoric*, 40.

[6] Desiderius Erasmus, *Copia: Foundations of the Abundant Style [De Duplici Copia Verborum ac Rerum Commentaris Duo]*, tr. Betty I. Knott (Toronto: University of Toronto Press, 1978), 604.

[7] Rigolot, 'Crisis of Exemplarity,' 557.   [8] Berger, 'Narrative as Rhetoric,' 5, 6.

earlier eras when paradigms and exempla were primarily stylistic. Lyons examines words cognate with *paradeigma* and concludes like Erasmus that they have a broadly rhetorical function, serving 'in view of an effect'; whereas unlike Rigolot Lyons associates the *exemplum* more with style than with conduct, connoting 'selection, excision, textual combination, and discontinuity.'[9] The vernacular term *exemplaire* thus connotes a 'sampler' for stylistic imitation. In 1538 Thomas Elyot defined 'exemplar' as 'a sample, wherby we attempt to make a thynge lyke to it.'[10] By 1587 Thomas Thomas had expanded the definition to include both positive and negative models, either 'to follow or eschew.'[11] When the term 'exemplarity' enters English usage in 1619, it refers to conduct, and an exemplar is synonymous more with an ethical precedent or 'president' than with a stylistic standard.

The blurring of stylistic and ethical exemplars owes to the long-standing contiguity of admirable words and actions. Consider the *Facta et Dicta Memorabilia* (or Memorable Deeds and Sayings) compiled by the Roman rhetorician Valerius Maximus in c.29 CE. Valerius's stated purpose is to compile 'a selection from famous authors... in order that those who wish to embrace the examples may be spared the toil of lengthy research.'[12] He deliberately conflates deeds with sayings 'because it [the exemplum] is always both.'[13] More recently, in 1551 Matthew Parker's funeral sermon for Martin Bucer depicted him as a living commonplace book, who collected and exemplified the *facta* and *dicta* of his models.[14] Just as Bucer's words were models of style, so were his own deeds models of behaviour. More recently still, Sidney defended poetry on the basis of its rhetorical power to relate deeds in efficacious words, to burnish inconsistent histories and biographies until they gleam with purpose.

The historical arc I am tracing is from stylistic to ethical exemplarity, under the influence of Protestantism and humanism. By the late sixteenth century the

---

[9] Lyons, *Exemplum*, 10. Lyons adds that the use of example 'is recommended strongly by all Roman rhetorical texts,' from Cicero to Quintilian (8). His discussion of Quintilian is limited to the rhetorician's distinction between simile and example.

[10] Thomas Elyot, *The Dictionary of Syr Thomas Eliot Knyght* (1538).

[11] Thomas Thomas, *Dictionarium* (1587); s.v. 'Exemplar,' *Lexicon of Early Modern English*. Thomas's definition is supported by Randle Cotgrave, *Dictionarie* (1611).

[12] Valerius Maximus, *Memorable Deeds and Sayings,* tr. David Wardle (Oxford: Clarendon Press, 1998), 12. This book of examples, notes Wardle, is for 'declaimers, oral performers in the recital halls of the early Principate, men who needed a wide range of material to provide the historical examples for their speeches' (12). '*Exempla* were a key mode of moral education for the Romans, for whom history provided a catalogue of actions and sayings worthy of praise or blame. [Valerius] provided such a catalogue with the morals inescapably highlighted by the arrangement and by his own introductions and conclusions to the individual *exempla*' (13).

[13] 'An exemplary action is already a saying because it transmits its authority to the community. An exemplary saying is already a doing because it produces a moral obligation which must be enacted' (Larry Scanlon, *Narrative, Authority, and Power: The Medieval Exemplum and the Chaucerian Tradition* (Cambridge: Cambridge University Press, 1994), 34).

[14] Jessica Martin, *Walton's Lives: Conformist Commemorations and the Rise of Biography* (Oxford: Oxford University Press, 2001), 19. Funeral sermons were 'the definitive Protestant instrument of commemoration' (Peter Marshall, *Beliefs and the Dead in Reformation England* (Oxford: Oxford University Press, 2002), 268).

example is also less doctrinal and devotional than the medieval *exemplum*.[15] It is also more variable than those that 'occur in the context of another text, hierarch-ically superior, which systematizes multiple examples and relates them to a maxim.'[16] But both the early modern example and the medieval *exemplum* are discontinuous interjections into the 'hierarchically superior' discourses whose purposes they serve.[17]

Rhetoricians of this later era cite a pantheon of ethical exemplars from classical, biblical, historical, and fictional sources to influence their objects. These encap-sulated biographies are for objects to imitate or repudiate. Let us define ethical exemplarity as the deliberate adaptation and inculcation of a biography to evoke a fitting response. It begins with a rhetorician using an idealized subject to provoke a suitable response from its object(s), either to imitate a positive exemplar or to repudiate a negative one.[18] This hortatory or cautionary provocation urges its object either to follow or to avoid the conduct and outcomes that it describes. So exemplarity is rhetoric with a virtuous aim: to educate its object effectually, informing their reason and provoking their emotions in order to stimulate their will.[19] Philip Melanchthon divides rhetoric's emotive and motivational appeals from dialectic's more sequestered pedagogical function: 'The end or purpose of dialectics is to teach, but the function of rhetoric is to move and stimulate minds and thus to affect a person' or audience.[20] In speech or in writing, rhetoric aims 'to

---

[15] Rebecca A. Davis defines the 'philosophical and theological concept of exemplarism, as distin-guished from the genre of the exemplum': 'It proposes that the created world, like a book written by God, bears the imprint of its creator and that human beings have the capacity to "read" or see spiritual lessons "reflected" in nature' ('"Save Man Allone": Human Exceptionality in *Piers Plowman* and the Exemplarist Tradition.' In *Medieval Latin and Middle English Literature: Essays in Honour of Jill Mann*, ed. Christopher Cannon and Maura Nolan (Cambridge: D. S. Brewer, 2011), 41). Larry Scanlon defines the exemplum, in both its sermonic and its public forms of the *Mirrors of Princes*, as 'a narrative enactment of cultural authority,' or an 'ideological representation of authority [with] a specific historical source' (34); Geoffrey Chaucer and fifteenth-century Chaucerians used it to give vernacular 'literary authority not only a sacral, but a sacerdotal cast that has persisted through modernity' (*Medieval Exemplum*, 349). For 'a critique of the notion that morality in the Middle Ages,' at least in Chaucer and John Gower, 'was...restricted to a uniform system of values, a naive conception of divine-command, or prescriptive ideological statements,' see J. Allan Mitchell, *Ethics and Exemplary Narrative in Chaucer and Gower* (Cambridge: D. S. Brewer, 2004).

[16] Lyons, *Exemplum*, 24. He underscores this discontinuity, even in medieval homilies where exemplum is often wrongly associated with narrative proper: 'Even if the narrations are intended for pleasure and not as illustrations of a doctrine or proposition of faith, the narration is conceived of as separate from the main body of the sermon, as an intercalated entity' (11).

[17] Lyons, *Exemplum*, 30. Lyons uses the term 'exemplary text' to refer to a text that uses exemplars in this way—'not one [i.e. the *exemplum*] that imposes or enjoins a specific example or a universal interpretation of example' (23). To appreciate the flexibility of examples and their potential meanings, we must dispel the understanding of exemplary texts as 'a small group of texts having an explicit doctrinal meaning...having the primary function of manipulating the reader into a position of learner' (23). The *exemplum* is not 'a self-contained and inherently definable type of discourse,' but rather 'the function of a unit of discourse within a whole' (17).

[18] I use 'ideal' throughout this study in the positive rather than the normative sense: the biography of a cautionary exemplar, for instance, is an idealized yet undesirable pattern of experience.

[19] Gray, 'Pursuit of Eloquence,' 500–1.

[20] Cit. Brian Vickers, *In Defence of Rhetoric* (Oxford: Clarendon Press, 1988), 281.

move a reader's affections, to quite properly affect his judgments; ... [to] move him to feel intensely, to will, to act, to understand, to believe, to change his mind.'[21]

Having defined exemplarity in primarily ethical terms, then, let us now distinguish its uses and aims among Protestant humanists from earlier practices. Examples originate in idealizations. Thomas Greene coins the term 'institute' for the Renaissance genre of 'ideal portraits of a society or institution or occupation' that 'might have been calculated to inhibit the vertical as well as horizontal flexibility of the individual by fixing him in a given role much as medieval society did. And yet on the whole the institutes did not do this.' Instead, they replaced medieval examples from devotional and hagiographical sources with public and civic models aimed at 'the surpassing of natural human limitations, undoing the constraints of the incomplete, the contingent, and the mortal ... It was difficult to know when the ideal of individual development approached the superhuman, the impossible, the divine.'[22]

Post-medieval examples came from a wider range of sources, learned or experienced, and could take many forms, verbal or visual. Erasmus describes exemplars taking a leading role, whether the speech is the sort that debates what action should be taken, or urges a particular course of action, or is intended to console someone in grief, or is laudatory or vituperative—in short, whether one is trying to convince an object, to move them, or to give them pleasure. Exemplars readily serve all three of Aristotle's branches of rhetoric: deliberative, seeking to encourage or dissuade; judicial, to accuse or defend; and epideictic, to praise or blame.[23]

Effecting change in an object may require comparisons with exemplars of varied origins, whose intrinsic meanings are less important than their extrinsic effects. These extrinsic effects in the circumstances of their reception determine the rhetorician's choice and use of exemplars. They outweigh the accidental features of exemplars' origins. For instance, an exemplar need not be true to be convincing; it need only be plausible to be persuasive. It originates somewhere in between truth and invention, and is limited only by taxonomic and generic

---

[21] Tuve, *Elizabethan and Metaphysical Imagery*, 183. 'Poetry and rhetoric share the power of moving readers,' she adds. 'All poetry, like other impassioned speech, makes use of the methods which the rhetorician lists' (183, 184). Sidney's discussion of the poet as rhetorician appears in 'Sidney's Subjunctives' in the present chapter.

[22] Thomas Greene, 'The Flexibility of the Self in Renaissance Literature.' In *The Disciplines of Criticism: Essays in Literary Theory, Interpretation, and History*, ed. Peter Demetz, Thomas Greene, and Lowry Nelson Jr. (New Haven and London: Yale University Press, 1968), 250–1. 'The Renaissance produced innumerable institutes; there is space here to recall at least the most familiar: the portraits of an ideal society (More and Bacon), of a family (Alberti), a prince (Pontano and Machiavelli), a courtier (Castiglione), a magistrate (Elyot), a gentleman (Della Casa and Spenser, in their very different versions), a schoolmaster (Ascham), a poet (Minturno and any number of other authors of *artes poeticae*), a lover (Ficino, Bembo, Leone Ebreo, and so on)' (250).

[23] Lanham, *Handlist of Rhetorical Terms*, 164–5.

decorum.[24] This departs somewhat from classical rhetoricians' emphasis on historicity. The Greek grammarian Aspines argues for a strict historical register of examples, particularly domestic ones, advice that Erasmus adopts in *De Copia*.[25] Cicero, after Aristotle, acknowledges that *historia* is more effective than *argumentum*, 'a fictitious narrative which nevertheless could have occurred'; and more effective still than *fabula*, whose events have no verisimilitude.[26] Yet the question of an exemplar's origins, again, is overshadowed by its desired rhetorical effect. Indeed the same example can serve contradictory purposes, as Erasmus writes of the death of Socrates; depending on the rhetorician's purpose, it 'can be turned to Socrates' praise or blame.'[27]

This flexibility freed rhetoricians but provoked anxieties about one's own posthumous legacy. Consider how exemplarity renegotiates the relationship between the living and the dead. Catholic obsequies spoke on behalf of the dead, to intercede for the sake of their souls. But the post-Reformation denial of purgatory and 'abolition of the whole vast industry of intercession,' as Michael Neill writes, 'placed the dead beyond the reach of their survivors.'[28] Accordingly when a preacher like Parker delivered a funeral sermon, not only was he relieved of praying for Bucer's soul, he also repudiated the habit of rehearsing the details of Bucer's life. Instead, like many Protestant biographers, Parker memorialized only those particular details that would instruct the living by providing a model for imitation:

---

[24] See 'Varieties of Decorum' in the Introduction.

[25] Aspines offers this advice for selecting examples from history: 'Examples must be familiar, clear, not too old nor mythic but in accord with the audience.' Moreover, 'every example takes its subject from actual occurrences and is drawn either from native or foreign events. Domestic examples are more striking and appropriate' (cit. and tr. W. Martin Bloomer, *Valerius Maximus and the Rhetoric of the New Nobility* (Chapel Hill: University of North Carolina Press, 1992), 4). As Erasmus writes, 'People are most impressed however by examples that are ancient, splendid, national, and domestic' (*Copia*, 608).

[26] Marcus Tullius Cicero, *De Inventione*, tr. Harry Mortimer Hubbell (Cambridge: Harvard University Press, 1968), I.xix.27. Quintilian similarly favours factual history, 'from which examples may be drawn if circumstances so demand, such illustrations being of the utmost value in every kind of case' (*Institutio Oratoria*, tr. Harold Edgeworth Butler (Cambridge: Harvard University Press, 1969), II.iv.20).

[27] Erasmus, *Copia*, 607. For a discussion of the 'polysemy' of 'multiple illustrative purposes' Erasmus allows to stem from Socrates' death, see Jeanneret, 'Vagaries,' 570.

[28] Michael Neill, *Issues of Death: Mortality and Identity in English Renaissance Tragedy* (Oxford: Oxford University Press, 1997), 38. Purgatory, argues Eamon Duffy, 'provided the rationale underlying the immense elaboration of the late medieval cult of intercession for the dead' (*The Stripping of the Altars: Traditional Religion in England, c.1400-c.1580* (New Haven: Yale University Press, 2005), 338). 'The impact of Protestantism upon this elaborate system of remembrance was wholly destructive' (Thomas, *Ends of Life*, 242). Davis describes this shift in post-Reformation France: 'All the forms of exchange and communication between souls in the other world and the living were to be swept away' ('Ghosts, Kin, and Progeny: Some Features of Family Life in Early Modern France.' *Daedalus* 106, no. 2 (1977): 94–5).

What comfort and edificatyon hys nyer aqueyntaunce receyved by hym in hys godlye wordes and communycation: I wolde wysshe for my self that it myghte be better counterfayted in example, than reported in worde.[29]

Active imitation among the living extends Bucer's edifying example, not mere praise of him. Melanchthon's funeral oration for Martin Luther (1549) similarly disavows 'the Encomye of the dead' in favour of admonishments to the heavens 'to be careful & pensive, what thinges we have special neede of, & to what examples we ought to direct our lyfe.'[30] So the Protestant funeral sermon's didactic purpose inverts the Catholic cult of the living in service of the dead, to a cult of the dead in service of the living.[31]

Elevating the recently dead to exemplary status was a process fraught with comparisons to iconography. Such was the case with a 1610 funeral elegy of John Donne's for the 15-year-old daughter of his acquaintance and patron, Robert Drury. The poem was prefaced by 'An Anatomy of the World' in Donne's first published volume of poetry (1611), and later subordinated to that poem and its companion-piece, 'Of the Progresse of the Soule' (1612).[32] The 'Anniversary' poems, as they are collectively known, describe young Elizabeth Drury's loss as a signal of the world's decline, disorder, and disjunction from heaven—or as the 1611 edition's subtitle puts it, 'Wherein, by occasion of the vntimely death of Mistris Elizabeth Drvry the frailty and the decay of this whole world is represented.'[33] The poem is thus an 'occasional' text, as its subtitle suggests—but Donne no more restricts his subject to his occasion than John Milton, later in the century, does for the death of Edward King in 'Lycidas.' Like Milton, Donne has another purpose in mind: to use the event of a particular death to diagnose a general problem, if not a cause; and to convey the meaning of this life in a rhetorical interpretation for present and future readers.

---

[29] Cit. Thomas, *Ends of Life*, 242–3. "Funeral sermons[']...commemorative function was very similar to that of the masses they superseded" (Thomas, *Ends of Life*, 244).

[30] Cit. Martin, *Walton's Lives*, 20, 16. On the biographies of Luther, Calvin, and other Continental reformers see Irena Backus, *Life Writing in Reformation Europe: Lives of Reformers by Friends, Disciples and Foes* (Aldershot: Ashgate, 2008); on the genre of German funeral biographies from the sixteenth to the eighteenth century see Cornelia Niekus Moore, *Patterned Lives: The Lutheran Funeral Biography in Early Modern Germany* (Wiesbaden: Harrassowitz, 2006).

[31] These sermons are also a frequent 'starting point for fuller biographies', because they outline the life of the deceased as a guide and precedent for readers (Pritchard, *English Biography*, 19).

[32] John Donne, *The Poems of John Donne*, ed. Herbert Grierson (London: Oxford University Press, 1966), 2:178, 186–9. On 'the tension between the ostensible exemplarity of Elizabeth Drury and her countermonumental significance' for Donne, see Anita Gilman Sherman, *Skepticism and Memory in Shakespeare and Donne* (New York: Palgrave Macmillan, 2007), 49–64. Drury 'represents the future regenerate state that Donne desires for his own soul' (64).

[33] Donne, *An Anatomy of the World* (1611); see also *The First Anniuersarie. An Anatomie of the VVorld* (1612).

Donne recounts few details of Elizabeth Drury's actual lived experience. He encourages readers to imagine encountering her incomplete life story in 'the booke of destiny':

> Hee which not knowing her said History,
> Should come to reade the booke of destiny,
> How faire, and chast, humble, and high she'ad been,
> Much promis'd, much perform'd, at not fifteene,
> And measuring future things, by things before,
> Should turne the leafe to reade, and reade no more,
> Would thinke that either destiny mistooke,
> Or that some leaves were torne out of the booke.

Donne uses subjunctive verbs—what she *had been*, what the reader *would think*—because this lost life, these missing leaves, require our agreement with his claims of proportion and continuity: 'Much promis'd.' At the poem's close a few lines later, Donne assigns us responsibility 'T'accomplish that which should have beene her Fate':

> They shall make up that Booke and shall have thanks
> Of Fate, and her, for filling up their blankes.
> For future vertuous deeds are Legacies,
> Which from the gift of her example rise;
> And 'tis in heav'n part of spirituall mirth,
> To see how well the good play her, on earth.[34]

Reading and admiring her example will become active 'playing' and imitating, one of Donne's favourite topoi. (In 'The Sun Rising,' 'Princes doe but play us;' he says to his beloved, 'compar'd to this, | All honor's mimique; All wealth alchimie.'[35]) It is the same language of imitative performances that Parker used for Bucer in 1551 ('counterfayted in example') to stress its aspirational, imperfect nature. Inadequate as they are, these 'future vertuous deeds' by Drury's 'deligate[s]' perform her legacy, deeds 'which should have' filled these blank leaves.[36]

Donne's idealization of his subject's virtues in the Anniversary poems ran against more cynical currents of his time. Ben Jonson memorably accused Donne of hyperbole, telling Drummond 'That Dones Anniversarie was profane and full of Blasphemies; that he told Mr Donne, if it had been written of the Virgin Marie it had been something; to which he [Donne] answered, that he

---

[34] Donne, *Poems of Donne*, 1:248; ll. 85–90, 101–6.   [35] Donne, *Poems of Donne*, 1:11; ll. 23–4.
[36] Donne, *Poems of Donne*, 1:248; ll. 103, 99, 100.

described / the Idea of a Woman, and not as she was.'[37] Jonson's charge misreads more than Donne's intent; it misreads the Protestant purpose of Drury's 'Legacies' for living readers. Donne parried Jonson's charge of crypto-Catholicism with a Neoplatonic ideal. His poems give Drury's particularities ('as she was') a broad exemplary purpose, for 'this whole World.'[38] But one reason for Jonson's objection—beyond spite, anyway—was what he saw as backsliding to the old ways, fuelled by nostalgia in those like Thomas Browne. Cataloguing his errors of religious judgement in *Religio Medici* (written 1634; printed 1642), Browne wishes that 'the prayer for the dead' was 'not offensive to my Religion,' because 'I could scarce contain my prayers for a friend at the ringing [out] of a Bell, or behold his corpes without an oraison for his soule: 'Twas a good way me thought to be remembred by Posterity, and farre more noble then an History.'[39] By 'history' I take Browne to mean the brief, exemplary biographies that Protestant writers and preachers (as we have seen) used to retell memories and summarize legacies. Nigel Llewellyn describes funeral monuments and portraits in Protestant churches that sought to capture 'the didactic potential of the lives and deaths of the virtuous.'[40] Browne's prayers are more 'noble' than the representations of heraldry, accomplishments, and lineages on funeral monuments—themselves subject to the decay and iconoclasm that betrayed 'the vanity of attempting to shape future memory.'[41] Browne's confession is a reminder, more generous than Jonson's critique, that people sought private means to pay homage to the dead, lacking the whole apparatus of masses, prayers, chantries, indulgences, and other intercessions.[42]

If the measure of a good occasional poem is that it outlasts its occasion, Donne's overreaching risks objections like Jonson's. His prescriptions far surpass his

---

[37] Ben Jonson, *Ben Jonson's Conversations with William Drummond of Hawthornden*, ed. R. F. Patterson. (London: Blackie & Son, 1923), 5.

[38] Donne, *Poems of Donne*, 1:229.

[39] Thomas Browne, *Religio Medici, The Works of Sir Thomas Browne*, ed. Geoffrey Keynes (London: Faber & Faber, 1964), 16–17. Robert Burton similarly confesses that ''tis a naturall passion to weep for our friends, an irresistible passion to lament, and grieve' (*The Anatomy of Melancholy* (Oxford and New York: Oxford University Press, 1989), 2:180).

[40] Nigel Llewellyn, *The Art of Death: Visual Culture in the English Death Ritual, c.1500–c.1800* (London: Reaktion, 1991), 28. Duffy writes that 'After the Reformation, funerary inscriptions would as a matter of course record not the desire for prayers but the Christian virtues of the deceased' (*Stripping of the Altars*, 332).

[41] Peter Sherlock, *Monuments and Memory in Early Modern England* (Aldershot: Ashgate, 2008), 154; see also 30, 94–5.

[42] On seventeenth-century 'elegists' compensation for the absence of Catholic rituals...and beliefs such as purgatory,' see Andrea Brady, *English Funerary Elegy in the Seventeenth Century* (New York: Palgrave Macmillan, 2006), 47–51. As Natalie Zemon Davis argues, the shift from dead souls to living lessons—or the 'ritual and devotional break with the dead'—was neither abrupt nor decisive: 'the ending of Purgatory and ritual mourning...may have left Protestants...less removed from their parents, more alone with their memories, more vulnerable to the prick of the past, more open to the family's future' ('Ghosts, Kin, and Progeny,' 96). Her descriptions of the 'ritual and devotional break with the dead' extend to English Protestants and Huguenots alike, though her emphasis on memory is largely concerned with private (family) life (95).

descriptions. Authors of occasional texts face a further danger, that their subjects will assert claims to accuracy or even to obscurity. When Donne gives Drury meanings to outlast her circumstances, he is largely indifferent to her interests, subsuming them in his own—namely of her moral exemplarity. Yet the rhetorical flexibility of one's future example, no matter how distant or immediate the interpretation, unsettled Donne himself. In 'The Relic,' he addresses his own future misinterpreters, 'by this paper taught' to know him as he lived.[43] Otherwise they will ascribe false meaning to his and his beloved's bodies, by misreading their love-tokens as pseudo-Catholic relics. Other poets were bitterly apprehensive of wilful distortions, like John Marston in 'To euerlasting Obliuion,' who bids 'hungry Obliuion | Deuoure me quick.'[44] And William Shakespeare's appeal in sonnet 72 is motivated less by speculative fears than by the broad threat of false praise:

> O, lest the world should task you to recite
> What merit lived in me that you should love
> After my death (dear love) forget me quite,
> For you in me can nothing worthy prove;
> Unless you would devise some virtuous lie,
> To do more for me than mine own desert,
> And hang more praise upon deceasèd I,
> Than niggard truth would willingly impart.
> O, lest your true love may seem false in this,
> That you for love speak well of me untrue,
> My name be buried where my body is,
> And live no more to shame nor me, nor you.
>> For I am shamed by that which I bring forth,
>> And so should you, to love things nothing worth.[45]

Donne, Marston, and Shakespeare speculate, in their personae as speakers, about a range of future motives: ignorance, vengeance, obeisance. But they share a common anxiety of misinterpretation, of the distortions necessary to any posthumous representation that ascribes them meanings to outlast their circumstances. Shakespeare addresses the young man in this and other sonnets, asking him not to praise the poet with epitaphs 'hung' on his hearse or monument.[46] He consigns his own writings to oblivion, as much as his ethical reputation. The common

---

[43] Donne, *Poems of Donne*, 1:63, l. 21.

[44] Marston, John, *The Poems of John Marston*, ed. Arnold Davenport (Liverpool: Liverpool University Press, 1961), ll. 5–6.

[45] William Shakespeare, *The Complete Sonnets and Poems*, ed. Colin Burrow. The Oxford Shakespeare (Oxford: Oxford University Press, 2002), 525.

[46] Shakespeare, *Sonnets and Poems*, 524.

interpretation of 'that which I bring forth' is that the poet is humble about his own writings, but Katherine Duncan-Jones includes the shameful actions and desires catalogued in Mark 7: 20–3: 'That which cometh out of the man, that defileth the man.'[47]

Shakespeare's chosen term for future praise, a 'virtuous lie,' encapsulates the powerful fiction of an ethical exemplar, particularly a positive one. The lie is virtuous because it is ethically praiseworthy, characterized by virtuous motives like Donne's speculative 'virtuous deeds... which from the gift of her example rise.' The lie provokes first admiration and then virtuous behaviour. Yet Shakespeare uses 'virtue' more in the ethical and political sense of efficacy,[48] of the Machiavellian 'man of energetic and conscious will,' of the humanist public servant.[49] Blair Worden defines these valent meanings of virtue for Sidney: 'It meant not only conformity to moral principles but the possession of divinely endowed gifts and powers. Those properties, if cultivated by education, would carry the authority of example and could change the world.'[50] Set aside the divinity of these innate qualities and consider, as Shakespeare does, their exemplarity: these are lies that turn knowledge into argument, wisdom into eloquence, ideas into policy, and a brief life into an imitable afterlife. This is virtue in the public sphere, not merely in one's private character. But it can make these shifts only if it is 'cultivated by education.'

Having defined ethical exemplarity against the Protestant habits of condensing lived experiences into imitable descriptions, or deeds into words, I now examine the humanist inverse transformation of words into deeds—starting with education and proceeding to poetry. In the closing section of this chapter I take up Horace's maxim that poetry serves to teach and delight, by identifying the humanist motive in Elizabethans who defended and wrote poetry with exemplary imitation in mind, namely to provoke what Sidney called 'well-doing and not of well-knowing only.'[51] But first I locate the origins of poetry's rhetorical motives in humanist educational methods, starting in the grammar schools.

[47] William Shakespeare, *Shakespeare's Sonnets*, ed. Katherine Duncan-Jones. The Arden Shakespeare, 3rd Series (Walton-on-Thames: Thomas Nelson, 1997), 254.

[48] William Shakespeare, *The Sonnets and a Lover's Complaint*, ed. John Kerrigan (London: Penguin, 2005). So Stephen Booth glosses 'virtuous' as '(1) morally good; (2) potent, efficacious' (*Shakespeare's Sonnets* (New Haven and London: Yale University Press, 1977), 258).

[49] This will is 'not just to form a wish but to act in such a way as to transform it into reality' (Francesco Ercole, *La politica di Machiavelli* (Rome: Anonima Romana Editoriale, 1926), 20, cit. John Humphreys Whitfield, *Machiavelli* (Oxford: Blackwell, 1947) in Niccolò Machiavelli, *The Prince: A Revised Translation, Backgrounds, Interpretations, Marginalia*, tr. Robert Martin Adams (New York: Norton, 1992)).

[50] Blair Worden, *The Sound of Virtue: Philip Sidney's Arcadia and Elizabethan Politics* (New Haven: Yale University Press, 1996), 23; see further 23–7. For an extended discussion of Sidney's conception of virtue see 'Sidney's Virtues' in Chapter 3.

[51] Sidney, *Defence*, 348.

Pedagogy, Prudence, and Politics

Donne and Shakespeare thought about future misinterpretations because of prevailing habits of turning past objects into relics and names into examples. The method of exemplarity is to assemble and translate such fragments of the past, from diverse alien circumstances and distant sources, into stylistic and behavioural lessons in familiar circumstances. That is also a workable definition of humanist methods with classical texts—and indeed most humanists used exemplars to isolate, epitomize, and propagate what was worth propagating from classical sources. Paul Oskar Kristeller defines humanism by its methodological instantiation in pedagogy, rather than by any innate qualities: 'not as such a philosophical tendency or system, but rather a cultural and educational program which emphasized and developed an important but limited area of studies'— namely of classical texts.[52] In other words, humanism inheres in transactional operations between readers and texts, objects and subjects, students and teachers. These operations rely on exemplarity to identify and promote ethical lessons in local circumstances, as I say—circumstances like the grammar-school classrooms where most of this period's rhetoricians of exemplarity studied.[53]

A grammar-school education promoted reading for the sake of extracting ethical principles and stylistic models. Virtue and eloquence were intertwined, for Ciceronian schoolteachers: 'if you mastered a good Latin style you might replicate the virtue of Cicero,' writes Colin Burrow.[54] Peter Mack adds that 'School pupils were trained to extract moral sentences from their reading and use them in their writing, to analyze and compose moral narratives, to collect historical examples illustrating ethical principles.'[55] So Richard Rainolde (1563) prescribed reading fables 'to frame and instruct our manners' through 'goodlie admonicion, vertuous preceptes of life.'[56] William Kempe (1588) likewise prescribed pupils to read *exempla* and sentences 'framing [them] to eloquence in talks, and virtue in deeds.'[57] Moral sentences included phrases (in Latin) like 'Know yourself,' or 'Ingratitude is the chief of all vices,' that taught both syntax

---

[52] Kristeller further defines humanism as motivated by prudent activations of knowledge 'which emphasized and developed an important but limited area of studies, the *studia humanitatis*'—namely rhetoric, grammar, poetry, history, and moral philosophy (*Renaissance Thought and the Arts: Collected Essays* (Princeton: Princeton University Press, 1990), 10).

[53] I focus on grammar-school rather than university rhetorical education also because the latter's more subtle disputations, syllogisms, and logical/dialectical analyses did not substantially affect exemplary rhetoric. (Would that it had, to temper its enthusiastic simplifications.)

[54] Colin Burrow, *Imitating Authors: Plato to Futurity* (Oxford: Oxford University Press, 2019), 294; he notes that this idea originates with Quintilian, quoting Cato.

[55] Peter Mack, *Elizabethan Rhetoric: Theory and Practice* (Cambridge: Cambridge University Press, 2002), 2.

[56] Richard Rainolde, *Foundacion of Rhetorike* (1563), sigs. 2r, 3r; cit. Mary Thomas Crane, *Framing Authority: Sayings, Self, and Society in Sixteenth-Century England* (Princeton: Princeton University Press, 1993), 43.

[57] William Kempe, *Education of Children* (1588), 223, cit. Crane, *Framing Authority*, 53.

and self-conduct; these textual fragments from diverse pagan or Christian sources replicated the scholastic habit of wrenching extracts out of their original contexts, even though humanists criticized such Lombardian methods.[58] Those contexts informed their original meaning, but did not circumscribe their new meanings in new contexts.

A pervasive practice among grammar-school masters was to teach the art of commonplacing, or compiling moral sentences from books; they 'encouraged readers to fragment their texts,' and '[b]oys were drilled on the moral lessons to be derived from the phrases and stories they read and learned by heart.'[59] Mary Thomas Crane describes the practice of excerpting fragments of texts in commonplace books as compiling a 'socially constituted subject' from excerpts, not from 'the assimilation and imitation of whole works.'[60] 'The point of reading a book,' as Rebecca W. Bushnell describes humanist reading, 'was a harvesting or mining of the book for its functional parts—useful to borrow for the reader's own writing or to serve as practical conduct rules or stylistic models.'[61] When grammar-school pupils graduated to become humanist rhetoricians, they used these excerpts to beautify their figurative language, or to substantiate assertions that readers should alter their conduct. So Crane describes the authors of rhetorical manuals—including the aforementioned Rainolde alongside Leonard Cox (1530), Richard Sherry (1550), Thomas Wilson (1560), and Henry Peacham (1577, 1593)—making their discourse 'seem grounded, authentic, under control, and able safely to assert control.' If rhetoricians could borrow from logicians 'the concepts of gathering and framing [excerpts] as the central means of making their form of discourse,' then their seemingly insubstantial discourse would be more trustworthy.[62]

---

[58] Charles G. Nauert describes the scholastic use of *sententiae* as 'the process of extracting isolated statements from a text and then treating those sentences as accurate reflections of the author's opinion, without attention to what the sentence implied in its original context' ('Humanism as Method: Roots of Conflict with the Scholastics.' *The Sixteenth Century Journal* 29 (1998): 434). For the conflict between Italian humanists and scholastics, see Kristeller, *Renaissance Thought*, 92–119; and Jerrold E. Seigel, *Rhetoric and Philosophy in Renaissance Humanism: The Union of Eloquence and Wisdom, Petrarch to Valla* (Princeton: Princeton University Press, 1968), 226–54.

[59] Mack, *Elizabethan Rhetoric*, 47. Mack resists Richard Halpern's claim that this educational system 'destroyed the content of the texts it taught in pursuit of style' (47).

[60] Crane, *Framing Authority*, 6, 2. Crane argues that 'English humanists often seemed to think of ancient literature as a space containing textual fragments, and... imagined their interaction with that literature as the collection and redeployment of those fragments' (2). Though her emphasis is on formulating 'cultural capital for upward mobility,' her account of self-constitution from textual fragments pertains to the rhetoric of exemplarity (6).

[61] Rebecca Bushnell, *A Culture of Teaching: Early Modern Humanism in Theory and Practice* (Ithaca: Cornell University Press, 1996), 129.

[62] Crane, *Framing Authority*, 39. 'By basing rhetoric as well as logic on the gathering and framing of textual fragments, rhetoricians could assert that rhetoric shared the material ground or authenticity of logic' (51–2). Crane is careful to claim that such rhetoric only *appears* grounded, as a means to claim prescriptive authority but not descriptive credibility.

Rhetoric has a long history of elevating the efficacy of its ethical guidance over the truth of its sources. Both Aristotle and Quintilian address the relative merits of fictional and historical examples, concluding that while true precedents are preferable they are also more scarce and unruly than invented *fabulae*.[63] Cicero, who depicts history instrumentally—as *magistra vitae* (the school of life), in *De Oratore* II.ix—follows Aristotle by subdividing *fabulae* as plausible or implausible; he proposes that rhetoricians simply choose any example that met their intentions.[64] Erasmus advises educators to use myths or natural analogies like industrious bees to illustrate precepts with whatever images will carry ethical weight.[65] As already noted, he echoes this advice to orators: use the most compelling example regardless of its source, whether from your culture or from another, or from myth, history, poetry, theology, or philosophy. The only consideration governing this choice is what effect it will have.

Having established that humanist educators and rhetoricians valued efficacy and praxis, I now examine the ends to which they put their examples: first in general terms, in exercising prudence; and then in two more specific realms of Elizabethan and Jacobean politics and poetry. If humanists, in Jeanneret's phrase, stressed 'an effective discourse about the world,' they were hardly the first to do so.[66] Men like the grammar-school masters amplified classical and medieval ideas of prudence, namely Aristotle's term *phronesis* ('practical wisdom') and the cardinal virtue of *prudentia*. '[T]o have *phronesis* is not just to have a virtue,' writes Daniel C. Russell, 'but to understand what a virtue is for.'[67] Victoria Kahn compares *phronesis* to 'its rhetorical equivalent in the rule of decorum,' namely in how it negotiates between the world and the mind; she adds that the design of humanist pedagogy was 'the reader's prudential judgement.'[68] Mack uses the same term to describe how grammar-school students learned an 'active conception of reading' designed to 'educate the reader's prudential judgement.'[69]

---

[63] 'Fables are suitable in deliberative oratory and have this advantage, that while it is difficult to find similar historical incidents that have actually happened, it is rather easy with fables.... Although it is easier to provide illustrations through fables, examples from history are more useful in deliberation; for generally, future events will be like those of the past' (Aristotle, *On Rhetoric*, 181). Quintilian is perhaps an exception to this separation of factuality from effect—at least for the education of youths, in which he advocates 'the praise of famous men and the denunciation of the wicked' not only for the moulding of character but for 'wide knowledge of facts ... from which examples may be drawn if circumstances so demand, such illustrations being of the utmost value in every kind of case' (*Institutio Oratoria*, II.iv.20).

[64] He categorizes illustrative examples as either history (*historia*), 'an account of actual occurrences remote from the recollection of our own age'; argument (*argumentum*), 'a fictitious narrative which nevertheless could have occurred'; or fable (*fabula*), 'a narrative in which the events are not true and have no verisimilitude' (Cicero, *De Inventione*, I.xix.27).

[65] Desiderius Erasmus, *The Education of a Christian Prince*, tr. Neil M. Cheshire and Michael J. Heath (Cambridge: Cambridge University Press, 1997), 147.

[66] Michel Jeanneret, *A Feast of Words: Banquets and Table Talk in the Renaissance*, tr. Jeremy Whiteley and Emma Hughes (Cambridge: Polity Press, 1991), 262.

[67] Daniel C. Russell, *Practical Intelligence and the Virtues* (Oxford and New York: Oxford University Press, 2009), 31; see also 1–34.

[68] Kahn, *Rhetoric, Prudence, and Skepticism*, 377.   [69] Mack, *Elizabethan Rhetoric*, 20.

The valorization of efficacy that this emphasis on prudential judgement promoted elevated the individual will and private self-interest over learning's other benefits. It meant that if a learned person wished to impose their will on others, they had both practical and principled reasons to do so. The result was an increase of what some have called 'politic ideology' among late humanists, a willingness to promote 'the self-interest of the individual agent' over 'the collective will toward the common good' as the motivating force behind politics, economics, and education.[70] Richard Halpern has recognized humanist pedagogy's role in simultaneously reinforcing 'ideological content' and 'economies of recreation and labor [*sic*], punishment and reward' to 'complement[] and reinforce[] the accumulation of capital' amid a transformation from feudalism to capitalism.[71] We need not adopt this materialist framework to recognize how late humanism served outcomes far beyond Marxist 'primitive accumulation'; we can look to the pragmatic and 'goal-orientated' readings of Gabriel Harvey,[72] or to the editions of Tacitus's *Annals* prepared by Justus Lipsius.[73] Both sought to replace abstract, ahistorical virtues with more instrumental uses of knowledge.

The road from instrumental to self-interested knowledge is short, but not inevitable; one person's self-interest is another's self-sacrifice. Such questions drive political divisions, particularly in this period. The decades from the 1580s to the 1610s were dominated by uncertainties regarding the succession and the threats of Catholic enemies, real and perceived, in foreign wars and domestic invasions or plots. Neither Elizabeth nor James decisively quelled these

---

[70] Amelia Zurcher, 'Untimely Monuments: Stoicism, History, and the Problem of Utility in *The Winter's Tale* and *Pericles.*' *English Literary History* 70 (2003): 910. John Hayward's *First Part of the Life and Raigne of King Henrie the IIII* (1599) is among the histories whose scepticism of political authority thus elevated the individual agent, 'whose ends were as likely as not to be opposed to any benefit for the commonwealth' (Zurcher, 'Untimely Monuments,' 910). On the new humanism, politic ideology, and affiliated modes of thought, see Alan T. Bradford, 'Stuart Absolutism and the "Utility" of Tacitus.' *Huntington Library Quarterly* 46 (1983): 127–55; Peter Burke, 'Tacitism, Scepticism, and Reason of State.' In *The Cambridge History of Political Thought 1450-1700*, ed. J. H. Burns (Cambridge: Cambridge University Press, 1991), 479–98; Martin Dzelzainis, 'Shakespeare and Political Thought.' In *A Companion to Shakespeare*, ed. David Scott Kastan (Malden: Blackwell Publishers, 1999), 100–16; F. J. Levy, 'Hayward, Daniel, and the Beginnings of Politic History in England.' *Huntington Library Quarterly* 50, no. 1 (1987): 1–34; J. H. M. Salmon, 'Stoicism and Roman Example: Seneca and Tacitus in Jacobean England.' *Journal of the History of Ideas* 50 (1989): 199–222; Mary F. Tenney, 'Tacitus in the Politics of Early Stuart England.' *Classical Journal* 37 (1941): 151–63; and Daniel R. Woolf, 'Genre into Artifact: The Decline of the English Chronicle in the Sixteenth Century.' *Sixteenth Century Journal* 19 (1988): 321–54, esp. 349–54 on politic history.

[71] Richard Halpern, *The Poetics of Primitive Accumulation: English Renaissance Culture and the Genealogy of Capital* (Ithaca, and London: Cornell University Press, 1991), 15. '[T]he rhetorical and literary culture of the Renaissance can be usefully situated within, if not quite "explained" by, the transition from feudalism to capitalism' (13–14).

[72] For Harvey reading was 'a public performance, rather than a private meditation, in its aims and character' (Lisa Jardine and Anthony Grafton, ' "Studied for Action": How Gabriel Harvey Read his Livy.' *Past and Present* 129 (1990): 31).

[73] On the Continent, Lipsius's *De Constantia* (1584) made Tacitus an advocate for resisting unjust rule. John Stradling translated the book into English in 1594, but Henry Savile's translations and Tacitean compositions were more influential.

uncertainties: she could be indecisive and capricious, he tolerant and pacific. This created fertile ground for charismatic or simply well-positioned public figures like Sidney, Essex, and Henry, who served (willingly or not) as a locus of hopes for disaffected and malcontented observers. Militant Protestants, for example, urged Essex to imitate Sidney's active virtues in overseas campaigns against Catholic aggressors—yet despite their proximity, as Paul Hammer has shown, circumstantial differences between subject (Sidney) and object (Essex) made this a classic case of exemplary disjunction.[74] Essex was prudent enough to read, and perhaps even to write, politic histories like Tacitus in the interest of serving his political ambitions;[75] but he was imprudent enough to allow his principles to attract dissenting ideas and foment rebellion at the end of his life. The calamity of Essex's 1601 rebellion did not prevent poets and polemicists from comparing Henry to recent military exemplars, but it did make the pantheon culminate in Sidney rather than Essex.[76] Henry's education was both theoretical and practical, though he seems to have favoured knowledge that he could apply in chivalric and militant pursuits. The poets Christopher Brooke and William Browne wrote that 'His Time by equall portions he diuided | Betweene his bookes and th'exercise of warre.'[77] Generals and foreign visitors to his court at Richmond would set out models of battles on tabletops, including horses and foot-soldiers, for the Prince to study. Moreover, '[n]either did he omit, as he loved the *Theoricke* of these things, to practice the same,' shooting pieces of ordinance and amassing a considerable stable of horses.[78] In time, the Prince would have met some of his admirers' aspirations while struggling (perhaps) to resist awkward comparisons with his father. But these events in the lives and deaths of Essex and Henry, as they addressed Sidney's legacy from the 1590s to the 1610s, are my subject in another chapter.[79] The relevant matter for this present argument is that the late humanist valuing of praxis over gnosis, present efficacy over past truth, manifested in the

---

[74] Hammer, *Polarisation of Elizabethan Politics*, 400. Essex's virtue conflicted with politics of court, of caution, of 'pragmatism' in the more decorous/rhetorical sense: it was principled and ideal; it demanded rewards for the virtuous; it was rude yet artless. See Hammer's sympathetic account (335–7) of the 1590s court as antagonistic to virtue, offering Essex poor rewards for his merits.

[75] 'Some contemporaries claimed that Essex was the real author of the epistle to the reader in Henry Savile's *The Ende of Nero and Beginninge of Galba* (1591), a landmark translation of key works by the classical Roman historian Tacitus' (Paul Hammer, 'Devereux, Robert, Second Earl of Essex (1565–1601).' In *Oxford Dictionary of National Biography* (Oxford: Oxford University Press, 2004)). Mordechai Feingold resists such claims (and those of David Womersley, Paulina Kewes, Alexandra Gajda, *et al.*) of ideological affinity between Essex and Savile ('Scholarship and Politics: Henry Savile's Tacitus and the Essex Connection.' *Review of English Studies* 67, no. 282 (2016): 855–7).

[76] However, Essex's son Robert Devereux, the third Earl (1591–1646), met favour with King James. He served as Henry's page, and in Robert Peake the Elder's 1605 painting of a royal hunt he is at Henry's side (Catharine MacLeod *et al.*, eds. *The Lost Prince: The Life and Death of Henry Stuart* (London: National Portrait Gallery, 2012), 70–1).

[77] Christopher Brooke, *Two Elegies* (1613), sig. B3v.

[78] John Hawkins, *Life and Death* (1641), 21, sig. B6r.   [79] See 'Sidney's Virtues' in Chapter 3.

educations and the exemplary rhetoric of two men amid their two political moments.

Sidney's Subjunctives

I turn now to poetry, and its own pursuit of the efficacy that motivates exemplary rhetoric. Connecting poetry with exemplarity depends not on analogy or subtle argument but on the evidence of poets' own assertions and practices. I begin with Sidney's assertions in the *Defence of Poesy* (written 1579/80; printed 1595) that poetry is defensible primarily for its rhetorical promotion of self-knowledge for the sake of 'virtuous action.'[80] Then I take up Shakespeare's apprehensiveness toward the 'virtuous lie' to address Platonic counter-assertions that poetry promotes delusive fictions, assertions that I myself make against unhistoricized exemplars. The closing argument in poetry's favour comprises Spenser's fictional enactments of exemplary rhetoric in the romance-world of *The Faerie Queene* (1590, 1596).[81] Its characters enact or avoid ethical exemplars in a narrative that parallels the experiential, historical world of Spenser's readers—particularly of his arch-reader Elizabeth, onto whom poets like Spenser projected narrative ambitions.

If you recall Drummond's elegy for Prince Henry, it shares with Donne's elegy for Elizabeth Drury a habit of describing foreclosed futures in the subjunctive tense.[82] Both poets use the image of a lost book—of Homeric epic, for Henry; and of destiny, for Drury—accounting for what its readers might have first enacted, then recounted, and finally imitated. The stark truth that none of that actually happened obliges Drummond and Donne to describe what was, even as they busily imagine what might have been. In this way elegists are in a comparable position to historians, whom Sidney in the *Defence* describes as constrained by the 'bare *was*' of factual events.[83] That puts historians in a dichotomy with poets, whom Sidney calls 'right' poets when their creative agency has a freer rein: 'they which most properly do imitate to teach and delight, and to imitate borrow nothing of what is, hath been, or shall be; but range, only reined with learned discretion, into the divine consideration of what may be and should be.'[84] The

---

[80] *A Defence of Poetry* (1595). In *English Renaissance Literary Criticism*, ed. Brian Vickers. (Oxford: Clarendon Press, 1999), 349. Citations throughout are from this edition. On its date of composition see Philip Sidney, *An Apology for Poetry or the Defence of Poesy*, ed. Geoffrey Shepherd and R. W. Maslen (Manchester and New York: Manchester University Press, 2002), 2–3.

[81] For an account of (moral) exemplarity in humanist pedagogy, the mirror-for-princes genre, and defences of literature on affective and transactional grounds, see Jane Grogan, *Exemplary Spenser: Visual and Poetic Pedagogy in* the Faerie Queene (Farnham and Burlington: Ashgate, 2009), 217, 47–53; she concludes that Spenser trusts his readers to 'make a pleasing Analysis of all' by recognizing and interpreting exemplary morals on their own.

[82] See 'Exemplarity in Occasional Texts' in the Introduction.   [83] Sidney, *Defence*, 355.

[84] Sidney, *Defence*, 346.

difference between 'may' and 'should' distinguishes poets from rhetoricians, insofar as Sidney intends a distinction. Both imitate nature with artifice created for the two ends of poetry that Horace defined in the *Ars Poetica*, 'to teach and delight.' For Sidney, poetry's functions surpass its form:

> it is not rhyming and versing that maketh a poet—no more than a long gown maketh an advocate, who though he pleaded in armour should be an advocate and no soldier. But it is that feigning notable images of virtues, vices, or what else, with that delightful teaching, which must be the right describing note to know a poet by.[85]

This latter conflation of poetry's Horatian ends, 'delightful teaching,' subordinates its imitative representations to its rhetorical purposes: the 'notable images' are notable for the same reason that they are efficacious, for persuasively exemplifying virtuous or vicious morals.

To teach is to conceive an imagined future, and then to persuade others to enact it. When Sidney says that poets 'borrow nothing of what is, hath been, or shall be,' the operative word is 'borrow': poets adapt nothing wholesale from history, but project it toward a possible future. Translating possibility into actuality depends on the reader's self-knowledge and motivation. Sidney uses the Greek term *architektonikē* to define this readerly impetus: 'the knowledge of a man's self, in the ethic and politic consideration, with the end of well-doing and not of well-knowing only.'[86] Doing is superior to knowing because 'the ending end of all earthly knowledge [is] virtuous action,' which like *architektonikē* is 'the highest end of the mistress-knowledge.'[87] Thus Sidney defends poetry's legitimacy based on its efficacy, its ability to conceive what may be and then to persuade readers that it should be. Moral efficacy was instrumental to humanist variations of poetry, according to Kristeller.[88] Poetry could mediate between human society and the imagination, as Stephen Greenblatt writes of rhetoric. He defines it as

> the common ground of poetry, history, and oratory; it could mediate both between the past and the present and between the imagination and the realm of public affairs.... It offered men the power to shape their worlds, calculate the

---

[85] Sidney, *Defence*, 347.

[86] Sidney, *Defence*, 348. See David Galbraith, *Architectonics of Imitation in Spenser, Daniel, and Drayton* (Toronto: University of Toronto Press, 2000).

[87] Sidney, *Defence*, 349, 348.

[88] Paul Oskar Kristeller, 'Humanism and Moral Philosophy.' In *Renaissance Humanism: Foundations, Forms, and Legacy*, ed. Albert Rabil Jr. (Philadelphia: University of Pennsylvania Press, 1988), 271–272. See also Arthur Kinney, *Humanist Poetics: Thought, Rhetoric, and Fiction in Sixteenth-Century England* (Amherst, MA: University of Massachusetts Press, 1986).

probabilities, and master the contingent, and it implied that human character itself could be similarly fashioned, with an eye to audience and effect.[89]

Greenblatt subtly couches grand possibilities in subjunctive 'could[s]' because rhetoric only 'offered' the illusion of mastering contingencies like death that are indifferent to such efforts. He is not the first to grant rhetoricians potential mastery and influence. Plato claimed rhetoric as the way for reason to overmaster passion, and Thomas Wilson used Plato's argument as the premise of the first English rhetorical manual, *The Arte of Rhetoricke* (1553). In 1579, Thomas Lodge prepared the way for Sidney by conflating rhetoricians with poets: 'poets were the first raisers of cities, prescribers of good laws, maintainers of religion, disturbers of the wicked, advancers of the well-disposed, inventors of laws, and lastly the very footpaths to knowledge and understanding.'[90] Sidney would then add to Lodge's jumbled catalogue of society, law, religion, justice, and self-knowledge the next step on this footpath: 'well-doing and not ... well-knowing only,' or virtuous action.

Sidney and Lodge know that defending poetry as rhetorical opens it to the same charge that rhetoric invites, not merely of indifference to truth but of a predilection for lies.[91] '[T]here is no need for rhetoric to know the facts at all,' writes Plato in *Gorgias*, 'for it has hit upon a means of persuasion that enables it to appear, in the eyes of the ignorant, to know more than those who really know.'[92] That poets share the rhetoricians' sophistry is a commonplace in classical oratory, from Isocrates to Cicero to Quintilian. It reverberates through Shakespeare's 'virtuous lie' and his claims like Touchstone's paradoxical defence of poetry in *As You Like It*: 'the truest poetry is the most faining.'[93] Francis Bacon memorably describes lies as an efficacious way to make stories more illustrative and persuasive in 'Of Truth': 'A mixture of a lie doth ever add pleasure.'[94] Yet when Plato banishes poets from his ideal polis in the *Republic* he offers them a chance at redemption:

> if poetic imitation designed for pleasure has any arguments to show that she should have a place in a well-governed city, we would gladly receive her back from exile.... And we might allow her patrons to speak on her behalf ... to

[89] Stephen Greenblatt, *Renaissance Self-Fashioning: From More to Shakespeare* (Chicago: University of Chicago Press, 1980), 162.

[90] G. Gregory Smith, *Elizabethan Critical Essays* (Oxford: Clarendon Press, 1904), 1.75.

[91] Sidney—like Thomas Wilson, Henry Peacham, John Hoskins/Hoskyns, and George Puttenham—conflates poets with orators for largely positive purposes. They all exhibit 'a striking inability, or unwillingness, to conceive that language could be applied to evil ends, or be used to deceive or corrupt' (Brian Vickers, '"The Power of Persuasion": Images of the Orator, Elyot to Shakespeare.' In *Renaissance Eloquence: Studies in the Theory and Practice of Renaissance Rhetoric*, ed. James J. Murphy (Berkeley: University of California Press, 1983), 412).

[92] Plato, *Gorgias*, tr. W. C. Helmbold (Indianapolis: Library of Liberal Arts, 1952), 459.

[93] Shakespeare, *As You Like it*, 3.3.17–18.

[94] Francis Bacon, *The Essays*, ed. John Pitcher (London: Penguin Books, 1985), 61.

show that she is not only a source of pleasure, but also a benefit to societies and human life.[95]

'But now indeed my burden is great,' writes Sidney in his confutation of poetry's opponents, 'now Plato's name is laid upon me.'[96] Sidney's burden is to turn poetry's disregard for truth from a liability into an asset, to claim that it enables poets to write the sorts of edifying poetry, like hymns to the gods or paeans to the great, that Plato endorses as beneficial. So Sidney puts 'virtuous action' at the centre of his defence, but he makes it rely on misrepresentation 'to guide men toward virtue and worthwhile goals, not to mislead them for vicious or trivial purposes.'[97] Sidney shares Bacon's belief that rhetoric is like logic and moral philosophy, guiding reason rather than overpowering it:

> Neither is the nature of man so unfortunately built, as that those powers and arts should have force to disturb reason, and not to establish and advance it: for the end of Logic is to teach a form of government to secure reason, and not to entrap it; the end of Morality is to procure the affections to obey reason, and not to invade it; the end of Rhetoric is to fill the imagination to second reason, and not to oppress it.[98]

That 'second reason,' that things could or should be other than what obtains, is rhetoric's persuasive design—relying, as I say, on the denial of 'what is, hath been or shall be.'

Sidney defends poetry on the basis of what it does, but he delineates those functions in a sort of negative space, defining them by what they are not. Most sententiously he asserts, again to confute Plato and his ilk, that 'the poet, he nothing affirms, and therefore never lieth.'[99] Having shown how Sidney's 'right' poet-rhetorician operates in the subjunctive realm 'of what may be and should be,' I turn now to how Sidney imagines poets actualizing these images without affirming them. The pivotal word for this delicate operation—delicate only insofar as it risks affirming untruths to credulous readers—is 'doctrinable,' by which Sidney means capable of achieving the poet's rhetorical motives. The word arises when Sidney illustrates the poet's need to depart from the historian's motive to recount an event as it occurred in time, 'as it was,' and rather 'to have it set down as it should be.'[100] For 'certainly is more doctrinable the feigned Cyrus of Xenophon than the true Cyrus in Justin, and the feigned Aeneas in Virgil than

---

[95] Penelope Murray, ed. *Classical Literary Criticism* (London: Penguin, 2000), 55.
[96] Sidney, *Defence*, 374.   [97] Seigel, *Rhetoric and Philosophy*, p. xiv.
[98] Francis Bacon, *The Advancement of Learning*, ed. Michael Kiernan. (Oxford and New York: Clarendon Press, 2000), 238.
[99] Sidney, *Defence*, 370.   [100] Sidney, *Defence*, 354.

the right Aeneas in Dares Phrygius.'[101] For 'doctrinable,' read imitable. A biography like the *Cyropaedia* can only inspire readers by making the life of Cyrus appear more purposeful than the meandering, contingent realities of his historical experience, subject to the caprices of fact. Sidney praises Xenophon's text as 'an absolute heroical poeme' because it propagates the 'idea' of Cyrus's virtues.[102] Such a poem should be judged by how 'substantially it worketh, not only to make a Cyrus, which had been but a particular excellency as Nature might have done, but to bestow a Cyrus upon the world to make many Cyruses,' when readers imitate his example.[103]

Spenser also describes Xenophon's *Cyropaedia* as 'doctrinable' in his letter to Walter Ralegh appended to the first three books of *The Faerie Queene* in 1590. But rather than comparing poetry to history, as Sidney does, Spenser contrasts it with philosophy—returning *ad fontes* to Plato's *Republic*. Spenser defends his use of 'Allegorical deuises' to present Arthur's ethic and politic virtues: for 'nothing [is] esteemed of, that is not delightfull and pleasing to commune sence. For this cause is Xenophon preferred before Plato,' whose *Republic* represents a commonwealth 'such as it should be, but the other in the person of Cyrus and the Persians fashioned a gouernement such as might best be: So much more profitable and gratious is doctrine by ensample, then by rule.'[104] For Spenser, then, the *Cyropaedia* is more 'delightfull' and 'profitable' doctrine than the philosopher's principles because it idealizes Cyrus as it narrates him. Although Sidney also denigrates philosophers' dry precepts to promote poets' vivid illustrations, for Xenophon his chosen contrast is with historians, 'captived to the truth of a foolish world.'[105] They like Justinian who tell a historical story 'hath many times that which we call fortune to overrule the best wisdom.'[106] 'Best wisdom' is like Bacon's 'second reason': it tells of Sidney's will to subject happenstance to wisdom, to posit ethical virtues behind visible outcomes, to tell a story 'for your own use and learning.'[107]

The Cyrus of Sidney and Spenser's *Cyropaedia* is an exemplar because he is not 'particular' but profitable to readers. Like all positive ethical exemplars, he is also a

---

[101] Sidney, *Defence*, 354. Justinian and Dares Phrygius are historians whose factual depictions of the Persian emperor Cyrus the Great and the Trojan Aeneas contrast unfavourably with their more poetic, memorable stories in Xenophon's *Cyropaedia* and Virgil's *Aeneid*.

[102] Sidney, *Defence*, 347. Francis X. Connor compares this 'idea' to Donne's in the Anniversary poems, in '"Delivering Forth": Philip Sidney's Idea and the Labor of Writing.' *Sidney Journal* 31, no. 2 (2013): 53–75.

[103] Sidney, *Defence*, 344. Erasmus repeats the commonplace that 'Xenophon wrote his *Cyropaedia* more as a manifesto on the training of the young than as a genuine historical record' (Erasmus, *Copia*, 613–14).

[104] Edmund Spenser, *The Faerie Queene*, 2nd edition, ed. A. C. Hamilton, Hiroshi Yamashita, and Toshiyuki Suzuki (London: Pearson Education, 2001), 716, ll. 23, 24–6, 26–8. On Spenser and Xenophon, see A. C. Hamilton *et al.*, eds. *The Spenser Encyclopedia* (Toronto: University of Toronto Press, 1997), 716, and Grogan, *Exemplary Spenser*.

[105] Sidney, *Defence*, 356.   [106] Sidney, *Defence*, 355.   [107] Sidney, *Defence*, 354.

fallacy. His virtues are sustained through time only by freeing them from the sorts of contingencies that befall his readers; aspiring 'many Cyruses' live in history, not in a 'heroical poeme,' and are subject to moral inconsistencies, errors, accidents, and other lapses of receptive decorum. Jane Grogan thus argues that Spenser's Letter to Ralegh responds to Sidney's *Defence* by 'testing moral virtue ... within a narrative framework' that purposefully 'relinquish[es] control of his reader's moral choices.'[108] As I suggest, the failings of 'many Cyruses' are also lapses of generic decorum: the narrative features of the hero's experience will never map onto those of the reader's. The hero's potential remains ever latent for readers who will never realize it. To understand why receptive indecorum owes to generic indecorum requires a definition of genre that applies equally to exemplary moments (an incident in the *Cyropaedia*) and to their surrounding texts (the *Cyropaedia* as a whole). Thus to conclude an argument focused on the cultural contexts encouraging instrumental and doctrinal uses of ethical exemplars, I will posit a definition of genre that poses it between ethics and their unfolding in time. Then in the next chapter I will address Spenser's uses of ethical exemplars in complaint, elegy, and epic romance.

Genre is the interaction of characters with circumstances. The scope or dur-ation of those circumstances defines the scale of the genre in question, whether of a single incident or an indefinite series of incidents. Naturally it is the poet's prerogative to delimit that series—to give the poem a beginning and an end, to define the hero's journey (say) as Xenophon does, and give the whole poem its genre. But incidents within the poem also have generic qualities. At smaller scales, internal text-features like tone, setting, mode, and above all character exert a disproportionate influence on localized genres: a farcical moment like Odysseus cross-dressing to evade military service can exist within an epic, just as comic interludes can heighten a tragedy's pathos.[109] In the case of an exemplary incident, the rhetorician elevates the ethical value of a character above other considerations. A complex character becomes an exemplary subject when a rhetorician reduces them to virtues or vices and describes incidents that encapsulate those qualities. Karlheinz Stierle argues that exempla simultaneously expand moral precepts and condense the stories from whence they originate:

---

[108] Grogan, *Exemplary Spenser*, 16. She argues, furthermore, that Xenophon offers Spenser the model of heroes who 'always have room to learn' through time in a series of adventures (62). Accordingly, Arthur's moral 'doubts and deviations' suggest that an ethos of contingency should 'replace the humanist imperative to extrapolate finite or fixed exemplars of virtues or vice' (66, 63).

[109] I opt to call such moments within texts 'localized genres' rather than 'modes' because I understand genre to include all elements of mode (including register/discourse, setting, types, etc.), but to further include narrative events and outcome. Thus tragedy or romance are genres, while satirical or pastoral are modes. For a discussion of Spenser's complaints as both mode and genre, see 'Generic Decorum' in Chapter 2.

The exemplum is a form of expansion and reduction all in one—expansion as regards its underlying maxim, reduction as regards a story from which is extracted and isolated that which the speech action of the exemplum needs in order to take on a concrete form.... The basic rule underlying the unity of the whole is the 'purpose' of the exemplum—the moral precept.[110]

This reduction of its original story is a timely reminder that the genre of a poem and of an exemplary incident are often more coextensive than I suggest. Stierle's formulation, based on exempla in Dante, Boccaccio, and Montaigne, also applies to positive ethical exemplars like Cyrus who embody virtues capable of inspiring readers' imitations. Though the hero suffers through adversity, their virtues persevere and ultimately prevail, even in defeat—owing to the representations of both their first poets (like Xenophon) and later rhetoricians (like Sidney and Spenser). A hero who masters the contingent exhibits virtues that prevail through any genre, even those antagonistic to those virtues: forbearance through tragedy, say, or dignity through farce. But when the same hero becomes an exemplary subject, they are often removed from their surrounding generic circumstances, reduced to an incident that illustrates whatever virtue (Stierle's 'moral precept') the rhetorician intends.

Lapses of receptive decorum owe partly to the disjunctions between represented exemplary experiences and lived experience, but the problem owes equally to a dichotomy that Jeff Dolven develops from Stierle and from Jerome Bruner, between paradigms and narratives.[111] Exemplars are paradigms first and narratives second; their narratives are packaged and selected for how well they illustrate their paradigms. Dolven argues that humanist pedagogues favoured paradigmatic maxims, epitomes, sentences, and examples because they stood apart from the flow of time—for instance, the historical time between a source and its reader. Hampton has also defined exemplars as atemporal and universal.[112] The trouble with atemporality arises when a decidedly temporal reader tries to imitate a positive ethical exemplar, as I have shown; so too has Dolven, in his study of education in romances including John Lyly's *Euphues*, Sidney's two *Arcadias*, and Spenser's *Faerie Queene*. Romance reinvests atemporal humanist teachings in time, testing their students' understandings when they attempt to translate concepts into behaviour, words into action. Dolven raises the epistemic question of how teachers know whether or not students understand something, and

---

[110] Karlheinz Stierle, 'Story as Exemplum—Exemplum as Story: On the Pragmatics and Poetics of Narrative Texts.' In *New Perspectives in German Literary Criticism*, ed. Richard E. Amacher and Victor Lange (Princeton: Princeton University Press, 1979), 398.

[111] Jeff Dolven, *Scenes of Instruction in Renaissance Romance* (Chicago: University of Chicago Press, 2007), 58–9; Jerome Bruner, 'Narrative and Paradigmatic Modes of Thought.' In *Learning and Teaching: The Ways of Knowing*, ed. Elliot Eisner (Chicago: University of Chicago Press, 1985), 97–115.

[112] Hampton, *Writing from History*, 11.

particularly whether they grasp an idea intrinsically and substantially, rather than extrinsically and superficially. Understanding may begin with mere repetition: 'Knowledge is a string of text; learning it is hearing or reading it; knowing it is repeating it.'[113] This can form the basis of *imitatio*, writing in the manner of a stylistic exemplar.[114] But to imitate an ethical exemplar is to grasp them intrinsically, to actualize their virtues in behaviours sustained through time. (In this way, as I have said, the exemplary cycle is a behavioural analogy to the linguistic and stylistic activity of double translation in the grammar schools.)

In Chapter 2, then, I begin by reading Spenser's *Faerie Queene* as a situation of exemplary virtues in fictional time, which mirrors the real time in which Elizabethans read Spenser's poem. Spenser's purpose is to invest positive ethical exemplars in time, to reveal disjunctions between them and their readers. He then uses the genres of complaint and elegy to contrast readers with his own higher representational ambitions for them, namely for chronicles and epics befitting higher actions than they deserve. The commonality among Spenser's various genres is their effort to make representations a cause rather than an effect of actions, to guide and provoke readers to do things worthy of his rhetoric.

[113] Dolven, *Scenes of Instruction*, 31.
[114] Dolven, *Scenes of Instruction*, 26. More recently, Burrow argues that Ben Jonson's imitations of Martial and Horace created a stylistic exemplary cycle: 'he imitated authors in such a way as to establish himself as an imitable author' (*Imitating Authors*, 11; see further 235–78).

2

Indecorous Spenser

The normal course of an occasional text's rhetorical decorum is for an event to provoke a suitable text: an elegy for a death, an entertainment for a royal visit, and so on. Circumstances provoke descriptions infused with praise or blame. But the latter has a more capacious grasp of its occasion. When you criticize events your occasional text is partly seeking to invert decorum's normal course of cause and effect, to itself cause events that would be worthy of praise. You seek to effect events, not merely to admire and describe them. Marian Zwerling Sugano gestures toward this inversion in her definition of the occasional text, which 'go[es] beyond a mere description or representation of an occasion to *effectuate* an act in language: it is itself an occasion in (and of) words.'[1] Arguably this is more difficult than writing, say, a panegyric for a positive exemplar—a comparatively straightforward exercise of amplifying their ethical virtues and actions to render them as more momentous than disinterested observers recognized. Surpassing description with critique, as in a complaint, requires the poet to identify what is lacking or latent in events as they are—the first task of any occasional author, regardless of their intent—but then to address apt solutions to the problems they have diagnosed. Critique inverts the normal course of rhetorical decorum by resisting its occasion and positing better ones.

My own definition of 'occasional text' builds on Sugano's and expands O. B. Hardison's to include more critical ambitions: satirical characterizations of public figures, for instance, or polemical interventions in controversies. Hardison's catalogue of their purposes and conventions imagines only conventional forms like elegies, panegyrics, commendations, epithalamia, and the like:

> The occasional forms dealt with contemporary events and living (or recently living) figures. They were particularly suited to arousing patriotism, stimulating interest in specific institutions or events, teaching admiration for a particular ruler, or demonstrating the existence of virtue in the society in which the reader actually lived.[2]

---

[1] Marian Zwerling Sugano, *The Poetics of the Occasion: Mallarmé and the Poetry of Circumstance* (Stanford: Stanford University Press, 1992), 44. She defines '[t]he best occasional poetry' as 'that which denies its status as such' (11).

[2] Hardison, *Enduring Monument*, 108.

The Rhetoric of Exemplarity in Early Modern England. Michael Ullyot, Oxford University Press. © Michael Ullyot 2022. DOI: 10.1093/oso/9780192849335.003.0003

Permit these celebratory purposes as a starting point for occasional texts, but let us also include the works of those who opt like Sidney's poet in *The Defence of Poesy* to critique the 'bare was' of events by comparing them to what they ought to be.

Spenser does that in the five texts that this chapter addresses. In an elegy, an eclogue, two complaints, and an epic romance, his standards for what deserves representation are higher than what his circumstances offer. Spenser's occasional texts seek to invert their causal relationship to events—effectively, to cause the events that his texts deserve. This is not mere ornamentation, as we might characterize his allegorical death for Sidney in *Astrophel* (1594); nor is it mere invention, as Spenser undertakes in *The Faerie Queene* (1590, 1596). In his 'October' eclogue from *The Shepheardes Calender* (1579) and in two poems in his *Complaints* collection (1591), Spenser devotes substantial attention to the paltry circumstances that effectuated them: inadequate patronage, uninspiring public figures, and neglected heroic exemplars. But he leverages his opposition to spur and provoke his readers into actions that deserve better genres, eulogies instead of elegies. These poems lament the paucity of matter that his present subjects offer in contrast to past subjects. I show how Spenser's bivalent uses of the word 'matter' give it meanings of both subject matter for his occasional poems to describe, and material support from his patrons. (For present purposes I focus only on the former.[3]) He does so in order to invert causality, as I say, but also to invert the course of decorum that informs exemplary rhetoric.

Recall that violations of any one of three varieties of decorum will scuttle this rhetoric: taxonomic (the right story); generic (the right structure); and receptive (the right response). More extensively than any other rhetorician, and in more genres, Spenser overtly uses taxonomic and generic decorum to provoke receptive decorum. His impetus is a disillusionment with exemplarity, evident only when comparing these generically diverse texts. Spenser's speakers and characters recount exemplary stories in judiciously chosen genres, each designed to provoke a particular response. Some work, and some do not. In four of these five texts, written for real audiences, failures are part and parcel of their occasions; if there was nothing to complain about, or no death to eulogize, none of these genres would be necessary. But in *The Faerie Queene*, where Spenser is the author of his fictional readers' responses to their readings, failures and successes reveal more of his disillusionment with exemplary rhetoric. Thus my argument begins with this epic romance.[4] In all five texts, Spenser also uses historical exemplars to foreclose

---

[3] I elaborate on both meanings in 'Spenser and the Matter of Poetry.' *Spenser Studies* 27 (2012): 77–96.

[4] Burrow defines 'epic romance' as his reformulation of Homeric emotions (sympathy, guest-friendship, supplication, and pity) and Virgilian digressions that encouraged Ariosto, Tasso, Spenser, and Milton to invent this hybrid mode. 'Underlying the work of all these writers is a perplexed sense that their language will not quite permit the coalescences of pity and piety, sympathy and combat, which shape classical epic' (*Epic Romance*, 5; see also 1–6).

any objections to their taxonomic decorum, because they are suitable models for the readers who are often their descendants, or at least their claimants. (As we see in this and the next chapter, a genealogical link between exemplary subjects and objects is the readiest way to posit taxonomic decorum. It is harder to ignore or repudiate your ancestors than more remote antecedents.)

In three episodes in *The Faerie Queene*, Spenser represents the readers or audiences of history in various forms—chronicles of the past, analogies to the present, and prophecies of the future.[5] The first is Arthur and Guyon reading their respective nations' chronicles in the House of Alma; the second is Merlin's prophecy to Britomart of her descendants with Arthur; and the third is Paridell retelling his Trojan ancestry for persuasive purposes at the house of Malbecco. In each episode, Spenser designs his readers' rhetorical circumstances, in moments that invite us to read over the shoulders of his intended and represented readers. We infer or witness those readers' imperfect interpretations, or receptive indecorum, of (pseudo-)historical exemplars. *The Faerie Queene*'s narrative turns in each episode on a character's recognition or ignorance of their identity as both the culmination of genealogical narratives and the potential subject of future narratives, or as both the end and means of history.[6] This object/subject has a bright future, rhetorically at least, if they learn from the example(s); or a dark future, if they either ignore the example(s) or the rhetorician wills it so. The worst outcome of all is oblivion, owing to the rhetorician's neglect. Spenser's real and fictional readers encounter all three possibilities: praise, blame, and obscurity.

'Spenser seems to have been especially concerned with the activity of the reader, however that person may be identified.'[7] Maureen Quilligan cites evidence for her claim in *The Shepheardes Calender* and *Amoretti*, but most extensively in his Letter to Ralegh on the first three books of *The Faerie Queene*, setting out his 'generall end' or intended effect—moving the reader to virtue—lest they misinterpret his allegory. He can equally be quite precise about his intended readers—including the seventeen named readers among Elizabeth's courtiers in the dedicatory sonnets accompanying the poem.[8] His persistent attention is on Elizabeth herself, however, in his overarching dedications and his proems to each book. At

---

[5] The division is Bart van Es's, in *Spenser's Forms of History* (Oxford and New York: Oxford University Press, 2002).

[6] While 'history' had a considerable range of meanings for Spenser and his contemporaries, I mean it specifically as a narrative of the distant or recent past, one that potentially extends from the present to the future. Sarah Smith complicates this historical continuity by analysing holy-well episodes in I.vii, I. xi, and II.i–ii as evidence that 'the nation's religious history presented a profound and durable obstacle to attempts either to celebrate the nation's past or to trust in its Protestant future' ('An Unyielding Past: Holy Wells and Historical Narrative in *the Faerie Queene* 1–2.' *Studies in Philology* 118, no. 2 (2021): 307).

[7] 'Reader in *The Faerie Queene*.' in Hamilton, *The Spenser Encyclopedia*, 585.

[8] On the placement of these sonnets in the 1590 volume, as Spenser's definitive intervention in the politics of Elizabethan readership, see Andrew Wallace, 'Reading the 1590 *Faerie Queene* with Thomas Nashe.' *Studies in the Literary Imagination* 38, no. 2 (2005): 35–49.

the start of Book II, for instance, he pointedly underscores the genealogical nature of his taxonomic decorum, to remind Elizabeth that Arthur and Britomart are her ancestors:

> In this faire mirrhour … behold thy face,
> And thine owne realmes in lond of Faery,
> And in this antique Image thy great auncestry.[9]

Thus when Arthur reads the *Briton monuments* historical chronicle in the House of Alma nine cantos later—a chronicle of famous precedents and virtuous examples for an indeterminate prince and an overdetermined queen—Elizabeth watches the scene as through a mirror. Arthur's ignorance of his own ancestry starkly contrasts with Elizabeth's ineluctable self-awareness, owing to poets like Spenser. He situates her in a narrative of historical expectations, as the crux between an overdetermining past and a grand narrative future—just as he situates characters like Arthur and Britomart, who reflect her ideal qualities.

This chapter begins with *The Faerie Queene*'s taxonomic decorum provoking varying receptions in Spenser's invented circumstances. First I investigate the nature of this decorum in late humanist cultures, confronting questions of what to read amid textual abundance. Then I read Spenser's Letter to Ralegh in conjunction with Sidney's poetic values of rhetorical invention and efficacy in *The Defence of Poesy*, before addressing *The Faerie Queene*'s three episodes of receptive decorum. In the latter half of the chapter, I read Spenser's *Astrophel*, his complaints *The Teares of the Muses* and *The Ruines of Time*, and his 'October' eclogue from *The Shepheardes Calender*—all occasional poems that attempt to surpass and overwrite their occasions.

Taxonomic Decorum

The rhetoric of exemplarity relies on the right story (for taxonomic decorum) in the right form (for generic decorum) provoking the right response (for receptive decorum), as I have elucidated.[10] Readings and other receptions are the obvious interim step between a story and its influence, and a reader's identity is one way to determine whether or not a narrative is the right one to effect its influence. I emphasize the reader's role in this rhetoric because thus far I have emphasized the rhetorician's, including Spenser's focused depictions of particular readers reading particular narratives. I foreground the reader's questions of what to read and how to read because I recognize that exemplarity is often asynchronous:

---

[9] Spenser, *Faerie Queene*, II.Proem.4.7–9.   [10] See 'Varieties of Decorum' in the Introduction.

writers often direct their rhetoric of praise or blame to readers that they cannot anticipate. Consider the frequent case of a pagan author read by a Christian reader: clearly a rhetorician like Virgil could not anticipate his early modern readers, Eclogue IV notwithstanding.

Taxonomic decorum in humanist cultures was for literate readers to determine for themselves. At few times in history has a flood of information been so sudden or widespread. Humanists exposed readers to vast numbers of potential sources of influence: by educating readers in ancient languages; by printing and translating ancient texts; and by asserting the timeless similarity of human beings, or a transhistorical *humanitas*.[11] Anthony Grafton describes a debate among humanists, whether 'to make the ancient world live again, assuming its undimmed relevance and unproblematic accessibility,' or 'to put the ancient world back into its own time, admitting that its reconstruction is a difficult enterprise and that success may reveal the irrelevance of ancient experience and precept to modern problems.'[12] The former opinion prevailed. 'Moderns can imitate the ancients because men have the same passions,' Niccólo Machiavelli wrote in his *Discourses on Livy*. This meant that the most distant, historical, or quasi-historical character could be localized to exert an immediate influence on the reader's self-conception and actions. The rediscovery, translation, and dissemination of classical texts, in particular, promoted 'a new sense of personal liberty and accomplishment.'[13] Erasmus praised Aldus Manutius for printing editions of Greek and Latin authors whose thousand-copy print runs quadrupled the usual quantities.[14] He praised the Aldine editions as a service 'for the benefit not of one province but of all nations everywhere and of all succeeding ages.'[15]

Yet these editions also created the novel problem of overabundance. For the first time, there was far too much verbal knowledge in circulation for any one reader to know. William Webbe complained in 1586 that 'this country is pestered, all shops stuffed, and every study furnished' with 'innumerable sorts of English books, and infinite fardles of printed pamphlets'; and in 1591 R. W. extended this objection to new writing: 'every red-nosed rhymester is an author, every drunken man's dream is a book.'[16] We can measure the problem of overabundance by considering the book trade, but we can also see this problem as an opportunity.

---

[11] Kristeller, *Renaissance Thought*, 271–2.

[12] Anthony Grafton, 'Renaissance Readers and Ancient Texts: Comments on Some Commentaries.' *Renaissance Quarterly* 38 (1985): 615–49. This essay was substantially reprinted as ch. 3 of Anthony Grafton and Lisa Jardine, *From Humanism to the Humanities: Education and the Liberal Arts in Fifteenth- and Sixteenth-Century Europe* (London: Duckworth, 1986).

[13] Kinney, *Humanist Poetics*, 3.

[14] Steven R. Fischer, *A History of Reading* (London: Reaktion, 2003), 211.

[15] Desiderius Erasmus, *The Adages of Erasmus*, tr. William Barker (Toronto: University of Toronto Press, 2001), 143.

[16] William Webbe, *A Discourse of English Poetrie* (1586) in Smith, *Elizabethan Critical Essays*, 1:226–7; R. W., *Martine Mar-Sixtus* (London: 1591), sig. A3v. Both sources cit. Bushnell, *A Culture of Teaching*, 119.

Humanist readers had access to hundreds of new or newly printed books. It is hard to quantify with certainty the number of books printed after 1450, but local and national statistics show that readers in the decades thereafter could choose from increasingly large numbers of books.[17] When readers could take inspiration from any period or source of recorded experience, internal and external criteria of judgement were vital to filter them for use.

New books introduced the new problem of belatedness and responsibility to the past, the duty of sufficient and suitable interpretation. Complaints took at least two forms: against inferior new books; and against bad interpretations of superior old books. Definitions of 'superior' were relative, as Ann Blair notes. Humanists like Erasmus promoted the best ancient authors, while reformers like John Calvin advocated for 'grave' biblical commentaries, 'erudite and solid coming from pious and right-thinking men.'[18] Readers might 'converse freely with the glorious dead,' in Aldus's words, but what precepts would they take from this conversation?[19] Some sources of potential influence could be highly problematic, if the differences between human beings then and now—or between the subjects and the objects of exemplarity—were more than circumstantial. The circumstances of an ancient text's reception could provoke hostility, particularly from those who resisted the influence of pagan literature on Christian readers. There are plenty of English examples, like the nostalgia of Thomas Howard—the father of Henry Howard, the poet Earl of Surrey—in 1540: 'It was merry in England afore the new learning came up.'[20] Humanism created rhetorical and linguistic circumstances for tensions between taxonomic and receptive decorum.

An earlier Italian controversy illustrates how humanists viewed classical texts with culturally agnostic curiosity. It suggests that ethical exemplarity, or receptive decorum, could determine a text's taxonomic decorum, and defeat arguments for censorship.[21] It also raises questions. If your reading should obey taxonomic decorum, how is that defined, and by whom? Or is your receptive decorum all that determines what you should read? Can you have it both ways, avoiding a text's moral taint while receiving its moral benefits? In 1378, the chancellor of

---

[17] On the problem of quantifying books printed in this period, see Elizabeth L. Eisenstein, *The Printing Revolution in Early Modern Europe* (New York: Cambridge University Press, 2012), 14–15. Blair also notes the difficulty of quantifying this increase, but adds that the *English Short-Title Catalogue* 'shows impressive increases, from 416 titles in the incunabular period to 4,373 titles printed between 1500 and 1550,' and some 500 titles per year after 1600 (*Too Much to Know: Managing Scholarly Information Before the Modern Age* (New Haven and London: Yale University Press, 2010), 54). For a synoptic view, see Michael E. Hobart and Zachary S. Schiffman, *Information Ages* (Baltimore: Johns Hopkins University Press, 2000).

[18] Cit. Blair, *Too Much to Know*, 56.   [19] Cit. Fischer, *History of Reading*, 211.

[20] William A. Sessions, *Henry Howard, the Poet Earl of Surrey: A Life* (Oxford and New York: Oxford University Press, 1999), 11.

[21] In the parallel realm of stylistic exemplarity, or *imitatio*, Burrow argues that adapting a source's vocabulary and conventions to new circumstances was predicated on their 'transhistorical principles' and value: 'Cicero or Virgil consequently could be thought of not as a specific body of texts or as a particular set of words, but as a set of principles for composition' (*Imitating Authors*, 9).

Florence Coluccio Salutati was forced to defend his desire to read Virgil's *Aeneid* against charges that it would corrupt him with pagan ideas.[22] Giuliano Zonarini, the Bolognese chancellor, refused to send Salutati an edition of Virgil on these grounds, calling the poet a '*vatis mentificus*' or lying soothsayer.[23] Salutati rebutted by reading Aeneas's flight from Troy as a narrative of Christian virtues, a repudiation of vice:

> Vergil may rightly be called a *vatis mentificus*, that is, 'one who edifies the mind.' He adorns Aeneas with every virtue and sets him forth as an example for us. He leads him in a marvellous progress fleeing from a corrupt city, a citadel of vice, the haughty Ilium . . . away from the fleshy lusts and mockeries of this present life to the peace of virtue.

The measure of the *Aeneid*'s worth lies in its subject's virtuous edification of its sensitive and pragmatic readers, not in the ethical (religious) status of its author. But Salutati's defence of Virgil does not always rely on Christian dichotomies like corruption and virtue, earthly flesh and transcendence. He uses familiar tropes to depict Aeneas as an instructor, a source of nourishment, and a mirror or exemplar of desirable virtues: 'If one is willing to examine all this in a lofty spirit he will find in that author not merely a delightful outside with the fragrant perfume of flowers, but such food at the marrow that it may well be said to nourish the thinking mind.'[24] He praises Virgil's hero on aesthetic, spiritual, mental, and rhetorical grounds: 'You will find in him delight for your eyes, food for your mind, refreshment for your thought, and you will gain from him no little instruction in the art of eloquence.'[25] Aeneas's origins, his religion—anything that renders him unfamiliar—are accidents, however 'delightful'; the 'marrow' instead will benefit readers capable of reading him through the right interpretive lens.

Salutati's elegant defence of Virgil reveals the pragmatism that characterizes humanist readings: one reads the *Aeneid* to reap educational benefits, to imitate its ethically universal virtues.[26] Salutati cites the patristic precedents of Jerome and

---

[22] On this anecdote, see Javier Lorenzo, 'Modeling the Self: Ontological and Political Uses of Exemplarity in Renaissance Literature.' (Diss., Pennsylvania State University, 2000), 19–25.

[23] Ephraim Emerton characterizes Zonarini's opposition, which was evidently sincere, as 'monkish' (*Humanism and Tyranny: Studies in the Italian Trecento* (Cambridge: Harvard University Press, 1925), 287–8).

[24] Emerton, *Humanism and Tyranny*, 299. In the simpler formulation of Pier Paolo Vergerio, 'the images of illustrious men combine pleasure and instruction, moving readers to virtuous imitation': *Illustrium virorum imagines cum delectatione insit doctrina magnopere se ad earum imitationem concitari* (*Il Epistolario di Paolo Vergerio*, 201; cit. and tr. Lorenzo, 'Modeling the Self,' 11; I have adapted his translation). On Salutati's reading more broadly, see B. L. Ullman, *The Humanism of Coluccio Salutati* (Padua: Antenore, 1963), 227.

[25] Emerton, *Humanism and Tyranny*, 300.

[26] In England in 1531, Thomas Elyot similarly cites Virgil's moral instruction for future governors: 'no one autor serveth to divers wittes as doth Virgile' (*A Critical Edition of Sir Thomas Elyot's* The Boke Named the Governour (New York: Garland, 1992), 45).

Augustine for his opinion that Christian readers can insulate themselves from moral taint by reading texts in this rhetorical frame of mind. In the latter two books of his *Genealogia deorum gentilium* (*Genealogy of the Pagan Gods*), composed in the late fourteenth century, Boccaccio had also justified Christian scholars' study of pagan texts; Salutati knew the work well enough to commission its first alphabetic index.[27] In another incident, he cites St Basil's letter 'On the Reading of the Books of the Gentiles' (so translated by Leonardo Bruni) in response to Giovanni da San Miniato's charge that pagan poetry corrupted young readers. Basil gives authority to Salutati's belief that moral philosophy is essentially secular.[28] '[T]he true Christian scholar reads the . . . heathen poets,' not to 'rest in them,' in Salutati's phrase, but to read them pragmatically: 'as I read I examine diligently to see if I can find anything that tends toward virtuous and honorable conduct.'[29] Salutati uses the rhetoric of exemplarity to justify his reading choices because it does not depend on contrived arguments of classical writers' intentions, as scholastic traditions like *Ovide Moralisé* made. He asks instead 'if I can find anything' imitable in the text, because its present effects determine its decorum more than its past origins. He also applies careful principles of selection, following Vives's injunction to Christian readers of pagan works 'to take from the only what is useful, and to throw aside the rest.'[30] So Salutati uses receptive decorum to obviate taxonomic decorum.

This Italian controversy illustrates how exemplarity served as a filter for humanists with too much to read. The imitation of good examples and avoidance of bad ones is predicated on the universality of human experience, and identifies moral benefits regardless of their sources. Exemplarity bridges cultural and historical differences—between an exemplar's making and their reception, and between their origins and their rhetorical invocation. This exemplarity is open to various critiques, from Jonson's ridicule of Donne to Zonarini's moral objections to Salutati. The former is against rhetorical exaggeration, and the latter

---

[27] Giovanni Boccaccio, *Genealogy of the Pagan Gods*, ed. Jon Solomon (Cambridge, MA, and London: Harvard University Press, 2011), 1.xxxi-xxxii; x.

[28] Leonardo Bruni, *The Humanism of Leonardo Bruni: Selected Texts* (Binghampton: Medieval and Renaissance Texts and Studies, 1987), 24, 14-15. Salutati similarly cites Jerome and Augustine to refute Zonarini's challenge on patristic as well as hermeneutic grounds (Emerton, *Humanism and Tyranny*, 288). The idea of poetry's moral qualities has a different meaning for Zonarini, who focuses on Virgil's foreignness and resists his influence because pagan literature does not satisfy his Christian ethic. For humanism's Christian antagonists as parodied by Erasmus, see Bushnell, *A Culture of Teaching*, 10. Yet elsewhere, Erasmus cautions princes against placing too much credence on a pagan author: 'he speaks with authority on many subjects, yet he by no means gives an accurate picture of the good prince. Measure everything by the Christian standard.' He also advises readers to practise discretion, to retrieve morals 'as you would a jewel from a dung heap' (*Education of a Christian Prince*, 199, 201).

[29] Emerton, *Humanism and Tyranny*, 288, 295. Emerton distinguishes between universal and Christian truths, writing that Salutati aims 'to draw from them ["the works of the heathen poets"] whatever of truth they may contain; and such truth cannot contradict the Truth' (288).

[30] Cit. Crane, *Framing Authority*, 58. She also cites Elyot's echo of this injunction with the same metaphor of distinguishing wholesome flowers from noisome weeds (58–9).

against a reader's receptivity. Both depend on the question of proximity between a subject and their objects. That is Hamlet's question when he asks, 'What's Hecuba to him, or he to her, | That he should weep for her?'[31] His question about the Player's show of grief for a fictional queen is about her emotional, not exemplary, proximity—but also her taxonomic decorum. Why should she have such an effect at such a cultural distance?

The Player is an immediate, if not a decisive, example of the emotional resonance that should spur Hamlet to action, to avenge his own father's murder. But the proximity of rhetorical exemplars is rarely so immediate. They tend to inhabit a more distant, universal sphere until a rhetorician decides to locate and localize them. Humanist assertions like Machiavelli's of transhistorical resonance conflict with exemplary rhetoric, in which 'a contingent past activity is raised to a momentary universality that makes discernible its value for the present.'[32] The tension within Hampton's canonical definition is between contingency and universality, and whether the past and the present can be sufficiently aligned to obviate their differences. So exemplarity relies on a world beyond contingent human experiences, a represented 'reality shared by speaker and listener, reader and writer.'[33] Its rhetorician aims to describe a past ideal that is reproducible in present reality, or for 'time itself' to be 'subordinated to a higher, more powerful order.'[34]

Consider again Hamlet marvelling at the Player's emotional response to Hecuba, underscoring his own inadequate response to his father's death. Both equate proximity with resonance, or narrative with responsive decorum (so to speak). Yet Hamlet mistakenly conflates the performance of grief with what passes show, with its inward moral effects. The Player's performance ends as it began, abruptly; its effects are transient because Hecuba is, in fact, inconsequential to him. Her present value is as a theme for performance, but no further.[35] The Player's is a receptive decorum without any taxonomic decorum. He appropriates—literally makes appropriate—the emotional resonances of Hecuba's grief, but undergoes no moral change owing to her influence.

That brings us to Spenser's *Faerie Queene*, whose real and fictional readers are confronted with explicitly historical examples whose taxonomic decorum is always extrinsic, if not always explicit. As a self-described 'Poet historical,' Spenser both rearranges historical narratives and fictionalizes their receptions in different circumstances. He surpasses Sidney's advice in *The Defence of Poesy* that poets revise history, by writing fictional receptive circumstances to show how

---

[31] William Shakespeare, *Hamlet*, Arden Shakespeare, 3rd Series, ed. Neil Taylor and Ann Thompson (London: Bloomsbury, 2006), 2.2.494–5.

[32] Hampton, *Writing from History*, 11.   [33] Lyons, *Exemplum*, 4.

[34] Lyons, *Exemplum*, 11–12. This order is invoked whenever authors of exemplary texts select and present models for their readers to follow.

[35] I use the term 'value' as Hampton does in his definition of exemplarity that I have quoted above.

rhetoricians distort and withhold history's details for ethical effect. Spenser's characters have the opposite problem to Salutati's: their factual exemplars' taxonomic decorum is irreproachable, but their fictional manipulations and half-truths problematize their receptive decorum. Having addressed the reader's role in adjudicating taxonomic decorum and enacting receptive decorum, I now turn to Spenser's conception of poetry's relationship to history, as manifested in his self-definition. As it owes to Sidney's *Defence of Poesy*, I address features of that treatise unaddressed thus far. Then I take up Spenser's characters confronting written histories as guides to present actions.

As Salutati's defence of Virgil has shown, receptive decorum lies with the reader's attitude, such as the humanist's openness to ethical influence regardless of its source. Spenser is interested in the taxonomic decorum of more proximate exemplary models, particularly ancestral ones—and more particularly, ancestral models who are withheld or misrepresented. Their proximity gives them ethical credibility, but only when their representations are unimpeded by circumstances or deliberate obfuscation.

The only trustworthy narrator of history in Spenser's *Faerie Queene* is Spenser himself. Only he trusts his arch-reader, Elizabeth, to interpret a history that aspires to encompass the present moment of its reading, by making rhetorical overtures in that moment. His proems, as cited, describe her readings of the poem's characters as a kind of self-examination. And his meta-poetic *Letter to Ralegh* sets out the poem's two principal ambitions: for completeness and for rhetorical influence along the lines of Sidney's conception.

Sidney focuses on the poet's two rival guides to virtue, the moral philosopher and the historian. Poetry is inventive and elaborate, Sidney writes, because its representations are better at fostering virtuous imitations than dry philosophical precepts or dusty historical chronicles. He dispenses with the philosopher's challenge readily enough, accusing them of offering pure precepts in paltry contrast to the poet's applied examples. 'For as Aristotle saith, it is not *gnosis* but *praxis* must be the fruit': that is, knowledge 'with the end of well-doing and not of well-knowing only.'[36] The former is from *Nicomachean Ethics* 1.3.1059: 'the end aimed at is not knowledge but action.'[37] Sidney characterizes 'the moralist' as teaching 'a disputative virtue': 'These men casting largesse as they go of definitions, divisions, and distinctions, with a scornful interrogative do soberly ask whether it be possible to find any path so ready to lead a man to virtue as that which teacheth what virtue is.'[38] Sidney refutes this on the basis only of style, not of substance: that 'the philosopher teacheth, but he teacheth obscurely, so as the learned only can understand him.'[39] Poetry's readers interpret it actively, turning 'things not affirmatively but allegorically and figuratively written,' into 'the imaginative

---

[36] Sidney, *Defence*, 357, 348.   [37] Cit. Sidney, *Defence*, 357 n. 84.

[38] Sidney, *Defence*, 349, 350, 349.   [39] Sidney, *Defence*, 353.

ground-plot of a profitable invention.'[40] Spenser echoes this ('So much more profitable and gratious is doctrine by ensample, then by rule') to justify his choice of a narrative to teach readers lessons that are 'clowdily enrapped in Allegoricall deuises,' not overt, like the lessons of sermons.[41]

I have already addressed aspects of Sidney's *Defence* that signal its debt to humanist pragmatism, such as the poet's disregard for truth—or preference, rather, for poetry's more 'profitable' or 'doctrinal' exemplarity than history's.[42] The salient idea for the present is that exemplary poets can propagate virtuous action only by sublimating history to 'the corrective genius of the writer in his quest to influence the future conduct of the reader or audience.'[43] Sidney painstakingly refutes the historian's challenge to the poet's pre-eminence. Whereas the philosopher, whose 'knowledge standeth...upon the abstract and general,' 'sets down with thorny argument the bare rule,' the historian can offer narrative examples that reveal 'the particular truth of things and not...the general reason of things.'[44] Like the poet, the historian traffics in stories—and his stories have a claim to truth, making them a particular threat to the poet's inventions. Sidney turns their virtues of sincerity and factuality against them. He attacks their claims to truth first by mocking the historian's reliance on 'old mouse-eaten records' and 'other histories, whose greatest authorities are built upon the notable foundation of hearsay.'[45] Such overstatements are, Vickers notes, 'not...[Sidney's] considered judgement, which was otherwise favourable,' but a necessary feature of his epideictic rhetoric.[46] Having conceded to historians their superiority to philosophers ('the one giveth the precept, and the other the example'), Sidney can only dispraise historians for their factuality, which gives their narratives efficacy.[47]

Sidney must make a virtue of poetry's untruth, if he is to persuade us of its superiority over history. The problems with historical truth are twofold: its particularity and its ethical inflexibility. The historian 'is so tied...to the particular truth of things and not to the general reason of things, that his example draweth no necessary consequence, and therefore a less fruitful doctrine.'[48] Sidney turns again to Aristotle—to his *Poetics*, this time—to define why poetry's 'universal consideration' is a more fruitful doctrine than history's particularities: because 'the universal weighs what is fit to be said or done...and the particular only marks whether Alcibiades [or who you will] did, or suffered, this or that.'[49]

---

[40] Sidney, *Defence*, 370.

[41] Spenser, *Faerie Queene*, 732. Yet in the two *Arcadias* and *The Faerie Queene*, the two poets differ in their use of what Sidney calls 'allegorie's curious frame' (Philip Sidney, *The Poems of Sir Philip Sidney*, ed. William A. Ringler (Oxford: Clarendon Press, 1962), 178). See Hamilton, *Spenser Encyclopedia*, 656; for exemplarity in the *Old Arcadia*, see Kenneth Borris, *Allegory and Epic in English Renaissance Literature* (Cambridge: Cambridge University Press, 2000).

[42] See 'Sidney's Subjunctives' in Chapter 1.   [43] Lyons, *Exemplum*, 14.

[44] Sidney, *Defence*, 351.   [45] Sidney, *Defence*, 349.   [46] Sidney, *Defence*, 349 n. 51.

[47] Sidney, *Defence*, 350.   [48] Sidney, *Defence*, 351.

[49] Sidney, *Defence*, 354; cit. *Poetics* 9.1451b 4–11.

This is the very problem that Spenser's taxonomic decorum addresses, as we will see: how to make a history's particular examples suit the particularities of a given reader. The lacuna in Sidney's argument for the efficacy of poetry's universals and general reasons is that poetry's readers are always particular.

Sidney's second criterion for history's inferiority to poetry is that it is 'captived to the truth of a foolish world,' a world in which virtue can go unrewarded and vice unpunished.[50] Sidney's verb tenses subsume the contrast between history and poetry. The historian, 'in his saying such a thing was done, doth warrant a man more in that he shall follow.' Precedents are persuasive. Yet 'if he stand upon that *was*,' leveraging the ethical weight of factual precedents, he will be constrained and undermined by their moral caprices: 'the historian in his bare *was* hath many times that which we call fortune to overrule the best wisdom.'[51] Not only 'must [he] tell events whereof he can yield no cause,' he will equally often tell events whose cause (vice or virtue) is obverse to his moral. Contrast his 'bare *was*' with Sidney's verb tense for what he calls 'right poets,' who 'most properly do imitate to teach and delight, and to imitate borrow nothing of what is, hath been, or shall be; but range, only reined with learned discretion, into the divine consideration of what may be and should be.'[52] In so doing, these poets depart from the divine and the philosophical poets in telling exemplary stories, in 'feigning notable images of virtues, vices, and what else, with that delightful teaching.'[53]

I close this discussion of Sidney's *Defence* where I began, with his phrase 'the best wisdom': the faculty of judgement and the rhetorical motivation that poets exercise to turn historical events into examples. It is a compelling job-description, and in *The Faerie Queene* Spenser does his utmost to fulfil it. He takes Sidney's idea of poetry's intrinsic features and applies those features to a series of extrinsic reading activities in fictional circumstances. Spenser combines, in other words, Sidney's wisdom with pragmatism; writing 'doctrinable' poetry with reading it; the general qualities of poetry with its particular reception. If readers are to achieve 'the ending end of all earthly learning[,] being virtuous action,' they must take poetry's precepts and apply them somehow to their immediate circumstances, to perfect an imperfect world.[54]

Sidney and Spenser trust the reader to interpret poetry's lessons decorously—to appropriate them appropriately, as it were. The poet's role in this process is to expose and expound, if subtly, the right examples to the right readers. Spenser's *Faerie Queene* invents receptive occasions, the fictional moments when characters read and respond well or poorly to real, historical exemplars. His motive is to show Elizabeth and other potential patrons how they ought to read—and not just any text, but historiographic texts. If these readers aspire to become exemplars in their own right, to take up their place in future historiography, they must be aware

[50] Sidney, *Defence*, 356.   [51] Sidney, *Defence*, 355.   [52] Sidney, *Defence*, 346.
[53] Sidney, *Defence*, 347.   [54] Sidney, *Defence*, 349.

of both the precedents it sets and the formation of those precedents, the gaps and manipulations involved in history's writing.

All this while Spenser practises and advertises his credentials as a 'Poet historical,' one who manipulates events to repurpose their persuasive effects in fiction. Spenser defends poetry not with a treatise like Sidney's, but by illustrating its effects in action.[55] He endorses Sidney's triad of poetry, history, and philosophy by combining philosophical precepts with historical stories in a narrative poem. He departs from Sidney's repudiation of history by integrating it into moments that show how useful it can be, how it can achieve the poet's rhetorical aims—precisely because it bridges the poem's fictional world with the reader's real one.

Spenser makes this case in the letter to Ralegh appended to his 1590 edition of the poem's first three books. This letter is the closest Spenser comes to a treatise, though it probably echoes some ideas in his lost, unpublished discourse *'the English Poete.'*[56] He is channelling Sidney channelling Horace, so his motive for rearranging events sounds familiar:

> For the Methode of a Poet historical is not such, as of an Historiographer. For an Historiographer discourseth of affayres orderly as they were donne, accounting as well the times as the actions, but a Poet thrusteth into the middest, euen where it most concerneth him, and there recoursing to the things forepaste, and diuining of thinges to come, maketh a pleasing Analysis of all.[57]

By rearranging history's sequence, the poet achieves a 'pleasing Analysis' which delights and teaches. But Spenser's goal is more than Horatian. Like Sidney, he adds a rhetorical imperative: to persuade, to move readers to virtuous action.[58] Spenser's self-definition as a 'Poet historical' gives him an epic poet's prerogative to rearrange a story's historical order, to begin *in medias res* and then to recall and foretell those elements of the story that are most pertinent to his aims. He gives the example of his opening line: 'A gentle knight was pricking on the playne. &c.'[59] Spenser deliberately withholds the knight's identity, and the quest's origins, for effect—even though his poem 'may happily seeme tedious and confused' without this knowledge of 'the wel-head of the History.'[60] The reader's discoveries that this

---

[55] For contrasts between Spenser and Sidney's defenses of poetry, see Joseph Campana, 'On Not Defending Poetry: Spenser, Suffering, and the Energy of Affect.' *PMLA: Publications of the Modern Language Association of America* 120, no. 1 (2005): 33–48; and Robert Matz, *Defending Literature in Early Modern England: Renaissance Literary Theory in Social Context* (Cambridge: Cambridge University Press, 2000).

[56] So titled by the anonymous editor of *Shepheardes Calendar* in Edmund Spenser, *The Yale Edition of the Shorter Poems of Edmund Spenser*, ed. William A. Oram et al. (New Haven: Yale University Press, 1989), 170.

[57] Spenser, *Faerie Queene*, 732.

[58] Maureen Quilligan, *Milton's Spenser: The Politics of Reading* (Ithaca: Cornell University Press, 1983), 33.

[59] Spenser, *Faerie Queene*, 717, l. 69.   [60] Spenser, *Faerie Queene*, 718, ll. 82, 84.

knight is the Redcross knight, and the future St George, are both deferred. It is Spenser's prerogative to withhold his 'conceit' until it suits the aims of his 'pleasing Analysis'—in this case, among other reasons, to defer the reader's recognition of Redcross in his personal and hagiographical guises until Redcross grasps them himself. And there are more deferrals planned, even if Spenser did not realize them all. 'The beginning therefore of my history, if it were to be told by an Historiographer should be the twelfthe booke which is the last'[61]—namely, the moment Redcross receives his commission at Gloriana's feast. Ten cantos after Spenser 'thrusteth into the middest' of his story, Redcross's vision of the New Jerusalem from atop the Hill of Contemplation reveals both his personal origins— his birth among the Britons from an ancient race of Saxons—and his future canonization as England's patron saint. Andrew Fichter uses Peter Marinelli's definition of the hero of dynastic epic, to speak of Redcross as the *homo historicus*: the creature of history who, paradoxically, can shape its course only by aligning himself with its intentions for him.[62]

The Faerie Queene is full of characters seeking their place in historical narratives, because those narratives define their identities. Some pursue knowledge, while others (like Redcross) have it thrust upon them. Redcross is the apotheosis of historical self-consciousness, because in an instant he grasps his ancestral origins and providential legacy. His hilltop epiphany gives his life both providential definition and historical roots, fitting his immediate experience and self-conception into a frame of surrounding experience. This is the 'pleasing Analysis' of Spenser's Book I: that characters are most fully realized when they conceive of themselves as both the end of history, its purpose and its culmination, and the means of its future continuity. The past consists of a chain of human experiences culminating in the present, and influencing present actions. Redcross's reluctance to descend back to the world is not dread at the fight awaiting him, but distaste for his former ignorance as a condition of the world below. His descent represents a return to partial understanding, at best, of disjointed historical narratives.

We see this partial understanding in the three episodes that Spenser uses in the subsequent books of the 1590 *Faerie Queene* to present Arthur, Britomart, and Paridell's readings or tellings of history. In those three episodes, Spenser offers a discontinuous but entire narrative of British imperial history, from the fall of Troy to the present-day succession crises that were incumbent on Spenser's reader

---

[61] Spenser, *Faerie Queene*, 717, ll. 49–50.

[62] Fichter defines the dynastic epic as concerned with 'the rise of *imperium*, the noble house, race, or nation to which the poet professes allegiance' (*Poets Historical: Dynastic Epic in the Renaissance* (New Haven: Yale University Press, 1982), 8). Merlin will likewise urge Britomart to confirm her decreed future. Yet the caveat from Hooker's *Laws of Ecclesiastical Politie* (1593–7), that 'Prescience . . . hath in itself no causing efficacy' underscores our heroes' imperatives to act, in order to actualize their futures (cit. Richard McCabe, *The Pillars of Eternity: Time and Providence in the Faerie Queene* (Dublin: Irish Academic Press, 1989), 187).

(Elizabeth) to resolve.[63] Before we turn to those episodes, consider the ways a poet like Spenser navigated between historical truth and rhetorical efficacy. These will set the terms for his interjections of British historiography into a narrative unfolding in Faeryland, a time and place on the margins of recognizable history. Spenser imagines readers asking, 'Where is that happy land of Faery[?].' He acknowledges objections that his fictional romance-epic is little more than a 'painted forgery,' rather than a matter of 'iust memory.'[64] This in an era when truth seems stranger than fiction, Spenser replies: the newly discovered world overseas adduces the limits of knowledge. Yet Spenser uses historiography as a touchstone in this fictional world, interjecting the 'iust memory' of truth into his 'painted forgery.'

But naturally, it is not that simple. These interjections are overtly selected and manipulated for immediate rhetorical effect, to say nothing of their internal manipulations; Spenser's characters, as we will see, withhold or amplify details to achieve these effects. They are fictional characters reading real histories—or *translatio imperii* mythologies in the case of Troy. In this way Spenser inverts the standard pattern of exemplary poets, whose real readers read fictional histories; he realizes the rhetorician's dream of writing both an exemplary text and a reader's response to it. Just as fortune (in Sidney's formulations) may overrule the best wisdom, and will force historians to recount the 'bare *was*' of the past, fortune can also overrule a reader living in the bare *is* of the present. They may die young, for instance, or lead rebellions, or disappoint expectations in myriad other ways. Spenser's *Faerie Queene*, at least, circumvents this problem of receptive indecorum that his *Complaints* and *Astrophel* confront. But set them aside for the moment, and consider Spenser's methods of telling persuasive and decorous histories in *The Faerie Queene*'s invented circumstances.

The Ends of History

Having established Redcross as the standard by whom to judge other characters' historical self-conceptions, I turn now to Arthur's, Britomart's, and then Paridell's readings of historiography in Books II and III. These three characters read, hear,

---

[63] See Michael O'Connell, *Mirror and Veil: The Historical Dimensions of Spenser's Faerie Queene* (Chapel Hill: University of North Carolina Press, 1977), 71. For a comprehensive treatment of Spenser's sources and a full explication of his history, see Carrie A. Harper, *Sources of British Chronicle History in Spenser's Faerie Queene* (Philadelphia: John C. Winston, 1910). By the sixteenth century there was a long tradition of building national histories on a mythic foundation. Heather James offers an explanation and numerous examples of Troy's position in the histories of many northern European nations as the 'transcultural, transhistorical model onto which poets...graft indigenous myths of origin' (*Shakespeare's Troy: Drama, Politics, and the Translation of Empire* (Cambridge: Cambridge University Press, 1997), 15).

[64] Spenser, *Faerie Queene*, II.Proem.1.7, 4, 5.

or relate histories that culminate in them—that is, histories whose deliberate ethical import is to persuade them either to follow a given course or to recognize their identity.

In the English historiographic tradition, the timeworn notion that history is a guide to action is as old as Bede.[65] It owes not just to patrons' self-concern but also to the cyclical pattern of genealogical history, a pattern that slots individual biographies into a sequential structure. Genealogies are a handy way to periodize and localize a long-range narrative. They also reflect how Elizabethans and Jacobean aristocrats 'saw the family as fundamentally definitive of an individual's potential to contribute to the commonwealth, and appealed to family heritage in asserting individual merit or virtue.'[66]

There are two false claims at play in genealogical history, which we might call the claim of descent and the claim of culmination. The first is driven by the second. When an emperor like Augustus or a king like James wants to claim descent from an ancestor like Brutus, he commissions a poet to write him a dynastic epic. The descent is patently fictional, but poets like Virgil have incentives to make it plausible. Elizabethan and Jacobean claims of descent appear in real and fictional histories, and in genres like panegyrics with an elevated sense of occasion. The second claim, of culmination, drives these efforts—as it drives Spenser's three historical episodes in *The Faerie Queene* that I now address. In each episode, Spenser uses the claim of culmination to localize the past in the present, or rather to make the past influence present readers to re-enact their ethical lessons. Who is to argue with their own ancestors? The claim of culmination based on genealogy is a more literal version of the claims that poets make when they link exemplars to readers.

The Faerie Queene provokes a reader to rhetorical self-consciousness. Spenser aims 'to make the reader interpret his or her own interpretations, to judge the moral quality of his or her response to reading, to feel the work as a large rhetorical appeal to the will.' Quilligan argues that John Milton's early reading of the poem signals this project's success.[67] In *Areopagitica*, Milton's argument against censorship relies on a claim that that moral goodness derives from familiarity with evil. Milton cites two episodes in Book II, Guyon's repudiation of Mammon and his destruction of the Bower of Bliss. In these episodes Spenser

---

[65] See Andrew Escobedo, *Nationalism and Historical Loss in Renaissance England: Foxe, Dee, Spenser, Milton* (Ithaca and London: Cornell University Press, 2004); Daniel R. Woolf, *The Social Circulation of the Past: English Historical Culture 1500–1730* (Oxford: Oxford University Press, 2003); and Arthur B. Ferguson, *Clio Unbound: Perception of the Social and Cultural Past in Renaissance England* (Durham: Duke University Press, 1979).

[66] Woolf, *Social Circulation*, 133; on ancestry and heraldry evincing a broader 'genealogical imagination' in this period, see 99–137.

[67] Quilligan, *Milton's Spenser*, 41. For Milton, goodness is predicated on *choice*, on intimate knowledge of, and rejection of, evil: knowledge of good only comes from acquaintance with evil. On Guyon as a reader see Quilligan, *Milton's Spenser*, 52–4.

tempts Guyon with wealth and pleasure, Milton writes, 'that he might see and know, and yet abstain.... And this is the benefit which may be had of books promiscuously read.'[68] *The Faerie Queene* often alerts readers to their interpretive duties. Not only does Spenser directly address Elizabeth in his proems to each book, anticipating and thus shaping his readers' responses; he also shows them (and us) characters reading, learning, and discovering things about themselves, their world, and their origins in the outlying narratives of history.

Spenser manipulates the historical narratives within his fictional narrative to make us see how rhetoric can alter a familiar story. But his manipulations are subtler than mere internal distortion; they often happen at stories' edges (beginnings and endings), or at the interfaces between stories and the circumstances of their narration and reception. In three particular episodes, the teller of a history either withholds or distorts elements of the story in order to convey less than its full truth. First Arthur and Guyon read their respective national chronicles, at the House of Alma in Book II; then Merlin offers Britomart a prophecy of her descendants in Book III; and finally, Paridell draws an analogy between himself and his Trojan ancestors to woo the young and beautiful Hellenore later in Book III. Each episode reveals how the truth-value of the past is subordinate to its present, rhetorical purpose: to urge their readers to do something (Hellenore); or to show Spenser's own readers how fictional readers (Arthur) and real readers (Elizabeth) are enacting what future historiographers and 'Poet[s] historical' will write, so they ought to conduct themselves with self-awareness.

In the first of these three episodes, Spenser assumes the role of history's narrator. In Book II, Guyon and Arthur come to the House of Alma, an allegory of the temperate human body, and make their way to its 'brain,' the library of Eumnestes, or 'Good Memory': 'This man of infinite remembrance.'[69] Among his decaying volumes and worm-eaten manuscripts, they find histories of their native countries, and devour them eagerly. Guyon, the Faerie knight, reads the 'Antiquitie of Faerie lond', a thinly veiled Tudor history of his queen Gloriana: 'brave ensaumples' to kings, but not necessarily to Guyon.[70] Meanwhile, the British knight and future king Arthur reads the *Briton moniments*, a chronicle culminating in the present.[71] Like Redcross, Arthur knows nothing of his past, or

---

[68] John Milton, *The Complete Poetry and Essential Prose of John Milton*, ed. William Kerrigan, John Peter Rumrich, and Stephen M. Fallon (New York: Modern Library, 2007), 939.

[69] Spenser, *Faerie Queene*, II.ix.56.1. For a study of Eumnestes's library in light of Spenser's Protestant nationalism, see Jennifer Summit, *Memory's Library: Medieval Books in Early Modern England* (Chicago: University of Chicago Press, 2008), 106, 121–8.

[70] On how the Elfin chronicles reflect Tudor and biblical genealogical habits of thought, see Margaret Christian, '"The Ground of Storie": Genealogy in *The Faerie Queene*.' In *Spenser Studies: A Renaissance Poetry Annual IX*, ed. Patrick Cullen and Thomas P. Roche Jr. (New York: AMS Press, 1991), 61–79.

[71] On connections between this chronicle and *The Ruines of Time*, see Thomas A. Prendergast, 'Spenser's Phantastic History, *The Ruines of Time*, and the Invention of Medievalism.' *Journal of Medieval and Early Modern Studies* 38 (2008): 175–96.

(consequently) of his identity—he knows only his future, his quest to find Gloriana.[72] The history of Britain is a revelation to him—of historical knowledge not only for its own sake, or for examples like Guyon's—but also for the sake of defining his identity through his place in the chronicle. It is a historic moment, in many senses of the word. But as Arthur reads the chronicle, it ends abruptly at the moment Uther Pendragon is to be succeeded by the unwitting reader. The poisoned Aurelius has been buried at Stonehenge, when

> After him *Vther*, which *Pendragon* hight,
> Succeeding..." There abruptly it did end,
> Without full point, or other Cesure right,
> As if the rest some wicked hand did rend,
> Or th'Authour selfe could not at least attend
> To finish it:[73]

As far as Arthur is concerned, the narrative ends at an arbitrary point in the past. Spenser underscores this gap in Arthur's understanding by having him eulogize the 'wonder of antiquitie' and decry his former ignorance (comparatively speaking): 'How brutish is it not to vnderstand' history, he enthuses, even as his own place in it remains withheld.[74] Spenser calls the end an 'untimely breach,' the moment when historiography reaches its limit in the present moment, in time that cannot be chronicled—only experienced, or prophesied. Spenser will write Arthur's history, but it will not come that easily: Arthur has to enact it first. When Spenser implies that the author faltered before finishing the chronicle, he means the inverse: it is the reader who needs to complete this story. The narrative's truncation ensures that Arthur remains ignorant of any connection to this past or any grand designs for his future.

As a dynastic epic, *The Faerie Queene*'s immediate story is subsumed within a narrative extending far beyond even what Spenser calls the 'whole intention' of his conceit—the poem's projected twenty-four books.[75] For royal readers, like Arthur and Elizabeth, dynastic history does not merely end in the present, it culminates in the present. Their ancestors give them a birthright, but it is not a passive inheritance. It imposes a set of expectations: at the very least, to live up to their

---

[72] E. M. W. Tillyard calls Arthur's search for Gloriana an inversion of the Tudor myth, which Spenser emphatically supports: 'Thy name, O soueraine Queene, thy realme and race, | From this renowmed Prince deriued arre' (II.x.4). This dispels any remaining doubts of the future king's identity—in all, that is, but Arthur himself. On parallels between Redcrosse's near-suicide and Arthur's patriotic fervour, see John Curran, 'Despaire and Briton Moniments: Moments of Protestant Clarity in *the Faerie Queene*.' *Reformation* 25, no. 2 (2020): 175–91.

[73] Spenser, *Faerie Queene*, II.x.68.1–6.

[74] Spenser, *Faerie Queene*, II.x.69.7. 'Arthur's wonder resides in the unknowable,' Summit writes. Thus 'the Spenserian library calls attention to the perennially fragmentary, incomplete nature of the post-Reformation [-dissolution] archive' (*Memory's Library*, 126).

[75] Spenser, *Faerie Queene*, 738.

examples. Unlike Guyon, Arthur has no choice whether or not to 'follow' these examples (in both senses of the word). The past culminates in the present, a time that is always relative to the reader's frame of reference.

Before the second episode involving a chronicle culminating in the present, Spenser invokes the muse of history to solicit her aid in writing an account that will end with Elizabeth:

> Begin, O *Clio*, and recount from hence
> My glorious Soueraines goodly auncestrie,
> Till that by dew degrees and long protense,
> Thou haue it lastly brought vnto her Excellence.[76]

Spenser dramatically shifts this frame of reference by extending British history to the Elizabethan present, from where he broke it off before Arthur's reign. Britomart has a vision of her beloved Artegall, and consults Merlin on how to find him in order to fulfil her quest. Merlin does more than that: he prophesies their future descendants up to and beyond the Norman invasion, ending on a high note with the Tudors' 'eternal vnion' (ending the Wars of the Roses) that heralds eternal peace. Then he arrives at Queen Elizabeth:

> Then shall a royall virgin raine, which shall
> Stretch her white rod ouer the *Belgicke* shore,
> And the great Castle smite so sore with all,
> That it shall make him shake, and shortly learne to fall.

> But yet the end is not.' There *Merlin* stayd,
> As ouercomen of the spirites powre,
> Or other ghastly spectacle dismayd,
> That secretly he saw, yet note discoure.[77]

Whether from incomprehension or alarm, Merlin stops at what Britomart considers an arbitrary point in the future.[78] From the vantage-point of this Elizabethan future, of course, the perspective is quite different; this moment would electrify Elizabethan readers who had just read Arthur's truncated history lesson. In an instant, Spenser turns all of his valorizing of Elizabeth's dynastic heritage into a reminder of the succession question: 'the end is not.' The narrative

---

[76] Spenser, *Faerie Queene*, III.iii.4.6–9.   [77] Spenser, *Faerie Queene*, III.iii.49.6–50.4.

[78] W. H. Auden wrote 'Secondary Epic' in response to the close of Anchises' prophecy in Book VI of the *Aeneid*. As he facetiously points out, the prophecy of this 'unborn nation['s] . . . coming historical drama' ends in 31 BCE: 'Wouldn't Aeneas have asked—"What next? | After this triumph, what portends?"' (cit. Fichter, *Poets Historical*, 2).

goes on, but Merlin refuses to disclose it. Britomart considers Merlin's whole prophecy as marvellous as Arthur's encounter with his history, but she is not Merlin's object. Merlin draws direct attention to Elizabeth's dynastic position—not to glorify it, but to reinforce its burden. No doubt, writes Richard McCabe, 'the queen was intended to ponder it deeply; only she held the key to succession, only she could [enact] the future toward which Spenser gestures.'[79] Spenser's poetry could gesture toward this future, but it could not tell Elizabeth what form it would take, or how to actualize it. The Queen faced a predicament worse than Britomart's: how to actualize a mysterious future.

While the same dynastic force impels all three of these figures—Arthur, Britomart, and Elizabeth—forward from their common past, the future remains withheld by the divine force of providence. Redcross's state of complete understanding is the ideal toward which they all strive: the sense not only that they are borne along by the same destiny that determined the fates of their ancestors but that they could willingly reconcile themselves to providence.

In these two episodes Spenser relates true, undistorted histories. His only rhetorical licence with these chronicles and prophecies is at their beginnings and endings, contexts and consequences. A third category of Spenser's forms of history is the analogy, to which we now turn.[80] Analogy gives a rhetorician far greater licence to manipulate historical events for exemplary effects. The rhetorician in question is not Spenser, but a knight named Paridell. Later in Book III when Britomart dines at the house of Malbecco (an old man with a young wife, Hellenore) Paridell tells the familiar story of the Trojan War. As their names suggest, Paridell, Hellenore, and Malbecco are ciphers for Paris, Helen, and Menelaus. Thus Paridell steals Hellenore away from her jealous husband, just as his ancestor Paris stole Helen. Paridell first tells his dinner companions that he is lineally descended from Paris of Troy, before his actions demonstrate that he owes more to him than a name. At Hellenore's eager request, Paridell narrates his ancestor's story in preferential terms.

Paridell departs from the traditional view of Paris as passionately ineffectual and Helen as the beautiful cause of wide-scale suffering, twisting historiography to woo a new Helen. In Paridell's version, Paris becomes the 'Most famous Worthy of the world.'[81] But when Britomart, a student of history, hears the story she cannot help asking if Paridell hasn't forgotten Aeneas, whose legacy after Troy was somewhat more glorious. Whether it is accurate or not, Paridell's story inflames Britomart's pity for the Trojans,

---

[79] McCabe, *Pillars of Eternity*, 193. Only Elizabeth *can* do so, as the historical allegories of Book V arise directly from her decisive rule, writes Berger in *Revisionary Play: Studies in the Spenserian Dynamics* (Berkeley: University of California Press, 1988), 130.
[80] These categories are Bart van Es's, in *Forms of History*.   [81] Spenser, *Faerie Queene*, III.ix.34.

> from whose race of old
> She heard, that she was lineally extract:
> For noble *Britons* spring from *Troians* bold,
> And *Troynouant* was built of old *Troyes* ashes cold.[82]

Before Britomart can elaborate on this lineal connection between the Britons and the Trojans, Paridell almost interrupts her lament for the ruined city with this version of the story. When Paridell tells the story of Aeneas's voyage to Latium, he deliberately glosses over the story of Dido, who isn't mentioned by name—presumably because this would put amorous visitors in an unfavourable light.[83] When Britomart interrupts him again, she earns a disingenuous apology from Paridell:

> Pardon I pray my heedlesse ouersight,
> Who had forgot that whilome I heard tell
> From aged *Mnemon*;[84]

He is making excuses, while downplaying Aeneas's importance. And so, with further prompting from Britomart, Paridell proceeds to tell Britain's founding myth: of Aeneas's grandson Brute sailing to Britain, slaying its native giants, and conquering it for Rome. Paridell's story takes the form of an analogy—in which an exemplary story mirrors, and influences, its present circumstances. Hellenore will leave Malbecco just as Helen left Menelaus.

This third episode differs from the first two in a few ways. For one, the descendant recounts his own story, provoking Paridell's dispute with Britomart about which of its details matter. Paridell's historiography is unreliable because he shapes it for rhetorical effect; he neglects to mention details like Aeneas's dalliance with Dido because it would warn women like Hellenore against this affair. Paridell's unreliability is the chief difference between his analogy and Spenser's other accounts of history, but Britomart naïvely corrects his manipulations.[85] Exemplarity's taxonomic decorum runs through all three episodes. Arthur and Elizabeth each hear about their ancestors, whether or not they recognize them as such; Britomart hears about her descendants, and asserts a more thorough history than Paridell's distortion; and Paridell and Hellenore reenact their namesakes, even if they follow vice instead of virtue.

---

[82] Spenser, *Faerie Queene*, III.ix.38.6–9.

[83] Thomas P. Roche, *The Kindly Flame: A Study of the Third and Fourth Books of Spenser's* Faerie Queene (Princeton: Princeton University Press, 1964), 65.

[84] Spenser, *Faerie Queene*, III.ix.47.2–4.

[85] Heather Dubrow, 'The Arraignment of Paridell: Tudor Historiography in *The Faerie Queene*, III. ix.' *Studies in Philology* 87, no. 3 (1990): 312.

In each of these three episodes, Spenser deploys historical narratives with resonant decorous relationships to their readers or audiences, in an effort to influence their self-conceptions and actions. He withholds either internal details, as in Paridell's lack of an Aeneas in his story, or external ones, like what happens (or might happen) after the story ends. Arthur, Britomart, and Paridell's ancestors influence their proclivities; their personal inclinations and actions are subject to comparisons with these exemplars. These episodes from *The Faerie Queene* give us Spenser's principles in action, showing readers how they ought to live up to past examples. But in his complaints, and in *Astrophel*, we see the decline from principles to reality, as Spenser confronts the compromised state of the present.

The present always fails to live up to the past. Spenser's task is to make his characters, and his real-world readers, aware of their duties to historical antecedents—or aware of their agency as subjects of future historiography. Their obligations to meet history with responsive decorum stem from that history's taxonomic decorum. Yet their responses are manifestly inadequate. Readers' lapses in receptive decorum—their inadequate responses—suggest that negative, cautionary examples are more universal than positive, idealized ones. Idealizations do the past a disservice; they distance it from an inadequate present. Only readers could make it adequate by re-enacting the past, meeting its standards, living up to its example. When they fail in this effort, or fail to undertake it at all, Spenser provokes their narrative self-consciousness by offering them texts that are manifestly insufficient. In short, readers' actions earn elegies and complaints, genres far less desirable than chronicles or epics, both for subjects to earn or poets to write.

I now turn from narrative to generic decorum, and consider a set of texts using exemplarity for rhetorical effect: his complaints, and his elegy for Sidney. Spenser's purpose in these texts is to move his objects through criticism, rather than praise. He induces the same historical self-consciousness (of objects as potential subjects in the exemplary cycle) that we saw in *The Faerie Queene*, but he uses unflinchingly negative depictions of the inadequate genres that his subjects deserve. Spenser holds fast to the rhetorical potential of generic decorum, to the belief that the right genre can provoke readers to earn better genres. He uses complaints to complain about inadequate subjects, and to exert pressure on readers to do better, to imitate better examples and cultivate better legacies. Just as he used taxonomic decorum (the right story) to provoke receptive decorum (the right response) in *The Faerie Queene*, his complaints and elegies use generic decorum (the right kind of story) to provoke receptive decorum in a real world of potential stories.

Generic Decorum

When Shakespeare's Theseus hears a 'brief' of the entertainments with which to pass the evening before the lovers' marriages in *A Midsummer Night's Dream*, one of the options he rejects sounds familiar to Spenserians: 'The thrice-three Muses mourning for the death | Of learning, late deceased in beggary.' Theseus rejects it as unsuitable on generic grounds, calling it 'some satire, keen and critical, | Not sorting with a nuptial ceremony.'[86] Shakespeare likely refers to Spenser's *The Teares of the Muses*, a poem from his *Complaints* (1591).[87] It is hard to imagine Spenser's complaint of the death of learning entertaining anyone, let alone these betrothed Athenians: it may not be a satire, but it is certainly keen and critical. Theseus has already banished melancholy from his own wedding, and will not risk its return with an indecorous genre.[88] Better an epithalamion, or a re-enactment of famous lovers—Pyramus and Thisbe, say—even if they are impersonated by rude mechanicals.

Theseus bases his choice on generic decorum, or the suitability of a text's genre to its occasion and audience. Generic decorum combines elements of social, literary, and rhetorical decorum: social circumstances dictate the writer's choice of genre, whose tonal, narrative, and other conventions influence its effects on a receptive audience.[89] It determines the appropriateness (decorum) of a generic choice based both on its social conditions, and on the rhetorical ends that a writer (or audience like Theseus) deems most suitable or necessary to those conditions.

Genres have a public function, a burden of circumstance. Their decorum is external, or social; not merely internal, or literary. An epithalamion suits a wedding because it celebrates marital unity; an elegy suits a funeral because it mourns human frailty. Their effects are variable and contingent, but they are limited (at least) by the determinate range of responses that each genre intentionally provokes: praise or blame, complacency or change, delight or dole. To continue in this Shakespearean vein, both mirth in funeral and dirge in marriage are starkly indecorous on generic grounds.

These decorous limits make the writer's choice and execution of an occasional genre sound reductively automatic. They also account for Samuel Johnson's snide, influential view that 'occasional poetry must often content itself with occasional praise.'[90] Occasional texts have both memorial and rhetorical aims: to describe

[86] William Shakespeare, *A Midsummer Night's Dream*, ed. Stephen Greenblatt (New York: W. W. Norton & Co., 2008), 5.1.42, 39, 52–3, 54–5. On the question of this allusion, see James Bednarz, 'Imitations of Spenser in *A Midsummer Night's Dream*,' *Renaissance Drama* 14 (1983): 79–102.

[87] The first to make this identification was Thomas Warton, in William Shakespeare, *The Plays of William Shakespeare: In Ten Volumes*, ed. Samuel Johnson and George Steevens (London, 1773), III.90n.

[88] 'Turn melancholy forth to funerals— | The pale companion is not for our pomp' (Shakespeare, *Midsummer Night's Dream*, 1.1.14–15).

[89] My use of the term 'generic decorum' refines its usual meaning, of the internal rules of particular genres. Aviva Freedman and Peter Medway coin the term 'generic rhetoric' for the choice of a genre to fulfil 'attendant felicity conditions or conditions of success' (*Genre and the New Rhetoric* (London: Taylor & Francis, 1994), 99). See the Introduction for a discussion of generic decorum in the context of the taxonomic and receptive varieties that also operate in exemplary rhetoric.

[90] Samuel Johnson, *Lives of the Poets* (1781), 159.

occasions as they are; and to influence readers to undertake given actions, departures from the way things presently are. These texts reflect their circumstances not only by representing things as they are, but also—and more importantly, to my purpose—by trying to alter those circumstances. Their effort to rewrite history is evidence of their indelible historicity.

Only in admittedly rare instances does such a text surpass the limits of its occasion, and earn the praise of readers in new circumstances. But if Johnson's charge is based on occasional poetry's transparent concern with quotidian conditions, it is too blunt for a poem like *The Teares of the Muses* at the Athenian court. Prompted by entirely different circumstances, this poem addresses those who deserve its 'keen and critical' scrutiny. More broadly, Johnson's claim is unsuited to occasional texts like complaint or satire, which criticize their conditions and demand better ones—just as it is unsuited to elegy, a 'reluctant genre' whose writers resist its necessity.[91] All are provoked by failures, though they vary in the specificity and degree of blame they assign their subjects. The generic decorum of these anti-occasional texts, as I call them, is necessarily discomfiting to the comfortable: these texts often posit alternate occasions, more memorable actions and the better memorials they would have provoked.

In *The Teares of the Muses* and in the 'October' eclogue of *The Shepheardes Calender* (1579), Spenser's rhetorical aim is more corrective than decorous. In his *Complaints* (1591), Spenser laments that his poetic ambition is impeded by failures of inspiration—at times underscored by the deaths or other failures of patrons, but always embroiled in the broader problem of worldly impediments to heroic verse.[92] Facing a paucity of subjects to praise, Spenser counsels patrons to liberate poets from the whims of occasion so they can write more monumental verse, whose endurance is more important than its veracity. In *The Ruines of Time*, another poem in the *Complaints* volume, Spenser rejects his occasions and his subjects to demand better ones. He urges prospective subjects to do things worth remembering, and prospective patrons to cultivate their legacies. He thus raises questions about poetry's cause and effects, or origins and reception. Having addressed Spenser's motive of inverting receptive decorum in these occasional poems, let us now turn to his execution of the strategy in practice.

---

[91] Michael Ullyot, 'The Fall of Troynovant: Exemplarity After the Death of Henry, Prince of Wales.' In *Fantasies of Troy: Classical Tales and the Social Imaginary in Medieval and Early Modern Europe*, ed. Stephen Powell and Alan Shepard (Toronto: CRRS, 2004), 269–90. Elegists lament not only the deaths that have occasioned them, but that elegies are necessary at all. 'Elegies are at once idealistic representations which seek to immortalise their subjects, and critical responses to the decadence of the age,' Brady writes in her study of the ritualized nature of seventeenth-century elegy, *English Funerary Elegy*, 2. For further discussion of the genre, see 'Lamentations' and 'Attributions' in Chapter 4.

[92] The rhetorical intentions of Spenser's *Complaints* have been noted as long ago as Gerald Snare, 'The Muses on Poetry: Spenser's *The Teares of the Muses*.' *Tulane University Studies in English* 17 (1969): 31–52. For the place of this text in Spenser's career, see Katharine A. Craik, 'Spenser's "Complaints" and the New Poet.' *Huntington Library Quarterly* 64, no. 1/2 (2001): 63–79.

Where do poems come from? Stephen Guy-Bray raises this faux-naïve question in the subtitle of *Against Reproduction: Where Renaissance Texts Come From.*[93] Early modern English responses focused on poetry's celestial origins, before it assumed an earthly habitation. The 'ancient-learned' opinion, according to Sidney in *The Defence of Poesy*, is that poetry is 'a divine gift, and no human skill.'[94] In his lost discourse 'the English Poete,' Spenser echoed this ancient opinion to describe poetry originating in 'celestiall inspiration.'[95] The poet's wit and labour then makes the ethereal concrete. Often the poet is inspired by the muses or other intermediaries, but all poets write under historical, material conditions. Theorists of poetry appreciated the need to manifest and materialize their subject matter— just as humanists saw the combination of wisdom and eloquence as essential to learning, and as orators saw the complementarity of *res* and *verba* (things and words) as essential to persuasion.

Spenser's complaints are both a genre and a mode, to judge from his own usage.[96] His 1591 collection of poems by that name (*Complaints: Containing Sundrie Small Poems of the Worlds Vanitie*) advertises in its subtitle that its poems lament the state of the world and the vicissitudes of Fortune.[97] More broadly, complaints are 'plaintive poems, or plaintive passages within larger poems, expressing grief or lamentation for any variety of causes: unrequited love, the speaker's affairs, or the sorrows of the human condition.'[98] As this definition suggests, a complaint either informs and shapes a whole text, such as *The Teares of the Muses*, or is subsumed by another text, such as Pastorella's 'pitifull complaints' of her captivity in *The Faerie Queene*, VI.x–xi.[99] The latter example suggests an analogy between complaint and pastoral. Both are modes that can preside over an entire text and can even accommodate one another: the pastoral *Shepheardes Calender* is punctuated by Cuddy's complaints from

---

[93] Stephen Guy-Bray, *Against Reproduction: Where Renaissance Texts Come from* (Toronto: University of Toronto Press, 2009).

[94] Sidney, *Defence*, 379. Sidney also refers to the poet endowed with 'the force of a divine breath' creating works that surpass God's own nature (344).

[95] Spenser, *Yale Edition*, 170. For a study of how poets' social positions affect their claims to poetic inspiration, see John Huntington, 'Furious Insolence: The Social Meaning of Poetic Inspiration in the 1590s.' *Modern Philology* 3 (1997): 305–26.

[96] See R. H. Nicholson, 'State of the Nation: Some Complaint Topics in Late Medieval English Literature.' *Parergon* 23 (1979): 21; Richard Rambuss, *Spenser's Secret Career* (Cambridge and New York: Cambridge University Press, 1993), 85; and John N. King, 'Traditions of Complaint and Satire.' In *A Companion to English Renaissance Literature and Culture*, ed. Michael Hattaway (Malden and Oxford: Blackwell, 2003), 367.

[97] Richard Danson Brown, *'The New Poet': Novelty and Tradition in Spenser's Complaints* (Liverpool: Liverpool University Press, 1999), 7.

[98] Hugh Maclean, '"Restlesse Anguish and Unquiet Paine": Spenser and the Complaint, 1579–1590.' In *The Practical Vision: Essays in English Literature in Honour of Flora Roy*, ed. James Doyle, Flora Roy, and Jane Campbell (Waterloo: Wilfrid Laurier University Press, 1978), 30. Brown concludes from his analysis of the 1591 *Complaints* that 'for Spenser it becomes a genre instinctively preoccupied with the status and value of poetry' (*Novelty and Tradition*, 24 n. 72).

[99] This is Spenser's description (6.10.44.2). To find this and other examples of Spenser's usage, I have searched his texts with Wordhoard: <http://wordhoard.northwestern.edu/>.

January to December. Both modes can also be inset within various genres; witness the pastoral modes that Shakespeare incorporates into a romance like *The Winter's Tale*, or a comedy like *As You Like It*.[100]

Complaints are elastic because they are prompted by the speaker's immediate subjects and experiences. Yet unlike satire, they concern abstract or conceptual problems over named, particular wrongdoers.[101] When the subject is historical, the speaker is 'Edmund Spenser'—and the result is a genre lamenting his persona's circumstances. When the subject is invented, like Pastorella's captivity, so too is the speaker—and the result is a mode inset in the poem, lamenting her own circumstances. Lamenting is not quite the right word, however: one laments in an elegy, but one criticizes in a complaint. Its speaker knows, and often says, that their circumstances could be otherwise. One account of late medieval complaints describes them as a 'rhetorical vehicle' to criticize social failings, even if (unlike satire) the particular 'source of these failings was not analyzed by the [complaint's] limited moral critique.'[102]

I began this argument with one faux-naïve question, and will now pose another. How can we reconcile Spenser's sense of poetry's idealized, ethereal origins with his complaints about its earthly impediments? To put it another way, if poems come as divine gifts from heaven, just what is Spenser complaining about? The answer is not simply the material debasement of the ethereal. Spenser's view of poetry survives in the paraphrase of his editor E. K., describing it as 'no arte, but a divine gift and heavenly instinct not to bee gotten by laboure and learning, but adorned with both: and poured into the witte by a certain ἐνθουσιασμὸς. [enthusiasmos] and celestial inspiration.'[103] The two denials in this definition distinguish poetry from rhetoric, that 'arte' or skill which can 'bee gotten by laboure and learning.' Sidney also argues that poetry requires more genius than brute-force industry. His definition is also indebted to rhetorical theory:

---

[100]   Mary Jo Kietzman argues that complaint is a mode within a range of genres, including 'medieval tragedy, allegory, epic, prose history, and picaresque' ('"Means to Mourn Some Newer Way": The Role of the Complaint in Early-Modern Narrative' (Diss., Boston College, 1993), 1–2). On mode (versus genre) as 'the literary manifestation, in a given work, of . . . its assumptions about man's nature and situation,' see Paul Alpers, *What is Pastoral?* (Chicago and London: University of Chicago Press, 1996), 50, esp. 44–5. On *As You Like It* in relation to this distinction, see 70–8.

[101]   John Peter, *Complaint and Satire in Early English Literature* (Oxford: Clarendon Press, 1956), 59; Kirk Combe, 'The New Voice of Political Dissent: The Transition from Complaint to Satire.' In *Theorizing Satire: Essays in Literary Criticism*, ed. Brian A. Connery and Kirk Combe (New York: St Martin's Press, 1995), 76–7.

[102]   Steven A. Owley, 'The Voice of Complaint: A Study in Political and Moral Rhetoric' (Diss., Ohio State University, 1999), 16; see also Nicholson, 'Complaint Topics'.

[103]   Spenser, *Yale Edition*, 170. On the relationship between E. K.'s glosses and Spenser's text, see Richard McCabe, 'Annotating Anonymity, or Putting a Gloss on *the Shepheardes Calender*.' In *Ma(r)king the Text: The Presentation of Meaning on the Literary Page*, ed. Joe Bray, Miriam Hadley, and Anne C. Henry (Aldershot: Ashgate, 2000), 35–54.

For poesy must not be drawn by the ears; it must be gently led, or rather it must lead; which was partly the cause that made the ancient-learned affirm it was a divine gift, and no human skill.... [S]ince all other knowledges lie ready for any that hath strength of wit; a poet no industry can make, if his own genius be not carried into it.[104]

Sidney's inquiry into the origins and effects of poetry in his *Defence* owes much to preceding writers on rhetoric like Ascham and Wilson, who themselves recapitulate Cicero, Quintilian, and the *Rhetorica ad Herennium*. Even if poetry can teach, delight, and persuade as rhetoric does, the poet is no mere rhetorician, trained up by the 'diligent practice and earnest exercise [that] are the only things that make men prove excellent.'[105] Rather, Sidney cites the proverb *orator fit, poeta nascitur*: an orator is made, a poet born.

That is the ideal. But Spenser's occasional poems temper his theory of poetry as a divine gift by emphasizing the circumstances of a poem's writing and reception. Occasional poems are closer to rhetoric than other poems because their words (*verba*) are more proximate to their subjects (*res*). Spenser's complaints are preoccupied with the decorous complementarity of *res* and *verba*: they emerge from and respond to their material circumstances, namely to be critical of them.

The elegy is an occasional text that similarly resists its occasion, if more surreptitiously than complaint. In a typical example, Thomas Heywood opens his 1612 elegy for Henry, Prince of Wales 'wishing with my soule, I might haue had a more pleasing subiect,' but conceding that 'since the Heauens haue giuen vs this cause it is a duty to entertaine the occasion, and an unswerable [*sic*] negligence to omit it.'[106] The 'duty to entertaine the occasion' implies a duty to acknowledge and receive the occasion with a decorous genre, in this case a death with an elegy. Heywood's claim that heaven gave poets this cause attributes the Prince's death to supernatural forces, as was conventional—and echoes what Sidney (again) calls the 'ancient-learned' opinion of poetry's divine origins. Heywood dutifully reconciles this divine matter with his earthly words, which he delivers only with reluctance.

I now address how Spenser's complaints are, like Heywood's elegy, occasional poems that resist their occasions. *The Teares of the Muses* focuses on poetry's subject matter, with Spenser assuming an adversarial role of resisting and criticizing it, in order to change it. This complaint counterbalances poetry's divine origins with a more material view of its circumstances. In *The Teares of the Muses*, each muse has a principled sense of the ideal form of her respective art. The

---

[104] Sidney, *Defence*, 379.
[105] Thomas Wilson, *An English Rhetoric (1560)*, *English Renaissance Literary Criticism*, ed. Brian Vickers (Oxford: Clarendon Press, 1999), 78.
[106] Thomas Heywood, *Funerall Elegie* (1613), sig. A2r. This elegy is discussed further in 'Decline and Fall' in Chapter 4.

Muses' main complaint is that poets are writing, instead, poems that are low in the generic hierarchy. They direct this frustration to the poetic subjects that fail to inspire better writing: error, folly, and spite prevail in place of virtue; infamy in place of fame. For instance, Erato finds no reception for her lyric poetry, nor for the 'high conceit of that celestiall fire' whence love is 'infused into mortall brests.' Among men's lewd 'dunghill thoughts' she finds no signs of love, 'the devicefull matter of my song.'[107] Melpomene, the muse of tragedy, uses the same word for poetic subjects when she complains that the petty tragedies of senseless men are poor 'matter' compared to the 'true Tragedies' she ought to relate: 'I mourne... Because that mourning matter I have none.'[108]

Spenser is ambitious to write genres more elevated in this hierarchy—but this is a bid for influence, not for mere prestige. Certain genres undeniably exert more rhetorical influence than others. Lyric and tragedy are better not only for what Erato calls their 'high conceipt[s]' but also for their rhetorical impact. Spenser's rhetorical ambition resembles Sidney's, who defines the 'right' poets as those who 'borrow nothing of what is, hath been, or shall be; but range, only reined with learned discretion, into the divine consideration of what may be and should be.'[109] The occasional poet must address 'what is' before ranging into these subjunctive aspirations.

Subject matter is particularly unavoidable in occasional texts. Spenser laments in his *Complaints* and in his elegies that his subjects are inadequate: he should be writing great histories about them, not doleful poems about their deaths. At the end of this complaint, Spenser's dissatisfied muses renounce this world and its writers. They break their 'learned instruments' in protest, a gesture that immediately silences the poet: 'The rest untold no loving tongue can speake.'[110] The finality of this gesture recalls Colin Clout hanging up his pipe at the end of *The Shepheardes Calender*, a gesture of resignation to age, cold, and the failures that Spenser will elaborate in *The Complaints* some years later.[111]

The October eclogue similarly addresses this paucity of subject matter. The shepherd Cuddy, 'the perfecte paterne of a Poete,' has found 'no maintenaunce of his state and studies.'[112] In the accompanying woodblock, Cuddy looks past the offered pipes to the classical temples, the courtly milieu that should supply poets with both kinds of matter. But it supplies no worthy makers of matter for poets to

---

[107] Spenser, *Yale Edition*, 283–4, ll. 391, 390. 393, 386.
[108] Spenser, *Yale Edition*, 275, ll. 155, 165, 167–8.   [109] Sidney, *Defence*, 346.
[110] Spenser, *Yale Edition*, 291, ll. 599, 600.
[111] Hugh MacLean, 'Complaints: *The Tears of the Muses.*' In *The Spenser Encyclopedia*, ed. A. C. Hamilton (Toronto: University of Toronto Press, 1990), 182. See also Lin Kelsey and Richard Peterson, 'Rereading Colin's Broken Pipe: Spenser and the Problem of Patronage.' *Spenser Studies* 14 (2000): 233–72.
[112] Spenser, *Yale Edition*, 170.

sing about.[113] When his companion Piers urges him to 'sing of bloody Mars, of wars, of giusts' and other heroic subjects, Cuddy complains that '[A]ll the worthies liggen wrapt in leade, | That *matter* made for Poets on to play.'[114] Spenser repeats this phrase in *The Faerie Queene* when he invokes the female knights 'That *matter* made for famous Poets verse,' immediately before he tells Britomart's story for the benefit of her descendant Elizabeth, 'O Queene, the *matter* of my song.'[115] The 'matter' that these worthies, knights, and queens made is his subject. That meaning is clear from Spenser's repeated uses of the phrase; it is also consistent with Puttenham's use of 'matter' interchangeably with 'subject' in *The Arte of English Poesie* (1589), wherein 'The Subject or Matter of Poesie' is one chapter heading. Puttenham uses the term 'the whole matter' to mean a complete thought or narrative, whether confined to a piece of writing or not; thus he describes a writer 'fashion[ing] his tale to his matter.'[116]

Spenser's repetitions of the word 'matter' and its cognate 'material', throughout his corpus, reveal the rhetorical quality of his combination of *res* with *verba*. Matter is the unformed source of all things, natural and artificial; it is always subject to interventions of a divine or poetic artificer. It emerges from Chaos, in one definition from *The Faerie Queene*, as the material cause of Creation itself: 'All things from thence doe their first being fetch, | And borrow matter, whereof they are made.'[117] Matter is also the cause of everything from private moods to pitched battles, in a range of instances. In the Proem to Book II of the poem, Spenser justifies his choice of poetic subject as a 'matter of iust memory' rather than as a painted forgery, an account of true events, not invented ones.[118] Spenser offers this justification particularly when addressing his subject's historicity, particularly as he prepares to interleave British with Faery histories in the House of Alma, later in Book II. In that episode, Spenser links matter to historical memory in ways that evoke Cuddy's appeal for memorable poetic matters.[119] Spenser abridges the book of Arthur's *Briton monuments*, glossing over 'much materiall.' It comprises 'seuen hundred Princes' whose 'sondry gouernments' are too tedious to recount, yet who stand as 'famous moniments, | And braue ensample, both of martiall, | And ciuil

---

[113] The woodcut also debates whether the poet's art ought to be solitary or social, mono- or dialogical (Rebeca Helfer, 'The Death of the "New Poete": Virgilian Ruin and Ciceronian Recollection in Spenser's "The Shepheardes Calender".' *Renaissance Quarterly* 56, no. 3 (2003): 728–30).

[114] Spenser, *Yale Edition*, 173, ll. 63–4; my emphasis.

[115] Spenser, *Faerie Queene*, III.iv.1.6, III.iv.3.8; my emphasis.

[116] George Puttenham, *Arte of English Poesie* (1589), book 3, chapters 2 and 5.

[117] Spenser, *Faerie Queene*, III.vi.37.1–2.

[118] Spenser, *Faerie Queene*, II, Proem.1.5. For a survey of sixteenth-century precedents to this privileging of truth in history see William Nelson, *Fact or Fiction: The Dilemma of the Renaissance Storyteller* (Cambridge: Harvard University Press, 1973).

[119] See 'Taxonomic Decorum' earlier in this chapter.

rule to kinges and states imperiall.'[120] Not all are worth recounting for his immediate purposes—to many readers' relief—but all remain firmly in the category of brave examples for princes from Arthur to Elizabeth. Matter and material are the origins of all histories, then, real and invented—of stories with the power to persuade and guide their readers.

Consider now the historical object of Spenser's provocations—to action and to patronage. Elizabeth is Spenser's arch-reader, as I have claimed. He aims to provoke the Queen's self-consciousness as a potential subject of future poetry, a subject to be read and imitated. In *Colin Clout's Come Home Again*, Spenser repeatedly refers to the historians and poets writing the Queen's life, and to his own ambition to join them. For instance, Colin praises William Alabaster's 'heroick' yet unfinished *Elisæis*, a Latin epic, in the hope that he can 'end thy glorie which he hath begun.'[121] Colin is ambitious for poetic immortality, specifically that 'long while after I am dead and rotten: | Amongst the shepheards daughters dancing rownd, | My layes made of her [Cynthia, or Elizabeth] shall not be forgotten.'[122] In *The Teares of the Muses* Spenser draws a sharp contrast between Elizabeth and lesser patrons. Calliope, muse of epic, pointedly repeats Erato's lament for the degenerate patrons careless both of 'the auncestrie | Of th'old Heroës' and 'that late posteritie | Shoud know their [own] names, or speak their praises dew.'[123] Like Clio, the muse of history, Calliope inspires poets to report past events; but her focus here is squarely on the present. As both 'the nurse of vertue ... And golden Trompet of eternitie,' she ensures that men choose to be good because it is more praiseworthy.[124]

Spenser's complaints about his subjects focus on the failures of patrons who are neglecting their duty to provide poets with matter fit for eulogies rather than elegies.[125] The muses 'Finde nothing worthie to be writ, or told' in potential patrons; they 'nothing noble haue to sing.'[126] The implications of this failure extend past the present; it is a disservice both to their ancestry and to their descendants. Clio protests that the Muses are mourning not because their poets are ill paid but (rather) because noble patrons are neglecting their duty:

> It most behoves the honorable race
> Of mightie Peeres, true wisedome to sustaine,
> And with their noble countenaunce to grace

---

[120] Spenser, *Faerie Queene*, II.x.74.4, 3, 6, 7–9. On this episode see Chloe Wheatley, 'Abridging the Antiquitee of Faery Lond: New Paths through Old Matter in *the Faerie Queene*.' *Renaissance Quarterly* 58, no. 3 (Fall 2005): 857–80.

[121] Spenser, *Yale Edition*, 541, ll. 404, 409.   [122] Spenser, *Yale Edition*, 550, ll. 640–2.

[123] Spenser, *Yale Edition*, 285, ll. 439–40, 441–2.   [124] Spenser, *Yale Edition*, 286, ll. 457–8.

[125] On Spenser's disillusionment with courtly readers after a poor reception in 1589–91, and the origins of the *Complaints*, see William A. Oram, 'Spenser in Search of an Audience: The Kathleen Williams Lecture for 2004.' *Spenser Studies* 20 (2005): 23–47.

[126] Spenser, *Yale Edition*, 273, ll. 100, 108.

The learned forheads, without gifts or gaine:
Or rather learnd themselves behoves to bee;
That is the girlond of Nobilitie.[127]

The peers are guilty of literally unbecoming behaviour. Their admiration for their ancestors amounts to resting on their laurels, without becoming admirable in their own right. This paucity of matter leads to paltry verses, debasements of what ought to be written—or at least, what the poets and Muses would prefer to write. A recurring question of *The Teares of the Muses* is whether or not the present will offer anything worth preserving in the future. If peers fail to sustain wisdom, the consequence for future ages will be a loss of memory:

So shall succeeding ages have no light
Of things forepast, nor moniments of time,
And all that in this world is worthie hight
Shall die in darknesse, and lie hid in slime:[128]

Spenser's implicit threats of slimy darkness and explicit promises of famous monuments are for the sake of provoking patrons—both to act, and to support poets who translate actions into words. Their 'moniments of time' are for succeeding ages to admire and imitate, just as Arthur read of *Briton monuments* in Eumnestes's library.

Spenser uses the word 'monuments' forty-six times in ten works, to mean a textual or physical aid to memory, or a medium of its preservation. He most frequently modifies it with adjectives like 'famous,' 'immortal,' 'eternal,' or 'endlesse.' But in another poem in his *Complaints* volume, *The Ruines of Time*, the narrator Verlame claims that 'Time all moniments obscure[s].'[129] Here Spenser is preoccupied with memory's passage into history, and the countervailing material media that preserves that memory.[130] This is memory in both the civic, or national, and the personal sense. '[T]hings forepast' here means ruined cities like the Roman city Verulamium, conquered by the Saxons and personified by the narrator. What remains are at most broken ruins, poor memorials that leave present-minded observers ignorant of their original grandeur.[131] *The Ruines of Time* borrows from Joachim du Bellay's influential sonnet sequence on Rome, particularly the role of poets and historians to create monuments more durable

---

[127] Spenser, *Yale Edition*, 273, ll. 79–84.   [128] Spenser, *Yale Edition*, 273, ll. 103–6.

[129] Spenser, *Yale Edition*, 240, l. 174. On Verlame see Carl J. Rasmussen, '"How Weak be the Passions of Woefulness": Spenser's *Ruines of Time*.' *Spenser Studies* 2 (1981): 159–81.

[130] On the vanity of earthly poetry and Spenser's relationship to predecessors like Sidney, see Hassan Melehy, 'Antiquities of Britain: Spenser's *Ruines of Time*.' *Studies in Philology* 102, no. 2 (2005): 159–83.

[131] See Helfer, 'Remembering Sidney, Remembering Spenser'.

than any other. Verlame's faith in the endurance of the written word reinforces her claims of poetic praise's evidentiary purpose.[132] Poets offer not flattery or false monuments like the pyramids she disparages, but 'wise wordes taught in numbers for to runne, | Recorded by the Muses' to outlast noble deeds and men's thoughts.[133] Verlame thus praises the chorographic historiography of the anti-quary William Camden, whose *Britannia* preserves 'the light of simple veritie, | Buried in ruines.'[134] Verlame uses the familiar trope of written memorials out-lasting physical monuments, claiming that Camden's 'just labours ever shall endure.'[135]

Both *The Ruines of Time* and *The Teares of the Muses* are anti-occasional complaints about their occasional subjects' limitations. Both address the inad-equacy of those subjects to provoke reactions in their readers, to generate the receptive decorum Spenser wants. Spenser dedicates *The Ruines of Time* to Mary Sidney to make this provocation more explicit: Philip Sidney's death in 1586, like that of his uncle Robert Dudley, Earl of Leicester in 1588, was symptomatic of a broader decline of virtue itself.[136] Verlame has witnessed Leicester's death, and testifies that his virtues will live as long as her verses persevere: 'For ever it shall live, and shall rehearse | His worthie praise, and vertues dying never.'[137] She excoriates those who have also neglected Leicester's memory, despite his good treatment of poets while he lived. Verlame also condemns men like William Cecil, Lord Burghley (without explicitly naming him) for their parsimonious 'scorn' of the Muses. Spenser's implicit goal is to goad patrons into supporting writers who can monumentalize their memories, and those of their predecessors like Leicester and Sidney.

All occasional poets aim to write enduring fictions from the passing personae and events of history. They aim to narrow the divide so that the fictionality seems more an elaboration or augmentation than an invention. *The Ruines of Time* and *The Teares of the Muses* illustrate what happens when inadequate subjects under-mine this poetic transmutation. Spenser's *Astrophel* elegy for Sidney, contrarily, illustrates what Spenser does when he is finished imploring patrons to act. Instead of waiting for them to respond, he offers an alternate biography of Sidney that

---

[132] Verlame acknowledges that any form of evidence of her past, verbal or physical, can be unconvincing: 'To tell the beawtie of my buildings fayre,' her riches and her forces, 'Were but lost labour, that few would beleeve, | And with rehearsing would me more agreeve' (Spenser, *Yale Edition*, 236–8, ll. 85, 90–1).

[133] Spenser, *Yale Edition*, 249, ll. 402–3.

[134] Spenser, *Yale Edition*, 240, ll. 171–2. Camden's Latin history had editions in 1586, 1587, 1590, 1594, 1600, and 1607 before its first English translation in 1610.

[135] Spenser, *Yale Edition*, 240, ll. 175, 174.

[136] Isabella Whitney, Mary Sidney, and Aemilia Lanyer, *Renaissance Women Poets*, ed. Danielle Clarke (London: Penguin, 2000), 307; Edmund Spenser, *The Shorter Poems*, ed. Richard McCabe (London: Penguin, 1999), 592.

[137] Spenser, *Yale Edition*, 243, ll. 255–6.

underscores Sidney's active life and heroic death.[138] An early sign of this impatience is Spenser's closing *The Ruines of Time* with an envoy for Sidney, or Philisides, who is stellified after his death. Having considered Spenser's resistance to constraints on his poetic matter, let us now turn to Spenser's more direct dealings with historical facts and occasions.

A curious feature of *Astrophel* is how belated it is. Spenser delayed writing his elegy until 1595, nine years after Sidney's death. He apologized to Mary Sidney in 1591 that 'I haue not shewed anie thankefull remembrance towards him,' nor to the Sidneys, nor the Dudleys, 'but suffer their names to sleep in silence and forgetfulnesse.'[139] He began to repair this ingratitude to Sidney's patronage of 'my young *Muses*' by memorializing him alongside Leicester in *The Ruines of Time*, as discussed. But despite what Heywood called every poet's 'duty to entertaine the occasion' of a public figure's death, Spenser remained silent in late 1586 when Sidney died of his injuries after the battle at Zutphen in the Low Countries. This put Spenser at odds with others who wrote Sidney dozens of elegies and poetic tributes after his grand public funeral in February 1587.

Spenser may have felt the disdain that he showed in a Horatian verse-epistle of 1579, *Ad Ornatissimum virum*, in which he praised Gabriel Harvey by excoriating the poets who seek public favour: 'Whoever has striven to please high-ranking men has studied folly,... [W]hoever desires... to ingratiate himself in public favour, learns to play the fool, and solicits the base applause of inglorious folly.'[140] Spenser may also have resisted the necessity of poetic mourning, a familiar sentiment that arises whenever there are outpourings of elegies for a public figure. He writes in his invocation to *Astrophel* that his poems 'are for such ones most fit, | Made not to please the liuing but the dead.'[141] Unlike his *Complaints*, then, *Astrophel* is (at least overtly) an effort to reframe his subject rather than to provoke responses from living objects.

Astrophel is not a monument to Sidney, the way that ruins are to Verlame's past. Rather, it is an alternate version: a pastoral allegory of Sidney's life and death, and the poetic community's posthumous mourning for him. Sidney's was a heroic death in defence of his country, so Spenser need not invent any matter to praise him. But Spenser alters it, to encourage readers to admire and to imitate Sidney—not the manner of his death, of course, but the virtues that provoked it. The poem

---

[138] On *Astrophel*'s role in situating Spenser among Sidney's successors in a poetic genealogy, see Raphael Falco, *Conceived Presences: Literary Genealogy in Renaissance England* (Amherst: University of Massachusetts Press, 1994), 95–123. Elisabeth Chaghafi also addresses Sidney's afterlife in *English Literary Afterlives: Greene, Sidney, Donne and the Evolution of Posthumous Fame* (Manchester: Manchester University Press, 2019).

[139] Spenser, *Shorter Poems*, 166, ll. 17–18, 19. Spenser's dedication of the poem (to the Countess of Pembroke) draws attention to his failure to mourn Sidney adequately (Alexander, *Writing After Sidney*, 172).

[140] This is Richard McCabe's translation, in Spenser, *Shorter Poems*, 577.

[141] Spenser, *Yale Edition*, 569, ll. 15–16.

relates the story of the pastoral shepherd Philisides—who has the name, and many of the same attributes, that Sidney often used for himself; who 'could pipe and daunce, and caroll sweet'; who loves his mistress Stella, as described in Sidney's sonnet sequence *Astrophil and Stella*; and who combines skills in writing with skills in action.[142] Spenser depicts Sidney as a man of action, capable of balancing poetry with wrestling, running, shooting, swimming, and hunting. He praises Astrophel for wooing Stella with 'brave deeds,' rather than 'ydle words' and 'verses vaine':

> Ne her with ydle words alone he wowed,
> And verses vaine (yet verses are not vaine)
> But with brave deeds to her sole service vowed,
> And bold atchievements her did entertaine.
> For both in deeds and words he nourtred was,
> Both wise and hardie (too hardie alas).[143]

This closing line expresses some hesitation about Sidney's boldness because Astrophel's 'brave deeds' and 'bold atchieuements' cause his death. Astrophel dies in what Gavin Alexander calls an 'allegorical fog,' on a hunting expedition, gored in the leg by a boar; the real Sidney was shot in the leg, and likely died of gangrene.[144] Astrophel is, in Spenser's conventional description, a 'sad ensample of mans suddein end'—yet he is also a tribute to Sidney's life.[145] Such a lesson would hardly '*please the liuing*,' to recall Spenser's invocation—but his cautionary example is regardless a valuable legacy.

Thus in *The Faerie Queene*, and in his complaints and elegies, Spenser uses generic decorum to make his poetry rhetorically effective, to provoke exemplary self-consciousness in his readers. A sense of generic decorum, he hopes, will provoke worthy readers to do things worth remembering, and to patronize writers who will write occasional poetry that endures. Spenser's broader ambition is to make poetry move past mere preservation and praise of uninspiring events, recent or distant. That includes Sidney's death. Like all elegies, *Astrophel* resists its occasion, or at least the inadequacy of its occasion to inspire Sidney's admirers without allegorical aid. *Astrophel* uses exemplary rhetoric in ways that are typical of elegy, as I elaborate in my discussion of Prince Henry's elegies.[146] Elegy often aims to memorialize the dead and explain their loss but also to make their successes and failures exemplary. Like Spenser's complaints, his elegy for Sidney

---

[142] Spenser, *Yale Edition*, 571, l. 31.   [143] Spenser, *Yale Edition*, 572, ll. 67–72.

[144] Alexander, *Writing After Sidney*, 174. For details of his wounding and death, see Alan Stewart, *Philip Sidney: A Double Life* (London: Pimlico, 2001), 312–20; and (for a more documentary focus) Katherine Duncan-Jones, *Sir Philip Sidney: Courtier Poet* (New Haven: Yale University Press, 1991), 294–303.

[145] Spenser, *Yale Edition*, 575, l. 134.   [146] See 'Lamentations' and 'Attributions' in Chapter 4.

tries to turn its own bad circumstances into better future ones. Complaints and elegies both focus on the inadequacy of their causes, to provoke better subjects. They use rhetorical methods like exemplarity to provoke receptive decorum. They use lamentations to provoke the reader to earn praise. But these ambitions are more rhetorical than real, as I will argue in Chapter 4.

I began the argument of this study with Spenser because he is well practised in the art of provocation, of contrasting readings with readers, exemplary subjects with objects. Spenser's contrasts can be subtle or overt, depending on the urgency of his rhetorical ambitions. In Chapters 3 and 4, I reveal how more direct ambitions—of patronage and other forms of recognition—lead other writers directly to voice their ambitions for Essex and Henry. I conclude that bad precedents are more common than good ones; elegies and complaints, not epics and chronicles, are the most that fallible human readers should anticipate.

3

The Exemplary Cycle

Thus far in this argument, the motives of exemplary rhetoric have been ethical, advising readers what they ought to think. All rhetoric attempts ethical persuasion. But exemplarity is rarely provoked by the rhetorician's desire to propagate knowledge for its own sake, or to reanimate subjects simply to admire them. It is a method of shifting beliefs to induce behavioural change. Nor is it a unidirectional imposition of ideals from a subject onto the life and conduct of its object. As I have said, exemplarity is both an intention to influence and a receptivity to being influenced. In this chapter I add a third stage to this transaction: it is also a desire for fame resembling that of one's models. This recursive drive turns the transaction between rhetorician and audience into a cycle of regenerative imitations. (To be exact, this cycle describes positive models, not cautionary ones—whose success or failure depends on audiences studiously avoiding similar infamy.) The rhetorician of exemplarity has prescriptive purposes: to encourage their objects to resemble their subjects, with the ultimate aim of turning them into new subjects. A poet invoking a positive exemplar implicitly or (often) explicitly suggests that readers who re-enact it merit not only favourable comparisons but their own comparable biographies. Those who interpret, adapt, and reanimate the ethical imperatives of exemplary biographies live lives worth recounting.

An apocryphal but oft-repeated anecdote about Alexander the Great's biographical envy of Achilles reinforces the prevailing view of Homer and Virgil that their poetry, not their subjects' deeds, is the cause of their subjects' fame. It is apocryphal because it aggrandizes the work of those who recounted it, starting with Arrian of Nicomedia (c.87–145), the Greek historian who styled himself 'the Alexander among writers.' Visiting the tomb of Achilles at Sigeum (near Troy), as Arrian reports at the beginning of *Anabasis*, Alexander was overcome not by the Greek warrior's military triumphs but by their descriptions in Homer's *Iliad*. As Hephaestus laid a garland on the tomb of Patroclus, 'Alexander laid one on the tomb of Achilles, calling him a lucky man, in that he had Homer to proclaim his deeds and preserve his memory.' 'And that is the reason why I have embarked upon the project of writing this history, in the belief that I am not unworthy to set clear before men's eyes the story of Alexander's life,' Arrian writes.[1]

---

[1] 'And well might Alexander envy Achilles this piece of good fortune; for in his own case there was no equivalent: his one failure, the single break, as it were, in the long chain of his successes, was that he had no worthy chronicler to tell the world of his exploits. No prose history, no epic poem was written

The Rhetoric of Exemplarity in Early Modern England. Michael Ullyot, Oxford University Press. © Michael Ullyot 2022.
DOI: 10.1093/oso/9780192849335.003.0004

Alexander's biographical envy made this anecdote compelling for early modern poets. Cicero and Plutarch recapitulated it.[2] Petrarch wrote a sonnet about it.[3] And like many other English poets, Spenser used it to buttress his argument for literary patronage.[4] In his gloss to Edmund Spenser's *October* eclogue in *The Shepheardes Calender*, E. K. cites it as evidence 'why Poetes were wont be had in such honor of noble men,' because 'Achilles had neuer bene so famous, as he is, but for Homeres immortal verses.'[5] Rhetoricians who cited this anecdote were more often prospective than retrospective; that is, they sought to provoke Alexander's envy in particular readers in order to remedy it themselves. Future subjectivity is the ultimate aspiration of any object, but particularly of a public figure inundated by exemplary subjects. They seek to become an exemplar themselves—to make their life sufficiently virtuous to earn them fame and admiration beyond their death. The reader or object's actions determine whether and how rhetoricians will turn them into that future subject.

This knowledge, or anticipation of this conversion, provokes narrative self-consciousness in potential subjects. Not only should they behave in ways that will be exemplary to others, they should also ensure that they leave a posthumous legacy. More pointedly, they should patronize the writers who promise to describe them in prescriptive, exemplary ways when they are dead. If rhetoricians are agents by which the past reactivates in the present, they will also retain this function in the future, reanimating present objects as future subjects. This knowledge is often implicit, as decorum demands; but as we will see, writers who promoted their descriptive services were more successful at attracting patrons than those who did not.

So positive ethical exemplarity follows a recurring cycle of prescriptive descriptions and self-conscious imitations. This cycle revolves through three stages of a reader's experience, from education to anticipation to representation. It begins with reading the experiences of others and comparing them to one's own; if successful, this stage provokes readers to actions that they anticipate others will read in turn. Consider how the exemplary cycle operates on men of high birth like Sidney, Essex, and Henry. First, they receive an exemplary education that presents them with virtuous models to imitate and vicious ones to shun. The rhetoricians

about him; . . . [yet] there has never been another man in all the world, of Greek or any other blood, who by his own hand succeeded in so many brilliant enterprises' (Arrian of Nicomedia, *Anabasis,* tr. Aubrey de Sélincourt (London: Penguin, 1971), 67–8).

[2] Marcus Tullius Cicero, *Pro Archia Poeta. The Speeches,* tr. N. H. Watts (London: Heinemann, 1961), 10.24; Plutarch, *Alexander* (London: Penguin, 1973), 15.

[3] He recounts Alexander thus 'sighingly' praising Achilles: 'O fortunate man who found so clear a trumpet' (Francesco Petrarch, *Sonnets,* tr. R. M. Durling (Cambridge: Harvard University Press, 1976), 187, 1–4; cit. and tr. Spenser, *Shorter Poems,* 563).

[4] Spenser's Verlame echoes Petrarch: 'O fortunate yong-man, whose vertue found | So brave a Trompe, thy noble acts to sound' (Spenser, *Yale Edition,* 251, ll. 433–4). For my discussion of *The Ruines of Time* see 'Generic Decorum' in Chapter 2.

[5] Spenser, *Yale Edition,* 180.

who present these exemplars call attention to their efficacy as representations, and pledge that the reader's innate worthiness and virtuous conduct will ensure that he is similarly represented and remembered in the future—with, implicitly, the present writer's help. The point is that these are representations to provoke exemplary self-consciousness, or thoughts about how the reader will provide both subject matter and material support for their posthumous legacy. In the chapters to come, I follow the exemplary cycle through one revolution: from Sidney to Essex to Henry to Charles. Having addressed the receptive decorum necessary for the cycle's revolution, I now focus on the education and anticipation that make up its first two stages.[6] The third, representation, follows in the next chapter. Promises of future representations initiate the third and final stage of the exemplary cycle, but that stage is usually the least developed or realized. It is more commonly a trope of disappointment, a template for what might have been, particularly among those elegists who are liberated from undertaking it—as we will see after the death of Prince Henry.[7]

I have already argued that rhetoricians of exemplarity fostered their objects' self-consciousness as future subjects, to see their reputations and their representations as intertwined.[8] The purpose of this chapter, which examines how writers presented their texts to Essex and Henry in particular, is to show how they did it. Before I conclude, I forearm readers with the warning that there is a wide gap between anticipation and reality, a gap that many early modern readers ignored. It is difficult to fault them for doing so, because this anticipation owed more to cultural commonplaces—and timeless human nature—than to any sense of self-aggrandizement or entitlement. In his synoptic study of these commonplaces, focused particularly on variable answers to the question of human fulfilment ('How should we live?'), Keith Thomas cites posthumous fame as a common answer:

> In the literary culture of early modern England it was commonplace to regard posthumous remembrance as the ultimate fulfilment of human life. No individual's felicity was complete unless he left a good name to be cherished by posterity. The fact that one would not be there to hear one's praises sung by posterity did not make the prospect any less enticing.[9]

In a method typical of his self-described 'retrospective ethnography,' Thomas cites multiple sources as evidence of this preoccupation, and for its concomitant 'horror of oblivion,' so rife among the social elite 'as to make one doubt whether the

---

[6] For receptive decorum see 'Varieties of Decorum' in the Introduction.
[7] See 'Lamentations' in Chapter 4.
[8] See 'Exemplarity in Occasional Texts' in the Introduction.
[9] Thomas, *Ends of Life*, 236–7. Early modern individuals inherited this preoccupation from the Greeks and Romans, but it was also consistent with medieval chivalric ambitions (235).

Christian doctrine of the afterlife can have been a living reality for those to whom posthumous fame was so overriding an objective.'[10] Later, he cites Francis Bacon in *The Advancement of Learning*:

> That whereunto man's nature doth most aspire is immortality or continuance; for, to this, tendeth generation, and raising of houses and families; to this tend buildings, foundations, and monuments; to this, tendeth the desire of memory, fame, and celebration; and in effect the strength of all other human desires.[11]

The sum of these desires is the memory that outlasts lived experience, the reputation that overwrites reality.

Writers relied on these habits of early modern thought to fuel exemplary self-consciousness in their readers. Sidney recognized their instrumental role in preserving experience in written representations at the close of his *Defence of Poesy*. If you believe that poets 'will [among other things] make you immortal by their verses . . . your name shall flourish in the printers' shops.' Otherwise, you are cursed to oblivion: 'when you die, your memory die from the earth for want of an epitaph.'[12] Oblivion is a fate worse than infamy. The motivating power of epitaphs will return in the next chapter, which focuses on posthumous reputations; it relies on the present argument that writers initiated the exemplary cycle by comparing their readers to their subjects.[13] It emerges from Chapter 2's conclusion that Spenser induced readers to take up Sidney's legacy so that Spenser would have more heroic subjects for poetry. I contrast Spenser's disillusionment over Sidney's legacy with the eagerness of elegists, biographers, and writers of dedications comparing Sidney to Essex after 1586. I then consider them in the broader context of a series of dedications to Essex and to Henry. Dedications structure my argument because they promulgate the exemplary cycle, from education to anticipation to representation, or from past to present to future.

Texts are the means by which actions are represented, and actions are informed by texts. But which texts? This argument turns on the reception of a few texts and genres that exerted particular influence on Essex and on Henry: military manuals; *Basilicon Doron* (1598, 1603); Chapman's translations of Homer's *Iliad* (1598, 1611); and histories. Each of them set exemplary precedents and defined expectations for these readers. They also gave their future, unwritten texts a tone and narrative shape of active, civic virtue.

The first part of this chapter considers the texts commemorating Sidney, and the military manuals—both of which were related and were dedicated to Essex. I begin with comparative readings of Sidney's exemplary qualities in the texts that compared him to Essex after 1586. Essex cultivated his reputation as the heir to

---

[10] Thomas, *Ends of Life*, 240–1.   [11] Cit. Thomas, *Ends of Life*, 261.
[12] Sidney, *Defence*, 390, 391.   [13] See 'Warnings' in Chapter 4.

Sidney's legacy, a reputation that many writers were glad to indulge. One of his motives for this was consistent with his behaviour before Sidney's death in 1586: his focus on chivalry to prepare him for military campaigns. More broadly, Essex was interested—as were many others—in militarism as the most evident and direct manifestation of his virtues, his beliefs in outward action, and his humanist education. The late humanist pragmatism that I have already described was particularly evident in pedagogical practices, which informed dedicatory epistles, particularly those prefacing military manuals.[14]

Henry's dedications betray the same pragmatism. His humanist education was influenced by his father's *Basilicon Doron*, which had a direct and lasting effect on his reputation as the object of influence. I offer a brief account of this reputation, and of Henry's pedagogical circumstances and principles. Each of these texts serves a pedagogical purpose, so writings on the educations of high-born men and princes, and particularly of these two, recur in this argument. They tell us how these books were part of a wider programme of influence, one that sought to teach Essex and Henry how to live—and inadvertently, how to be self-conscious of both their reputations and their legacies.

The key text for the next section of this argument is Homer's *Iliad,* a model of the literary monument to which any historical figure with militant ambitions aspired. I turn to Chapman's citation of Alexander in his dedication to Henry of his 1611 complete translation of Homer's *Iliad.* Chapman had previously dedicated his *Seaven Bookes* of the same translation to Essex in 1598, because both men were ideal models not only of achievement and notoriety but also of (Alexandrian) appreciation for the (Homeric) function of writers to preserve reputations. Chapman's serial dedications also draw attention to the function of patronage, the system by which an object like Henry or Essex becomes a subject. The patronage system drives these narrative forecasts. Every potential subject knew that it required a lot of artifice to transmute natural, contingent, private experience into an artificial, consistent, and public exemplary text.

In the chapter's final section I turn to the histories dedicated to Essex and to Henry. They set the standard for both men's future, and underscore how those futures were informed by texts (as originating in written histories) and imagined as texts (as resulting in written legacies). Like Spenser, the rhetoricians who encouraged this historiographical self-consciousness treated their rhetorical objects as potential subjects. And as Elizabeth was to Spenser, Essex and Henry were to many writers both the ends and the means of history, both its culminations and its agents. In Henry's case, writers used the term 'abridgement' to describe both his readings and his distillations of their exemplary rhetoric. Throughout his life, Henry read abridgements of virtuous lives—of Hercules,

---

[14] For pragmatism, see 'Pedagogy, Prudence, and Politics' in Chapter 1; for the military manuals, see 'Words and Actions' in this chapter.

Hector, Alexander, the Black Prince, Henry V, Sidney—and aspired to be abridged himself, as a comparable exemplar of virtue. Instead, when Henry died prematurely, he became another kind of abridgement: a truncated text. But that is an argument for the next chapter.

Sidney's Virtues

Dedications and other paratexts are a tempting category of evidence for the climate of ideas and intentions surrounding a reader.[15] They can also be a red herring, particularly in cases where we cannot know whether a dedicatee even read a text. Some would be unsolicited or even unwelcome—as a case like Stephen Gosson's dedication of *The School of Abuse* (1579) to Sidney attests.[16] So dedications tell us far more about their dedicatees' public image and their writers' aspirations than about anything that might have penetrated further. It is worth noting that dedications are evidence in the history of ideas—not in the history of reading, which would require evidence closer to a dedicatee's habits of mind.

What dedications reveal, in their choice of language to describe their potential objects and their narrative subjects, is how the idea of exemplarity was manifested. Consider the constellation of meanings surrounding the word 'virtue,' which privileges rhetorical efficacy over moral goodness or veracity.[17] This connotation is explicit in many of the eighty-six dedications in print and manuscript that Essex attracted between 1577 and 1601. Their number testifies to Essex's public reputation as a potential patron and as the Queen's favourite (after 1587).[18] Their language is conventional, but noteworthy for their repeated use of the word

---

[15] Gérard Genette defines paratexts before and after texts (title pages, frontispieces, dedications, epistles, tables of contents, glossaries, appendices, subscription lists, etc.) as 'the means by which a text makes a book of itself and proposes itself as such to its readers, and more generally to the public' ('Introduction to the Paratext.' *New Literary History* 22, no. 2 (1991): 261). See also Randall Anderson, 'The Rhetoric of Paratext in Early Printed Books.' In *The Cambridge History of the Book in Britain, 1557–1695*, ed. John Barnard and D. F. McKenzie (Cambridge: Cambridge University Press, 2002), 636–44. On paratexts negotiating relations between early modern books and readers, see Michael Saenger, *The Commodification of Textual Engagements in the English Renaissance* (Aldershot: Ashgate, 2006).

[16] Spenser reported that Sidney 'received with scorn' Gosson's dedication, and a common theory of the *Defence of Poesy*'s origins is that it repudiates Gosson's 'pleasaunt invective against Poets, Pipers, Plaiers, Jesters, and such like' (cit. Philip Sidney, *A Defense of Poetry, Miscellaneous Prose of Sir Philip Sidney*, ed. Katherine Duncan-Jones and Jan van Dorsten (Oxford: Clarendon Press, 1973), 62; Gosson cit. Sidney, *Apology*, 2–3). For a fuller account of the *Defence*'s origins and Gosson's role, see Sidney, *Apology*, 2–3, and 3 n. 4.

[17] I make this claim in 'Virtuous Lies' in Chapter 1.

[18] This number of dedications is exceeded only by those to the Queen, Lord Burghley, and the Earl of Leicester. See Hugh Gazzard, 'The Patronage of Robert Devereux, Second Earl of Essex, c.1577–1696' (Diss., University of Oxford, 2000), 11. Alistair Fox's date-range of 1590–1603 overlaps with Gazzard's (see 'The Complaint of Poetry for the Death of Liberality: The Decline of Literary Patronage in the

'virtue' to identify what their authors expected Essex to inherit from his models. Those models began with his patrimony, starting in 1577 with Edward Waterhouse's epistle prefacing Richard Davies's funeral sermon for Essex's father.[19] Throughout his son's life, Walter Devereux was a pattern of noble virtues to follow. John Hester wrote in 1590 that he 'leaft at his death, so liuely a pattern for you to imitate' that 'neither our present age can affoord you any more vertues, nor any age past.'[20]

Yet Hester's claim was belied by the considerable number of dedications that compared Essex to Sidney, whose fatal injury and Essex's knighthood were both earned at the battle of Zutphen in 1586. The coincidence of these events, along with the end of Essex's wardship the same year—granting him full control of his estates—effectively thrust one man into view as the other withdrew. When Sidney was interred after an elaborate funeral at St Paul's on 6 February 1587, his 700 mourners remembered him as an exemplar of learning, of nobility and chivalry, of Protestant militarism.[21] In *The Life and Death of Sir Phillip Sidney* [sic], which John Phillip (or Phillips) dedicated to Essex, Sidney's 'want in Court, Towne, and country, be bewailed of Prince, nobilitie, Gentlemen, rich and poore.'[22] Sidney's death created an exemplary vacuum, one that Essex had every necessary qualification to fill: high birth, chivalric training, military success, and an instrumental view of learning.[23] Before Sidney died, he led a generation of militant Protestants that included Essex, who aspired to lead it himself.[24] After Sidney's death, and that

1590's.' In *The Reign of Elizabeth I: Court and Culture in the Last Decade*, ed. John Guy (Cambridge: Cambridge University Press, 1995), 229–57), but together they are incomplete; there is no comprehensive index of the dedications to Essex from 1577 (Richard Davies's sermon on the death of his father) to 1601 (his rebellion, trial, and execution). Hammer lists five books associating Essex with Sidney (*Polarisation of Elizabethan Politics*, 215). He also notes that half of all the books dedicated to Essex in the 1590s were of a religious character (*Polarisation of Elizabethan Politics*, 212).

[19] The epistle (Richard Davies, *Fvnerall Sermon* (1577)) also urged Essex to spend his life wisely in pursuit of virtues befitting his patrimony (Hammer, *Polarisation of Elizabethan Politics*, 21–2).

[20] Joseph Duchesne, *The Sclopotarie of Iosephus Quercetanus*, tr. John Hester (1590), sig. A2r. The book concerned cures (or 'spagericke antidotary of medicines') for gunshot wounds; *sclopetaria* are severe contusions.

[21] Sander Bos, Marianne Lange-Meyers, and Jeanine Six, 'Sidney's Funeral Portrayed.' In *Sir Philip Sidney: 1586 and the Creation of a Legend*, ed. Jan van Dorsten, Dominic Baker-Smith, and Arthur F. Kinney (Leiden: Leiden University Press, 1986), 37–67. See also John Buxton, 'Mourning for Sidney.' *Renaissance Studies* 3, no. 1 (1989): 46–56, and Alexander, *Writing After Sidney*, 155.

[22] John Phillip, *Life and Death of Sidney* (1587), 2, 1. The poem that follows is a *prosopopoeia* of Sidney's ghost, in which (among other things) he addresses Essex directly and tells him not to mourn.

[23] Thomas Nashe, John Harington, Samuel Daniel, and the range of authors who contributed elegies to *The Phoenix Nest* (1591) created Sidney's posthumous status as the originator of an Elizabethan literary community, particularly after the posthumous discovery of his poetry and prose narratives. Yet Alan Hager argues that Sidney was actually 'a critic of human aspiration', opposed to 'the very idealism with which he has been traditionally identified' ('The Exemplary Mirage: Fabrication of Sir Philip Sidney's Biographical Image and the Sidney Reader.' *English Literary History* 48, no. 1 (1981): 2.) The prevailing view was of a man who combined thought with action, or well-knowing with well-doing.

[24] Hammer, *Polarisation of Elizabethan Politics*, 52–4. But Kevin Windhauser argues against critical orthodoxy that Fulke Greville's *A Dedication to Sir Philip Sidney* (written c.1614, published 1651) dissociates Sidney from both his militant legacy and from Essex, 'whom Greville contrasts with Sidney as someone whose militaristic proclivities had led to a well-known disastrous end' ('"This Steady

of Essex's stepfather Robert Dudley, Earl of Leicester in 1588, Essex became 'the leading advocate of the overseas Protestant cause in English politics,' writes Paul Hammer.[25] He was viewed as his generation's last hope to achieve decisive military victories against the lingering Counter-Reformation. By 1590, 'Essex fully committed himself both to the Sidneian pursuit of knightly honour and to the political cause [of anti-Spanish Protestant militancy] which Sidney had espoused,' as his command of the 1591 Rouen campaign confirmed.[26]

Essex conspicuously modelled himself on Sidney, both in ways that Sidney encouraged and in ways that he might have found unsettling. He bequeathed Essex his best sword, and three years later Essex married Sidney's widow Frances (née Walsingham). We cannot judge the emotional sincerity of these oft-repeated facets of the Sidney-Essex inheritance, but these gestures feel self-consciously public. The sword connoted Sidney's Protestant militarism that Hammer has described as central to his public image, 'the linkage between war, virtue, and faith,' and 'the pattern of a perfect Protestant knight who had defeated death by the exemplary display of virtue during his own lifetime.'[27] Essex was thus Sidney's successor both in love and in war. In George Peele's *Polyhymnia*, a description of the 1590 Accession Day tilts, Essex appears 'Yclad in mightie Armes of mourners hue':

> As if he mourn'd to thinke of him he mist,
> Sweete *Sydney*, fairest shepheard of our greene,
> Well lettred Warriour, whose successor he
> In loue and Armes had euer vowed to be.
> In loue and Armes ô may he so succeede,
> As his deserts, as his desires would speede.[28]

While Sidney is '[w]ell lettred,' his love of Frances and his military arms are still paramount in 1590—because these are the areas where Essex's inheritance is most direct.

Accordingly, a considerable number of Essex's dedications compare him directly to Sidney. The word 'virtue' appears in nearly every description of Sidney's ethical legacy for Essex. In every instance, dedication-writers associate virtue with

---

Counsel": Fulke Greville's Transformation of Sidney in *A Dedication.*' *Studies in Philology* 118, no. 1 (2021): 102). For the biography itself, see Fulke Greville, *A Dedication to Sir Philip Sidney, The Prose Works of Fulke Greville, Lord Brooke*, ed. John Gouws (Oxford: Clarendon Press, 1986).

[25] Hammer, *Polarisation of Elizabethan Politics*, 79, 107.

[26] Hammer, *Polarisation of Elizabethan Politics*, 54. Hammer describes Essex, like Sidney before him, undertaking to unify his faith, his militancy, and his noble virtues to lead a generation (20; 400).

[27] Hammer, *Polarisation of Elizabethan Politics*, 400.

[28] George Peele, *Polyhymnia* (1590), sigs. A4r–A4v. As Reid Barbour aptly and acidly writes, 'Peele's occasional verse offers historical evidence about Elizabethan politics, patronage, and manners with little in the way of literary merit': 'Peele, George (bap. 1556, d. 1596).' In *Oxford Dictionary of National Biography* (Oxford: Oxford University Press, 2004).

a living reader's power to imitate those qualities of a dead subject. Phillip uses a conventional formulation: '[H]is virtues in this life haue made a conquest of death by fame in this life.'[29] 'Virtue' also describes Sidney's innate qualities in a way that makes them instrumental. In Robert Dallington's dedication to Essex of *Hypnerotomachia* (1592), 'the euer-lyuing vertues of that matchlesse Knight Syr *Phillip Sydney*' become the very virtues that Essex embodies.[30] Even more assertive is George Peele's *Eglogve Gratvlatorie* (1589), a Spenserian pastoral celebration of the Portugal expedition in which Essex drove his lance into the gates of Lisbon. Peele praises Essex's prowess, compares him to Sidney (or 'Philisides,' Sidney's familiar pastoral guise), and cites the need to 'royallize his fame': 'that iolly groome is dead, ... Yet in this louelie svvaine, ... Mun all his Vertues svveet reuiuen bee.'[31] Phillip urges Essex, among others, to hear Sidney's voice through him: '[H]is virtues so reuiue him from the graue, that he in truth speaketh vnto you.'[32]

These connotations of efficacy and revival resonated with Sidney's own conception of virtue. Blair Worden describes Sidney's use of the word as a humanist variation on a Ciceronian theme. In essence, humanist virtue is instrumental. 'Behind virtue,' Worden writes, 'there stands an ethical system which trains us for, and tests us in, both our public and private lives.'[33] This duality echoes Sidney's definition of poetry's ultimate aim, in the *Defence of Poesy*. One of the charges against poetry is that it encourages idleness, so Sidney's mission is strenuously to assert that poetry provokes virtue—indeed, that it possesses virtue in this efficacious sense: 'the ending end of all earthly learning being virtuous action, those skills, that most serve to bring forth that, have a most just title to be princes over all the rest.'[34] Worden cites a broader range of Sidney's uses of the word from the *Defence*: 'The poet's purpose is to "teac[h] what virtue is", to inspire "virtuous action", to accomplish, through "virtue-breeding delightfulness", "the winning of the mind from wickedness to virtue".'[35] He also cites Sidney's *Old Arcadia*, wherein the Princes Musidorus and Pyrocles are 'Born to the exercise of virtue' and 'desirous more and more to exercise their virtues' when they enter Arcadia.

Sidney led men to virtue—to piety, truth, loyalty, and military service—but he was also a model of virtue's afterlives. In other words, his virtue was both animating and reanimating; it implied his death-defying power, efficacy, and exemplarity. It seems that the former, at least, was a lifetime ambition. In his *Life of Sidney*, Fulke Greville recalls the poet's purpose in writing the *Arcadia* in

---

[29] Phillip, *Life and Death of Sidney*, n.p.

[30] Francesco Colonna, *Hypnerotomachia. The Strife of Loue in a Dreame*, tr. Robert Dallington (1592), sig. A2r.

[31] George Peele, *Eglogue Gratulatorie* (1589), sig. A3v.

[32] Phillip, *Life and Death of Sidney*, n.p. Phillip makes good on this promise when Sidney's ghost directly addresses Essex, telling him not to mourn.

[33] Worden, *Sound of Virtue*, 23. For a discussion of humanist pedagogy instilling virtues, see M. C. Horowitz, *Seeds of Virtue and Knowledge* (Princeton: Princeton University Press, 1998).

[34] Sidney, *Defence*, 349.   [35] Worden, *Sound of Virtue*, 24.

terms that echo Sidney's *Defence*: 'both his wit and understanding [were] bent upon his heart to make himself and others, not in words or opinion, but in life and action, good and great: in which *architectonical art* he was such a master.'[36] Phillip elaborates on the meanings of Sidney's virtue:

> This *Phenix* sweet *Sidney* was the flower of curtesie, who in his life time gaue a perfect light in his conuersation to leade men to virtue, the fruits whereof so glistered in the eies of mortall creatures, that by his example they might both learne to feare God, to glory in sincerity, to abound in loyalty, & to become carefull louers of their natiue countrie.[37]

Thus virtue is the power of exemplars to provoke imitation, to make things happen in the world. It is the pivot from reading to doing, from rhetorical gnosis to ethical praxis.[38] Thus for Essex reading Sidney, the word 'virtue' encapsulated the instrumental qualities that made Sidney's example both persuasive and powerful. For this reason writers frequently associate the word with the purposes of humanist learning, particularly as they are applied (as we will see) to Henry—a prince who 'from his Cradle liu'd in vertues Court,' whose educators foster 'those rare vertues, which his mind adorn'd.'[39]

The pedagogical meaning of virtue has deep roots. The aim of education, after Aristotle, is to give students *proairesis*, or the faculty to judge between good and evil. It begins with admiring virtue, to follow it, and hating vice, to repudiate it. Virtue and vice are insufficiently motivating as abstract principles, as Sidney argues in the *Defence*: you need a poet who 'yieldeth to the powers of the mind an image of that whereof the philosopher bestoweth but a wordish description.'[40] And you need an exemplary story to illustrate virtue sustained and rewarded and vice punished, through time. (The poet's other rival, the historian, 'being captived to the truth of a foolish world, is many times a terror from well-doing, and an encouragement to unbridled wickedness.'[41])

Both in his father and in Sidney, Essex recognized the sources of his own virtues—but beyond them, he recognized and practised Sidney's 'architectonical

---

[36] Sir Philip Sidney, *The Defense of Poesy, Sidney's 'The Defence of Poesy' and Selected Renaissance Literary Criticism*, ed. Gavin Alexander (London: Penguin, 2004), 328, my emphasis. As I discuss in 'Sidney's Subjunctives' in Chapter 1, Sidney borrows this word from the Greeks—*architektonikē*—to mean 'the knowledge of a man's self, in the ethic and politic consideration, with the end of well-doing and not of well-knowing only,' and it is the highest end of knowledge, which poetry serves (Sidney, *Defence*, 348).

[37] Phillip, *Life and Death of Sidney*, n.p.

[38] For 'the intellectual history of the alliance of rhetoric and prudence during the Renaissance,' see Kahn, *Rhetoric, Prudence, and Skepticism*, 10. My Introduction also addresses prudence and exemplarity at length.

[39] 'To the sad houshold of Prince Henry,' in Anon., *Great Brittans Mourning Garment* (1612), sigs. C4r; B4r.

[40] Sidney, *Defence*, 351.   [41] Sidney, *Defence*, 356.

art' of converting well-knowing to well-doing. So John Gibson, dedicating his *Sacred Shield of Al Trve Christian Sovldiers* to Essex, specified that 'it is neither to be read nor studied for speculation and contemplation onely, ... and to be able to dispute & discourse vpon the same: but to become such in practice & following.' Moreover, Gibson's readers

> shall have herein the light of your Honors [Essex's] example dayly before their eyes: so God giue them grace to haue the same in that reuerent and dutifull regard for effectuall imitation that it deserueth at their hands.[42]

Sidney and Essex's active pursuit of virtue repudiated aristocratic idleness, an ethical and religious imperative owing to the providence that had granted them noble birth. 'By undertaking virtuous actions and by drawing others to imitate him through the power of his personal example, a nobleman could—and should— change the world for the better.' Essex, in particular, viewed himself as 'a public person, superior to other men because his actions had ramifications for the good of the commonwealth.'[43]

For this reason, the education of young noblemen is a recurrent preoccupation in the humanist pedagogical tradition, which emphasizes learning's practical applications and its actualizations in the public sphere.[44] Repudiating the scholastic emphasis on vocational training, humanist educators promoted the ethical and public purposes of education, which 'should fit youths to take up leadership roles in courts and civic life.'[45] Treatises on the education of princes and other young noblemen, such as those by Battista Guarino, Erasmus, Aeneas Silvius Piccolomini (later Pope Pius II), and Thomas Elyot reinforced the need to prepare these pupils for public service.[46] From Elyot to Milton, early modern pedagogues

---

[42] John Gibson, *Sacred Shield* (1599), sigs. A5v–A6r.

[43] Hammer, *Polarisation of Elizabethan Politics*, 20, 21.

[44] See David Rundle, '"Not So Much Praise as Precept": Erasmus, Panegyric, and the Renaissance Art of Teaching Princes,' In *Pedagogy and Power: Rhetorics of Classical Learning*, ed. Yun Lee Too and Niall Livingstone (Cambridge and New York: Cambridge University Press, 1998), chapter 7 on Erasmus's use of panegyric to teach (through praise). See also Anthony Grafton, 'The Humanist as Reader.' In *A History of Reading in the West*, ed. Guglielmo Cavallo and Roger Chartier (Cambridge: Polity Press, 1999), 179–212.

[45] Craig W. Kallendorf, 'Introduction.' In *Humanist Educational Treatises*, ed. Craig W. Kallendorf (Cambridge: Harvard University Press, 2002), p. vii.

[46] Among other educational treatises Battista Guarino, *A Program of Teaching and Learning*, *Humanist Educational Treatises*, ed. Craig W. Kallendorf (Cambridge: Harvard University Press, 2002); Erasmus, *Education of a Christian Prince*; Aeneas Silvius Piccolomini, *The Education of Boys*. In *Humanist Educational Treatises*, ed. Craig W. Kallendorf (Cambridge: Harvard University Press, 2002); and Elyot, *Boke Named the Governour* are discussed in this and successive chapters.

propose that students read exemplary narratives, in particular, to learn the prudence required for public and private affairs.[47]

Recommended readings return us to dedicatory epistles, which are (as I say) tempting but dangerous to read as guides to a reader's private thoughts—unless readers like Essex and Henry leave firsthand evidence of how dedications and other readings influenced their self-perceptions. In both of their cases the archival record of their self-perceptions is vastly outweighed by the perceptions and intentions of others. Yet the record is there. I will consider Henry's in due course. In Essex's case, I am indebted to Hammer for attributing manuscripts to him. One in particular reveals that Essex understood the need not simply to read dedications, but to dedicate himself to combining their materials into models of good conduct. He wrote to Greville about the network of scholars he employed to research histories and other authorities on a given question: the scholars could 'like labourers bring stone, timber, morter, & other necessaries to your [the patron or employer's] building, but yow should put them together and be the master workman yourself.'[48]

The student of virtue has a responsibility to reanimate his exemplars. In the words of a 1593 dedication to Essex, he must revive those 'honorable and matchlesse vertues, [which are] deriued in part from your noble Father, but more plentifully inriched with your inuincible minde, and peerelesse indeuors.'[49] These two sources, his patrimony and his endeavours, must combine. We will see this emphasis, on the necessity for high-born readers to live up to the models of their ancestors, again in the dedications to Henry. In the interim, however, let us consider the subset of military books that were dedicated to Essex and Henry. In so doing, we will discover how many dedications shared a pedagogical aim, to educate readers in subjects that would lead them to perform acts of service in the public sphere.

Words and Actions

Military manuals and histories are two genres that regularly offered pragmatic advice to exemplary rhetoric's objects. The reason is not only because those objects were men poised to enact public roles, though that is essential; the reason

---

[47] See Natasha Glaisyer and Sara Pennell, *Didactic Literature in England, 1500–1800: Expertise Constructed* (Aldershot and Burlington: Ashgate, 2003) for more detailed discussion of exemplary readings.

[48] Cit. Hammer, *Polarisation of Elizabethan Politics*, 312; on the attribution to Essex see Hammer, 'The Earl of Essex, Fulke Greville, and the Employment of Scholars.' *Studies in Philology* 91 (1994): 167–80.

[49] Simon Kellwaye, *Defensative against the Plague* (1593), sig. A3v. Essex's debts to his ancestors could also be vague and peremptory. Silver described the Earl as 'one in whom the true nobility of our victorious Auncestors hath taken vp his residence' (*Paradoxes of Defence* (1599), sig. A5v).

owes to the very purpose of a humanist education, and its emphasis on public service. David Lawrence has studied these manuals, translations, and treatises of practical use for warfare (cartography, navigation, field medicine, and so on)—and compares them to the 'knowledge transactions' between employers and professional researchers that Essex used, as Lisa Jardine and William Sherman have described.[50]

After religious books, military books were the second most prevalent category of books dedicated both to Essex and to Henry, each the object of what William Hunt calls 'the values and policies of the Elizabethan war party.'[51] Between 1577 and 1601 Essex attracted eighty-six dedications in print and manuscript. Henry received dedications of more than a hundred books and manuscripts before 1612, particularly after his father's accession and his family's arrival in London in 1603. Henry's dedications are a heterogeneous collection of sermons, prayers, panegyrics, histories, and treatises.[52] Most set out their expectations for this future King Henry IX, ranging from Samson Lennard's and Richard Niccols's calls for his conquest of Rome to Chapman's appeals for peace and temperance; from Thomas Coryate's and Thomas Palmer's enthusiasm for foreign reportage to Samuel Daniel's endorsement of domestic self-sufficiency.[53] The loudest and most dogmatic voices were those of militant Protestants like Lennard, George More, Robert Pricket, and George Marcelline.

[50] David Lawrence, *The Complete Soldier: Military Books and Military Culture in Early Stuart England, 1603–1645* (Leiden: Brill, 2009); Lisa Jardine and William Sherman, 'Pragmatic Readers: Knowledge Transactions and Scholarly Services in Late Elizabethan England.' In *Religion, Culture and Society in Early Modern Britain: Essays in Honour of Patrick Collinson*, ed. Anthony Fletcher, Peter Roberts, and Patrick Collinson (Cambridge: Cambridge University Press, 1994), 103–24.

[51] 'This was the faction of Leicester, Walsingham and Philip Sidney, which the Earl of Essex inherited after their deaths,' as did Henry after Essex's; thereafter 'King Henry IX would lead the Protestant crusade of which Leicester and Sidney had dreamed' (William Hunt, 'Spectral Origins of the English Revolution: Legitimation Crisis in Early Stuart England.' In *Reviving the English Revolution: Reflections and Elaborations on the Work of Christopher Hill*, ed. Geoff Eley and William Hunt (London and New York: Verso, 1988), 311).

[52] John A. Buchtel has verified 107 individual books and reprints dedicated to the Prince between 1599 and 1612 ('Book Dedications and the Death of a Patron: The Memorial Engraving in Chapman's *Homer.*' *Book History* 7 (2004): 1–29). His list relies on what are presently the most comprehensive studies of (respectively) dedications specifically to Henry, and dedications in general: Elkin Calhoun Wilson, *Prince Henry and English Literature* (Ithaca: Cornell University Press, 1946); and Franklin Burleigh Williams, *Index of Dedications and Commendatory Verses in English Books Before 1641* (London: Bibliographical Society, 1962). For details of Henry's bibliographic acquisitions, see Roy Strong, *Henry, Prince of Wales, and England's Lost Renaissance* (London: Pimlico, 1986), 154–7; and Timothy Wilks, 'The Court Culture of Prince Henry and his Circle 1603–1613' (Diss., University of Oxford, 1987), 54–70.

[53] See Philippe de Mornay, *Mysterie of Iniqvitie*, tr. Samson Lennard (1612); Richard Niccols, *Three Sisters Teares* (1613); Chapman, *Euthymiae Raptus; or the Tears of Peace* (1609); Michelle O'Callaghan, 'Coryats Crudities (1611) and Travel Writing as the "Eyes" of the Prince.' In Wilks, ed. *Prince Henry Revived*, 85–103; Thomas Palmer, *Essay of the Meanes* (1606); and John Pitcher, *Samuel Daniel: The Brotherton Manuscript: A Study in Authorship* (Leeds: University of Leeds School of English, 1981).

Both Essex and Henry were expected to take up careers in military service. Well into the seventeenth century, the educations of high-born young men sought to prepare them for public service, and that service was most readily measured by their ability to wage war.[54] War was the most immediate way these men could prove their mettle while preserving the nation's 'moral well-being': both Sidney and Essex believed the 'commonplace of classical Roman thought' that victories in foreign wars could prevent corruption and decay.[55] Reading about military matters, accordingly, would prepare the officer class to develop knowledge beyond their limited experience, another commonplace that Essex espoused in matters of policy, particularly in history.[56] More underscores this emphasis on prudent behaviour in *Principles for yong Princes* (1611): 'it being more necessary for a Prince to doe well, then to speake well,' More writes, he 'ought to bee a Martiall man, stoute and couragious, as well to defend his subiects, as to offend his enemies.'[57]

The other reason for this prevalence of military books is that they directly translate knowledge into action, or well-knowing into well-doing. Militarism was a proxy for the active life. When Sidney defends poetry, one of the four charges to which he responds is that 'before poets did soften us, we were full of courage, given to martial exercises, the pillars of manlike liberty, and not lulled asleep in shady idleness with poets' pastimes'; or 'that before poets began to be in price our nation had set their hearts' delight upon action, and not imagination, rather doing things worthy to be written, than writing things fit to be done.'[58] He refutes this sentiment by claiming that 'poetry is the companion of [military] camps,' and repeatedly cites Xenophon's *Cyropaedia* as 'an absolute heroical poem' capable of motivating readers to action. His other text for this argument is Homer's *Iliad*, which Alexander is alleged to have read on campaign:

Alexander left his schoolmaster, living Aristotle, behind him, but took dead Homer with him. He put the philosopher Callisthenes to death for his seeming philosophical, indeed mutinous stubbornness, but the chief thing he was ever

---

[54] On military prowess as the pre-eminent aristocratic virtue see Thomas, *Ends of Life*, 44–77.

[55] Hammer, *Polarisation of Elizabethan Politics*, 225–6. For Essex's public representations as a military hero, see Alzada Tipton, 'The Transformation of the Earl of Essex: Post-Execution Ballads and "The Phoenix and the Turtle".' *Studies in Philology* 99, no. 1 (2002): 60–4, and Richard McCoy, *The Rites of Knighthood: The Literature and Politics of Elizabethan Chivalry* (Berkeley: University of California Press, 1989), 79–102.

[56] Hammer, *Polarisation of Elizabethan Politics*, 306–11. So John Hayward writes to readers in his notorious *First Part of The Life And Raigne of King Henrie the IIII* (1599), also dedicated to Essex: history offers both precepts and examples, 'whereby in shorte time young men may be instructed, and ould men more fullie furnished with experience then the longest age of man can affoorde' (*Life and Raigne of King Henrie* (1599), sig. A3r).

[57] George More, *Principles for yong Princes* (1611), sig. A9v. Barnabe Riche similarly tells Henry that 'in a Prince there is nothing so glorious as to be called a great captain or a worthy soldier' (*Frvites of long Experience* (1604), sig. A3v).

[58] Sidney, *Defence*, 369, 372. The other three charges are that there are better pastimes; that it is 'the mother of lies'; and 'that Plato banished them out of his commonwealth' in *The Republic* (369).

heard to wish for was that Homer had been alive. He well found he received more bravery of mind by the pattern of Achilles than by hearing the definition of fortitude.[59]

This trope was, or would become, a convention of many dedications—not least Chapman's 1611 *Iliad*.[60] Authors asserted that, as Alexander valued his Homer for teaching him virtues and how to actualize them in behaviour, so patrons ought to value whatever text the author was presenting. Alexander's Homeric education in militant fortitude is part of a broader emphasis on education serving 'all the offices, both private and public, of peace and war,' as Milton writes in *Of Education*.[61] Milton's terms to describe those offices emphasize masculine courage: students must be 'inflamed with the study of learning and the admiration of virtue—stirred up with high hopes of living to be brave men and worthy patriots, dear to God and famous to all ages.'[62]

Essex and Henry both received dedications of military histories, manuals, and like discourses to guide the educations of 'brave men and worthy patriots,' in Milton's terms. 'The beginning of all good successe, is good counsell and direction,' writes Matthew Sutcliffe in his dedication to Essex of *The Practice, Proceedings, and Lawes of armes* (1593). Even the experienced soldier 'shall hee learne much by reading of Military discourses, more then euer his owne experience could teach him.'[63] Sutcliffe's promotion of his own treatise draws on dedicatory tropes of guiding all readers, regardless of their experience with the subject: both young and old, green and wizened, can benefit from this knowledge. The aim of Sutcliffe's dedication—and others like it—is to encourage soldiers like Essex to read. Sutcliffe offers Essex useful knowledge to supplement his experience and thus improve his chances of military success. This is reading for explicitly practical and immediate purposes. Sutcliffe cites a series of 'ancient histories and discourses of deedes of armes' like the *Cyropaedia* and Vegetius's *De Re Militari*, both to underscore the historical precedents of this practice and to elevate his own text's authority: 'he must be very arrogant that would [claim to] profite nothing, nor adde any thing to his owne experience' from these texts.[64]

Similarly, Henry was the object of numerous dedications urging him to follow a militant path. By most accounts he was a receptive object of advice and education, as his dedications reflect. In the remainder of this chapter I largely focus on Henry: his military dedications, his education, and his readings of historiography.

---

[59] Sidney, *Defence*, 373, 347, 373–4. See 'Exemplarity in Occasional Texts' in the Introduction for more discussion of the Alexander trope.

[60] See 'The Education of a Stuart Prince' in the present chapter.

[61] John Milton, *Complete Poems and Major Prose*, ed. Merritt Y. Hughes (New York: Macmillan, 1957), 632.

[62] Milton, *Poems and Prose*, 633.　　[63] Matthew Sutcliffe, *Lawes of armes* (1593), sigs. A2r, A4r.

[64] Sutcliffe, *Lawes of armes*, sig. A4v.

Although Essex earned considerable attention and dedications, Henry's education was unconventionally public in its conduct and its outcomes.[65] I have argued that King James's *Basilicon Doron* (1598), a book of advice to Henry, sparked a widespread interest in his education, particularly after 1603.[66] It acknowledged that kings, 'being publike persons,' stand 'vpon a publike stage, in the sight of all the people'; they could thus expect to become the objects of their ambitions and expectations.[67] James tried unsuccessfully to preclude Henry's objectification in his preface, writing that *Basilicon Doron* was intended not to instruct general readers in 'the perfite institution of a King; but onely to giue some such precepts to my owne Sonne, for the gouernement of this kingdome.'[68]

Basilicon Doron's publication, its progress from a coterie manuscript to what Peter W. M. Blayney calls 'the runaway bestseller of 1603,' is a story of the unintended dissemination, reception, interpretation, and recapitulation of ideas about princely education, specifically that of his heir.[69] Henry became an object not only of his father's pedagogical influence but of his subjects' rhetoric and imaginations—of unsolicited advice that drew inspiration from his father's own counsel. After 1603, James's new English subjects eagerly took up the King's lessons for his heir by writing and dedicating books to Henry with educational themes. Some adapted James's lessons to their own texts—in a few cases, literally translating the book into their own words. Translation was one way to praise Henry and James simultaneously, as William Willymat did in his preface to *A Princes Looking Glasse* (1603). Willymat enthuses that, after reading *Basilicon Doron*, he read it 'againe and againe' before excerpting 'the fittest and principallest

---

[65] The stronger rationale is that no scholar has done for Henry what Hammer did for Essex in *Polarisation of Elizabethan Politics*; the only efforts thus far have been Wilson, *Prince Henry and English Literature*; J. W. Williamson, *The Myth of the Conqueror: Prince Henry Stuart, a Study in Seventeenth Century Personation* (New York: AMS Press, 1978); Strong, *Henry, Prince of Wales*; and the contributors to Timothy Wilks, ed. *Prince Henry Revived: Image and Exemplarity in Early Modern England* (London: Paul Holberton, 2007).

[66] See Michael Ullyot, 'James's Reception and Henry's Receptivity: Reading *Basilicon Doron* after 1603.' In Wilks, ed. *Prince Henry Revived*, 65–84.

[67] James VI and I, *Basilicon Doron, Cambridge Texts in the History of Political Thought*, ed. Johann P. Sommerville (Cambridge: Cambridge University Press, 1994), 4. Jason Scott-Warren cites this passage as an illuminating example of the alterations that James made to *Basilicon Doron* between its Scottish printing in 1598 and its English printing in 1603—adapting his private counsel to Henry for broader public consumption, and acknowledging that 'The king's most private sphere is a theatrical sphere' (*Sir John Harington and the Book as Gift* (Oxford: Oxford University Press, 2001), 8).

[68] James VI and I, *Basilicon Doron*, 9.

[69] I am grateful to Blayney for sharing his unpublished research on *Basilicon Doron*'s English printings: 'Nothing Succeeds like Succession: The Runaway Bestseller of 1603' (2001), 5. On the manuscript (British Library, Royal MS 18. B. 15), its publication, and its piracy, see Jane Rickard, *Authorship and Authority: The Writings of James VI and I* (Manchester: Manchester University Press, 2007), 113–20, and Jenny Wormald, 'James VI and I, *Basilikon Doron* and *The Trew Law of Free Monarchies*: The Scottish Context and the English Translation.' In *The Mental World of the Jacobean Court*, ed. Linda Levy Peck (Cambridge: Cambridge University Press, 2005), 36–54. See also James Doelman, '"A King of Thine Own Heart": The English Reception of King James VI and I's *Basilikon Doron*.' *The Seventeenth Century* 9 (1994): 1–9.

precepts and instructions' and translating them into Latin and English verse.[70] Willymat's excerpts reflect humanist pedagogy's traditional emphasis on sententiae. They also distort James's emphasis on practical matters of 'perfite' kingship. Willymat praises James for urging Henry to foster honesty, justice, and temperance, and to be valiant, with emphasis on this lattermost quality.

Like Willymat, many of Henry's admirers emphasized his chivalric exercises as preparatory to future war. The association of Henry with militancy was established at birth, when the classical scholar Andrew Melville forecast his conquest of Catholic Europe, particularly Spain and Rome.[71] Warlike formulations of Henry's future were common enough to inflame even Ben Jonson, who (like Walter Ralegh and Robert Cotton) would later urge Henry toward more peaceful endeavours like trade and civil industry.[72] In 1609 Jonson would speculate about the arenas of Henry's future actions to suggest his readiness to chronicling them:

> if my Fate (most excellent Prince, and *only Delicacy of mankind*) shall reserue mee to the Age of yor Actions, whether in the Campe, or the Councell-Chamber, yt I may write, at nights, the deeds of yor dayes; I will then labor to bring forth some worke as worthy of yor fame, as my ambition therein is of yor pardon.[73]

But in 1603, as the 9-year-old Henry approached London from Edinburgh for his father's coronation, Jonson closed his entertainment at Althorp with this eulogy:

> And when slow Time hath made you fit for warre,
> Looke ouer the strict Ocean, and thinke where
> You may but lead vs forth, that grow vp here

[70] William Willymat, *A Princes Looking Glasse* (1603), sig. A3r. These dual-language verses are printed on facing pages.

[71] See Barbara Lindsay and J. W. Williamson, 'Myth of the Conqueror: Prince Henry Stuart and Protestant Militancy.' *Journal of Medieval and Renaissance Studies* 5, no. 2 (1975): 204–5. They cite dedications that urged Henry to pursue a military path to glory: Dudley Digges's *Of the Worthiness of War and Warriors* (in his father Thomas's *Foure Paradoxes, or Politique Discourses* (1604)); and Riche's *Frvites of Long Experience* (1604). Lindsay and Williamson claim that a fifth of all the books dedicated to Henry between 1603 and 1612 concerned subjects like horsemanship, archery, navigation, exploration, military history, political history, and the education and training of princes. Their estimate of the number of dedications Henry received is inaccurate, but there is no doubt that Henry received a considerable number of military books.

[72] The question of whether Henry ought to pursue a military future was played out in a series of manuscript treatises and poems advocating opposite positions: Ralegh's included 'Observations and Notes concerning the Royal Navy and Sea Service' (1609?); 'Concerning a Match...between the Lady Elizabeth and the Prince of Piedmont' (1611); and 'Touching a Marriage between Prince Henry and the Daughter of Savoy' (1612). See Leonard Tennenhouse, 'Sir Walter Ralegh and the Literature of Clientage.' In *Patronage in the Renaissance*, ed. Guy Fitch-Lytle and Stephen Orgel (Princeton: Princeton University Press, 1981), 248–9. Cotton's treatise was more pointed: 'An answer made by command of Prince Henry, to certain propositions of war and peace, delivered to his Highness by some of his military servants' (Pitcher, *Brotherton Manuscript*, 21).

[73] Ben Jonson, *The Masque of Queens*, ed. C. H. Herford, Percy Simpson, and Evelyn Simpson (Oxford: Clarendon Press, 1941), 281.

Against a day, when our officious swords
Shall speake our action better then our words.[74]

This language is uncharacteristically militant for Jonson. In 1610 Richard Davies used a very similar phrase to urge Henry to lead his people in active service: 'in thy right, our Hearts, Liues, Limmes, and Swords, | Shall stretch our Actions farre beyond our Words.'[75] Both Jonson and Davies praise the Prince as a leader of military campaigns that will 'speake' or 'stretch' his subjects' actions. That same year, Arthur Gorges presented Henry with a manuscript treatise 'tendinge to the wealth and strength of this kingedome', urging the future king to purge his father's court of dissolute luxury and invest in the royal navy.[76]

These encouragements of the young prince to prepare for war through chivalric exercises were enthusiastically received, despite Jacobean scepticism of Elizabethan chivalry.[77] By most accounts, Henry was more than willing to expend his energy riding horses, handling weapons like the pike, tilting at barriers, camping outdoors, and enduring privations as if on campaign, re-enacting battles with toy soldiers, and revelling in drums and trumpets.[78] He regularly undertook mock expeditions, designed to prepare him for future military campaigns.[79] Marcelline uses Homer's episode of single combat between Hector and Ajax in the Iliad to illustrate Henry's eagerness to prove his valour:

This young Prince is a warrior alreadie, both in gesture and countenance, so that in looking on him, he seemeth vnto vs, that in him we do yet see *Aiax* before *Troy*, crowding among the armed Troops, calling vnto them, that he may ioyne

---

[74] Ben Jonson, *The Entertainment at Althorp*, ed. C. H. Herford, Percy Simpson, and Evelyn Simpson (Oxford: Clarendon Press, 1941), 7, 119–31, 131. Jonson reinforces Henry's preference for action over words, a convention of military rhetoric that recurs in Brooke, *Two Elegies*: 'Hee knew that Souldiers vs'd n'affected words, | Whose Tongues are speares, their Oratory swords' (sig. B4v).

[75] Richard Davies, *Chesters Trivmph* (1610), sig. A2r.

[76] See Aysha Pollnitz, *Princely Education in Early Modern Britain* (Cambridge and New York: Cambridge University Press, 2015), 352–3 on this treatise amid Henry's schoolbooks at the Wren Library, Trinity College Cambridge.

[77] On the decline of Elizabethan chivalry in the early seventeenth century see Arthur Ferguson, *The Chivalric Tradition in Renaissance England* (London: Associated University Press, 1986), 139–52.

[78] Among other sources, see Norman Egbert McClure, *The Letters of John Chamberlain* (Philadelphia: American Philosophical Society, 1939); and Hawkins, *Life and Death*, 20–5, sigs. B5v–B7r. For the pike, see Timothy Wilks, 'The Pike Charged: Henry as Militant Prince.' In Wilks, ed. *Prince Henry Revived*, 180–211 and Figure 3 in Chapter 4.

[79] This anticipation was partly conventional: the Italian humanist educator Pier Paolo Vergerio recommended exercises such as tournaments and 'war-games' to prepare future soldiers, but also praised camping in the fields as reinforcing military discipline among future kings and generals (*The Character and Studies Befitting a Free-Born Youth, Humanist Educational Treatises* (Cambridge: Harvard University Press, 2002), 79–81).

body to body with *Hector*, who standes trembling with chill-cold feare, to see him seek to determine the difference in the inclosed Field or Lists.[80]

Marcelline refers to a famous incident in 1610 when Henry defeated fifty-eight combatants in the tiltyards, soon after his Creation ceremony.[81] This mock-battle was Henry's way of bolstering his future reputation at the moment when he anticipated erupting onto a larger field of military endeavours. His victory impressed upon Hawkins 'that *Great Brittaines* brave *Henry* aspired to immortality.'[82] Observers also counselled Henry to wait for the proper time and place for his conquests. '[L]et it not be immagined,' Marcelline reassures him, 'that the execution of great desseignes [*sic*], are vtterly lost by deferrence and delay.'[83] Until his 'fit season,' Henry's 'stronger desire' to wage war must be checked by the 'order of Nature': his youth, inexperience, and filial obedience.

Though some have suggested that Henry's militarism overtly conflicted with his father's pacifism, this exaggerates their differences and ignores the degree to which James himself advised military readiness.[84] Thinking and doing, words and actions, were as complementary as arts and arms, the pen and the sword. Many writers described James and Henry as complementary in exactly these terms. In his *Parænesis to the Prince*, a 1604 poem advising Henry on princely conduct and virtues, William Alexander urges the Prince to 'bring eternall Trophees to the North: | While as thou doest thy fathers forces leade, | And art the hand, while as he is the head.'[85] Alexander foresees Henry leading James's forces into battle as the active complement of his father's more contemplative persona (his 'hand' enacting the will of James's 'head'), his 'eternall Trophees' a sign of his worthiness to rule 'this glorious yle.' Alexander also praises Henry's military training as a son's duty to his father, because kings are well served by martial prowess ('In Mars his mysteries t'acquire renowne, | It giues Kings glorie, and assures their place'):

> This well becomes the courage of thy Sire,
> That traines thee vp according to thy kind.

---

[80] George Marcelline, *The Triumphs of King James* (1610), sig. L3v. By 'vs' Marcelline means Protestant militants like More, Davies, Lennard, Andrew Melville, and Robert Pricket.

[81] In Hawkins's admiring recollection of this episode, Henry issued this challenge to the knights of Britain 'not onely for his owne Recreation, but also that the World might know, what a brave Prince they were likely to enjoy' (*Life and Death*, sig. A8v).

[82] Hawkins, *Life and Death*, sig. B2r. Ironically, the accolades Henry received after this contest only encouraged him to pursue further tests of his physical strength, causing his fatal illness.

[83] Marcelline, *Triumphs of King James*, sigs. L3v–L4r.

[84] Richard Badenhausen typifies these overstatements about James's 'vigorous campaign to halt the growth of a potentially dangerous myth' in 'Disarming the Infant Warrior: Prince Henry, King James, and the Chivalric Revival.' *Papers on Language and Literature* 31, no. 1 (1995): 20–37. The conflict owes less to personalities than to the differences between ambition and duty, prospective and actual power. See Ullyot, 'Reading *Basilicon Doron*,' 75.

[85] William Alexander, Earl of Stirling, *A Paraenesis* (1604), sig. B1r.

> He, though the world his prosp'rous raigne admire,
> In which his subiects such a comfort find,
> Hath (if once mou'd the bloudie art t'imbrace)
> That wit for to make warre, which now keepes peace.[86]

So Henry's militarism accords with his father's wishes: James has the 'wit' to wage war, but chooses instead to maintain peace. 'His pen hath made way for your sword,' Lennard describes James to Henry, 'and his peace, if God giue long life, may farther your warres.'[87] Moderating military strength with civil government, war with peace, and action with contemplation were commonplaces. Like Lennard, Marcelline posits king and prince as a conjoined figure whose books and swords are equally instrumental to military success:

> Yours [Henry's] shall bee the arme and strength, but his [James's] the head and Counsel; Yours the paine and endeauour, his the effect; Yours the Action, but he the Agent: You for him, & he for you, and you and hee ioyntly together, shall win an immortal glory; to the end, that al the world may see you in effect after the same manner, as one figured Cæsar, aloft, deposing or treading a Globe vnder him, holding a book in one hand, and a sword in the other: so that it may be saide of you, *That for the one & other you are a Cæsar.*[88]

James's pen had, in its way, underscored this simile; Marcelline is recalling the King's advice to Henry in *Basilicon Doron* to read, and thus to re-enact, Caesar's commentaries for their 'precepts in martiall affaires.'[89] James advises Henry to balance contemplation with physical activity, and to learn and practice the arts of war. He counsels him to enter into war with the necessary provisions, to hazard himself in battle but not rashly, and above all to 'be slow in peace-making,' for 'a honourable and iust warre is more tollerable, then a dishonourable and dis-aduantageous peace.'[90]

Despite these heroic urgings, neither James nor Henry would lift a sword in battle. Neither was capable of doing so: James because of the balance of power in Europe and because his own insolvency prevented him from waging war (even to intervene on behalf of his daughter, Elizabeth of Bohemia, besieged in Prague by Spanish troops in late 1620); and Henry because his youth and position delayed

---

[86] Alexander, *Paraenesis*, sig. C3v.   [87] Mornay, *Mysterie of Iniqvitie*, sig. ¶3r.
[88] Marcelline, *Triumphs of King James*, sigs. M2v–M3r. He describes James as holding both a book and a sceptre (sig. E2r). After Henry's death under what some viewed as suspicious circumstances, there was a certain urgency to reinforce James and Henry's mutual love. Chapman describes their bodily conjunction in terms similar to Marcelline's: 'The Humor bred | In one heart, straight was with the other fed; | The bloud of one, the others heart did fire; | The heart and humour, were the Sonne & Sire' (*Epicede* (1613), sig. B3r). Henry's alleged dying words to James call him 'Soule to my life, and essence to my Soule' (sig. D4v).
[89] James VI and I, *Basilicon Doron*, 33.   [90] James VI and I, *Basilicon Doron*, 33.

his confronting the same exigencies.[91] Had he lived to 1625, Henry IX might have succumbed to pride and tyranny, as Gorges speculated in *The Olympian Catastrophe*.[92] Or he might have been as ill-fated as his brother Charles I. 'The truth is,' Osborne reflects through the lens of regicide, '*Prince Henry* never arrived at the great test, *Supremacy in power*, that leaves the will wholly to its owne guidance.'[93] Until that emancipation, Henry would remain—has remained—an object of others' interpretive ambitions.

Dedications to Henry, like those to Essex, seek to provoke aspirations aligned with the writer's values and desires. Having shown that Sidney represented the exemplary virtues that Essex's actions ought to reanimate, I have argued in this section that military books articulated a very pointed subset of those virtues—but that their values evidently aligned with Henry's own. They also articulated suitably pragmatic and active outcomes of his reading, aligned with the ethos of much humanist pedagogy. In the next section of this chapter, I explore how Henry's education promoted both active readings and exemplary ambitions.

The Education of a Stuart Prince

The education of princes is a subject of abiding interest in the humanist peda-gogical tradition, because of its claims of learning's practical applications in the public sphere over which the Prince will rule.[94] Xenophon's *Cyropaedia* was the narrative of princely education commonly idealized by writers of humanist educational treatises for princes and governors from Guarino to Ascham, Piccolomini to Elyot—and to King James himself.[95] A more recent influential text was Erasmus's 1516 *Institutio principis Christiani* (*The Education of a Christian Prince*), which Erasmus dedicated to Henry VIII. It outlines the ideal educational programme for the future emperor Charles V, and asserts the prin-ciple that princes require extensive instruction in the liberal arts and sciences, as Guillaume Budé's 1547 *L'Institution du prince* similarly argued.

---

[91] I am grateful to R. Malcolm Smuts for this point.

[92] Arthur Gorges, *The Olympian Catastrophe*, *The Poems of Sir Arthur Gorges*, ed. Helen Estabrook Sandison (Oxford: Clarendon Press, 1953), 172–3.

[93] Francis Osborne, *Historical Memoires* (1658), 115, sig. M2r. He offers a sober comparison of Henry's lost future with his brother's fate: 'though I may concurre so farre with the generall voyce of the whole Kingdome, as to allow him the highest epithets…yet I want not cause in experience, by suspending my future Judgment, To avoid their common mistake, who think all such virtues lost in the untried dead, as are found absent in him that had the luck to Succeed' (113–14, sigs. M1r–M1v). On Henry's presumed circumvention of the civil war, see Wilson, *Prince Henry and English Literature*, 174.

[94] Pollnitz, *Princely Education* is the pre-eminent study of this subject.

[95] James borrowed from Xenophon so heavily that James Cleland would later claim that 'his Maiesties instructions haue worne Xenophon out of credit in al other Countries' (*Hērō-paideia* (1607), sig. T4). (I am grateful to Jane Grogan for this reference.) Two of these treatises appear in *Humanist Educational Treatises*, tr. Craig W. Kallendorf (Cambridge: Harvard University Press, 2002): Guarino, *Program*; and Piccolomini, *Education*. For Elyot, see n. 98.

A prevailing theme of these treatises was how to read texts correctly, with an attitude of detachment from circumstantial differences yet with alertness to their ethical qualities. This was crucial when prescribing texts for impressionable students and future rulers, as Erasmus knew when he advised tutors to illustrate *sententiae* with examples: 'The deeds of famous men fire the minds of noble youths, but the opinions with which they become imbued is a matter of far greater importance, for from these sources the whole scheme of life is developed.'[96] While 'famous men' are instrumental to a nobleman's education, he must not read them without guidance, interpreting them as he pleases. His teachers must 'package' ancient books, 'processing them and transforming them from jagged, unmanageable, sometimes dangerous texts into uniform, easily retrievable, reproducible bits of utterance and information.'[97]

Cultivation was a prevailing metaphor, originating with Quintilian, for the educations of young noblemen.[98] This metaphor depicted the pupils' education as a flowering of innate abilities, with the aid of conscientious teachers and a favourable environment for growth. In *The Boke named the Governour* (1531), Elyot describes the ideal method of 'forming the noble wits of noble men's children, who ... shall be made propitious or apt to the governance of a public weal' as 'the policy of a wise and cunning gardener' overseeing the placement, nourishment, and protection of his seedlings in rich (noble) soil.[99] Thus in *Foure Birds of Noahs Arke* (1609), a compilation of prayers for the royal family and other public figures, Thomas Dekker prays for those 'set ouer him [Henry] as tutors or guardians': 'As yet he is but a greene plant; O drop the deaw of thy graces vpon his head, that he may flourish till the shadow of his branches be a comfort to this whole Iland.' Dekker's arboreal and fountain metaphors, as conventional in pedagogical treatises as gardening metaphors, reinforce the public aims of Henry's education. They also underscore the importance of his educators' cultivations to realize his potential.[100]

---

[96] Erasmus, *Education of a Christian Prince*, 145.   [97] Grafton, 'Humanist as Reader,' 199.

[98] Quintilian compares 'dry' teachers to 'a dry and arid soil for plants that are still young and tender' in *Institutio Oratoria*, 229. For a discussion of cultivation imagery to signal the divisions and the 'fruition' of knowledge in human affairs in Bacon's writings, see Brian Vickers, *Francis Bacon and Renaissance Prose* (Cambridge: Cambridge University Press, 1968), 193–8.

[99] Cit. Bushnell, *Culture of Teaching*, 82. Alan Stewart calls Elyot's *Boke named the Governour* (1531) 'the first major vernacular articulation of an English humanism' (*Close Readers: Humanism and Sodomy in Early Modern England* (Princeton: Princeton University Press, 1997), p. xxix). Bushnell identifies in Elyot 'an ambivalence in concert with *The Governour*'s pervasive oscillation between the teacher/adviser's self-promotion and his subservience.' Moreover, she finds in humanist pedagogy more broadly 'a persistent and productive tension between a compulsion to order and a respect for nature's claims' (*Culture of Teaching*, 83, 90). Bushnell outlines how the contest between nature and nurture or art takes in a wide array of subjects in Renaissance literature, including innate or learned virtue and character, and agency and social difference (*Culture of Teaching*, 75 n. 5).

[100] Thomas Dekker, *Foure Birds of Noahs* (1609), 12–13, sigs. E4r–E4v. For an extended discussion of gardening analogies for humanist pedagogy see Bushnell, *A Culture of Teaching*, 73–116.

The premise of much writing on royal educations is that the pupil must receive an education commensurate with their high birth. Everyone who dedicated a book to Henry knew that it had more to do with birth than worth. But they focused on his education in order to make his worth commensurate with his birth. As in Essex's dedications, those to Henry repeatedly use the language of 'virtue' to connote his ancestry, to suggest that he actively follow it as a model. Henry's ancestry is reason enough for most observers to find ways for him to deserve his social position. But in 1604, William Alexander is forthright about the Prince's duties both to the past and to the future:

> happie Henrie, that art highly borne,
> Yet beautifiest thy birth with signes of worth,
> And though a child, all childish toyes doest scorne,
> To show the world thy vertues budding forth.[101]

This 'yet' is a reminder of the expectations of virtue that accompany high birth. Alexander acknowledges and approves of Henry's maturity, his scorn of childish toys, because it signals his budding virtues. Henry's own father used opportunities to praise Henry in similar terms, such as in James's 1610 address to Parliament on Henry's investiture as Prince of Wales. Its witnesses, said James, 'may see his [Henry's] Fortunes established, in whome their owne, are so much secured; and in whome, the world obserueth so many rare and eminent gifts of nature, and choise parts of vertue and reuerence to vs his Father.'[102] These 'choise parts of vertue,' the pearls gleaned from Henry's education, combine with such 'rare and eminent gifts of nature' as his patrimony, youth, strength, and intellect to 'establish' the Prince's fortunes, his promised inheritance to (and in) which his subjects' hopes 'are so much secured'—in both senses of the word.[103]

Henry was born at the right time and of the right parents, both the culmination and the agent of dynastic narratives. 'To haue good ancestors t'is a great gaine,' Alexander succinctly concludes after a lengthy discourse on Henry's 'annointed blood.'[104] But it is also a great burden. Ancestors, having set the Prince on what James Cleland calls his 'vertuous course,' are imperative guides for its remainder. Cleland writes to Henry in 1607 that 'Nobility consisteth not in the glorious

---

[101] Alexander, *Paraenesis*, sig. B1r. In *The Triumphs of King Iames the First* (1610), George Marcelline refers to 'my *Parænesis*, or accomplishment of my wish' (*Triumphs of King James*, sig. M4v). In 1637, Alexander rededicated the poem to Charles.

[102] *Calendar of State Papers Domestic: Edward VI, Mary, Elizabeth, and James I*, ed. R. Lemon and M. A. Everett Green. (London: HM Stationery Office, 1856–72), 9:597. The preamble James read was in Latin, composed by Francis Bacon and Henry Hobart; this anonymous translation is the more elegant of two written soon after Henry's creation.

[103] The figure Amphion addresses the Prince in typical terms in Anthony Munday's royal entry for his Creation: 'the Sunne of true-borne Majestie shines in your bright eye' (*Londons Love* (1610), 21, sig. D1r).

[104] Alexander, *Paraenesis*, sigs. B3r, B2r.

images of ancestors, nor ... should it bee worne in the shoo-heeles, but their vertue should be a pattern for thee to imitate, and a spur to pricke thee forward in that vertuous course, wherein they haue placed thee.'[105] Henry's own virtues would only be realized if his actions resembled his ancestors', if he views them as 'a spur' to reflect their virtues. Thus Barnabe Riche suggests in 1604 that Henry's past foretells his future:

> as you are knowne to be descended from a most royall and princely progenie, and
> to be the vndoubtfull heire of your worthie fathers Crowne and Scepter, so you
> may growe in renowne & honour equall to your auncestors, & may succeed your
> royall parents in their vertues.[106]

These writers' recurring argument is that while Henry deserves lavish praise, he also has a duty to match the standards of his ancestors. The translator W. C. is one of few voices amid the zeal attending the Stuart accession to warn Henry against this onrush as he adjusted to his new privileges and duties: '*accustome your selfe, in your yong yeares, to a diligent consideration of all those vnspeakeable blessings, that are heaped vpon you.*'[107] To keep a steady eye on his future required a sense of his innate character.

The paradox of a princely education becomes visible in such formulations. Henry was tasked with realizing what he innately was, or what he was born to become; his status was auspicious, but hardly guaranteed his future. The attribute conventionally used to describe the Prince is his maturity, as if his youth was a prologue to his adulthood. As early as September 1603, Thomas Chaloner, Henry's governor until 1610 (and thereafter his Chamberlain) and the principal agent in the formation of Henry's household, praised him in a letter to Gilbert Talbot, seventh Earl of Shrewsbury: 'what noble parts may be required in a prince do every day shew themselves moast lively in him.'[108] In June 1607, the Venetian Ambassador Nicolo Molin described Henry as 'about twelve years old, of a noble wit and great promise. His every action is marked by a gravity most certainly beyond his years.'[109] And in March 1609, when Cornwallis (then James's

---

[105] Cleland, *Hērō-paideia*, sig. B1r. Cleland's equestrian metaphor owes to Henry's lifelong interest in horsemanship, particularly in chivalric tilts and tournaments.

[106] Riche, *Frvites of long Experience*, sig. A3v.

[107] W. C., *False Complaints* (1605), sig. A3r. Alexander also warns Henry to 'flatter not thy selfe with those faire showes' of love (*Paraenesis*, sig. B1r).

[108] Thomas Chaloner, 'Letter to Gilbert Talbot, Seventh Earl of Shrewsbury' (28 September 1603); cit. Wilks, 'Court Culture,' 39. Wilks adds that Chaloner was involved with Henry's upbringing from this early age, overseeing his armoured tournaments, his court masques, and his growing collections of paintings and medals (see 4, 8, 39–40, and 47).

[109] *Calendar of State Papers and Manuscripts Relating to English Affairs Existing in the Archives and Collections of Venice*, ed. Rawdon Brown and G. Cavendish Bentinck (London: HM Stationery Office, 1864–1947), 12:513; in fact, Henry turned 13 on 19 February 1607. See further Robert Ashton, ed. *James I by his Contemporaries: An Account of his Career and Character as Seen by Some of his Contemporaries* (London: Hutchinson, 1969), 95–7.

ambassador in Spain) sought to join Henry's household, he wrote to the Prince in terms that echo these reports:

> Myself, as a diviner of your future greatness, and out of what I hear of your heroical disposition, who in this spring of your age incline yourself, not to what those years do usually affect, but to the understanding of the greatest and most weighty affairs, that may hereafter ingreat your fame, and make the people happy, that shall be committed to your government.[110]

Cornwallis would become Henry's treasurer and, later, his first biographer.[111] The conventionality of his letter of application is revealed when he repeats this claim in his 1626 biography, describing Henry's 'countenance and aspect inclining, in those his young years, to gravity and shew of majesty.'[112] Other posthumous descriptions conventionally have Henry exhibiting gravity and maturity in his youth: 'Me thought his Royall person did fore-tell, | A Kingly statelines, from all pride cleare' Wither recalls in his elegy.[113]

Great expectations encircled Henry's future. Despite his youth, his 'childhood promis'de greater hope of praise, | Then ever Prince attained in his time.' Robert Allyne's wistful recollection of 1613 recalls that Henry's inborn royalty seemed augmented by his acquired virtues. Notably, Allyne recalls witnessing not hope of greater praise but an enlargement of hope itself, for

<blockquote>
a Prince,
Whome nature grace'd with such divine perfection,
That all that e're were borne before, or since,
Did choose him for their chiefe by rare election.
    Famous for learning, valor, wisedome, worth:
    Royall by vertue, beauty, bounty, birth.[114]
</blockquote>

---

[110] Cit. Thomas Birch, *Life of Henry* (1760), 145, sig. L1r.

[111] Cornwallis (d. 1629), who had been Henry's treasurer, cites his position in Henry's court as 'not onely meanes to observe his actions, but to become particularly acquainted with the most of his thoughts' (*Discourse of Prince Henry* (1641), 5, sig. A3r). On his tenuous position in Henry's court, see Wilks, 'Court Culture,' 31–2. An earlier source is Joel Morris Rodney, 'Henry Frederick, Prince of Wales, and his Circle' (Diss., Cornell University, 1965), 178–220. Though it was not printed until 1641, Cornwallis claimed to have written this biography—the first full account of Henry's life—in 1626, both to memorialize Henry and advise Charles to imitate his brother. It describes how the Prince devoted his life to knowledge of civil and military affairs. (See further 'The Book of Henry' in Chapter 5.) These were conventions of heroic biographies, from William Alexander's to Fulke Greville's life of Sidney.

[112] Cornwallis, *Discourse of Prince Henry*, 528.

[113] George Wither, *Prince Henries Obseqvies* (1612), sig. D1r.

[114] Robert Allyne, *Funerall Elegies* (1613), sig. B2r.

Nostalgia has distorted Allyne's memory, but he neatly summarizes the distinction that informed every address or entreaty to this future king: between his acquired 'worth' and natural, if socially determined, 'birth.' Allyne, like Alexander, cites Henry's virtue because it reinforces the election of birth that has placed Henry in a position to rule. But virtue necessitates, in Allyne's words, 'learning, valor, wisedome, worth': in sum, a princely education to 'beautify' birth by eliding its distinction from worth.

Let us turn now to the conduct and character of Henry's education, before addressing how it informed his exemplary ambitions. Not surprisingly, his father exerted considerable influence over his education. Its earliest stages were essentially those that Elyot prescribed for high-born children: the first by a governess until the age of 7, and the second by a male tutor without female company, to avoid the risk of falling prey to their 'voluptuositie.'[115] Against Queen Anne's objections, James sent Henry to be raised by the Earl and Countess of Mar almost immediately after his baptism in 1594.[116] A few years after the family moved to London in 1603, James established Henry's household, which was designed explicitly for the Prince's education.[117] James decreed that it should 'rather imitate a College than a Court.'[118] In 1607, Henry's chamberlain Thomas Chaloner recalled that the household 'was intended by the King for a *Courtly College*, or a *Collegiate Court*.'[119] Henry's household was distinct from those of his parents, beginning in 1606 as a primarily educational institution before its independence and self-sufficiency were increased after his 1610 creation. Henry's tutors, including Adam Newton and James Cleland, made his household a centre of humanist learning, attracting young men from worthy families despite its lesser status to the

---

[115] Williamson, *Myth of the Conqueror*, 31.

[116] This separation of Henry from Queen Anne caused a rift with her husband. See Williamson, *Myth of the Conqueror*, 16–21; Wilson, *Prince Henry and English Literature*, 5–6; and J. Leeds Barroll, *Anna of Denmark, Queen of England: A Cultural Biography* (Philadelphia: University of Pennsylvania Press, 2001).

[117] Henry's first households were at Oatlands Palace (in Surrey) and Nonsuch Palace; after 1610 the household moved to St James's Palace (Graham Parry, *The Golden Age Restor'd: The Culture of the Stuart Court, 1603–42* (Manchester: Manchester University Press, 1981), 70). His tutor from 1600 was the Latinist and art collector Adam Newton (Strong, *Henry, Prince of Wales*, 13–14). Peacham's 1612 emblem-book includes an emblem dedicated to Newton (*Minerua Britanna* (1612), sig. G3v); another presents an armoured knight on horseback and praises Henry's militarism (sig. D4v). See Pollnitz, *Princely Education*, 325–6 on the establishment and constitution of Henry's court.

[118] National Archives LS 13/280/304.

[119] Cit. Parry, *Culture of the Stuart Court*, 69–70. Chaloner had the charge of Henry after 1603, when he accompanied the Prince and his mother from Edinburgh to London; in 1610 he was granted the position of Lord Chamberlain (Strong, *Henry, Prince of Wales*, 13). Daniel Price would lament the dissolution of 'this *Collegiate societie*' in a sermon addressed to the household the day before their master's funeral (*Spiritvall Odovrs* (1613), sig. O2v).

King's court.[120] Other young men joined the household to study Latin, geometry, history, and other subjects to prepare for their public duties.[121] So James surrounded his son with influential men to groom him for his future, creating 'an academy filled with aristocratic youths' in each of the Prince's successive households.[122] Henry's commitment to virtuous self-presentation extended to his household. Cornwallis praised Henry's government over a household of nearly five hundred men, 'many of them young Gentlemen, borne to great fortunes, in the prime of their years when their passions and appetites were most strong, and their powers and experiences to temper and subiect them to reason most weake, [yet] his judgement, his grave and Princely aspect, gave temper to them all.'[123] Cleland, tutor to one of Henry's fellow pupils, recommended the Prince's court as 'the true Panthæon of Greate Britaine, where Vertue herselfe dwelleth by patterne, by practise, by encouragement, admonitions, & precepts of the most rare persons in Vertue and Learning that can be found.' Praising its 'glorious and laudable emulation among Peeres,' Cleland described Henry 'sympathising' with his teachers and other exemplars to the degree that he was a model of virtue himself.[124]

No facet of Henry's education was undertaken for his private benefit alone, but always with a public benefit in mind. As a public figure and exemplar of virtue, a prince serves his people as a law-book, as his own reading has served him. This commonplace of humanist pedagogy informed poets' praise of the King—while encouraging others to offer Henry their own advice.[125] James himself described the Prince's public responsibility to exemplify virtue:

---

[120] Even before Henry's creation, James mentioned the three courts as distinct entities in a proclamation of 2 June 1610 ('A Proclamation for the due execution of all former Lawes against Recusants [2 June 1610].' In James Francis Larkin and Paul L. Hughes, *Stuart Royal Proclamations* (Oxford: Clarendon Press, 1973), 1: 247). Neil Cuddy characterizes queens' and princes' 'satellite courts' throughout the Stuart era (1603–88) as 'dwarfed by the patronage and power at the direct disposal of the monarch'—a sweeping generalization, but a reminder of the relative status of these households ('Reinventing a Monarchy: The Changing Structure and Political Function of the Stuart Court, 1603–88.' In *The Stuart Courts*, ed. Eveline Cruickshanks (Stroud: Sutton, 2000), 63). For treatments of Henry's household, see Wilks, 'Court Culture,' 38–70; and Parry, *Culture of the Stuart Court*, 64–93.

[121] Thomas Chaloner, Henry's chamberlain from 1610, thus described Henry's household in 1607. See Pollnitz, *Princely Education*; Wilks, 'Court Culture'.

[122] Strong, *Henry, Prince of Wales*, 20. Among these youths were John Harington (cousin to the poet of that name) (1592–1614); Robert Devereux, 3rd Earl of Essex (1591–1646); and William Cecil, Lord Cranborne, later 2nd Earl of Salisbury (1591–1668) (Strong, *Henry, Prince of Wales*, 20–3). Adds Wilks, 'From 1603...and for as long as he lived, Henry was the receptive object of unrelenting and painstaking instruction' ('Court Culture,' 55).

[123] Cornwallis, *Discourse of Prince Henry*, 9, sig. C1r.

[124] Cleland, *Hērō-paideia*, sigs. E2r–E2v. Cleland was Harington's tutor (Parry, *Culture of the Stuart Court*, 69).

[125] See Erasmus, *Education of a Christian Prince*, 157. Samuel Daniel praised James in 1604 as a 'great exemplare prototipe of Kings' whose subjects behold him, and read his words, to 'see what we must be, and what thou art' (*Panegyrike Congratvlatorie* (1603), sig. A3v). Augustine Taylor concurred: 'Our King's, our stay, | Whose actions we may imitate' (*Encomiasticke Elogies* (1614), sigs. B1r–B1v).

And therefore (my Sonne) sith all people are naturally inclined to follow their Princes example (as I shewed you before),[126] let it not be said, that ye command others to keepe the contrary course to that, which in your owne person ye practice, making so your wordes and deedes to fight together: but on the contrary, let your owne life be a law-booke and a mirrour to your people; that therein they may see, by your image, what life they should leade.[127]

James's conventional warning in *Basilicon Doron* that kings and princes stand 'upon a publike stage, in the sight of all the people,' might also have encouraged Henry's desire to do service to his subjects.[128] Cornwallis repeatedly cites Henry's desire to serve as an example 'imitable to all other Princes': 'This became to this Prince so great a motive, as hee thought not fit to lose any houres of the life that upon this earth were appointed unto him, but so to bestow them, as they might not onely become profitable to himselfe, but imitable and exemplary to others.'[129] Some of these sentiments about Henry's moral rectitude and exemplarity are in implicit contrast to his father's court, which had a more licentious reputation. Henry's goal was, as his father wrote, to show others 'what life they should leade.' Cornwallis describes Henry's beliefs about the difference between high- and low-born men in terms that echo *Basilicon Doron*:

In persons private it may suffice to be Religious, honest and just within themselves. To Princes and men constituted in high places, it behoveth to bee also givers of good example to others. Inferiours and Subjects cast their eyes more upon what Princes doe, then upon what they command, their examples with them are of more force then any Law of letters.[130]

This emphasis on deeds over words, on the Prince's exemplary actions speaking more forcefully than his commandments, was a guiding principle. From Silius Italicus's *Punica* Henry adopted the motto *fax mentis honestae | gloria,* which Haydon translated as 'Renowne is a furtherer of an honest mind.'[131]

What emerges from these half-admiring, half-aspirational descriptions of Henry's education is the importance not simply of living up to his exemplars, but of living and behaving in a manner conducive to his becoming an exemplar himself. Yet it is difficult to gauge whether this imperative penetrated any deeper than other people's perceptions of and representations to Henry. Historians must

---

[126] '[T]each your people by your example: for people are naturally inclined to counterfaite (like apes) their Princes maners' (James VI and I, *Basilicon Doron*, 20).
[127] James VI and I, *Basilicon Doron*, 34.   [128] James VI and I, *Basilicon Doron*, 4.
[129] Cornwallis, *Discourse of Prince Henry*, 8, 15; sigs. B4v, C4r.
[130] Cornwallis, *Discourse of Prince Henry*, 14, sig. C3v; paragraph breaks are silently removed.
[131] Italicus Silius, *Punica* (Cambridge: Harvard University Press, 1934), 6.332–3; William Haydon, *True Picture* (1634), 11. In his *Discoveries*, Ben Jonson claimed to have given the Prince this motto.

rely on the ambitions and recollections of his observers because so little remains of the Prince's own recorded thoughts. Those records are vastly outnumbered by other people's writings, but I will now address those that do remain, among the Harleian and Lansdowne manuscripts of the British Library and the Wren Library of Trinity College, Cambridge—including his copybooks and composition books from his tutor Adam Newton.[132]

The most significant among these records is Henry's New Year's gift to James in 1608/9, a Latin prolusion whose 'main point was to shew, that learning is more necessary to Kings, Princes, and persons in the highest stations, than to others; and then to answer what might be alledged on the contrary side of the question.'[133] 'It does not suffice that the Prince's mind is pure, healthy and immune to contaminating vice,' Henry opines in Newton's transcription. '[H]e should also aim towards decorum by instruction's honoured and fortified path.'[134] To some degree Henry performs this declaration to show James that he embraces the values of *Basilicon Doron*: he rehearses the Platonic ideal of learned philosopher-kings, balanced by the political skills that a prince needs to rule effectively. The subject of Henry's oration is the necessity for princes to learn from the past—or more particularly, to recognize the causes of military conflict and to change the fortunes of war. Private men may take delight in reading histories, he says, but the Prince will recognize his own affairs borne by another person: '*At Princeps qui suum sub aliena persona negotium geri videt.*'[135] This suggests that Henry thought about the representations of others in historiography as an analogy for his own reputation—which is consonant with his exemplary self-consciousness. Evidently, exhortations to be conscious of his future representations provoked his concern about what forms his legacy might assume.

The expectations that surrounded Henry after 1603 are in some ways particular to their moment in time, when the Stuart royal family represented a fledgling new dynasty. But they also reflect conventional habits of exemplary rhetoric, particularly the habit of using historical precedents as guides to conduct and forecasts of representations. Rhetoricians hoped, often in vain, that high-born readers would provide narrative and financial material worthy of their forebears. We have

---

[132] British Library, Harleian MSS 6986, 7007; Lansdowne MS 1236 and Trinity College, Cambridge, Wren Library MS R.7.23*. For a recent study of these collections, see Pollnitz, *Princely Education*, 314–77.

[133] Birch, *Life of Henry*, 138, sig. K5v. A prolusion was an educational exercise, outlining opposing positions on a given question. Henry Stuart, Prince of Wales, 'Oratio Serenissimi Principis ad Regem' (1 January 1609) defends the necessity of a liberal education for princes. 'The prodigal son could not have framed an oration more likely to please his royal audience than one that combined filial piety, intellectual engagement with James's *Basilicon Doron*, a readiness to demonstrate his *inventio* and belated gratitude for the Erasmian liberal education (*bonae litterae*) that his father and schoolmaster [Adam Newton] had foisted upon him' (Pollnitz, *Princely Education*, 349).

[134] '[I]ta non sufficit ut mens sit pura, sana atq a vitiorum contagione immunis; sed ad decorum requiritur ut sit disciplinarum accessione munita et condecorata' (230r).

[135] Stuart, 'Oratio Serenissimi Principis', 230r.

already seen how Spenser explicitly hoped as much in *The Faerie Queene* and his complaints.[136] Hayward and countless occasional poets (including Daniel, Drayton, Jonson, and Dekker) expressed the same hopes for Essex and then for Henry. They suggested that each man's genealogical descent not only put him in a position to be praised but obliged him to live up to his precedents.

Dedication-writers used the same familiar metaphor for their readers' obligations to their ancestors. Just as Spenser exhorted Elizabeth to 'In this faire mirrhour' of the *Faerie Queene* to 'behold thy face,' Richard Grenewey (or Greenwey)'s dedication of his 1593 translation of Tacitus's *Annals* to Essex calls it 'a glasse, representing in liuely colours of prowesse, magnanimitie and counsell; not onely woorthie personages of ages past and gone, but also your L. owne honorable vertues, wherof the vvorld is both vvitnes & iudge.'[137] Like Henry viewing historical personae as extensions of himself, Essex ought to see his virtues reflected upon himself as (or if) he reads his Tacitus. William Jones's 1595 translation of Giovanni Nenna's *Treatise of Nobility* similarly uses 'glass' as a verb for Essex reading himself in the book: 'He here shal glasse himselfe, himselfe shal reed.' And more explicitly, Jones elaborates that 'if your H. would behold a truer *Idea* of right, & accomplished Nobility, then this Author writeth of, your L. need but as in a glasse to view your selfe, and thereby to set downe what you see in your selfe.'[138]

As I address in the Introduction, some historical mirrors violated taxonomic decorum.[139] The most notorious book dedicated to Essex is John Hayward's history of the deposition of Richard II, *The First Part of the Life and Raigne of King Henrie the IIII* (1599).[140] This history revealed '*not onely precepts,*' Hayward wrote in his address to the reader, '*but liuely patterns, both for priuate directions and for affayres of state.*'[141] Although Hayward failed to secure Essex's patronage, crown officials saw fit to question him after Essex's rebellion.[142] Thirteen years later in the summer of 1612, Henry summoned Hayward. In Hayward's self-

---

[136] See 'The Ends of History' in Chapter 2.

[137] Spenser, *Faerie Queene*, II, Proem.4; Cornelius Tacitus, *The Annales of Cornelius Tacitus. The Description of Germanie*, tr. Richard Grenewey (1598), n.p.

[138] Giovanni Battista Nenna, *Nennio, or A Treatise of Nobility*, tr. William Jones (1595), sigs. A5v, A2v.

[139] See 'Varieties of Decorum' in the Introduction.

[140] A holograph copy of this book, in various hands, is among the Prince's schoolbooks in the Wren Library of Trinity College Cambridge (MS R. 7. 24).

[141] Hayward, *Life and Raigne of King Henrie*, sig. A3r; for a more recent edition see *The First and Second Parts of John Hayward's The Life and Raigne of King Henrie IIII*, ed. John J. Manning (London: Royal Historical Society, 1991).

[142] The interrogation was probably because Hayward's dedication explicitly linked Essex with Henry Bolingbroke, as Arthur Kinney has shown ('Essex and Shakespeare versus Hayward.' *Shakespeare Quarterly* 44, no. 4 (1993): 464–6). Alzada Tipton has since argued that Hayward used Bolingbroke to teach Essex how to manage his public image ('"Lively Patterns... for Affayers of State": Sir John Hayward's *The Life and Reign of King Henrie IIII* and the Earl of Essex.' *Sixteenth Century Journal* 33 (2002): 769–94). Hayward ironically had little success with this dedication to Essex, who in 1599 was

aggrandizing account of their meeting, the Prince underscored the importance of choosing the right author for writing his future story:

And is not this (said he) an errour in vs, to permit euery man to be a writer of Historie? Is it not an errour to be so curious in other matters, and so carelesse in this? We make choise of the most skilfull workemen to draw or carue the portraiture of our faces, and shall euery artlesse Pensell delineate the disposition of our minds? . . . Shall euery filthie finger defile our reputation?

Hayward reports that Henry then praised him for preserving true history, and elaborated on the need to respect his ancestors' legacies:

Wee are carefull to prouide costly Sepulchers, to preserue our dead liues, to preserue some memorie of what wee haue bene: but there is no monument, either so durable, or so largely extending, or so liuely and faire, as that which is framed by a fortunate penne; the memory of the greatest Monuments had long since perished, had it not bene preserued by this meanes.[143]

Hayward puts this endorsement of literary monuments in Henry's mouth in the dedicatory epistle preceding his *Lives of the III. Normans, Kings of England* (1613). He says that Henry requested this history before leaving to join his father's progress in Nottinghamshire in early August 1612. On the Prince's return to London, when Hayward presented him with '*certaine yeeres of Queene* Elizabeths *Reigne,*' Henry expressed his pleasure with the manuscript, and asked for it to be printed. But '[n]*ot long after he died; and with him died both my endeauours and my hopes.*'[144]

Henry's unexpected death in November 1612 prompted Hayward, like many others, to rededicate his book to Henry's younger brother Charles, Duke of York. Having received none of the stipends Henry promised him for this work, Hayward urged Charles to take up the project his elder brother had praised lavishly but rewarded poorly. '[H]*ee did so farre esteeme his descent from them* [his ancestors] *as he approached neere them in honourable endeauours,*' Hayward writes. He insinuates that Charles ought also to support historical writers for '*his owne instruction*'—not in '*rude and absurd writings,*' but in well-composed histories

preparing for his Lord Lieutenancy in Ireland and would not consider literary patronage; Fritz J. Levy situates the history among others seeking to influence current events ('Beginnings of Politic History,' 1–3, 15–21).

[143] Hayward, *Lives of the III. Normans*, sig. A2v.

[144] Hayward, *Lives of the III. Normans*, sig. A3r. In sweltering heat, Henry rode from Richmond to Belvoir Castle (96 miles) in two days; this incident is discussed in 'Decline and Fall' in Chapter 4. '*Hereupon, beautifying his face with a sober smile, he desired mee, that against his returne from the progresse then at hand, I would perfect somewhat of both sorts for him*' (Hayward, *Lives of the III. Normans*, sig. A3r).

by writers like, as it happens, Hayward himself.[145] We would expect to find dedication-writers praising historiography about their readers' ancestors; it upholds the taxonomic decorum of the ancestors' exemplarity, and promotes the writer's future services.

The broader context is that readings of history, both for ethical precedents (to see virtue rewarded and vice punished) and rhetorical examples (for character sketches and orations), had long been a tenet of a grammar-school education.[146] That was partly Sidney's motive in the *Defence of Poesy* for denigrating history, like philosophy, in favour of poetry. But the practice had deep roots. Willymat, in his enthusiastic translation of *Basilicon Doron,* recalls Plato's advice to teach courage by considering historical examples along with the study of theoretical principles and the development of physical fortitude. Plato's teachers, he writes, exposed princes to 'many things concerning fortitude, theoricall vertues [*sic*], and the worthie acts of kings, Princes, and noble men, and exhorted them diligently to imitate good examples, and to eschew, hate, and vtterly detest the badde examples, and shamefull enterprises of wicked tyrants.'[147] *Basilicon Doron* had briefly advised Henry to read 'authenticke histories and chronicles,' to apply 'the bypast things to the present estate,' but largely to appreciate the variability of human fortunes.[148]

A word, before proceeding, on the word 'history.' Writers like Willymat and Dallington used it without James's qualifying adjective 'authenticke,' or true, because like Henry they were more concerned with reputations than with authenticity. To repeat a point I have made, a history's rhetorical purpose could outweigh its truth-value in this culture of humanist pragmatism and Protestant commemoration.[149] A 'history' was any instrumental narrative.[150]

The case of Alexander the Great conveys how exemplarity deliberately blurred the line between heroic pseudo-history and 'authenticke' history. Rhetorical imperatives will do that. The example of Alexander encouraged many writers, including James, to convert their intended reader's learning from historical exempla into his intentions to find a Homer or a Hayward to commemorate his actions after death. Feats of arms, especially, are nothing without poets to propagate them among future admirers—a fact that Alexander acknowledged by carrying Homer's books on every campaign, it is said, in a silver casket he captured from Darius.[151] So Sidney used Alexander as evidence of heroic poetry's public good ('he received more bravery of mind by the pattern of

---

[145] Hayward, *Lives of the III. Normans,* sig. A3r.   [146] Mack, *Elizabethan Rhetoric,* 37–8.
[147] Willymat, *Princes Looking Glasse,* sig. A2v.   [148] James VI and I, *Basilicon Doron,* 46.
[149] See 'Sidney's Subjunctives' in Chapter 1.
[150] Benjamin Griffin argues that 'history' and 'story' were interchangeable in early modern usage (*Playing the Past: Approaches to English Historical Drama, 1385–1600* (Woodbridge: D. S. Brewer, 2001)). For a more synoptic view see Woolf, *Social Circulation.*
[151] Plutarch, *Alexander,* 8, 26; Pliny, *Natural History,* 7.29.108; cit. Spenser, *Shorter Poems,* 564.

Achilles than by hearing the definition of fortitude'), as we have seen. After James urged his son Henry to read *Basilicon Doron* as Alexander had read Homer, multitudes of eager authors made the same comparison to associate their texts with Henry's future achievements and fame.[152] Cornwallis wrote him a letter in 1609 beginning with an extended comparison of Henry with Alexander. In 1610 Daniel Price compared Henry to Ptolemy, Alexander, and Josiah; and Marcelline wrote that 'Honour was all his nouriture, and Greatnesse his pastime (as it was saide of Alexander) and Triumph the ordinary end of al his Actions.'[153]

But certainly the most justified use of Alexander comes in Chapman's dedication of the *Iliad*, the very book that Alexander had carried in his campaigns, and credited with his victories.[154] After dedicating excerpts of the poem in 1598 to Essex, Chapman completed his translation in two instalments dedicated to Henry in 1609 and 1611.[155] We have seen in the Introduction how, in Chapman's dedicatory poem, Alexander 'would affirme that Homers poesie | Did more advance his Asian victorie | Than all his Armies.'[156] Like Sidney before him, Chapman uses Alexander's reverence for Homer to suggest that Henry treat his translations of the *Iliad* with similar anticipation. Chapman implicitly offers Henry his own services, something William Alexander (for one) more explicitly promises when he describes Henry's future military campaigns and offers to 'be thy *Homer*, when the warres do end.'[157] Homer's immortal verses on worthy subjects are what every poet wants to write. He is a touchstone of dedicatory poems and other bids for patronage because he is also the kind of mirror in which any patron would want to see himself reflected. Greek and Roman writers and historians elevated modern subjects to the status of classical heroes. Authorial invocations of them were a familiar part of the humility topos; so John Hawkins protests at the beginning of his *Life and Death* of Henry that he is hampered by 'conscience of my unworthiness, & insufficiencie to performe so high a task, (which rather would become some *Homer*, *Virgil*, *Demosthenes*, *Cicero*, or rather some one in whom all their excellencies are combined, to performe aright).'[158]

---

[152] See Pollnitz, *Princely Education*, 317–24 and 337–49 on *Basilicon Doron*'s influence on both Henry's and Charles's educations.

[153] Marcelline, *Triumphs of King James*, sig. L3v. Price reflects the breadth of Henry's exemplarity: 'such a hope for the young, such a comfort for the old, such happinesses for all; such a young *Ptolomey* for studies and Libraries; such a young *Alexander* for affecting martialisme and chiualrie, such a young *Iosiah* for religion & piety' (*Creation of the Prince* (1610), sig. D2r).

[154] Plutarch, *Alexander*, 8, 26; Pliny, *Natural History*, 7.29.108; cit. Spenser, *Shorter Poems*, 564.

[155] Chapman dedicated both *Seaven Bookes of the Iliades* and *Achilles Shield* to Essex in 1598, whose disgrace and execution led Chapman to dedicate his *Homer Prince of Poets ... in twelve Bookes of his Iliads* (1609) to Henry, followed by the complete *Iliads of Homer Prince of Poets* (1611). Both Essex and Henry died before realizing the ambitions of those who praised them as Protestant warriors. 'No poet was ever so unlucky in his choice of patrons' (Soellner, 'Caesar and Pompey and Henry,' 138).

[156] Chapman, *Iliad*, 3, ll. 27–9.   [157] Alexander, *Paraenesis*, sig. C4v.

[158] Hawkins, *Life and Death*, 3.

Domestic history is more aligned with the 'authenticke' sources that James advised Henry to read, so many writers followed Hayward's example of comparing Henry to his English forebears like Henry VIII.[159] Some went a step further and inserted him directly into their company. In 1606 Robert Fletcher offered the Prince *The Nine English Worthies*, a domestic rendition of the Nine Worthies consisting of brief biographies of Henry himself, alongside the eight English kings of the same name. Fletcher writes that he expects 'a transparent passage of their vertues into you, and a reflexion from you,' as Henry has '(herein) meanes, examples, and leasure to heare, learne, beholde, and obserue the singular goodnesse of God, in that, which hereafter shall be your owne greatnesse and happinesse.'[160] These kings are mirrors to Henry, that he may 'transparently' reflect his own comparable 'greatnesse.' By installing the Prince in this pantheon, Fletcher's *Nine English Worthies* realizes Henry's aspiration to epitomize his forebears. The volume's longest biography is that of Henry V, whom Fletcher praises for fortitude, endurance, and fastidiousness—virtues that will recur in the early biographies of Henry. Fletcher also signals his preferential treatment of Henry V by invoking Homer, Virgil, and Cicero to write the king's epitaph, just as the worthies collectively propose Wyatt and Surrey as authors of Prince Henry's praise.[161]

Fletcher's emphasis on Henry V also echoes Michael Drayton's description of the Prince in 1604.[162] Drayton uses the word 'abridgement' to describe Henry's encapsulation of his ancestors, a word that writers used during Henry's lifetime to refer to his exemplars. But Henry also aspired to earn a similarly selective biography—to become, as Marcelline described him in 1610, 'The *Index, Abstract,* or *Compendium* of the very greatest Princes whatsoeuer.'[163] Witnessing the Stuart royal family's first royal entry in March 1604, Drayton describes 'the faire Prince' as one

> in whom appear'd in glory
> As in th'abridgement of some famous story,
> Ev'ry rare vertue of each famous King
> Since *Norman Williams* happie conquering:
> Where might be seene in his fresh blooming hopes,
> *Henry* the fifth leading his warlike troupes,

---

[159] Mark Rankin compares depictions of Henry VIII as a prototype of Prince Henry in two Jacobean history plays (Rowley's 1605 *When You See Me, You Know Me* and Shakespeare's 1613 *Henry VIII, or All is True*) in 'Henry VIII, Shakespeare, and the Jacobean Royal Court.' *Studies in English Literature* 51, no. 2 (2011): 349–66.

[160] Robert Fletcher, *The Nine English Worthies* (1606), sig. A3r. In the Introduction to this study I cite this dedication as an instance of taxonomic decorum.

[161] Fletcher, *Nine English Worthies*, sigs. F2r–F3r, F4r, K2v.

[162] On Drayton's 'Ballad of Agincourt' and the poet's relationship to Henry, see Marlin E. Blaine, 'Drayton's Agincourt in 1606: History, Genre, and National Consciousness.' In *Renaissance Papers*, ed. George Walton Williams and Philip Rollinson (Columbia: Camden House, 1996), 53–65.

[163] Marcelline, *Triumphs of King James*, sig. A2r.

> When the proud French fell on that conquered land,
> As the full Corne before the labourers hand.[164]

Henry's appearance on horseback 'abridge[s]' these exemplary and 'famous' stories of his ancestors, in Drayton's words. The poet anticipates a future in which this 11-year-old prince, who contains both the germ and culmination of Henry V's conquests, realizes his narrative potential. Drayton's word choice, like Marcelline's, evokes the humanist pedagogue's methods of condensing knowledge into packets of wisdom for readers to digest; their words depict Henry in textual terms, already recapitulating exemplary histories.[165] Another occurrence of the term 'abridgement' to describe the living Henry reinforces the textual quality of these plans for his future. In 1611, Francis Davison included in his *Poetical Rapsody* a eulogy 'To my Lord the Prince,' whom he praises as one 'On whose faire structure, written is the *story* | Of natures chefest skill.' He then wishes Henry everlasting fame after a long life:

> *Abridgement* of all worth, the mighty Ioue,
> Long lengthen your good daies, and still your name,
> And when you shall haue honoured long this land
> Grant you a glorious Saint in heauen to stand.[166]

Davison uses 'abridgement' to mean an epitome of 'all worth,' or at least a summation of the stories of that worth—stories of nature's skill that will persevere after Henry's eventual death. He glances forward to the legacy Henry will earn posthumously—though after a long life.

There are two meanings of abridgement. The first is a condensation or epitome of a longer text, the meaning that both Drayton and Davison use in their comparisons of Henry to his famous and worthy ancestors. Shakespeare uses this meaning numerous times with reference to the economics of staging events 'Which cannot in their huge and proper life | Be here presented,' as the Chorus to Shakespeare's *Henry V* explains when asking audiences to 'brook abridgement'

---

[164] Drayton, *Paean Trivmphall*, in *The Works of Michael Drayton* (Oxford: Published for the Shakespeare Head Press by B. Blackwell, 1961), 1:481; ll. 55–62. For other descriptions of Henry in this entry, see *CSPV 1603–1607*, 10:139; Gilbert Dugdale, *Time Triumphant* (1604), sigs. B2v–B3r; and David Bergeron, *English Civic Pageantry, 1558–1642* (Tempe: Arizona Center for Medieval and Renaissance Studies, 2003), 36. On the rhetoric of these panegyrics, see Richard McCabe, 'Panegyric and its Discontents: The First Stuart Succession.' In *Stuart Succession Literature: Moments and Transformations*, ed. Paulina Kewes and Andrew McRae (Oxford: Oxford University Press, 2019), 19–36. McCabe argues that addresses to James amplify those to his heir: 'The celebratory literature of 1603–4 is valuable not least for exposing the dynamics of political panegyric to comparative scrutiny as competing factions attempted to flatter the king into compliance with their view of him' (36).

[165] Grafton, 'Humanist as Reader'; Chloe Wheatley, *Epic, Epitome, and the Early Modern Historical Imagination* (Farnham: Ashgate, 2011).

[166] Francis Davison, *Poetical Rapsody* (1602), 208; sig. K2v; my emphasis.

and allow him to describe events between the acts.[167] Shakespeare uses the word apologetically, in the same spirit that he asks the audience to 'Piece out our imperfections with your thoughts.' Elsewhere, Shakespeare uses 'abridgement' more narrowly, for a narrative shortened to distil both its moral and its entertainment value: in *A Midsummer Night's Dream*, Theseus asks Egeus for an 'abridgement' to pass the evening, a term he interchanges with 'masques,' 'dances,' and 'revels.'[168]

The second meaning of abridgement is a premature end or interruption. In *Hamlet*, Shakespeare uses the word's two meanings when the eponymous prince describes the visiting players as 'the abstract and brief chronicles of the time' and then, interrupted by their entrance, says: 'look where my abridgement comes'; they are both Hamlet's interruption, and his abstracted chronicles.[169] When other writers use 'abridgement' with reference to 'days' or 'lives' rather than to entertainments, the word has more overtly threatening overtones. Christopher Marlowe uses variations on this phrase to refer to murder, in *Edward II*, or suicide, in *1 Tamburlaine*; and variations on the phrase 'to abridge one's days' imply a premature death in plays, romances, and elegies by Emanuel Ford (1598 and 1607), Thomas Rogers (1603), and Gervase Markham (1607), among others.[170] Jonson's *Volpone* urges rich men to purchase health with good physicians, so as not 'to abridge the naturall course of life.'[171] In Sidney's expanded *Arcadia* (pr. 1593), Zelmane laments 'that hatefull death can abridge ['human mindes'] of powre.'[172] Similar phrases appear in romances or moral histories by Henry Roberts (1590), Thomas Beard (1597), and Richard Johnson (1597).[173] Finally, 'abridge' simply means 'limit' in the anonymous *Life and Death of Jacke*

---

[167] William Shakespeare, *King Henry V*, ed. T. W. Craik. (London: Routledge, 1995), 5.0.45, 4, 5–6.

[168] William Shakespeare, *A Midsummer Night's Dream*, The Oxford Shakespeare, ed. Peter Holland. (Oxford: Oxford University Press, 1994), 5.1.39, 32, 36.

[169] William Shakespeare, *Hamlet*, ed. Richard Proudfoot, Ann Thompson, and David Scott Kastan. The Arden Shakespeare Complete Works (Walton-on-Thames: Nelson, 1998), 307; 2.2.421.

[170] Usage data and textual quotations in this paragraph are from *Literature Online* <http:lion. chadwyck.com> [accessed 7 October 2011], using a keyword search for 'abridg*' and limiting the date range from 1590 to 1610. See Emanuel Ford, *Parismus* (1598), part 1, and *Ornatus and Artesia* (1607), sig. K4v; Thomas Rogers, *Anglorum Lacrimae* (1603), sig. B2r; and Gervase Markham, *English Arcadia* (1607), sig. R4v.

[171] Ben Jonson, *Volpone* (1607), sig. E1r.

[172] Philip Sidney, *The Covntesse of Pembrokes Arcadia* (1593), sig. G6v.

[173] In Henry Roberts, *Defiance to Fortune* (1590), Andrugio wishes that he could have been spared his life's torments by poisoned serpents in his cradle (like those of Hercules) 'which might haue abridged my life' (sig. B3r). Abridgements of journeys, discourses, and of lives—using the same expression for a wish for death to relieve suffering—appear in Thomas Beard's macabre translation from Jean de Chassanion's French of various histories illustrating divine reprobation against apostates and other sinners (*The Theatre of Gods Iudgements* (1597): 'to the end to abridge his miserable daies, hee resolued to hunger starue [sic] himself to death' (93; sig. G2r).) In Richard Johnson, *History of the seauen Champions of Christendome* (1597), the knight of the Black Castle threatens St George that if the English champion's wife and children were present he would 'abridge their liues that thy accursed eyes might be witnesses of their bloodie murthers' (sig. M1v). In the same text Rosana laments her mother's death: 'the gloomy fates doe triumph in your death, and abridge your breathing ayre of life' (sig. K2v).

Straw (1593), when Richard II knights the Lord Mayor with the promise that 'Time, shall nere abridge thy fame.'[174]

What Henry wanted, and what Drayton and Davison implicitly promised, was just that: to earn the kinds of abridgements that time would never abridge. I close this chapter's argument with the positive, exemplary meaning of abridgement, as an epitome that claims to encapsulate the essence of a longer text. I consider how rhetoricians used abridgements for pedagogical ends, specifically for the purpose of 'profiting' readers; they encouraged Henry to read abridgements as guides both to his own experience and to his own textual legacy. Finally, I conclude by contrasting these exhortations and representations with the truth of Henry's experience in the final weeks before his premature death, an event that proved him incapable of distinguishing between abridgement's two meanings.

But first, to Henry's reading. In 1606 Matthew Sutcliffe, dean of Exeter and anti-Roman polemicist, dedicated his *Abridgement or Svrvey of Poperie* to the Prince, seeking to refute a Catholic pamphlet dedicated to King James—but also to summarize that religion's 'heresies and superstitions' and 'impious and wicked doctrines.'[175] The manner and quality of Sutcliffe's survey is less revealing than his motives, which make transparent what most abridgers conceal. I mean their decisions about what to include, what to emphasize, and (concomitantly) what to exclude from an abridgement of some topic or text. Those decisions cause readers to hold certain beliefs at the expense of more nuanced or even contrary beliefs. When the thing abridged is a text or a biography rather than a topic, the chosen parts may do an injustice to other parts that might convey a different or opposing meaning.[176]

Sutcliffe wrote in a culture of necessary abridgements, for a prince whose preference for the form was likely due to his impatience with reading. The satirist Henry Fitzgeffrey tells us something about who read these texts when he urges the clerks to 'Roule up the *Records* of *Antiquity*, | To frame *Abridgements* for youth's *Liberty*.'[177] Abridgements were designed to compress long texts' essential stories or information into a readable size, or at least into a form that readers could skim to find key information. Ann Blair describes them as a response to the number and range of texts disseminated by the printing press:

> Printing shaped both the nature of the information explosion, by making more books on more topics available to more readers, and the methods for coping with it, including a wide range of printed reference tools. Printing diffused more broadly than ever before existing techniques for managing information and

---

[174]   *Life and Death of Iacke Straw* (1593), Act 4.

[175]   Matthew Sutcliffe, *Abridgement or Svrvey of Poperie* (1606), sig. A2v.

[176]   This is what I call the problem of metonymy, which disrupts a reader's expectations to reanimate most exemplary narratives; see the introduction to Chapter 5 for a definition of this term.

[177]   Charles Fitzgeffrey, *Satyres* (1617), sig. B4v.

encouraged experimentation with new ones, including new layouts, finding devices, and methods of comparison.[178]

These tools included miscellanies and abridgements, both steeped in the humanist textual exercises of *translatio, paraphrasis, metaphrasis, imitatio*, and *declamatio*, designed 'to supplement reading and encourage eloquence.'[179] They began as rhetorical exercises in compression or restraint, reducing long texts to a readable size by stripping away all but their essential meaning.

The necessity of abridgements is evidenced by their ubiquity. To take just the English context, in the late sixteenth and early seventeenth centuries there were printed abridgements or epitomes of laws, of Roman history, of John Foxe's *Book of Martyrs*, and most famously of the chronicles (begun by John Stow). These texts provided readers not only with compact summaries of complex subjects and long narratives but also with guidance (as Sutcliffe offers Henry) on how to interpret those subjects or imitate their models. In this, they could point to ancient traditions of rhetoricians offering their abridgements or miscellanies to economize reading and guide interpretations. In the exemplary tradition, Valerius Maximus had compiled his *Factorum et Dictorum Memorabilium* (*Memorable Deeds and Sayings*) in c.29 CE 'in order that those who wish to embrace the examples may be spared the toil of lengthy research.' '*Exempla* were a key mode of moral education for the Romans, for whom history provided a catalogue of actions and sayings worthy of praise or blame,' notes Valerius's editor and translator David Wardle, adding that he 'provided such a catalogue with the morals inescapably highlighted by the arrangement and by his own introductions and conclusions to the individual *exempla*.'[180] Valerius's miscellany differs from an abridgement insofar as it compiles exemplary material from a range of sources rather than compressing a single text, but its motive (to 'spare[] [readers] the toil') and effect on suitable readers ('who wish to *embrace* the examples') is similar. Readers with the right judgement and disposition will reap benefits from these texts, according to the raconteur and gentleman-scholar Richard Brathwaite who describes miscellanies as 'the abridgement of all relations, and in themselues sufficient to produce incredible effects: they require especiall reading, ripe iudgement, and an apt disposition.' Brathwaite's emphasis on the miscellany's 'incredible effects' on readers is key to understanding the pragmatic ambitions of abridgements, miscellanies, and other epitomes.[181]

Abridgements of texts were explicitly intended to save readers the tedium of reading them in full. Thomas Langley, for instance, uses a string of adjectives to

[178] Blair, *Too Much to Know*, 13–14.
[179] Wheatley, 'Abridging the Antiquitee,' 861. I rely throughout this argument on Wheatley's analyses of Renaissance 'epitome culture' (see *Epic, Epitome*, esp. 9–38).
[180] Valerius Maximus, *Deeds and Sayings*, 12, 13.
[181] Richard Brathwaite, *Schollers Medley* (1614), 62; sig. I3v.

distinguish the unpleasant labour of reading the original to the benefits one can gain from his 1551 abridgement of Polydore Vergil:

> Althoughe the booke translated might have bene for the diversitiee of matter *profitable*: and for the authours high lernyng *laudable*, and finally to a good translatoure *commendable*, yet in so muche, as for the greatnes, it should have bene to the berers *grevouse*, and for length to the reders *tediouse*.[182]

A '*profitable*' reading with less difficulty than the original recurs as the cited purpose of many abridgements in this period. Consider the King James translation of the preface to the apocryphal *2 Maccabees*, which condenses Jason of Cyrene's story of the Jewish struggle for religious freedom into what the Vulgate calls *uno volumine breviare*. The translators describe the purpose of 'this painefull labour of abridging,' 'that all, into whose hands it comes might haue profit.'[183]

Thomas Mason's *Christs Victorie ouer Sathans Tyrannie* (1615), 'abstracted' from John Foxe's *Actes and Monuments*, offers a similar example. Its author acknowledges that Foxe's book is '*one of the most profitablest Bookes that is for Gods Children, except the Bible.*' Mason has '*made it tractable for all sorts of people*', so that those who find purchasing Foxe too dear and reading him too onerous '*shall reape as much profit by reading this abridgement, as by reading of the Booke at large.*'[184] Even in Foxe's compilation, whose fourth edition (1583) grew to 3,800,000 words, individual narratives like the travails of Elizabeth during the reign of her sister Mary avoid 'importunate length' by using 'brevity and moderation' for 'the profit of the reader,' among other ends.[185] Mason followed in the footsteps of Foxe's abridgers beginning with Timothie Bright's in 1589, whose full title addresses itself to '*such as either through want of leysure, or abilitie haue not the vse of so necessary an history*'; Bright undertakes to offer readers '*an assay, an appetite, to know further, whereof thou maist here take (as it were) the taste.*'[186] There is a pleasant and recurring fiction among more scrupulous abridgers, like Mason, that readers will progress from ease to difficulty—that is, that they will be ready (if not eager) to '*know further*' by reading the unfiltered Foxe. This is a departure from most other prefaces to abridgements, as we have seen, which more expressly anticipate that they will replace reading '*the Booke at large.*'

Thus for much the same reasons they do today, condensed versions of long texts or summaries of complex subjects both frustrate and fulfil humanist

---

[182] Cit. Wheatley, *Epic, Epitome*, 14, my emphasis.
[183] John Rainolds et al., *King James Bible* (1611), 2:26, 2:25; sigs. 5B2r–5B2v.
[184] Thomas Mason, *Christs Victorie* (1615), sig. A3r.
[185] John Foxe, *Foxe's Book of Martyrs: Select Narratives*, ed. John N. King (Oxford and New York: Oxford University Press, 2009), xxi, 265–6.
[186] Timothie Bright, *Abridgement of the booke of Acts and Monvmentes* (1589), sig.¶1v. For other abridgements of Foxe in this period see David Scott Kastan, 'Little Foxes.' In *John Foxe and his World*, ed. Christopher Highley and John N. King (Aldershot: Ashgate, 2002), 117–29.

educators' aims. Reading abridged accounts of famous exemplars might teach readers how to behave, but only by reducing nuanced, thorough histories to simplified formulae. Ascham dismissed abridgements as 'a silie poore kinde of studie,' suited only to 'those that be learned already' in a subject—that is, as an aid not to learning, but to memory. He thus called them 'a way of studie, belonging, rather to matter, than to wordes: to memorie than to utterance.'[187] It is not difficult to sympathize with Ascham's objections to abridgements when the reader entrusts them so far as to replace the original texts. They are selectively interpreted versions of those texts, inflected by fallible abridgers. A genealogy of rulers replaces a thousand years of political history, and the particular lessons in statecraft each might impart. Similarly, a hero's purposeful life downplays their doubts and misfortunes along the way. All abridgements are contingent, and leave readers susceptible to misinterpretations. But some are more transparent than others about their motives, and more deferential to their source-texts' authority.

In the analogy I am drawing between Henry's abridged life (prematurely concluded) and Henry's abridged readings, the former's source-text is akin to the unfiltered nature of experience itself—which includes unpredictable events like illness and death. Aspirations to condense the lives of famous kings and other ancestors are powerfully compelling, but powerless to turn expectations into experience; they are susceptible to human frailty.

Henry's death on 6 November 1612 is a case in point. Defying rhetorical optimism, political expectations, and medical interventions, he succumbed in his eighteenth year to an undiagnosable infection—likely typhoid fever. In the final week of his life, there was a contrast between hope and frailty that succinctly illustrates a problem that all positive exemplarity faces. On 31 October, the Prince lay on his deathbed in St James's Palace while a player impersonated him in a civic pageant in the streets of London. The contrast between these two men represents the gap between experience and expectations, and the note on which this chapter closes—before the next takes up the mad scramble after Henry's death to represent his indecorous death.

We cannot fault Thomas Dekker for bad timing; his *Troia-Nova Triumphans* suited its occasion perfectly. Dekker's Lord Mayor's Show fulfilled the form's didactic and allegorical conventions.[188] 'This was that day for Antique deeds

---

[187] Roger Ascham, *Scholemaster* (1570), sig. O2r; cit. Wheatley, 'Abridging the Antiquitee,' 861.

[188] David M. Bergeron describes the occasion of this pageant in *English Civic Pageantry*, 113–114. On sources of the iconographical and allegorical elements of English civic pageantry, see his 'Symbolic Landscape in English Civic Pageantry,' *Renaissance Quarterly* 22, no. 1 (1969): 32–7, and 'The Emblematic Nature of English Civic Pageantry.' *Renaissance Drama* NS1 (1968): 167–98. For a synoptic anthropological account of royal entries as charismatic expressions of authority through allegorical symbolism, see R. Malcolm Smuts, 'Public Ceremony and Royal Charisma: The English Royal Entry in London, 1485–1642.' In *The First Modern Society: Essays in English History in Honour of Lawrence Stone*, ed. A. L. Beier, David Cannadine, and James M. Rosenheim (Cambridge: Cambridge University Press, 1989), 65–93. For a description of Dekker's entertainment amid expectations both of Henry's

renown'd, ' recalled Richard Niccols, when 'people, yeare by yeare, with triumph crownd | To honour their elected Magistrate.'[189] Dekker praised the King, the city, its new mayor Sir John Swinnerton, the twelve livery companies, and particularly his own company Merchant Taylors, of which both Swinnerton and Henry had been made free. His final device 'and highest honour,' the *'Throne of Vertue,'* paid tribute to his own company and to its noblest member. There, alongside Fame herself, 'In other seuerall places sit Kings, Princes, and Noble persons, who haue bene free of the *Marchant-tailors*: A perticular roome being reserued for one that represents the person of *Henry* the now Prince of *Wales*.'[190] As Niccols recalled, there were also 'Antique deeds' in the shape of Henry's illustrious ancestors like Henry VII, who grafted the red rose to the white: '*A* Sprig *of which* Branch, (Highest *now but* One) | *Is* Henry Prince of Wales, *followed by none*.'[191] Dekker's pageant mingled civic celebration with this symbol of national pride, the young prince whose virtues are both inherited and intrinsic. Players represented these ancestors to suggest that Henry's virtue and fame would resemble theirs.

Like epitomes, these images of the 'kings, Princes, and Noble persons' standing alongside Henry in Dekker's House of Fame were simplified formulae. They projected the confident self-assurance that characterizes civic pageantry and royal panegyrics, the genre from which Dekker borrowed most directly.[192] *Troia-Noua Triumphans* foreshadows the royal entries Dekker might have written for King Henry IX. It posits a distinguished future for Henry, 'Highest *now but* One,' namely King James, and followed by none—absenting his younger brother, the unwitting future King Charles I. Henry's death will disrupt the smooth transition into the future Dekker proposes for him, belying the poet's implicit

future and Elizabeth's marriage see Gregory McNamara, ' "A Perfect Diamond Set in Lead": Henry, Prince of Wales and the Performance of Emergent Majesty' (Diss., West Virginia University, 2000), 220–3.

[189] Niccols, *Three Sisters Teares*, sig. B3r. On this customary annual date of Tudor-Stuart mayoral inaugurations, see Lawrence Manley, *Literature and Culture in Early Modern London* (Cambridge and New York: Cambridge University Press, 1995), 219.

[190] Thomas Dekker, *Troia-Noua Triumphans* (1612), C1r, C1v. The Merchant Taylors' Company attracted a significant number of honorary members from the reigns of Edward III to James I, including Henry VII and Prince Henry: 'seven Kings, one Queen, seventeen Princes and Dukes, two Duchesses, one Archbishop, thirty one Earls, five Countesses, one Viscount, fourteen Bishops, sixty six Barons', and so on (Birch, *Life of Henry*, 93, sig. G7r). For a complete list, see the roll presented to James on Henry's investiture: Charles Clode, *Memorials of the Guild of Merchant Taylors* (London: Harrison & Sons, 1875), 1:292–304; for an account of the ceremony in June 1607, see Birch, *Life of Henry*, 92–4, sigs. G6v–G7v. Henry was made free of the company in 1607, with an elaborate entertainment written by Jonson and planned in part by Swinnerton, a second-generation Merchant Taylor since 1589 (Clode, *Memorials*, 1:263; Gabriel Heaton and James Knowles, ' "Entertainment Perfect": Ben Jonson and Corporate Hospitality.' *Review of English Studies* 54 (2003): 593, 595).

[191] Dekker, *Troia-Noua Triumphans*, C2r. As Bergeron notes in *English Civic Pageantry*, references to the union of York and Lancaster recur in civic pageantry from Elizabeth's first royal entry of 1559 to the last Jacobean Lord Mayor's Show of 1624, Webster's *Monuments of Honor* (173). James spoke to parliament in 1603 of 'my descent lineally out of the loynes of Henrie the seuenth,' both to legitimize his succession and to assert his reunion of the divided kingdoms (*Kings Maiesties Speech*, sig. A4v).

[192] On relations between civic entertainments and royal entries, and particularly on the mutual dependence of city and crown, see Manley, *Literature and Culture*, 216–21.

promises: that by reanimating the virtues of his historical exemplars, not only would Henry IX enjoy a long reign, his kingdom would also be immune to misfortune.

Troia-Noua Triumphans typifies the disjunction between occasions and their representations that exemplary rhetoric demands. Its projections of Henry's future and his protection of London are based on a selective view of the past—emphasizing civic and military glory without human vulnerability. It distorts and denies any negative features of its positive exemplars to impose unrealistic expectations on its objects. It relies on gaps between experience and its representations, between the Prince who lives (for now) and the king he will (not) become. *Troia-Noua Triumphans* is undone only by bad timing, by presenting an image of Henry's future and London's perpetual triumph eight days before the Prince's death.

In hindsight, Niccols marvels at this presumption that Henry's life would have resembled the long and illustrious lives of his exemplars. His recollection of Dekker's pageant is full of references to the wanton excesses, fashionable displays, prodigal consumption, and general idleness of its audience: 'VVith diuers change of fashions and of face, | That stately townes proud streets did ebb and flow.' The benefit of hindsight permits Niccols to paraphrase their mood with ironic detachment:

> Let not vaine doubt disturbe our strengthned state,
> Nor feare awake our peace with warres alarm's, [...]
>
> Inioy we not the Sonne of such a King
> So faire a branch, which now such fruit doth beare,
> That from such fruit, such hopes already spring,
> That our great Fortunes shake the world with feare?[193]

Henry's spectators anticipate this common future unimpeded by 'vaine doubt' or hesitation. Niccols overstates the exuberance and ignorance of these spectators to reinforce the effects of Henry's death on the people of London. Yet he accurately reflects the eulogistic aim of civic pageantry, to praise the city's public figures by (at least) exempting them from past tragedies. If we remove its moralizing overtones, Niccols's account is indistinguishable from Dekker's description of Henry's future.

That confidence is undone by the experience of Henry's death, an event that required numerous writers—beyond the unfortunate Dekker—to reframe their eulogistic depictions of Henry for elegiac purposes. The subject of my next chapter

---

[193] Niccols, *Three Sisters Teares*, sigs. B2v, B3v. Niccols excoriates the 'vaine opinion of Soule-blinded men | To thinke that ought on earth may be secure,' when 'Vnlookt for chance may change such ioyfull mirth | To dolefull mourning' (sig. B4r).

is this renegotiation that such a lapse of receptive decorum imposes on occasional poets. They suffered under the conditions that experience imposes on all occasional poets, the necessity to represent events as they really happened—and to address the cautionary lessons that such experiences impose. In sum, they suffered the consequences of historicizing exemplary rhetoric, which undermines positive exemplarity.

A life can serve an array of exemplary purposes, of which few are foreseeable and none are certain. In one of his chaplains' final sermons for the Prince, preached immediately before his fatal illness, Robert Wilkinson refers to the Prince of Wales's motto: 'what meaneth that *Ich dien*, the word or Imprease of the English Prince, but *I serue*, A Prince, and yet serues.' Referring to the Prince's *pluma triplex* device, Wilkinson urges Henry not to pursue fame, but service: 'yea & he shakes vp his feathers, & flourisheth when he speaks it, as if it were his glory as yet to serue.'[194] Henry intended to serve as an exemplar, but not as a cautionary tale of human frailty; that was not Cornwallis's meaning when he reported Henry's wish to be exemplary to others. In the chapter to come, I describe the experiences that reformulated those expectations.

---

[194] Robert Wilkinson, *Paire of Sermons* (1614), 78; sig. L2v. See Peacham, *Minerva Britanna*, sig. A1v for an epigrammatical anagram of Henry's motto beneath an illustration of his device encircled by Tudor roses and Scottish thistles.

4

The Reluctant Genre

When William Drummond of Hawthorden laments Prince Henry's death by claiming that 'A booke had been of thy illustrous deeds,' he measures the loss in narrative terms.[1] Like Spenser's Muses whose 'Eulogies turne into Elegies,' Drummond cites the genres that Henry's life ought to have occasioned, in pointed contrast with those that his death necessitates.[2] Elegy, like complaint, is a reluctant genre: no poet takes it up eagerly, and many call attention to its sad necessity as a response to undesired events or circumstances. I have already characterized Spenser's complaints and his elegy for Sidney as anti-occasional poems, in the context of *The Faerie Queene*'s fictional and actual readers enacting the exemplary cycle of alternate readings and descriptions.[3] Occasional texts form the interface between this cycle's stages, or between deeds and books (in Drummond's terms). Only when the deeds are unworthy of imitation, as Spenser has shown, do the authors of books resist their occasions.

Dedications try to begin a new cycle with prescriptive, exemplary rhetoric. As their numbers attest, they are among the least reluctant genres that a rhetorician can offer.[4] Their prescriptions distinguish dedications from descriptive genres like complaint or elegy, yet they too are born of occasions that seem inadequate or insufficient in ways that readers can assuage by following their guidance. What all of these genres have in common, regardless of their author's eagerness to write them, is the historicity of their exemplary rhetoric. They are proximate in time to the occasions they praise or blame, or to the circumstances they try to influence. The relationship between an occasional text and its circumstances is one of cause and effect, and can go in either direction—even if the category 'occasional text' customarily means a text reflecting its occasion rather than trying to influence it.[5] An occasional text typically commemorates fortunes or misfortunes, like a noteworthy birth, marriage, or death. Yet few authors of occasional texts are satisfied with description alone; most describe their subjects rhetorically, in judicial terms for deliberative purposes. They praise or blame in order to exhort or dissuade.

The circumstances of Henry's death and its immediate occasional texts (elegies, epitaphs, and sermons) concern me here, not only because they are so proximate

---

[1] Drummond, *Death of Meliades*, sig. A2v.   [2] Spenser, *Yale Edition*, 283, l.372.
[3] See 'Generic Decorum' in Chapter 2.   [4] See 'Sidney's Virtues' in Chapter 3.
[5] See the introduction to Chapter 2 for Spenser's inversion of the causal relationship between occasional texts and events.

The Rhetoric of Exemplarity in Early Modern England. Michael Ullyot, Oxford University Press. © Michael Ullyot 2022. DOI: 10.1093/oso/9780192849335.003.0005

to their occasion but also because Henry was unlike his immediate exemplary forebears. Unlike Essex and Sidney, Henry died before he was able to achieve much of note, and in a manner that seemed entirely unsuited to his life. All three men were objects of similar expectations during their lives, but Henry's illness and death at the age of 18 left writers with far less material for posthumous descriptions than Sidney's fatal wounding in battle, aged 31, or Essex's heroic exploits before his disgrace and execution, aged 35. Yet the shock of Henry's death, and its foreclosure of his future, was enough to provoke an outpouring of more than forty memorial anthologies and single-author volumes in print and manuscript.[6] 'Never was any Prince's death more universally and cordially Lamented,' Roger Coke recalls, 'and the more, by how much the suddenness of his Death being known, before his Sickness was scarce heard of, was surprizing.'[7]

The volume and range of those lamentations for Henry exceeded those for Sidney or for Essex, because (I argue) he inspired greater expectations and fulfilled so few of them. Yet his death posed a narrative problem that Sidney's death did not: how to extract an inspiring ethic from such a manifest failure of expectations. The apparent blamelessness of Henry's death, unlike Essex's, gave writers licence to discuss it at some length—even to attribute it to supernatural causes, as my readings of Gorges's and Chapman's allegories show. My comparison between these elegies and Spenser's for Sidney also show marked differences between their qualities of tone and attribution. Sidney's death was the last time a comparable public figure died, but in heroic circumstances that better suited the expectations of his life.

Indecorous is perhaps the unkindest way to describe Henry's death; it violated the receptive decorum of so many texts dedicated to him in his lifetime. Henry's experience offered writers a subject more intriguing than his immediate forebears: a life informed by expectations, mostly narrative; and an early, blameless death,

---

[6] 'Posthumous testimonials to the talents and virtues of that very promising Prince, Henry Frederick ... were so numerous, that a mere enumeration of them would run on to considerable extent' (Egerton Brydges, *Restituta: Or Titles, Extracts, and Characters of Old Books in English Literature, Revived* (London: T. Bensley & Son, 1814–16), 3:477). The appendix to this study is a complete bibliography of the poetry composed for Henry's death; it is the first to answer George W. Pigman's appeal in 1985 (*Grief and English Renaissance Elegy* (Cambridge: Cambridge University Press, 1985), 143 n. 2). For incomplete lists, see Brydges, *Restituta*, 4:172; John Nichols, *The Progresses, Processions, and Magnificent Festivities of King James the First, his Royal Consort, Family, and Court* (London: J. B. Nichols, 1828), 2:504–12; and John Philip Edmond, 'Elegies and Other Tracts Issued on the Death of Henry, Prince of Wales, 1612.' *Publications of the Edinburgh Bibliographical Society* 6 (1901–4; published 1906): 146–58.

[7] Roger Coke, *Detection of the Court and State* (1719), 61. Coke's previous (1694) edition declares that it offers '*many Secrets never before made publick.*' His secondhand account of 1612 is as follows: 'This year was wound up in a mournful *Catastrophe*, for upon the 6th. of *November*, Prince *Henry* died in the beginning of the Blossom of his Youth, being 18 Years, 8 Months, and 17 Days old: A Prince adorned with Wisdom and Piety above his Years, strength and ability of Body, equal to any Man; of a Noble and Heroick Disposition, and an hater of Flatteries and Flatterers....I have heard my Father (who was about the Prince's Age) tell several Stories of him,' many involving hunting-dogs and other tiresome adventures (Coke, *Detection of the Court and State*, 60).

suggesting incompletion rather than closure. Many respondents argued that Henry's life would have inspired multiple volumes of heroic biographical writings; they often leveraged those claims into offers to new patrons to write biographies of them instead. Many expressed their disappointment in textual terms, mirroring the terms used during Henry's lifetime, and the tropes we have seen in Donne's elegy for Elizabeth Drury. But writers had to contend with the unavoidable truth that Henry's text now looked wholly unlike the texts he had patronized in his lifetime. This is a truth universally ignored in exemplary rhetoric, that its cyclical promise of future descriptions and future readings relies on humans who are fallible, and that historical accidents like an illness can easily defeat rhetoricians' predictions or subjects' intentions. In this chapter I make the core argument of this whole study: that when you historicize exemplarity, you cannot ignore the uncertainty of its success and likelihood of its failure. The immediacy of Henry's death made it impossible for the authors of his posthumous descriptions, his elegies and epitaphs and sermons, to ignore his cautionary meaning.

This is the story of how a life surrounded by positive expectations became a cautionary tale against such expectations, owing to a historical accident. It follows the development of Henry's reputation through three stages: from the events surrounding his death in November 1612, when rhetoricians tried to preserve his fame and commemorate his virtues; to the rhetorical resistance and allegorical counter-narratives of his death that rationalized it as a supernatural event that left him blameless; and finally to the rhetoricians' acceptance that he was a cautionary exemplar of human fallibility. In this lattermost formulation the elegists came to accept lessons that Henry's chaplains had preached long before his death, lessons occluded by pageantry and optimism. The story of Henry's transition from life to death is unlike those of his immediate forebears, because it renegotiates the narratives that followed him through this transition from expectation to experience, exhortation to caution, and exemplary object to subject.

Decline and Fall

In 1612, two years after his creation as Prince of Wales, the 18-year-old Henry was the picture of youthful vitality and resilience.[8] Richard Niccols recalls that 'Nature in constructure of those parts' of Henry's physical body, 'The grace of all good feature gaue to him | In euery Muskle, member, ioynt and limbe.'[9] His

---

[8] Hence John Davies's recollection: 'He di'de [sic] but in his prime' (The Mvses-Teares (1613), sig. D1r). My narrative of Henry's decline borrows historical details from Williamson, Myth of the Conqueror, 151–2; Ethel Williams, Anne of Denmark: Wife of James VI of Scotland, James I of England (London: Longman, 1970), 150; and from the primary sources cited throughout this chapter.

[9] Niccols, Three Sisters Teares, sig. D2v.

Comptroller John Holles describes Henry's 'able, graceful, body never wearied with labour, eminent in all princely exercises on horseback and on foot, a great sufferer of cold and heat, and in all things and to all things so framed as he promised us not only a great ableness but a long-lasting ableness.'[10] 'He was tall and of an high stature,' adds William Haydon, his senior Groom of the Bedchamber, 'his body was strong and well proportioned, his shoulders were broad...the colour of his face some what swarte and scorched with the sunne.'[11] John Hawkins describes the Prince as 'of a fearelesse, noble, Heroicke, and undanted courage, thinking nothing unpossible, that ever was done by any.'[12]

But in the late summer of 1612, his mother Anne was alarmed to see him growing increasingly listless and pale. When Henry complained of a fever, the King's royal physician Theodore Turquet de Mayerne attributed his illness to excessive and repeated chafing of the blood.[13] In early October, Mayerne ordered the Prince to rest more frequently at his residence in Richmond Palace. However, in Mayerne's blunt post-mortem assessment, Henry soon began to 'extinguish[] the beginnings of life through naughtinesse.'[14]

After two weeks of illness, writes his tutor Adam Newton, Henry intended 'by the vigour of his spirit and strength of his body, to overcome it in such sort.'[15]

---

[10] *Historical Manuscripts Commission Portland*, 9:8–11; cit. Strong, *Henry, Prince of Wales*, 2.

[11] Haydon, *True Picture*, sig. D4r. I owe the attribution of this 1634 biography to Roy Strong, who misdates its first printing as 1641 (*Henry, Prince of Wales*, 5).

[12] Hawkins, *Life and Death*, 94, sig. G1v. Given the Prince's recurring interest in testing and promoting his physical endurance, Hawkins is likely referring to Henry's riding and jousting.

[13] Mayerne moved to London from Paris after the assassination of Henri IV in 1610, served as royal physician to James I and Charles I, and was knighted in 1624. He was instrumental in establishing the Worshipful Society of Apothecaries (Roy Porter, *The Greatest Benefit to Mankind: A Medical History of Humanity* (New York: W. W. Norton, 1997), 206). His casebook of Henry's death and autopsy, BL Sloane MS. 1679, is a detailed account of Henry's symptoms and physiology; for a summary see Brian Nance, *Turquet De Mayerne as Baroque Physician: The Art of Medical Portraiture* (Amsterdam: Rodopi, 2001), 171–90. Library of the Royal College of Physicians MS. 444 contains Mayerne's assorted casebooks from 1607 to 1651 (Lucinda McCray Beier, *Sufferers and Healers: The Experience of Illness in Seventeenth-Century England* (London: Routledge, 1987), 276 n. 4). The definitive biography of Mayerne is Hugh Trevor-Roper, *Europe's Physician: The Various Life of Sir Theodore De Mayerne* (New Haven: Yale University Press, 2006).

[14] Haydon, *True Picture*, 46, sig. F3v. This diagnosis is the basis of my assertion that Henry's displays and tests of his physical endurance in late 1612 contributed to his death. However, the exact cause of his illness was unknown to his doctors. Norman Moore concludes that only the pathology of Mayerne's time prevented him from recognizing Henry's illness as enteric fever, a malaria-like illness inducing delirium, convulsions, stupor, and 'spots like flea-bites, which usually began like a tertian, but soon became a continued fever' (*The History of the Study of Medicine in the British Isles* (Oxford: Clarendon Press, 1908), 96). Yet as retrospective diagnoses are unreliable, we now know little more about Henry's illness than the English Ambassador to Venice knew in December 1612, when he described it as 'a continuous fever that became violent and malignant, refusing to yield to any medicine or remedy' (*CSPV 1603–1607*, 12:464). Chamberlain wrote that 'Yt is verelie thought that the disease was none other then this ordinarie ague that hath raigned and raged allmost all over England since the later end of sommer' (McClure, *Letters of Chamberlain*, 1:388). The least—perhaps most—that we can say is that Henry's physical exertions did not cure his illness; we cannot know whether he would have recovered by convalescing earlier.

[15] Newton thus explains why Henry 'scarce omitted his ordinary exercises of running at ring and playing at tennis' (Nichols, *Progresses of James*, 2:471 n. 2).

Ignoring his symptoms and his physician's advice not only allowed Henry to pretend that nothing was wrong; it also upheld his well-laid plans that were coming to fruition in October 1612. The impending marriage of his sister, Princess Elizabeth, to Frederick V, Count and Elector Palatine of the Rhine, would cement Henry's allegiances with Continental Protestants in their struggle against Habsburg Spain and other Catholic regimes.[16] Judging from the enthusiastic predictions, this formal union between Britain's and Germany's princes in a pan-European Protestant coalition would be the first step toward Henry's vigorously anti-Catholic foreign policy, and would have struck fear in the heart of Rome.[17] In the negotiations for Elizabeth's hand, both Henry and King James 'did onely fancy the Palsgraves motion' above other offers, 'for great Britaines eternal felicity, and terrour of all Papists.' Hawkins also recalls that, in the summer of 1612, with marriage offers arriving from Spain and from the Duke of Savoy, Henry entertained Frederick's ambassador in order to secure the match.[18]

Thus at this pivotal moment in October, following Mayerne's order to convalesce would have been both inconvenient and impolitic. Henry's desire to promote allegiances with Frederick's entourage of barons and other continental Protestants overcame any personal considerations.[19] Had he restricted himself to mere

---

[16] Henry's affection for the German Protestant princes and their courts' adaptations of Italian Renaissance culture is evidenced by his library holdings. Thomas A. Birrell notes that Henry owned a number of books by and about the *stadholder* of Schleswig-Holstein, Heinrich Rantzau, 'a model for Prince Henry because he was Protestant, Germanic, and essentially modern: a humanist with an interest in science and a patron of Italian culture who could adapt it to a Northern civilisation.' Henry also owned Franciscus Modius's *Pandectæ Triumphales* (Frankfurt: 1586), which explained the medieval origins of tournaments, barriers, and other chivalric martial displays for the Germanic nobility and aristocracy (*English Monarchs and their Books: From Henry VII To Charles II* (London: British Library, 1987), 31). Strong describes Henry's admiration of other foreign cultures that could inspire domestic industry through patronage, particularly the new architecture of Paris and the commissions of Henri IV, and the artistic legacy of Medicean Florence (*Henry, Prince of Wales*, 17).

[17] In an address delivered perhaps at Frederick's arrival, and certainly before Henry's death, William Fennor jointly praised the Princes of England, the Palatinate, Brandenburg, Brunswick, and Hesse: 'Fiue heires, true youths, Fiue kinsmen, and Fiue princes | Of one Religion, though in fiue Prouinces... Each of these are their Countries ioyfull hope, | friends to the Gospell, foes to th' Diuell and Pope' (*Fennors Descriptions* (1616), sigs. C1v, C2v). Hans Werner cites 'internal evidence' for dating this poem ('The Hector of Germanie, or The Palsgrave, Prime Elector and Anglo-German Relations of Early Stuart England: The View from the Popular Stage.' In *The Stuart Court and Europe: Essays in Politics and Political Culture*, ed. R. Malcolm Smuts (Cambridge: Cambridge University Press, 1996), 124 n. 41).

[18] Hawkins, *Life and Death*, 23, sig. B6r; he overestimates James's anti-Catholic sentiment. The marriage of Frederick and Elizabeth has been described as 'Henry's pet project' and 'a victory for his ideological and militarist agenda' (Werner, 'Anglo-German Relations,' 124). See further Strong, *Henry, Prince of Wales*, 57–8.

[19] Frederick's retinue comprised more than thirty-six barons and assorted gentlemen, eight counts, and fifty pages and grooms. Three of these men were of the House of Nassau, including Prince Maurice of Orange, with more than sixty gentlemen and servants in his own 'private suite,' and his brother, Count Henry of Nassau (*CSPV 1603–1607*, 12:443; see also Williamson, *Myth of the Conqueror*, 153–4). Hawkins recalls that Henry was 'wonderfully busie in providing, and giving order for every thing belonging to his care, for his Sisters Marriage, advancing the same by all meanes possible, keeping also his Highnes the *Palsgrave* company, so much as conveniently he could, together with Count *Henry* his Excellencie, *Grave Maurice* his Brother, whom he also much honoured and esteemed, belike because of a Noble and Heroicke disposition, which he saw in him, fitting his humour' (*Life and Death*, 33, sig. C3r).

socializing, all might have been well. But truer to form, Henry overtaxed his fragile health in a vain attempt to overcome it with physical strength. Ignoring both his illness and the dictates of the weather, in the chill of late October he played an outdoor tennis match with Count Maurice of Orange, wearing only a shirt— '(neither considering the former weake estate of his body, danger, nor coldnesse of the season) as though his body had been of brasse,' Hawkins recalls, 'during which time, he looked so wonderfull ill and pale, that all the beholders tooke notice thereof, muttering to one another what they feared.'[20] They rightly feared that Henry's evident disregard for his physical limits, so highly praised throughout his life, would prove fatal.[21]

The next day, Henry's illness forced him to withdraw from all public appearances in order to recover.[22] In the course of his apparent convalescence, he was surrounded by men with 'good hopes' but inadequate medical knowledge.[23] Hawkins recalls messages of optimism with 'no creature surmising the least danger.'[24] Henry's early symptoms—headache, fever, thirst—gave little cause for alarm. These soon gave way to light-headedness and a vulnerability to fainting, for which the Prince's physician-in-ordinary, John Hammond, prescribed a mild clyster or enema. As his symptoms worsened, Henry was forced to remain in bed, tended by Hammond, Mayerne, and John Nasmith, the King's surgeon; they

---

[20] Hawkins, *Life and Death*, 33–4, sigs. C3r–C3v. Henry's athleticism was frequently cited as evidence of his self-control, but in this instance they were at odds. Cornwallis recalls it in his *Discourse*: 'at tennis play ...he neither observed moderation, not what appertained to his dignity and person, continuing oftentimes his play for the space of three or four hours, and the same in his shirt.... Of this and of his diet, wherein he shewed too much inclination to excessive eating of fruits, he was, as in all other things, content to hear advice, but in these two particulars not to follow it' (*Discourse of Prince Henry*, 16–17).

[21] This contest suggests Henry's binary attitude toward illness: if he was not sick, as he evidently convinced himself, then he was as capable as ever of physical exertion.

[22] Mary Bradford Whiting adds that Henry heard another sermon that day at Whitehall Palace in the company of his father, but offers no attribution or further detail: 'Henry, Prince of Wales: "A Scarce Blown Rose".' *Contemporary Review* 137 (1930): 499.

[23] Hawkins, *Life and Death*, 39, sig. C6r. Lucinda McCray Beier argues that 'Modern conventions regarding privacy simply did not exist' for bedridden convalescents ('The Good Death in Seventeenth-Century England.' In *Death, Ritual, and Bereavement*, ed. Ralph Houlbrooke (London: Routledge, 1989), 55). 'Dying is a public spectacle in a crowded room, governed by its own code of conduct,' adds Gittings, describing the death of Sir Henry Unton ('Sacred and Secular: 1558–1660.' In *Death in England: An Illustrated History* (Manchester: Manchester University Press, 2000), 154; on the public nature of death see Edward Muir, *Ritual in Early Modern Europe* (Cambridge: Cambridge University Press, 1997), 46). Unton's famous memorial tableau represents different moments in his life and death, including an image of the Elizabethan gentleman on his deathbed. This inset image from 1596 has elements in common with Henry's death in 1612. The bed itself is surrounded on all sides by mourning and praying servants, and by doctors administering futile medical treatments; bowls of blood cover a bedside table. For other analyses of this portrait, see Roy Strong, *The Cult of Elizabeth: Elizabethan Portraiture and Pageantry* (Berkeley and Los Angeles: University of California Press, 1977), ch. 3; Llewellyn, *The Art of Death*, 13–16; and Neill, *Issues of Death*, 272–4.

[24] Hawkins, *Life and Death*, 39, sig. C6r. Similarly, King James's death from 'a tertian ague' in March 1625 followed his refusal to 'suffer himself to be ordered and governed by phisicall rules [i.e. of his physicians]' (McClure, *Letters of Chamberlain*, 2:606). Alan Stewart calls this stubbornness 'characteristic' of the King, although few would have expected it to be fatal; as the Countess of Bedford described the King's illness in a letter to Jane Lady Cornwallis, 'there was no more doubt of his safety than of every man's that hath an ordinary tertian ague' (*The Cradle King: The Life of James VI and I, the First Monarch of a United Great Britain* (New York: St Martin's Press, 2003), 343).

were joined on 28 October by William Butler, the renowned physician and Fellow of Clare Hall, Cambridge.[25] While his doctors argued over treatments, their ministrations relieved Henry of his symptoms but could not cure his condition.[26] Despite hopeful signs of his recovery, Henry's fatal illness confounded both treatments and expectations, wrote his chaplain Daniel Price: 'when *Natures* frame seemed firme, and a countenance of *continuance* appeared in this *Divine Prince*, Death led him into the vnavoidable passage of the farthest & fairest path of nature, & kept him 13. daies in this *Labyrinth*.'[27] By the twelfth day of Henry's withdrawal, there was a marked shift of tone from hope to despair. His condition had so deteriorated that 'newes was sent unto his Majesty of the undoubted danger, and that there now remained no hopes or means of his Highnesse recovery, but with desperate and dangerous attempts.'[28] 'In this desperate case,' Mayerne echoes, 'euery one hasted to hinder this unspeakable losse, and out of the abundance of their affection, propounded that, which they thought might do any good.'[29] The doctors' regimen in Henry's final days reflects their mounting anxiety. They administered juleps and laxatives before shaving Henry's head, letting his blood, and ending with the traditional 'last remedy' of applying pigeons to his body.[30] Finally, they yielded their patient to the prayers of the Archbishop George Abbot, and 'the rest into the hands of God.' By eight o'clock on Friday evening, 6 November 1612, Henry was dead.[31]

---

[25] Beier notes that seventeenth-century patients in danger of death were often examined by multiple physicians to ensure that their treatments were 'proper and sufficient.... Such consultations helped to reassure patients and their families that everything possible was being done. They also served as protection for the medical practitioners involved, should the patient fail to improve or die.' Yet she also claims that physicians were rarely blamed for the deaths of their patients (*Sufferers and Healers*, 245, 258). Henry's status would have merited more than the usual number of physicians.

[26] 'Mayerne would continue to favour bleeding [as opposed to purging] as the best therapy, against the more hesitant recommendations of his fellow physicians' (Nance, *Art of Medical Portraiture*, 175). As a Paracelsan, Mayerne also used chemical cures (Porter, *Greatest Benefit to Mankind*, 205). On the disagreement between Mayerne and Butler, see Chamberlain, McClure, *Letters of Chamberlain*, 1:388. Beier argues that in seventeenth-century England, 'whatever their hopes, people did not actually expect healers and medicines to cure them,' citing the 'modern inflation of expectations' as the main difference between early modern and later medical practices (*Sufferers and Healers*, 5). For a contemporaneous daily account of Henry's illness, treatment, and death, see Hawkins, *Life and Death*, 37–75, sigs. C4v–E8r; for a more recent account, see Williamson, *Myth of the Conqueror*, 155–61.

[27] Price, *Second Anniversary* (1614), sig. E4v. William Browne develops the labyrinth metaphor with an extended analogue of the Perseus myth: '*When last he sickned, then we first began* | *To tread the* Laborinth *of* Woe *about:* | *And by degrees we further inward ran,* | *Hauing his* thread *of life to guide vs out* | ... *When we were almost come into the* Center, | *Fate (cruelly) to barre our ioyes returning,* | *Cut off our* Thread, *and left vs all in* mourning' (*Britannia's Pastorals* (1616), 93, sig. N3r).

[28] Hawkins, *Life and Death*, 62, sig. E1v.   [29] Haydon, *True Picture*, sig. F2r.

[30] So called by Alice Thornton in her diary of the death of Christopher Wandesford in 1640 (cit. Beier, 'Good Death,' 53 n. 26). Lemnius recommends shaving of the head 'for the redresse of certayne diseases of the head.' 'For by this meanes all they that are encombred wyth Rhewmes, Cararrhes, and headach, fynde much ease' (*Touchstone of Complexions* (1576), 23).

[31] Haydon, *True Picture*, sig. F2r; Haydon, *True Picture*, 32, sig. D4v. The Venetian Ambassador Antonio Foscarini erroneously reports the time of death as two hours after midnight on Friday (*CSPV 1603–1607*, 12:448). The month of November was widely perceived as a time of calamity; see Wrenn, '*At usque, & usque*' for a characteristic lament. John Davies asks that future anniversaries of 'this curst day' be commemorated as a 'black *Death-day*' (*The Mvses-Teares*, sig. C1r). On the second anniversary

Reports of the Prince's death provoked disbelief and suspicion. In the weeks that followed, London was consumed by misinformation, accusations, and general hysteria. Rumours of his poisoning circulated in diplomatic circles; charges of privy counsellors consorting with Jesuits were broadcast from the pulpits; and a raving naked man 'sayeng he was the Princes ghost come from heaven with a message to the King' attracted thousands of spectators. Both the chaplain who levelled the charge ('One Baylie [Lewis Bailey] a chaplain belonging to the Prince') and the naked impersonator (whom John Chamberlain described admiringly as 'A very handsome young fellow much about his age and not altogether unlike him') were quickly silenced.[32] To quell the poison rumours, the day after Henry's death the King's surgeons autopsied his corpse and declared that he had died of natural causes.[33] 'To satisfy public opinion, as the times are full of evil deeds and men's tongues prone to wag,' reported the English Ambassador to Venice, 'the body was opened and a careful examination showed that this blow came solely from the hand of God.'[34]

Tongues were prone to wag because this vigorous, athletic, 18-year-old had been widely viewed as invulnerable. As John Holles recalled, Henry's vigour had promised 'not only a great ableness but a long-lasting ableness.'[35] Price concurred: 'It is true, the very *outside* and rinde, the very raiment of his *soule*, his body was so

---

of Henry's death, Price cites the disasters that befell in Novembers past, including the Flood itself: 'It would rather fill a *Library*, then a *volume* to descend to *particulars*' (*Second Anniversary*, 41, sig. F1r). Price makes much of the rumour that on the first day of November 1612, a rainbow was seen over St James's Palace, signalling the revocation of God's covenant: 'But now God seemeth for our *sinnes*, to haue taken downe his *bow* againe, it was an arrow he shot with the *fervency* of his *furie*, the Court was *wounded*, the *Commonwealth*; the *Church*, the whole *Protestant* world receaved a wound, in the death of Gods *deareling*, the *Renowned Prince* now in *heaven*' (*Second Anniversary*, 42, sig. F1v). In his *Lamentations*, Price cites the proximity of Henry's death to the anniversary of the Gunpowder Plot (5 November 1605) and to rumours, which he feeds, of Henry's poisoning (*Second Anniversary*, 449, sig. C1v). He develops the theme of divine wrath: '*O God*, how hast thou plagued vs, . . . In that *moneth* thou once gauest vs *Queene Elizabeth*, to take away *Prince* Henry; in that *moneth*, thou gauest vs noble *Prince Charles*, the succeeding *Charlemaine*: In that *moneth* to take away his blessed *Brother*; In the *moneth* thou diddest preserue vs from that furious *sulphureous Plot* of our enemies, in the same *moneth* are wee for our great *sorrowes* insulted on by our *Enemies*' (*Second Anniversary*, 481, sig. G1v).

[32] Chamberlain, McClure, *Letters of Chamberlain*, 1:391, 392.

[33] Haydon, *True Picture*, 44, sig. F2v. Coke itemizes the results: 'First, They found his Liver paler than ordinary, in certain places somewhat Wan; his Gall without any choler in it, and distended with Wind. Secondly, His Spleen, in divers places, more than ordinarily black. Thirdly, His Stomach was in no part offended. Fourthly, His Midriff, in divers places, black. Fifthly, His Lungs were very black, and in divers places spotted, and of a thin watry Blood. Sixthly, That the Veins of the hinder-part of his Head were fuller than ordinary, but the Ventricles and hollowness of the Brain were full of clear water' (*Detection of the Court and State* (1694), 62).

[34] *CSPV 1603–1607*, 12:464. Foreign gossips included the Duke of Savoy and Vicenzo Gussoni, the Venetian Ambassador to Savoy (*CSPV 1603–1607*, 12:455, 459, 473). For recollections of these rumours in seventeenth-century historiography, see Francis Bacon, *In Henricum Principem Walliae Elogium Francisci Bacon*, in *The Works of Francis Bacon in*, ed. James Spedding, Robert Leslie Ellis, and Douglas Heath. (Boston: Brown of Taggard, 1860), 22; Osborne, *Traditionall Memoyres*, 119–22, sigs. M4r–M5v (in Walter Scott, *Secret History of the Court of James the First* (Edinburgh: James Ballantyne, 1811)); Coke, *Detection of the Court and State* (1694, 1719), 61–2. For a more recent account, see David Bergeron, *Shakespeare's Romances and the Royal Family* (Lawrence: University of Kansas Press, 1985), 233–4 n. 53.

[35] *Historical Manuscripts Commission Portland*, 9:8–11; cit. Strong, *Henry, Prince of Wales*, 2.

faire and *strong* that a soule might haue been *pleased* to liue an *age* in it.'[36] So the poet and playwright Cyril Tourneur wondered, 'How hath death (then) found a way | To One so able? Hee was yong and strong.'[37] Wither recalled his disbelief first of the 'sad rumour' of Henry's sickness, and then of the 'sad newes' of his death 'when one had forc't vnto my eare, | My Prince was dead.' He cited similar reports after the Gunpowder Plot of 1605. When he confirmed the news from other sources, Wither's resolve faded as he repeatedly heard 'what I did least desire.'[38] These recollections come in Wither's *Prince Henries Obseqvies or Movrnefvll Elegies vpon his Death*, a collection of forty-five sonnets entered on the Stationers' Register on 18 December 1612.[39] That was eleven days after the Prince's funeral procession on 7 December, an event that quelled this tumult by confirming Henry's death.

The funeral was a public ceremony on the grandest scale.[40] Two thousand mourners attended Henry's chariot (Figure 1) through the streets of London and Westminster, from St James's Palace to Charing Cross to Westminster Abbey (Figure 2).[41] The procession was so long that, it was said, 'as the head of the procession entered the Church the tail had not yet left the Palace.'[42] The chariot,

---

[36] Price, *Spiritvall Odovrs*, 16, sig. B4v. For Henry's resilience see also Haydon, *True Picture*, sig. D4r.
[37] Cyril Tourneur, *A Broken Elegie* (1613), sig. B2r.
[38] Wither, *Prince Henries Obseqvies*, sigs. B4v, C1r.
[39] The publisher commemorates its timing with a title-page woodcut engraving of Henry's funeral chariot—the sole extant image of this wheeled cart. (See Figure 1.) Images of his hearse—the immobile structure in Westminster Abbey where the coffin and effigy stood—were more common; see Figure 2. On distinctions between hearse, chariot, and bier, see Llewellyn, *Art of Death*, 64.
[40] For descriptive accounts see Jennifer Woodward, *The Theatre of Death: The Ritual Management of Royal Funerals in Renaissance England, 1570–1625* (Woodbridge: Boydell Press, 1997), 148–65; and Gregory McNamara, '"Grief was as Clothes to Their Backs": Prince Henry's Funeral Viewed from the Wardrobe.' In Wilks, ed. *Prince Henry Revived*, 259–79.
[41] Isaac Wake offers this rarely noted detail on the route of Henry's funeral procession, describing 'ye corse from Saint James to Westminster ye farthest waye about by Charing Cross' (SP 14/71/68, (1612)). Many of the details that follow are from the anonymous *Fvnerals of the High and Mighty Prince Henry* (1613). Hawkins, *Life and Death*, 89, sig. F7r refers to this slim quarto, though Wake is impatient for its appearance: 'euery daye we expect ye relation of it in print.'
[42] *CSPV 1603–1607*, 12:468. See also Hawkins, *Life and Death*, 85–6, sigs. F5r–F5v. Foscarini repeats this estimate of 2,000 mourners in *CSPV*, as cited; see his description of the procession for minor variations. John Davies equated the collected nobility of these mourners to the worth of the deceased: 'Now; all we see, of *worth*, go all in *blacke*, | For *Him* whose *worth* all *times* shall *loue* and *lack*' (*Mvses-Teares*, sig. C4r; this is the first line of the volume's second poem, titled 'Sobs for the losse of the most Heroick Prince Henry,' sigs. C4r–C4v). Every member of the Prince's household—from his tradesmen, artificers and servants to his secretary, treasurer, and chamberlain—preceded this chariot, performing 'these last *ceremonies* of service, and sorrow' as Price (attending among Henry's twenty-four Chaplains in Ordinary) had counselled them the day before (Price, *Spiritvall Odovrs*, 3–4, sigs. M3r–M3v). They were followed by the attendants of the Count Palatine and of Prince Charles, Duke of York; a series of barons and earls; and the Archbishop of Canterbury, George Abbot. Phineas Pett, who marched in the procession, recalled its length at more than five hours: 'It was three of the clock before his body was placed under the hearse.' His memory may be unreliable, however: there were often long delays between events and his recording of them (*The Autobiography of Phineas Pett* (London: Navy Records Society, 1918), 101, vii–ix).

Figure 1 The title leaf of George Wither's elegy depicts Henry's effigy atop his funeral chariot (*Prince Henries Obseqvies*, sig. *Π*r; RB 79898, The Huntington Library, San Marino, California).

Figure 2 Prince Henry's effigy and hearse in Westminster Abbey.[43] William Hole's engraving was affixed to Chapman's *Epicede or Funerall Song*. The Latin verses are by Hugo Holland and English by George Chapman (RB 98538, The Huntington Library, San Marino, California).

[43] See Elizabeth Goldring, "So iust a sorrowe so well expressed': Henry, Prince of Wales and the Art of Commemoration,' In Wilks, ed. *Prince Henry Revived*, 285–95; MacLeod, *Lost Prince*, 165.

'set with Plumes of blacke feathers' and laden with heraldic arms, was 'drawne by eight black horses, decked with his several Scutcheons and Plumes,' bearing Henry's coffin under a canopy of black velvet.[44]

The size and accoutrements of Henry's heraldic funeral reflected his stature. David Cressy describes 'the transportation of the dead' in funeral processions as 'a civil affair, balancing the estate and circumstance of the deceased with the social and cultural concerns of the living.'[45] Henry's also gave spectators an object for their grief—most directly for its unusual inclusion of the Prince's effigy recumbent atop his coffin, its wooden frame dressed in the robes worn for his 1610 creation as Prince of Wales and topped with a wax head in his likeness.[46] '[T]he goodly image of that lovely prince,' observed Isaac Wake, 'did so liuely represent his person, as that it did not onely draw teares from the severest beholder, but cawsed a fearefull outcrie among the people as if they felt at the present their owne ruine in that loss.'[47] Wither describes the display of Henry's effigy as his first concrete confirmation of the Prince's death: 'when I saw the Hearse, then I beleeu'd, | And taking breath, thus fell to vowelling.'[48] Like other eyewitness accounts of the funeral in poetry and prose, *Prince Henries Obseqvies* modulates Wither's inward grief into public, and then published, expressions of mourning.[49]

These accounts had various purposes, but the conventional aim among the earliest to be published and circulated was to ensure that Henry received his deserved fame. Fame and funerals were often paired together, with poets offering self-serving claims to a memorial power that would outlast other forms.[50] Like

---

[44] Hawkins, *Life and Death*, 85–6, sigs. F5r–F5v; Anon., *Fvnerals of the High and Mighty Prince Henry*, sig. B4v. The latter notes that the chariot was 'drawne by six Horses couered,' though Hawkins, as quoted, recalls eight horses. Six are shown in Figure 1.

[45] David Cressy, *Birth, Marriage, and Death: Ritual, Religion, and the Life-Cycle in Tudor and Stuart England* (Oxford: Oxford University Press, 1997), 436; see 450 on heraldic funerals.

[46] Woodward, *Theatre of Death*, 150. For the effigy's design in 1612, and subsequent public exhibition and fate, see Julian Litten, 'The Funeral Effigy: Its Function and Purpose.' In *The Funeral Effigies of Westminster Abbey*, ed. Anthony Harvey and Richard Mortimer (Woodbridge: Boydell Press, 1994), 59–62. Its most detailed image is Figure 3. I am indebted to Tony Trowles at the Westminster Abbey Library for sharing Martin Rivington Holmes's unpublished 1986 lecture 'A Carved Wooden Head of Henry Frederick, Prince of Wales.' The wooden frame, property of the Abbey's Undercroft Museum, was part of the National Portrait Gallery's 2012 exhibit on the quadricentenary of Henry's death; for an image see MacLeod, *Lost Prince*, 164.

[47] TNA SP 14/71, fol. 128r; cit. Strong, *Henry, Prince of Wales*, 7.

[48] Wither, *Prince Henries Obseqvies*, sig. C1r. As noted, Wither in fact saw Henry's funeral *chariot*; his immobile *hearse* stood in Westminster Abbey; see Figure 2.

[49] James Doelman argues that the elegies for Henry reflect tensions between public and private grief in *The Daring Muse of the Early Stuart Funeral Elegy* (Manchester: Manchester University Press, 2021), 28–60. Other accounts include Chapman's *Epicede*, with an extended poetic description of the funeral procession; and the anonymous pamphlet *Great Brittans Mourning Garment. Given to all faithfull sorrowfull Subiects at the Funerall of Prince Henry* (1612).

[50] In the Unton portrait, his image is flanked by skeletons and the figure of Fame. As late as 1646, the funeral chariot of the Parliamentary commander Robert Earl of Essex was surmounted by Fame with her trumpet (Gittings, 'Sacred and Secular,' 161). The commonplace of poets upholding Fame also appeared in Robert Johnson's elegy for Robert Cecil, Earl of Salisbury: 'Though fames arch enemies do striue, | To canker greatnesse with times rust: | Yet spiritfull Poets may reuiue, | Their true deseruings from the dust' (*Life and Death of Salisbury* (1612), sig. C2r).

Wither, the anonymous author of *Great Brittans Mourning Garment* describes the funeral procession as it unfolds. (This pamphlet's subtitle suggests its immediacy: '*Given to all faithfull sorrowfull Subiects at the Funerall Of Prince Henry.*') The twelfth of its nineteen sonnets begins by invoking Fame ('Euterpe') whose 'melodious thundring blastes' 'powre new fire into my frozen stile' and revives the poet's 'fainting fury' and 'dull drooping Song' on dolorous themes like the uncertainty of man: 'The mournfull shadowes from infernall deepe, | ... know best how t'adorne a Funerall.' The poet then shifts from morbid to celebratory tones:

> No: Rest you ghosts, possesse your quiet peace,
> My griefes forbid me to disturbe the dead,
> And rest fond teares, and fruitlesse Dirges cease,
> But thou that with thy Trumpet shril dost spread
>   The praise of worthies (oh impartiall fame)
>   Helpe me to celebrate Prince Henries name.[51]

Christopher Brooke, another eulogist, more explicitly lays out this memorial purpose, effectively to reverse his subject's death with praise: 'A Poets Magicke yet, prevailes in death; | Adds Life to Vertue; and gives Honor Breath.'[52]

None of these claims or promises were unique to Henry's elegists; they echoed those written for the recent deaths of public figures from Sidney to Elizabeth.[53] Their self-promotional contrasts with the gilded monuments of princes, the 'marble lines' that Edward Gibson claims would be inadequate to praise Henry, were also typical. Gibson bemoans that no medium can contain his praise: 'No pen can take so high or low a straine, | Nor marble lines so britle be or strong'— overstating that 'Him then to prayse would doe his prayses wrong.'[54] The Venetian Ambassador reported on plans to build 'A rich tomb of marble and porphyry ... and many statues,' which he added 'will take a long time and cost much,' but like the King's other profligate plans it was put on indefinite hold.[55] Poets found 'the classical trope of poetry-as-monument' irresistible, particularly in

---

[51] Anon., *Great Brittans Mourning Garment*, sig. B3r. The poet's qualifications, reversals, and workmanlike style evoke the maxim that occasional poetry is worth only occasional praise. But I come to study this poetry, not to praise it; I use it as evidence for the climate of ideas surrounding Henry's death and afterlife. His funeral is the beginning of that afterlife, with the impulse toward celebration and 'The praise of worthies' that *Great Brittans Mourning Garment*'s author displays.

[52] Brooke, *Two Elegies*, sig. B2r.

[53] For a discussion of the elegies for Sidney, see Dennis Kay, *Melodious Tears: The English Funeral Elegy from Spenser to Milton* (Oxford: Clarendon Press, 1990), 68–78; for Elizabeth, 78–90.

[54] *Epicedium Cantabrigiense* (1612), sig. O2r. In this volume of Latin verses, Gibson's is a rare elegy written in English.

[55] *CSPV 1603–1607*, 12:469.

the absence of Henry's unbuilt tomb.[56] The poet G. B. offered his manuscript elegy in exactly those terms:

> Great Prince if worde [sic] a Tombe to thee could frame
> perhaps with others I could make thee one
> But loe I buyld it to thy Sacred name
> In thy eternall Soule in steed of stone.[57]

Robert Allyne forecast that even if Henry were to join the stone effigies of Westminster Abbey, or the painted portraits of historical worthies, poetry would 'brave oblivion' better than any such monument:

> While thou pure marble shalt possesse a place,
> Amongst the best of English Potentates
> And with thy Princely presence there shalt grace
> The glorious crew of great Plantagenets.
>   Where *Henries, Edwards, Richards*, still surviue.
>   In Marble bodies as they seem'd aliue.
> Why then thogh art can saue from earth's corruption,
> The earths owne body, which is due to wormes:
> Yet cannot so paint out the Soules perfection,
> A greater taske then Painters art performes,
>   To braue oblivion with his memorie,
>   Concernes the sacred art of Poetrie.[58]

The Henry that would 'possesse a place' in this historical pantheon is the same Henry that Dekker imagined and portrayed in *Troia-Nova Triumphans* a week before his death.[59] Allyne and Dekker are like many of Henry's rhetoricians, full of praise explicitly for their subject and implicitly for their craft. The difference is that the elegists' praise feels more forced, more self-willed, more adulterated by its impotence.

Yet if anything, poets seemed more eager to praise Henry after death than before. 'Never before,' writes Dennis Kay, 'had so many elegies been written on a single occasion, by such a wide range of practitioners: poets of all kinds, all

---

[56] Neill, *Issues of Death*, 42; see e.g. John Weever's 'Author to the Reader' in *Ancient Funerall Monuments* (1631), sigs. *4r–A2v.

[57] G. B., '*Cestria Lugens*': *A Collection of Epitaphs and Elegies on Prince Henry by one 'G. B.'* In *Melodious Tears: The English Funeral Elegy from Spenser to Milton*, ed. Dennis Kay (Oxford: Clarendon Press, 1990), 234. Similarly, Michael Neill notes Weever's invocation of 'the classical trope of poetry-as-monument to insist that literature itself constituted the most enduring monument of all' (*Issues of Death*, 42).

[58] Allyne, *Funerall Elegies*, sig. B1v.   [59] See 'The Education of a Stuart Prince' in Chapter 3.

(or most) religious and political persuasions.'[60] Thomas Heywood began his *Fvnerall Elegie* 'wishing with my soule, I might have had a more pleasing subject,' while conceding that 'since the Heavens have given us this cause it is a duty to entertain the occasion, and an unswerable [*sic*] negligence to omit it.'[61] Nearly every active poet in London, Edinburgh, and both English universities contributed to the memorial anthologies and single-author volumes in print or manuscript.[62] They numbered more than forty: eight Latin and English anthologies, with multiple authors; thirty individual poems or (more often) collections of poems; eight anonymous poems, including five ballads; at least four sermons and 'state prayers"; and two madrigals or 'songs of mourning.'[63]

If a sense of 'duty to entertaine the occasion' (to borrow Heywood's phrase) motivated many of the authors of these texts, the social pressure must also have been intense. To remain silent might have been a conspicuous signal that one did not think Henry merited such grief.[64] Wither asserted the contrary rationale that Henry's own qualities merited this outpouring: Henry could not be praised adequately 'Though all the Muses were imploy'd at once, | And write as long as Helicon would runne.' The task is so immense that it requires 'Many a Pen, and many yeares of daies,' as the quantity of elegies makes clear. In Wither's succinct estimation, 'the subject, matter infinit affords.'[65] 'Pity it were that Pen should euer more cast inke,' adds Heywood, 'that would not make the whitest paper mourne in so vniuersall a sorrow.'[66]

Mourning, as Heywood suggests, is self-evidently the initial purpose of post-humous writing: every author responds to the death first with surprise and then

---

[60] Kay, *Melodious Tears*, 124. The elegies for Henry outnumber those written for either Sidney (1586) or for Elizabeth (1603), attests Kay, though Sidney's reputation was more analogous to Henry's (as Protestant warrior, national hero, and patron of the arts) (67). Kay's bibliography considers six volumes of memorial anthologies, sermons, and biographies for Sidney; nine for Elizabeth; and twenty-six for Henry. Adrian Streete describes how elegists (Chapman, Campion, Brooke, Donne, Allyne, Davies, Wither, Webster, and contributors to Sylvester's 1613 *Lacrimae Lachrymarum*) use the prophetic mode to express a range of political views in 'Elegy, Prophecy, and Politics: Literary Responses to the Death of Prince Henry Stuart, 1612–1614.' *Renaissance Studies* 31, no. 1 (2015): 87–106.

[61] Heywood, *Funerall Elegie* sig. A2r. For further discussion of Heywood's elegy see 'Generic Decorum' in Chapter 2.

[62] The Scottish historian John Philip Edmond would write that 'the printing press literally rained tears of black ink' ('Elegies and Other Tracts,' 143). For a vivid illustration of one such page, see Brooke, *Two Elegies*, sig. *Π2r; see also Figure 3 in this chapter, and Figure 4 in the Conclusion.

[63] For a comprehensive list of these volumes, see the Appendix.

[64] William Browne describes a vast reserve of grief leading to superfluous displays: 'Is Henrie *dead, and do the Muses sleepe? | Alas! I see each one amazed stands, ...All are so full, nought can augment their store: | Then how should they | Their greifes display | To men, so cloyde, they faine would heare no more?'* (*Britannia's Pastorals*, 90, sig. N1v). Heywood is less fulsome: 'Is all the Land in sorrow, and can I | Still silent be? when every *Muse* exclames | On *Time*, on *Death*, and on sad *Destiny*, | For Henries losse' (*Funerall Elegie*, sig. A4r). G. B. opposes this conversion of sorrows into verse: 'Conuert to teares thy Ink, to Signes thy Pen, | Striue not in wordes to wayle this Prince of men | Thy Muse could play her prize could verses rayse him | Oh therefore feede on Sorrowes, cease to prayse him' (*Cestria Lugens*, 233). On the insincere 'impulse to compose an elegy' on learning of a death, particularly as a bid for patronage, see Pigman, *Grief and Elegy*, 43–4.

[65] Wither, *Prince Henries Obseqvies*, sigs. C2v, D3r.   [66] Heywood, *Funerall Elegie*, sig. A2r.

HENRICVS PRINCEPS

SEe here the portraite of that matcheles wight
Whose valour paralel'd the God of fight:
— At Tilt, at Barriers, both with sword and speare
He made his hopefull prowesse oft apeare:
His shadow's here, the world his substance misses
That was this Isles *Achilles* and *Vlisses*.
His soul's inthroan'd aboue Heauen's spangled frame,
And earth's adorn'd with his resounding fame.

A

Figure 3 The mourning page surrounding the prince's *imprese* (John Taylor, *Great Britain, all in Blacke*, sigs. *IIv*–A1r; RB 17295, The Huntington Library, San Marino, California). The woodcut of Henry practising with the pike is based on an engraving by William Hole after a drawing by Isaac Oliver, now lost.[67]

---

[67] See Wilks, 'Henry as Militant Prince'; MacLeod, *Lost Prince*, 176–7.

with a rhetorical purpose, whether to lament or commemorate or console or rationalize. I will address this range of purposes momentarily; it is necessary first to address posthumous writing categorically. It encompasses a range of forms, genres, and modes, from sermons and broadsheets to epicedes and madrigals. Let the single term 'elegy' encompass all of those forms that respond to the event of a death, and have some mix of judicial and deliberative purposes, to describe their subject (the dead) and influence their object (the reader).[68] Elegy has many subtypes, which I dissect and anatomize in this chapter, but as a category it presents two features:

1. First, elegy obeys generic decorum, or the author's choice of a genre suitable to its occasion and circumstances. An elegist is less enthusiastic about meeting an occasion than they would be to write a panegyric, say, but they uphold decorum nevertheless.[69]
2. Second, elegy is always a reluctant genre (as I stated above). Its author responds to the death with acts of commemoration and consolation, but first struggles against the turn of events that has provoked this response.

These features create conflicts within many elegies, particularly between their necessity and their futility. Their authors write these elegies because of a historical accident, yet they also try to change their circumstances with their rhetoric. I say 'many' elegies suffer thus because the tension depends on their rhetorical goals. The less ambitious an author is to change the future, to influence readers' actions based on their beliefs about what has happened, the more efficacious the elegy can seem. For instance, when an elegy merely laments the dead it can offer powerful consolation. When that consolation relies on speculative counter-narratives that attribute the event to supernatural or otherwise invisible forces, the elegy assumes a power that only credulous readers will accept. Only when the elegy warns readers against over-credulity, against believing in unreliable ideas like fame and immortality for earthly princes, is it both ambitious and efficacious. These three

---

[68] I use 'elegy' to refer to the genre of memorial verse, not the form (i.e. verse in elegiac meter). Elegies for Henry are titled with a variety of terms, including epitaph, song of mourning, epicede, and funeral song—but 'elegy' is the most common. George Puttenham notes that the epicede or monody (sung by many or one, respectively) were 'used at the enterment [*sic*] of Princes and others of great accompt' (*Arte of English Poesie*, sig. G4r). See 'Elegy: A Note on Terms' in Brady, *English Funerary Elegy*, 11–12. For an anthropological take on public elegies, see Matthew Greenfield, 'The Cultural Functions of Renaissance Elegy.' *English Literary History* 28, no. 1 (1998): 75–94. For an account of the emergence of sixteenth- and seventeenth-century elegies from medieval antecedents, see Scott Wayland, 'Religious Change and the Renaissance Elegy.' *English Literary Renaissance* 39, no. 3 (2009): 429–59.

[69] This is similar to the theory of historical formalism, which posits that textual forms emerge from their moments in time: 'not only that literary texts have historical roots and functions, but that they do so by virtue of their discourse-specific forms and conventions as well as their . . . ideological content' (Stephen Cohen, *Shakespeare and Historical Formalism* (Aldershot: Ashgate, 2007), 14).

aims—to lament, to attribute, and to warn—are my successive categories now for addressing Henry's elegies.

Lamentations

The hundreds of elegies written for Henry in the aftermath of November 1612 range from the immediate 'vowelling' of Wither at the funeral to the annual anniversary sermons of Price. Amid this chorus, whose individual laments are too voluminous and conventional to divide, there is a category that feels particularly poignant for this literary critic (at least): the lament for lost texts. John Webster's extended elegy, *A Monvmental Colvmne* (1613), finds the pathos of Henry's death in the trope of lost narratives. Surveying the elegies by frustrated poets, abandoned courtiers, erstwhile soldiers, and cloistered academics, Webster takes aim at both their ignorance and their conventionality:

> Fames lips shall bleed, yet nere her trumpet fill
> VVith breath enough, but not in such sicke aire,
> As make waste Elegies to his Tombe repaire,
> VVith scraps of commendation more base
> Then are the ragges they are writ on, ô disgrace
> To nobler Poesie. This brings to light,
> Not that they can, but that they cannot write,
> Better, they had, nere troubled his sweet trance,
> So, silence should haue hid their ignorance:
> For hee's a reuerend subiect to be pend
> Onely by his sweet *Homer* and my frend.[70]

Only in this penultimate line do we learn why Webster is so scornful of these 'scraps' and 'ragges' displacing 'nobler Poesie,' because he has a nobler poet in mind for his 'reuerend subiect.' Henry deserves worthier textual monuments, so Webster turns to his 'frend' Chapman's most recent English translation of Homer's *Iliad*.[71] Let us return to Chapman after we consider how conventional Webster's disdain for 'ragges' actually was. Donne used the same word to denigrate his own paltry offerings for the life of Elizabeth Drury (as addressed in the Introduction), three years before Webster. In *An Anatomy of the World*, Donne ends 'The First Anniuersarie' resolving to write more elegies for Drury, though he

---

[70] John Webster, *Monvmental Colvmne* (1613), sig. C1r. Thomas P. Anderson addresses relations between Webster's poem and Henry's effigy in ' "We Cannot Say Hee's Dead": Writing Royal Effigies in Marvell's Poetry.' *English Literary Renaissance* 35, no. 3 (2005): 507–13.

[71] Browne also refers to Homer's translator as 'My friend' in Browne, *Britannia's Pastorals*, 88, sig. M4v.

adds that her life is 'matter fit for Chronicle, not verse' (l. 460). Yet by the beginning of 'A Funerall Elegie,' this volume's next poem, Donne's attitude has shifted:

> Can these memorials, ragges of paper, giue
>   Life to that name, by which name they must liue?
> Sickly, alas, short-liu'd, aborted bee
>   Those Carkas verses, whose soule is not shee.[72]

However elegies may suit the decorum of a death, the hierarchy of genres plainly puts chronicles and epics above these 'ragges of paper.' Drury differs from Henry only in the domains of her life, and the absent Homeric projections of her unrealized future. 'The world containes | Princes for armes, and Counsailors for braines,' writes Donne, 'and shee | Being spent, the world must needes decrepit bee.'[73]

Chapman's translations were not the sole, direct cause of these Homeric projections; it was conventional for ambitious military biographers to compare their work to Homer's war epic. Daniel had begun his account in *The Civil Wars* of Henry V's French campaign, culminating in the famous Battle of Agincourt, by lauding 'What euerlasting matter here is found, | Whence new immortal *Iliads* might proceed.'[74] And in 1603, Alexander enthused about the prospect of recounting Henry's military exploits in exactly those terms:

> I (*Henrie*) hope with this mine eyes to feed,
> Whilst, ere thou wearst a crowne, thou wear'st a shield,
> And when thou making thousands for to bleed,
> That dare behold thy count'nance and not yeeld,
> Sturres through the bloudie dust a foaming steed,
> An interested witnesse in the field,
>   I may amongst those bands thy Grace attend,
>   And be thy *Homer*, when the warres do end.[75]

Alexander emphasizes that he will bear witness to these exploits: his 'eyes' will 'behold' them as a 'witnesse' as he 'attends' the Prince, necessary preconditions for the poet to 'be thy Homer' in retrospect. His diction resembles that of Price, who in an anniversary sermon years later said that Henry 'would have been *subiect* for all pens, and *obiect* for all eies.'[76] The Homeric terms of such projections fuelled Webster's disdain, perhaps as much as Chapman's translations did. And yet the very terms of his disdain are, not surprisingly, conventional too. Recall how Drummond laments Henry's lost military biography:

---

[72] John Donne, *Anatomy of the World* (1612), sig. B7r.
[73] Donne, *Anatomy of the World*, sig. B7v.   [74] Daniel, *Certaine Small VVorkes*, sig. K3v.
[75] Alexander, *Paraenesis*, sig. C4v.   [76] Price, *Spiritvall Odovrs*, sig. C4v.

A booke had beene of thy illustrous deedes.
So to their nephewes aged Syres had told
The high exploits perform'd by thee of olde;
Townes raz'd, and rais'd, victorious, vanquish'd bands,
Fierce Tyrants flying, foyl'd, kild by thy hands.
And in deare Arras, Virgins faire had wrought
The Bayes and Trophees to thy countrie brought:
While some great *Homer* imping wings to fame,
Deafe *Nilus* dwellers had made heare thy name.[77]

It would certainly be easier to bemoan lost *Iliads*, as Drummond does, than to promise them, as Alexander had done; Henry's death freed poets from the obligation to write them. Drummond concedes that his elegy is a poor substitute for the 'booke' that 'had been' of Henry's 'high exploits,' which deserve virgins and poets to represent them. All that distinguishes his regret from Alexander's prospect is their verb tenses.

Chapman was at most partially responsible for fomenting these Homeric expectations of Henry's future. His *Epicede or Funerall Song* (1612) recalls how classical models once inspired his former patron with their abstracted rules of justice and of war:

O that thy life could haue disperst deaths stormes,
To giue faire act to those Heroique forms,
with which al good rules had enrich thy mind,
Preparing for affayres of euery kinde, . . .
Of which lawes, thy youth, both contain'd the text
And the contents; ah, that thy grey-ripe yeeres
Had made of all, *Cæsarean* Commentares,
(More then can now be thoght) in fact t'enroule;
And make blacke Faction blush away her soule.[78]

The image of Henry's youth as a table of contents for his prospective story recalls Drayton and Davison's descriptions of him as an 'abridgement.'[79] These poets

---

[77] Drummond, *Death of Meliades*, sig. A2v. Cicero compares the deafening roar of the Nile (or 'dull-making cataract of Nilus,' in Sidney's phrase) to man's deafness to the music of the spheres (Sidney, *Defence*, 390 n. 230).

[78] Chapman, *Epicede*, sig. C3r. On Henry's associations with Caesar see Soellner, 'Caesar and Pompey and Henry,' 137, and Jonathan Gibson, 'Sir Arthur Gorges (1557–1625) and the Patronage System' (Diss., University of London, 1998), 256–9. On the Commentaries' early modern reception by soldiers wielding both swords and pens, see Matthew Woodcock, '"The Breviarie of Soldiers": Julius Caesar's Commentaries and the Fashioning of Early Modern Military Identity.' In *Early Modern Military Identities, 1560–1639: Reality and Representation*, ed. Matthew Woodcock and Cian O'Mahony (Woodbridge: Boydell & Brewer, 2019), 56–78.

[79] See 'The Education of a Stuart Prince' in Chapter 3.

measure Henry's loss in textual terms because, in part, they are no longer obliged to write the lost texts. In 1614 Walter Ralegh would close his *History of the World* lamenting that its second, third, and fourth volumes 'which I also intended, and have hewne out; besides many other discouragements, persuading *my silence*; it hathe pleased God to take that Glorious Prince out of the world, to whom they were directed.'[80] But Chapman departed from Drayton, Davison, and Ralegh by undertaking in his *Epicede* to relate an elaborate supernatural narrative of Henry's life and death. In the section to come, I compare Chapman's narrative to analogous accounts of Henry's and then Sidney's deaths. Their common motive is to supercede lamentations—the conventional end of elegies—with supernatural attributions.

Attributions

Both Chapman and Arthur Gorges wrote elaborate allegories of Henry's death to uncover what Gorges called the 'veiled mystery' of its supernatural causes. Both had the precedent of Spenser's allegorical elegies for Sidney (*Astrophel*) and for Gorges's late wife, Douglas Howard (*Daphnaïda*), among others. But they also did novel things with this conventional form, by explaining the unexpected and unthinkable death of an object of great expectations. All three poets responded to the idea that their subjects deserved better stories than the elegies they offered as compensatory substitutions. But their stories were of otherworldly causes, rather than worldly effects.

Their three elegies—Spenser's *Astrophel* (1594), Gorges's *The Olympian Catastrophe* (1612), and Chapman's *Epicede* (1612)—are allegorical renditions of Sidney's or Henry's deaths. Aforementioned differences between Sidney's heroic death in 1586 and Henry's ignoble, pathetic death from illness in 1612 meant that Spenser could follow true events more closely; he merely allegorizes Sidney's gunshot during the battle of Zutphen as an Adonis-like boar attack during a hunting expedition. Both Sidney, who died (probably) of gangrene, and the pastoral shepherd Philisides, who dies from his wounds, exemplify human mutability ('sad ensample of mans suddein end')—but then, so too do the subjects of most elegies.[81] There was something fitting about Sidney's heroic death, suiting the pattern of his heroic life, that was missing from Henry's.

Whether or not Sidney's actions were blameworthy, they fit exemplary precedents like Memnon, the Ethiopian king proud of his armour, killed by Achilles. Francis Bacon called Memnon 'a youth too forward' in his compilation of classical

---

[80] William E. Engel, *Death and Drama in Renaissance England: Shades of Memory* (Oxford: Oxford University Press, 2002), 177, see also 113–33.

[81] Spenser, *Yale Edition*, 575, l. 134.

'fables,' *De Sapienta Veterum* (*The VVisedome of the Ancients*, 1609). Translating it into English, Gorges described Memnon's story as a warning against 'the unfortunate destinies of hopefull young men' who 'attempt actions above their strength' like combat with heroes, 'so that (meeting their ouer-match) [they] are vanquished and destroyed, whose untimely death is oft accompanied by much pitty and commiseration.'[82] The aftermath of Henry's death was no time to blame him for 'attempt[ing] actions above [his] strength,' particularly when those actions were on a tennis court rather than a battlefield—but Bacon's summary of Memnon (in Gorges's translation) seems apt for Henry: '[A]mong all the disasters that can happen to mortals, there is none so lamentable and so powrefull to moue compassion as the flower of vertue cropt with too sudden a mischance.'[83] This is more specific than Spenser's generalized lament for Sidney as a 'sad ensample of mans suddein end'; these are men who are 'the flower of vertue' whose ends come suddenly through some 'mischance.' The question of blame is set aside, addressed only if necessary.[84]

Henry resembled others who were blameless for their mischance, like Douglas Howard or Elizabeth Drury. The former was the subject of Spenser's other notable elegy, *Daphnaïda* (1591). Howard, Drury, and Henry share an attribute that complicates their mourning: all died in their youth, leaving poets to speculate about their lost adulthoods. 'For age to dye is right, but youth is wrong' was Spenser's stark assessment in 1591; and in 1612 Gorges directly quoted this lament in *The Olympian Catastrophe*.[85] In the complex history of mutual borrowings and recapitulations between Spenser and Gorges, both repurpose one another's work (its words, images, even stanzaic forms) for emergent circumstances. Gorges's love poetry to his wife (as Daphne) became his laments (as Alcyon) in Spenser's *Daphnaïda*; Spenser's reference in *Colin Clout's Come Home Again* (1595) to 'Sad Alcyon bent to mourn,' who 'for Daphnes death doth tourn | Sweet lays of loue to endlesse palints of pittie' suggests a collaboration between the two poets. Gorges certainly felt entitled enough to these words to reassign them to Henry's sister Elizabeth in *The Olympian Catastrophe*, amended to remove its 'most reprehensible, selfish elements' of 'misanthropy and suicidal impulses.'[86] Alcyon's mourning dominates *Daphnaïda*, more than Daphne's lost qualities; the poem is a warning to readers and to Alcyon's immediate audience of damsels, pilgrims, and shepherds that his 'sorrowful annoy' could be theirs: 'such mishap, as chaunst to me, | May happen unto the most happiest wight; | For all mens states alike unstedfast be.'[87]

---

[82] Francis Bacon, *VVisedome of the Ancients*, tr. Arthur Gorges (1619), 71, sig. C12r.

[83] Bacon, *VVisedome of the Ancients*, 71–2, sigs. C12r–C12v.

[84] For further discussion of *Astrophel* see 'Generic Decorum' in Chapter 2.

[85] Spenser, *Yale Edition*, 503, l. 243; rewritten as Gorges, *Olympian Catastrophe*, 177, l. 1080.

[86] Gibson, 'Gorges and Patronage,' 197. See also Gorges, *Olympian Catastrophe*, 237.

[87] Spenser, *Yale Edition*, 513, ll. 515–17.

By the time he wrote *The Olympian Catastrophe* some two decades later, Gorges borrowed *Astrophel*'s chivalric allegory and stanzaic form (ABABCC) rather than *Daphnaïda*'s sombre warning that the 'mortall miseries' of human affairs are an ever-renewing source of 'new matter fit for Tragedies.'[88] In his opening stanzas, Gorges explicitly disavows Melpomene, the muse of tragedy, because this is not to be a mournful tale of grief but a eulogy of the Prince's achievements.[89] It is conceivable that Gorges wrote parts of his elegy during Henry's lifetime, intending them for more celebratory occasional texts. The poem consists of five scenes, alternating between the Olympian and Jacobean courts. It begins with a contention between the three goddesses Bellona, Minerva, and Juno over their respective claims to the 'princlie paragon' whose chivalric feats they admire. The scene shifts to 'Th'olympian games' of wrestling, running, fencing, archery, and chivalric tournaments, where a mysterious knight reveals his British origins through both emblems (of intertwined roses) and unmatched prowess in the field. This is clearly Henry, whom Gorges identifies thereafter as 'Brittains Prince.'[90] Gorges's choice of Olympian metaphors was a conventional way to conflate chivalric, athletic, and artistic feats as pre-eminent among nations; the previous year Daniel had praised Sidney for defending English against foreign (particularly Italian) arts in these terms:

> Let them produce the best of all they may...
> They cannot shew a Sidney, let them shew
> All their choice peeces, and bring all in one
> And altogether shall not make that shew
> Of wonder and delight, as he hath done:
> He hath th'Olimpian prize (of all that run
> Or euer shall with mortall powers) possest
> In that faire course of glory.[91]

The association with more recent Jacobeans was also conventional, thanks in part to Jonson's masques; in 1612 Chapman's *Epicede* referred to Henry's 'court-schoole; this *Olimpus*,' 'where all contention of vertues were practised.'[92]

The Olympian Catastrophe then takes a turn more catastrophic than any Jonsonian masque. After winning the garland victory, Henry has portentous and unsettling dreams of visiting the Elysian fields; the next morning his squires reassure him that providence will prevail over such 'dreamimge fancyes.'[93] The tournament resumes, where Gorges describes the Prince felling two opponents—before our

---

[88] Spenser, *Yale Edition*, 500, ll. 152, 154.   [89] Gorges, *Olympian Catastrophe*, 139, ll. 7–11.

[90] Gorges, *Olympian Catastrophe*, 140, 146, ll. 20, 36, 195.

[91] Daniel, *Certaine Small Workes*, sig. E4v. The context is Daniel's dedicatory epistle of *The Tragedie of Cleopatra* to Mary Sidney, Countess of Pembroke.

[92] Chapman, *Epicede*, sig. B4v.   [93] Gorges, *Olympian Catastrophe*, 149, l. 281.

scene abruptly shifts back to the quarrelling goddesses on Olympus, who learn that Jove has sent the fury Atropos to cut the thread of Henry's life. Minerva laments that their disagreement has caused his death: 'O most unhappy strife, | That twixt us deityes did earst beginne! | Wee were the cause that thou [Atropos] didst end his life.'[94] Gorges has underscored this attribution, much earlier in the poem, in case we missed it: 'from this strife arose | That hope-confounding harme.'[95] Atropos consoles them with claims that Henry's virtue exceeds 'earthes base pomp' and has been spared earthly decrepitude, but there is no doubt that he, rather than Henry, is to blame for it.

The conversation between Minerva and Atropos is one of the longest in the poem, yet it gives no details of exactly how Henry died in this chivalric contest. We are left only with supernatural interests and motives for this strike of 'fates tennis-ball,' a conventional metaphor and sidelong glance at Henry's sporting display.[96] Gorges tells a version of events that is consistent with what earthly spectators actually saw, but gives those events a more valiant and cosmic setting consistent with heroic poetry. He is more interested in uncovering their causes than in discussing their particulars. In his envoy to the poem, Gorges strikes a defensive tone that seems to address criticism of this lacuna. He rails against readers

> whom ignoranc so blinds,
> To count this Poeme Idle Ballatrye
> Because themselves with hood-winct blunddringe mynds
> Cannot discearne a vailed misterye.[97]

His poem has the power to impart lessons beneath its veiled meaning, so it is not 'idle'; and it has the power to reveal the hidden truth or cause of Henry's death, the earthly manifestation of a divine catastrophe. His term 'misterye' means (broadly) things surpassing human understanding, subject to faith rather than to reason. That is the definition of Thomas Wilson's *Christian Dictionary* (1612), published the same year, and it is consistent with uses of the term in the Authorized Translation the preceding year, describing the mysteries of iniquity, of godliness, and of worship. Fulke Greville's sonnet sequence *Caelica* (1633) enjoins men to 'dream no more of curious mysteries,' to accept God's omniscience as a consolation for human ignorance of things—like what pre-existed the universe or where heaven and hell are.[98] John Milton's archangel Raphael similarly advises the inquiring Adam to 'Be lowly wise,' and 'Solicit not thy thoughts with matters

---

[94] Gorges, *Olympian Catastrophe*, 166, ll. 757–9.
[95] Gorges, *Olympian Catastrophe*, 140, ll. 31–4.   [96] Gorges, *Olympian Catastrophe*, 170, l. 890.
[97] Gorges, *Olympian Catastrophe*, 177, ll. 1189–92.
[98] Emrys Jones, ed. *The New Oxford Book of Sixteenth Century Verse* (Oxford: Oxford University Press, 1991), 359, 216.1.

hid' from human understanding.[99] Gorges takes on Raphael's task in *The Olympian Catastrophe*, interpreting mysteries for Christian readers by paganizing them. Meanwhile on earth, the effects of this divine cause are familiar: 'Sorrow in playntes, in teares, in mourninge weedes, | Was Epilogue to all the royall sporte.'[100] Henry's observers immediately begin recounting his life and virtues, rather than the manner of his death. So Gorges turns his indecorous illness and death into something more heroic and inspiring, complete with a chivalric setting and supernatural cause.

Let us turn now to Chapman's *Epicede* to consider how he attributes the same event to different causes, following Gorges's motive to acquit Henry of blame. If Gorges deflects his readers' attention from the events of Henry's illness and death, Chapman takes them directly to 'the fatall Bed' in St James's Palace where Henry 'hid his white lyms,' and then encroaches further into 'his breast,' aflame with heat; 'his heart,' chilled with cold; and 'his vaines,' suffused with venom, before 'Death, Death, O Death, jnserting, thrusting in, | Shut his faire eyes.'[101] Unlike Gorges, Chapman leaves no doubt that the Prince succumbed to a fatal illness; but like Gorges, he offers an allegorical autopsy attributing it to supernatural forces. He begins by invoking 'an Angels tongue' to 'Tell thy astonisht Prophet' the real story: how 'Rhamnusia (Goddesse of reuenge, and taken for Fortune) in enuy of our Prince, executed Feuer against him.'[102] She gathers it from ethereal vapours to infect Henry's heart with 'A præternaturall heat; which through the vaines | And Arteries, by'th blood and spirits meanes | Diffus'd about the body.'[103] Rhamnusia's agent is the hideous fury Echidna, whose face, entrails, and vapours Chapman vividly describes; at Rhamnusia's command ('His pure Life, poyson') she bursts into the sickroom 'and cast | A fire in him, that all his breast embrac't.'[104] Rhamnusia's motive is 'sulphurous spight' for a prince who seems all futurity and self-assurance, 'who joyes securely in all present *State*, | Nor dreams what *Fortune* is, or future *Fate*.' So Echidna mocks him, standing over his bedside: 'why tak'st thou thus thy rest secure? | Nought doubting what Fortune and fates assure.'[105] Chapman turns Henry's misplaced self-assurance, his death despite his 'health,' 'continence' and 'pious feare,' into a moral for others:

> Now Princes, dare ye boast your vig'rous states
> That Fortunes breath thus builds and ruinates?
> Exalt your spirits? trust in flowry youth?
> Give reynes to pleasure? all your humours sooth?

[99] John Milton, *Paradise Lost*, Norton Critical Editions, ed. Gordon Teskey (New York: W. W. Norton, 2020), 8.173, 167.
[100] Gorges, *Olympian Catastrophe*, 174, ll. 1009–10.
[101] Chapman, *Epicede*, sigs. D3r, D2v, D3r.   [102] Chapman, *Epicede*, sigs. C4r, C4v.
[103] Chapman, *Epicede*, sig. D1r.   [104] Chapman, *Epicede*, sigs. D2r, D3r.
[105] Chapman, *Epicede*, sigs. C4v, D2r, D3r.

> Licence in rapine? Powers exempt from lawes?
> Contempt of all things, but your own applause?[106]

By 'states' Chapman means states of health, or (as before, in 'present *State*') states of being, that princes too often presume will last.

There is considerable irony in Chapman delivering this warning. Although he couches his criticisms in terms like 'spirits,' 'pleasure,' and 'humours,' as I have shown he also directly encouraged the Prince to exalt his spirit with thoughts of epic futurity in successive dedications of *Iliad* translations. Now that he is writing elegies, Chapman bemoans that Henry will never fulfil the heroic potential that his exemplars possessed, namely by waging war:

> O that thy life could haue disperst deaths stormes,
> To giue faire act to those Heroique formes,
> With which al good rules had enricht thy mind,
> Preparing for affayres of euery kinde,
> Peace being but a pause to breathe fierce warre.[107]

The 'Heroique formes' are Henry's ethical exemplars who impart 'good rules' of conduct in peace and war alike. Chapman struggles with a contradiction in his *Epicede*: between warning princes against predictions and wishing that this prince had met the poet's predictions. Chapman also reluctantly renegotiates the meaning of the city of Troy, where previously he set his very predictions. Suffice it to say the Troy he describes in his *Epicede* is not the same as in his *Iliad* dedications:

> O what a frame of Good, in all hopes rais'd
> Came tumbling downe with him! as when was seisde
> By Grecian furie, famous Ilion,
> VVhose fall, still rings out his Confusion.
> VVhat Triumphs, scatterd at his feete, lye smoking!
>   ... And how amaz'd
> The change of things stands![108]

Chapman's elegy is a monument to his epic, as a ruin is to a city '[t]hat Fortunes breath ... builds and ruinates.' It remains only for the poet to lament the 'state' of things that once seemed assured, in a manner reminiscent of Spenser in *The Ruines of Time*:

---

[106] Chapman, *Epicede*, sig. B2v.   [107] Chapman, *Epicede*, sig. C3r.
[108] Chapman, *Epicede*, sigs. B4v–C1r.

> And as the ruines of some famous Towne,
> Show here a Temple stood; a Pallace, here;
> A Cytadell, an Ampitheater;
> Of which (ahlas) some broken Arches, still
> (Pillars, or Columns rac't; which Art did fill
> With all her riches and Diuinitie)
> Retaine their great, and vvorthy memory:
> So of our Princes state, I nought rehearse
> But show his ruines, bleeding in my verse.[109]

Coming from the poet whose own 'Art' embellished Henry's hopes, this recognition of his vulnerability is rather belated. Yet it also provokes greater pity for the poet who was ambitious only to make Henry's intrinsic qualities extrinsically admirable:

> So had thy sacred Frame beene rais'd to height,
> Forme, fulnesse, ornament: the more the light
> Had giuen it view, the more had Men admir'd.[110]

Note Chapman's preference for the passive voice, hedging the role that he and others played in 'rais[ing] to height' this temple to Henry. Thus Gorges and Chapman both reiterate and rethink Spenser's treatment of Sidney, for an array of reasons—including their own investments in Henry's future and their disappointment in his failure to meet the Olympian and Trojan potential they once foresaw.

In what remains of this chapter's account of Henry's posthumous legacy, I extend my perspective to a wider range of writers articulating his cautionary lessons. If the immediate reaction to the news of Henry's death was lamentation; and if Gorges and Chapman saw their primary purpose as attribution; then the function of other responses was to warn their audiences that Henry's fate was hardly unique. I will address two prevailing genres that offered those cautionary lessons: first epitaphs, whose purpose is to warn readers more sharply than elegies do; and then sermons, which both before and after Henry's death consistently warn auditors against trusting in worldly things, particularly princes. A concluding section will address the frailty-of-princes topos pervading epitaphs and sermons, to consider Henry as an exemplar of human frailty.

Warnings

Epitaphs differ from elegies in both their medium and their message. Both genres attempt to preserve their deceased subject on what John Davies of Hereford called

---

[109] Chapman, *Epicede*, sig. C3v–C4r.   [110] Chapman, *Epicede*, sig. C3v.

'this ground of Fame.'[111] But epitaphs stand on more physical than metaphorical ground, conventionally (if not actually) carved in monumental marble. Until the early seventeenth century, epitaphs were defined only by their medium ('An inscription or writing set vpon a toombe'), though by 1616, John Bullokar refined the inscription's purpose as being 'in lamentation or praise of the party there buried.'[112] It was a key distinction, lamentation or praise, that determined whether the dead would be famous or infamous. Henry Peacham, substituting the term 'epicede' for elegy, notes that epitaphs ought to follow elegies, even if some poets break that rule: 'The difference is that the Epicedium is propper to the body while it is unburied, the Epitaph otherwise; yet our Poets stick not to take one for the other.'[113]

Regardless of their timing, two qualities distinguish epitaphs from other post-humous writings: their permanence and their impertinence. David Shaw's observation on Romantic epitaphs extends to all: 'What is laboriously carved on stone should have the status of a fixed feeling, whereas a feeling too transitory or poignant to be inscribed on stone may be entertained as a fugitive impression in an elegy.'[114] We can see this transitory quality in the descriptions of emotions provoked by Henry's funeral, in elegies like Wither's and Chapman's and in the anonymous *Great Brittans Mourning Garment*. Elegists evidently are less invested in their words when they are circulated in manuscript or print rather than carved in stone, even metaphorically. (We will see momentarily how Wither transitions from poignant 'vowelling' lamentations at the funeral to his more laboured address to readers in the epitaph closing his 1612 volume.) Epitaphs assume the burden of speaking not only for the living but also for the dead, impersonating them through an autobiographical 'voice-from-beyond-the-grave.'[115] Whether the dead speak directly or through the poet, using them as an indirect exemplar, they issue injunctions to living readers who, Paul de Man argues, are 'struck dumb, frozen in their own death' by this address.[116]

Consider whether these theorizations, largely based on English Romantic epitaphs, obtain for the voices and the auditors of early modern epitaphs. They

---

[111] Davies pledged to preserve the name of Elizabeth Dutton (d.1611)—the eldest daughter of Thomas Egerton, 1st Viscount Brackley (1540–1617)—using conventional tropes: 'For, knowing *Tombes* haue *ends* as well as *wasts*, | And that strong *Rime* their *ruine* farre out-lasts, | My *Muse* shall labour on this *ground* of *Fame*, | To raise a Pile of *Rime*, whereon thy *Name* | Shall euer shine' (*Mvses Sacrifice* (1612), sigs. P8r–P8v). For funeral monuments replacing religious icons with the figure of Fame after the Reformation, see Sherlock, *Monuments and Memory*, 197–230.

[112] J. B., *An English Expositor* (1616); cit. Scott L. Newstok, *Quoting Death in Early Modern England* (New York: Palgrave Macmillan, 2009), 8; for a thorough study of epitaphs' etymology and early modern usage, as distinct from elegy, see 33–58.

[113] Henry Peacham, *Period of Mourning* (1613), sig. C4v.

[114] David Shaw, *Elegy and Silence: The Romantic Legacy* (Lethbridge: University of Lethbridge Press, 1992), 2, 4. He defines epitaphs with reference to Romantic literature, whose critics have most extensively treated this genre—largely in response to Wordsworth's *Essays Upon Epitaphs*.

[115] Paul de Man, *The Rhetoric of Romanticism* (New York: Columbia University Press, 1984), 77.

[116] De Man, *Rhetoric of Romanticism*, 79.

are, as a rule, somewhat less autobiographical. They are also more informed by Continental models, often by reputation—though some Jacobean Englishmen would have seen epitaphs on tombs lining the Via Appia and Via Flaminia on their educational tours to Rome. One anonymous poet seems to address English travellers in search of more exotic foreign marvels, asking in their epitaph for Henry published in 1613, 'Why Pilgrime doest thou stray | By Asia's floods renown'd?' In Henry, this traveller could find better marvels at home: 'By Isis streames if thou'l [*sic*] but daigne to stay, | One thou shall finde surpassing all the told.'[117] This pilgrim is a river traveller, as Henry's place of internment (Westminster Abbey) is set beside a waterway (the Thames) rather than a high-way. But the poet's address to him as a traveller owes to the Roman practice of erecting monuments alongside highways, with epitaphs enjoining travellers to 'stay' or 'pause' (*siste, viator*) mid-route.[118]

If the English epitaphs' defensive tone betrays a nationalist insecurity, it is because their authors are aware of foreign competitors for fame and recognition. Drummond, identified only as W. D. in the collection that his epitaph shares with the unattributed one quoted above, addresses travellers en route:

> Stay Passenger, see where enclosed lyes,
> The Paragon of Princes, fairest Frame,
> Time, Nature, Place could show to mortall eyes,
> In Worth, Wit, Vertue; wonder vnto Fame.
> At least that part the Earth of him could claime,
> This Marble holds, *hard like the Destinies*:
> For as to his braue Spirit, and glorious Name,
> The one the World, the other fills the Skyes. ...
> > Then goe and tell from Gades vnto Inde,
> > Thow saw where Earths perfections were confinde.[119]

Drummond enjoins the traveller, embarking on the most important British trade route then being developed ('from Gades vnto Inde'), to extend Henry's

---

[117] Anon., *Mavsolevm* (1613), n.p.

[118] This was not the Jacobean practice, though it was imagined often enough. Consider the epitaph on Roger Manners (1576–1612), 5th Earl of Rutland and Dallington's patron, seemingly composed by the Earl himself and dated 11 December 1607, beginning: 'See here the paterne of true noble blood,' and ending, 'that men of virtuous mind | May—passing by—thy losse lament and mone' (HMC Rutland MSS, II.318).

[119] Anon., *Mavsolevm*, n.p. Drummond, *Death of Meliades* contains an epitaph very similar to this one reprinted in *Mavsolevm*; they share the same opening line, closing couplet, and thematic contrast of earthly elements with heavenly reputation (sig. B2r). Both were printed in 1613 by Andro Hart in Edinburgh, but the subtitle of *Mavsolevm* reveals that this anthology was printed later: *The Choisest Flowres of the Epitaphs, written on the Death of the neuer-too-much-lamented Prince Henrie*. The *Mavsolevm* text of Drummond's poem is evidently a revised version of the epitaph in *Death of Meliades*.

reputation internationally. Although Drummond lauds Henry at length before issuing this command, he also deliberately contrasts his former qualities (worth, wit, virtue, spirit, and name) with the limits of 'This Marble,' containing merely his mortal remains, 'that part the Earth of him could claime.' All of his qualities and 'Earths perfections [are] confinde' in these inadequate words, so Drummond's epitaph enjoins the traveller to disseminate them further.

Drummond's epitaph aspires to be entirely laudatory of "the most hope-fvll and all-vertvovs" Henry, but it is cautionary in spite of itself. This contradictory purpose is evident in the double meaning of a word like 'confinde,' which can mean both contained and restricted, both encapsulated and limited. Epitaphs need travellers to unconfine their subjects' qualities, or they will languish within what Wither calls 'a litle scope':

> Stay Trauailer, *and read; did'st neuer heare*
> *In all thy iourneyes any newes nor tales,*
> *Of a great* Heros [*sic*], *to the world once deare,*
> *They cal'd him* Henrie *the braue* Prince of Wales?
>
> *Looke here, within this litle place he lyes,*
> *Eu'n he that was the* Vniuersall Hope:
> *And almost made this Ile* Idolatrize,
> *See, he's contented with a litle scope. ...*
>
> *So this, to mocke vaine* Hopes, *in him began*
> *Dide; and here lyes, to shewe he was a man.*[120]

More pointedly (or forthrightly) than Drummond, Wither contrasts Henry's 'vaine Hopes' with this 'litle place' where he lies buried. If his tone is more mocking than laudatory, it is because he addresses those who revered Henry to the point of idolatry, to restore a sense of proportion and humility to their 'newes' and 'tales.'

Wither's candour fulfils expectations of an epitaph, offering a blunt, corrective lesson of human frailty: 'he was a man.' It is corrective, namely, of the ambitions both for a life of achievements and an afterlife of fame, ambitions that thread through the exemplary cycle like a pattern in a carpet. Epitaphs' permanent medium, even if it is more tropological than true, contrasts with the evanescence of those they memorialize. This tension is even more acute in the manuscript *Cestria Lugens*, written and circulated by one G. B. and otherwise unattributed.[121] Despite its less permanent medium, this metaphorical epitaph is more explicitly

---

[120] Wither, *Prince Henries Obseqvies*, sig. D3v.
[121] Dennis Kay has edited the manuscript, from Bodley MS Rawl. Poet. 116, fols. 1–16, in *Melodious Tears*, 233–50, Appendix A.

negative even than Wither's. G. B. describes Henry as a pre-eminent example of human frailty: 'Further example seeke thou none | Of deaths spoile, then vnder this stone.' More voluble than most, 'this stone' speaks for Henry as his epitaph:

> Admir'd of euery harte & eye
> Mirror of Princes here am I
> vntymely laide in graue full lowe
> fortune & death wold have it soe
> And if thou aske a reason why
> Kings are but men & men must die.[122]

G. B. underscores this *de casibus* (or mirror-for-princes) message with an ironic tone: 'Prince Henry here lies under grounde full lowe | Mirror wherein kings may theire glories knowe.'[123] Both Wither's and G. B.'s epitaphs are a long way from Alexander envying Achilles for his stone and textual monuments. Yet their emphasis on the mortality of kings puts both poets in good company.

Let us now put these epitaphs in a broader professional and generic context: the chorus of voices from the pulpits, both before and after Henry's death. Sermons were a far more regular feature of the Jacobean courts than they had been during Queen Elizabeth's reign. Peter McCullough goes so far as to argue, against literary scholars, that 'The sermon—not the Shakespearean drama, and not even the Jonsonian masque—was the pre-eminent literary genre at the Jacobean court.'[124] Even before he arrived in London in 1603, James instituted regular Tuesday sermons along with the usual Sunday sermons, with mandatory attendance for all residents of court. When these sermon days coincided with hunting days, which were frequent for James, his chaplains accompanied him to preach in the fields. When the King appreciated a good sermon he slept with it under his pillow, or so John Chamberlain reported.[125] James commanded regular court sermons, not only on different days of the week but on the anniversaries of calamities like the Gowry conspiracy and the Gunpowder Plot. In this respect Henry imitated his father. Henry's deliverance from the Gunpowder Plot 'made so strong an

---

[122] G. B., *Cestria Lugens*, 241, 243.

[123] G. B., *Cestria Lugens*, 234. The *de casibus* genre was still active in Shakespeare's and Webster's plays of this period; the *Mirror for Magistrates* was popular enough for a final edition as late as 1610. See Harriet Archer, *Unperfect Histories: The Mirror for Magistrates, 1559–1610* (Oxford: Oxford University Press, 2017); Harriet Archer and Andrew Hadfield, eds. '*A Mirror for Magistrates' in Context: Literature, History and Politics in Early Modern England* (Cambridge: Cambridge University Press, 2016); and Paul Budra, *A Mirror for Magistrates and the De Casibus Tradition* (Toronto: University of Toronto Press, 2000).

[124] Peter McCullough, *Sermons at Court: Politics and Religion in Elizabethan and Jacobean Preaching* (Cambridge: Cambridge University Press, 1998), 125, 130.

[125] The sermon in question was preached at court by Lancelot Andrewes on Christmas Day 1609 'with great applause,' after which 'the King with much importunitie had the copie delivered him . . . and sayes he will lay yt still under his pillow' (McClure, *Letters of Chamberlain*, 1:292, 295).

impression of religious gratitude upon the mind of his Highness, that ... he would never after suffer himself to be prevented by any business from being present' at anniversary sermons.[126]

Ideologically and stylistically, Henry's chaplains were more cohesive than those who preached before James; the King favoured variety, but the Prince's chaplains held more uniform political beliefs.[127] They considered it their duty to educate the Prince, 'and in harsh terms,' claims McCullough. This duty was partly due to the educational emphasis of Henry's household, and to his father's evident respect for sermons' educational and memorial purposes. Chief among Henry's chaplains was Daniel Price, who favoured sermons whose lessons would correct their audiences' tendencies toward sin.[128] In his own words addressed to Henry in 1608, he aimed 'to let you [sic] blood in the swelling vaines of pride, to launce the impostumes of greedy desires, to purge your ambitious, malitious, voluptuous thoughts, to cure wantonnes, & to curbe the lest thought of wickednesse.'[129] This pledge, part of the sermon Price delivered to Henry before he became his chaplain, typified the admonitions that men like Price preached to Henry in his lifetime. After his death those chaplains had, at least, the consolation of consistency. Reviewing the sermons of royal chaplains (Price at Henry's court and Robert Wilkinson at James's) and of the Archbishop of Canterbury (George Abbot), we can appreciate the devotional origins of his epitaphs and other posthumous laments. Their sermons' moral goals derive from scriptural themes and exemplars, so they confront the difficult lessons that other genres tend to avoid or ignore.[130]

Sermons have a complex relationship with exemplary rhetoric. Examples had biblical precedents, including Solomon's praise of the dead exceeding his praise of the living, who 'by their praises, held out the *light* of their vertuous *Lampe*, to lead others into those *wayes*.'[131] Yet sermons are occasional texts like any other, reflecting on current events and addressing their moral dimensions. As such, they document the crisis of faith in human exemplarity that Henry's death provoked. We can appreciate the depth of that crisis in Price's distinction between faith in God and faith in his earthly representatives, when he advises princes' subjects to 'yeeld *them faithfulnesse* and *obedience*, but settle not in *them* your

---

[126] Birch, *Life of Henry*, 61–2, sigs. E7r–E7v. On these and other annual remembrances of 5 November, see David Cressy, *Bonfires and Bells: National Memory and the Protestant Calendar in Elizabethan and Stuart England* (Stroud: Sutton, 2004), 141–55.

[127] For a lucid account of the origins and preaching styles of Henry's chaplains, and of their influence on the Prince's character and politics, see McCullough, *Sermons at Court*, 183–94. Many would later speak out against the Spanish match and James's refusal to aid his daughter Elizabeth and her husband Frederick, Elector Palatine, under siege in Prague (187, 188). For an account of James's response to the Bohemian uprising, see Stewart, *The Cradle King*, 297–309.

[128] McCullough, *Sermons at Court*, 190.   [129] Price, *Recvsants Conversion* (1608), 15, sig. C1r.

[130] For rhetorical techniques in sermons, see Vickers, *In Defence of Rhetoric*, 290–1.

[131] Price, *Second Anniversary*, 1, sig. A1r.

faith and *confidence*.'[132] Wilkinson addresses Henry's brother and heir, Charles Duke of York, with a diatribe against 'the life of fame, the Memoriall life, whereby euen dead men are said to live.' Reputations are won and lost in this world, Wilkinson adds, where 'fame hath her wings, not onely to flie about the world, but suddenly to vanish and fly cleane away: for how many haue there been of wonderfull note in their times, yet now not remembred so much as by name?' In an address that seems explicitly concerned with Henry, Wilkinson then counsels Charles to learn humility, rather than relying on the flattery of poets and other sycophants to preserve his posthumous honour:

> while you liue, oh how wise, how worthy, how wonderfull are you! yea it is your matchlesse wisedome, your incomparable valour, your equitie, piety, and Princely Maiestie, your excellence and immortall honour; but when the Lion once is dead, then euery Hare dare dance vpon his carkase, and dogs dare barke, and Poets then dare raile and rime with pen and tongue, and then this immortall honour dies, and is as mortall as your selues.[133]

In this world of empty praise, Wilkinson adds, men should be concerned equally with slander as with forgetfulness.

Price is more permissive of exemplarity in his address to Charles on the second anniversary of Henry's death. If anything, he is motivated by the need for Charles to benefit from his brother's memory. Price's dedication of his sermon to Charles reveals this motive with a commonplace: 'Not only the *praise* of the *dead*, but also the *profit of the living* be my inducements to this worke.'[134] These didactic and memorial functions were conventional; '[o]ur Theologians,' wrote Puttenham in 1589, 'use to make sermons, both teaching the people some good learning, and also saying well of the departed.'[135] But Price adds a spiritual function, to promote both 'religious *Pietie* towards God; and obsequious *dutie* towards man, [memorial sermons] doe both warne and warrant, our gratefull and faithfull remembrances of those *Worthies, of whom the world was not worthy*.'[136] In 1612 Edward Chetwynd was dean of Bristol, yet to become Queen Anne's chaplain, when he dedicated his funeral sermon to Charles, Elizabeth, and Frederick. Using the same formulation as Price, Chetwynd urges the three to 'alwaies set before your eies, the

---

[132] Price, *Lamentations* (1613), 480, sig. G1r.
[133] Wilkinson, *Paire of Sermons*, 20, 21, sigs. D1v, D2r. In the latter sermon in this volume, delivered to Charles in January 1614, Wilkinson uses a similar zoological metaphor for the same lesson on 'the honour of a King': 'while he liues, euery man praises him, and admires, and adores him; . . . but when he is once dead, his honour oft dies with him, and his light put out in darknes; . . . that as this *Salomon* said, *It is better to bee a liue dog, then a dead Lion*, Eccles. 9.4' (83, sig. M1r).
[134] Price, *Second Anniversary*, n.p., sig. *2r.   [135] Puttenham, *Arte of English Poesie*, sig. G4r.
[136] Price, *Second Anniversary*, 1, sig. A1r. Price cites the same verse (Hebrews 11) in *Spiritvall Odovrs*: 'I will say of him as S. Paule to the *Hebrewes* spake of those with whome our Master is nowe in Company, Prince Henry was hee of whom the *world* was not worthy' (24, sig. C4v). It recurs in other tributes to Henry, including *Hayward, Lives of the III. Normans,* sig. A3v.

Princely patterne of vertue and pietie, so happily expressed in the example of that blessed *Soule, whom the world was no longer worthy to enioy*: who . . . hath now left a sweet (though mournefull) memory, of his graces amongst vs.'[137] So praise of the dead would, ideally, serve the living in the same breath, by treating them as a 'patterne' or 'example'—so long as the living did not pursue 'the life of fame' that Wilkinson deplored.

Henry's death did a perverse favour for the living. It reminded them that they, too, were mortal and fallible. Price directs all of the 'Noble and worthy Gentlemen, who were sad spectators of the blessed passage of his Princely soul, [to] sequester all humane wisdom and policy, all Court vanitie or glory, looke upon the Glasse of mortalitie.'[138] This didacticism is reminiscent of Henry's epitaphs, as is this direct address to auditors who must renounce their trust in worldly things like princes. Two days after Henry's death, Price preached a sermon on exactly that lesson—intended, it seems, to correct the former misperceptions of his courtiers and subjects:

> Let your *deare* bought *experience* teach you the lesson that *Dauid*, a great *Prince*, gaue to his People; *Trust not in Princes*, for they be *sonnes of men*, there is no *health* in them, their *breath* departeth, and euery one of them *returneth* to his earth; . . . If a man may speake any *thing* worthy of the greatest *admiration*, it is this, *Trust not in Princes*, they themselues are not in *safety*; their *sublimitie* is but *sublunary*; they are within the *verge*.[139]

This lesson, drawn from Psalm 146, recurred in the aftermath of Henry's death. Wither repeats it in a poem castigating himself and all Henry's subjects for provoking God's corrective ire:

> Nay, I can name the chiefest murth'ring sinne:
> And this it was, how ere it hath bin hid.
> *Trust not* (saith *Dauid*) *trust not in a Prince*:
> Yet we hope't lesse, in God Ile sweare we did,
> In ielousie he therfore tooke him hence.
>   Thus we abuse good things, and through our blindnes
>   Haue hurt our selues, and kild our Prince with kindnes.[140]

The 'kindnes' of Henry's subjects, contravening with their 'blindnes' the message of David's psalm, made God 'jealous' by Henry's attraction of the trust and

---

[137] Edward Chetwynd, *Votiuæ Lachrymæ* (1612), sig. D4v.

[138] Price, *Spiritvall Odovrs*, 43, sig. F2r. The image of Henry as a 'glasse' recurs in his epitaphs; see in particular G. B.'s description of Henry as the 'Mirror of Princes,' already quoted.

[139] Price, *Lamentations*, 479–480, sigs. F4v–G1r.

[140] Wither, *Prince Henries Obseqvies*, sig. C2r.

affection they owe properly to Him. Both Prince and Wither use the same formulation to disavow trust in changeable princes, whose 'sublimitie is but sublunary.' And John Davies of Hereford similarly attributes Henry's death to lunar influences and divine grace:

> Nothing is certaine, but vncertainty
> Beneath the *Moone*; which varies like our *Mindes*:
> For, *Man's* a *Maze* of *Mutability*,
> Wherein both *Sin* and *Grace* stil turnes, and winds![141]

The word 'sin' recurs in both sermons and elegies as an explanation for why God would decide to take Henry from his subjects.

Archbishop Abbot's two-hour funeral sermon for Henry, at the service in Westminster Abbey, fuels these lessons of mutable princes and their culpable subjects. He uses Henry's death to gloss Psalm 82, whose sixth and seventh verses ('I have said, Ye are gods; and all of you are children of the most High. | But ye shall die like men, and fall like one of the Princes') were conventional reminders of princes' mortality, even in Henry's lifetime.[142] In Hawkins's account, Abbot offers Henry as the latest instance of this theme:

> for ocular proofe and use of all, inviting their eyes to the present dolefull spectacle of their late ever renowned *Prince*, who, not long agoe, was as fresh, brave, and gallant as the best of them, unto whom all the delights and pleasures of the World did begge for acquaintance, lacking nothing which heart could wish for, who yet now for our sinnes lay thus low, bereaved of life and all being, forced to prove the truth of this Text, not onely to fall, but to fall as others.[143]

Abbot removes any sense of the dead's culpability—which was only appropriate for the occasion. Henry's death reveals the Christian theme of the transience of greatness, rather than demonstrating any personal failure; this theme only requires events to make it manifest. The Archbishop makes Henry an example of mutability, distinguished from others by his very Christ-like cause of death, his people's sins.[144] This cause 'prove[s] the truth of this Text.' Henry's Christian

---

[141] Davies, *Mvses-Teares*, sig. B1v. For an analysis of the poem's impolitic audacity masked by an 'abstract and turgid style' see Doelman, *Early Stuart Funeral Elegy*, 51–7.

[142] This citation is from the Authorized Version (1611). It is also quoted in John Hawkins's account of this sermon: *Life and Death*, 88, sig. F6v. Andrew Willet quotes these verses in his dedication to Henry of *An Harmonie* (1607).

[143] Hawkins, *Life and Death*, 88–9, sigs. F6v–F7r.

[144] Joseph Hall associates it with original sin in 'Farewell Sermon,' in *Works of Joseph Hall* (1625), 465, sig. 2R5r.

virtues and the manner of his death make his comparison with Christ inevitable.[145] But others, like Joseph Hall, object to the comparison: 'It was one of our sinnes I feare, that wee made our Master, our God; I meane, that we made flesh our arme; and placed that confidence in him, for our earthly stay, which we should haue fixed in heauen.'[146] Joshua Sylvester agrees that responsibility for Henry's death lay with his subjects' sins. In a characteristic list, he blames the sins of every estate for bringing divine justice down on Henry's head: clergy, nobility, magistrates, gentles, courtiers, lawyers, citizens, and countrymen. Sylvester ends with an accusation that succinctly displays his poetic ability: '*Each hath thrown a* Dart, | *A Dart of Synne, at* HENRY's *princely hart.*' '*How e'r it were,*' he sobs, 'Wee *were the* Moving Cause | *That sweet* Prince HENRY *breath no longer drawes.*'[147]

The raw immediacy of these responses, not only of Sylvester and Hall but also of every preacher and elegist discussed in this chapter, lends them some credibility. I mean credibility in their relative lack of premeditation. I make this claim not as a naïve reader, credulous that Chapman or Sylvester or even Wither necessarily believed their own claims about Henry's death. With the possible exception of Gorges, few poets would have anticipated writing these moralizing or allegorical accounts before Henry died. But the events of October and November 1612 forced poets to draw premature conclusions about Henry's life—to commit, in writing, to discomfiting formulations of his legacy. Preachers experienced none of this moral disruption; their job had always been to moralize events for devotional lessons. A year later Price preached against the 'senselesse and stupid and horrid' neglect of Henry's cautionary legacy:

Religion wept, vertue bled at his death & the Christian world was ready to expire, yet gracious Prince Henry is forgot, the Jewel of Nature, modell of grace, religions Champion, *humani generis deliciae*, the light and life of mankind is already forgot: so senselesse and stupid and horrid is our vnthankfulnesse.[148]

---

[145] The scholar James Maxwell noted Henry's figuration of Christ's Passion: 'He [Henry] yeilded vp the Ghost into Gods hands the same day of the weeke, and about the same time of the day that Christ Iesus did yeild his into the hands of his Father; to wit, on friday the sixt day of the weeke, being likewise the sixt day of the ninth moneth, when he was not full 19 years olde' (*Laudable Life, And Deplorable Death* (1612), sig. B1v). Yet it was a conventional comparison; for Erasmus's Christian Prince the ultimate exemplar was Christ, 'who alone is in all ways to be imitated' (*Education of a Christian Prince*, 177).

[146] Hall, *Works of Joseph Hall*, 465, sig. 2R5r. Hall continues: 'Our too much hope hath left vs comfortlesse: Oh that we could now make God our Master, and trust him so much the more, as we haue lesse in earth to trust to.'

[147] Joshua Sylvester, *Lachrimae Lachrimarum* (1612), sigs. B3r, A4r. On Henry's patronage of Sylvester, see Leila Parsons, 'Prince Henry (1594–1612) as a Patron of Literature.' *Modern Language Review* 47 (1952): 503–7.

[148] Price, *Allegeance to Iervsalem* (1613), 16–17, sigs. B4v–C1r.

It is difficult to remember cautionary lessons after their urgency fades, but a chaplain's task is ever consistent: to call to mind such lessons of humility and vulnerability. A chaplain reminds the living that the dead teach us how to die.

To represent Henry's legacy in more appealing, positive terms required more selective representations, like the exemplary lives Henry attracted and commissioned himself. If the elegies, epitaphs, and sermons of this chapter respond directly to the circumstances of their composition, their historicity is a product equally of their moment and their generic predispositions. It stands to reason, then, that later moments will prompt different genres to address the same subject—genres with their own predispositions and qualities. The next chapter considers those biographical genres that are less immediate than Henry's elegies, epitaphs, and sermons, and accordingly are less obliged or inclined to attend to his cautionary meaning. Indeed they are inclined to realize exactly the sorts of incautious formulations that Henry had pursued in his brief lifetime, the sorts that might even make Price prefer forgetfulness.

5

The Problem of Metonymy

Rhetorical arguments from anecdotes are susceptible to objections that their evidence is incomplete. The possibility always exists that their chosen evidence is incompatible with other, conflicting evidence—either unknown or undiscovered at the time of writing. What a biographer asserts, for example, about a subject's motives or movements at a given moment may be subject to corrections when new documents are discovered about that moment.

But let me contextualize these claims. Recall that rhetorical arguments subdivide into three branches with three discrete aims: deliberative (aiming to exhort or dissuade), judicial (aiming to accuse or defend), and epideictic or demonstrative (aiming to praise or blame, using 'the ceremonial oratory of display').[1] The deliberative rhetorician is concerned with future action, with exhorting or dissuading their audience. They could cite the choice of Achilles, or some other commonplace, to induce courage in a young soldier. The judicial rhetorician makes forensic inquiries into past action, asking 'whether something has happened or not,' often to accuse or defend someone.[2] They might use eyewitness testimony to confirm the details of an act. The third, demonstrative rhetorician is concerned with the present; their audience acts more as spectator than judge. Richard Lanham suggests that 'deliberative and judicial rhetoric are fundamentally purposive in motive, [and] epideictic fundamentally playful.'[3] Yet rhetoric can easily combine elements of two or more branches; a demonstrative rhetorician might quote *Aeneid* 2.49 ('*Timeo Danaos et dona ferentes*'—or 'I fear the Greeks, especially bearing gifts') to display erudition while blaming some false friend.[4]

Return to our biographer making assertions about their subject. Their rhetoric is not primarily demonstrative, exhibiting the biographer's own skills; so is it primarily deliberative or judicial? The answer, alas, is that it depends on their aim and orientation: if the life is exemplary, exhorting or dissuading audience responses, their rhetoric is deliberative; whereas if the life aspires to past truth, describing things that have happened, their rhetoric is judicial. Our biographer uses anecdotes either to accentuate exemplary features or to represent accurate

---

[1] Lanham, *Handlist of Rhetorical Terms*, 164; Aristotle, *Rhetorica*, tr. W. Rhys Roberts (Oxford: Clarendon Press, 1924), I.1358a.

[2] Aristotle, *On Rhetoric*, 51; I.1359a; see also 47–50.

[3] Lanham, *Handlist of Rhetorical Terms*, 164.

[4] Virgil, *The Aeneid*, tr. Robert Fagles (New York: Viking, 2006), 76.

The Rhetoric of Exemplarity in Early Modern England. Michael Ullyot, Oxford University Press. © Michael Ullyot 2022. DOI: 10.1093/oso/9780192849335.003.0006

truths about their subject's life. Either way, conflicting anecdotes will threaten the rhetorical project.

As anecdotes are mere parts of a surrounding narrative, they may be called metonymic—that is, like the trope, consisting of parts that represent other parts.[5] Metonymic phrases like 'lend me your ears' or 'the head that wears the crown' connote other parts of the physical and mental faculties of those doing these actions, like paying attention or embodying authority. (Metonymy thus differs from synecdoche, which uses parts to refer to wholes: spears or boots for soldiers, for instance.) Anecdotes in biographies are metonymic in the following manner. If I describe one part, one moment, of any subject's life I am implicitly suggesting that it relates to other parts, its characteristics either typifying or clashing with them. If I suggest that it testifies to their generosity, for instance, for you then to discover incidents of parsimony would harm my credibility. You might then suspect me of having an agenda, or (worse) of doing slipshod research.

Thus the assumption that an anecdote can represent other parts of a life is belied by conflicting parts, should they emerge. I call this the problem of metonymy, and in this closing chapter of this study I argue that this problem is an intractable condition of exemplary rhetoric. Conflicting evidence may never emerge, but it always can. The only requirement is that a new rhetorician discovers new, conflicting evidence.

Thus far in this study I have traced a historical arc through the life and death of Henry, Prince of Wales. I began by discussing how Sidney answered an essential question of late humanism, what to read and how.[6] I showed how Spenser answered this question for real and fictional readers in *The Faerie Queene*,[7] and how Essex and Henry's educations and public images answered it more pragmatically: read to learn how to live.[8] Be an object of exemplary rhetoric, so you might deserve to be its future subject. Then I showed how Henry's death foreclosed these plans. When the praise and the paroxysms of grief were over, the prevailing view among elegists and chaplains was of Henry as a cautionary tale for his readers, most immediately for his brother Charles.[9] I concluded the last chapter with these occasional texts because their immediacy caused their caution. That is my core argument, that historicizing the rhetoric of exemplarity reveals that caution is the only universal; the only lesson of history is to avoid repeating it.

I wish that I could close this story of Henry's exemplary journey, so to speak, with a chapter about Charles reading cautionary tales of his brother and

---

[5] The philosopher of history Eelco Runia posits metonymy as historiography's means to make absent, discontinuous historical realities present to us, using their attributes metaphorically (*Moved by the Past: Discontinuity and Historical Mutation* (New York: Columbia University Press, 2014), 49–83). See also Eelco Runia, 'Burying the Dead, Creating the Past.' *History and Theory: Studies in the Philosophy of History* 46 (2007): 313–25.

[6] See 'Sidney's Subjunctives' in Chapter 1.   [7] See 'The Ends of History' in Chapter 2.

[8] See 'Sidney's Virtues' and 'Words and Actions' in Chapter 3.   [9] See 'Warnings' in Chapter 4.

assiduously avoiding his errors. Even had he done so, Charles might have met his own unforeseen premature death. But instead, what Charles read in most texts addressed or dedicated to him after 1612 were selective versions of Henry's life, separating his fame from his fate. Writers who used this formulation repeatedly tried to reassure Charles that he could inherit the conditions of Henry's life (his position and reputation) without the necessity of his death. In this chapter I analyse their texts to reinforce my claim that exemplary rhetoricians distort even the most immediate events to meet their immediate goals. They not only suffer from the problem of metonymy, they invite it.

Such claims will hardly surprise the reader who has followed my argument to this stage. So my goal for this chapter is not merely to extend the historical arc of Henry's posthumous reputation. Its end would be arbitrary, in any case. If I closed with the biographies dedicated to Charles, I would be ignoring representations of Henry's legacy for others, including his nephew Frederick Henry;[10] and if I closed with the seventeenth century, I would be ignoring Henry's longform biographies beginning in 1760.[11] My goal instead is to show how this problem of metonymy— of parts misrepresenting other parts—pervades the rhetoric immediately sur- rounding Henry. I want to historicize exemplarity, not to be its historiographer. I historicize it by surveying the rhetoric of tutors and biographers who surround Henry like concentric rings. The first, or innermost ring, uses deliberative rhetoric to influence his reading and his actions. The second uses judicial rhetoric to describe his susceptibility to influence and his resulting actions as virtuous and imitable. (There is a third, outermost ring of rhetoricians in which I situate myself, the critic, in this study's Conclusion.)

Consider metonymy. The reason I defined this representational problem as metonymic, rather than synecdochic, is because parts are the only kind of evi- dence that rhetoricians have. The synecdochic 'whole' to which they refer, or from whence they come, is a prince whose unmediated, historical experiences are lost— yet who attracted a torrent of exhortations, lamentations, and other representa- tions. We can, as I have done, examine this constellation of archival records of Henry's experiences; but even those most proximate to his mind—the household records, autograph exercise books, diplomatic letters, speeches on the utility of history for statesmen—are overtly performative, obedient, or otherwise informed by others' expectations.[12] We can perform what Cyndia Susan Clegg calls 'archival poetics' to interpolate and infer Henry's unmediated experience, but our specula- tions will be littered with subjunctive verbs: 'must haves' or 'cannot but haves' or 'would haves.'[13]

---

[10] Henry Peacham, *Prince Henrie Revived* (1615).   [11] Birch, *Life of Henry.*
[12] See 'The Education of a Stuart Prince' in Chapter 3.
[13] Cyndia Susan Clegg, 'Archival Poetics and the Politics of Literature: Essex and Hayward Revisited.' *Studies in the Literary Imagination* 32 (1999): 115–32.

So why would we? Because we know that what Hayden White calls 'the real' must be narrated to create the illusion of truth.[14] Paul Ricoeur describes historiography as a 'true allegory' of 'the enigma of being-in-time' not only because it plots discrete, inchoate moments in a narrative but also because its exclusions of other moments are necessary to make that narrative intelligible.[15] Historiography gives meaning to history, as biography does to life or criticism to texts: by excluding what is unsuited to the rhetorician's emergent understanding of their constructed subject. In the familiar domain of exemplary rhetoric, comprised of 'a multitude of discrete metonymically related segments or moments' (in Hampton's canonical definition), the overt metonymy of those segments renders them unreliable—but this problem pervades all deliberative and judicial argumentation.[16] Return with me now to this familiar domain, to consider a historical moment in Henry's life that I will use to lead you outward through the rhetorical rings encircling it, from tutors and biographers in this chapter to critics in the Conclusion.

Papirus Cursor

I begin with an anecdote about anecdotes. In Henry's household at St James's Palace there was a custom that after meals, the Prince and his companions would 'tell euery one a History by turne, all of them deliuering some obseruation upon the Historie told.'[17] This was table-talk with a humanist purpose, to distil history's ethical lessons in order to imitate them.[18] One day after dinner, the Prince's tutor Adam Newton recounted an anecdote from ancient Rome, of Lucius Papirus Cursor's clemency toward an offending captain:

> Papirus Cursor, a severe and rigorous Commander among the Romanes, commaunded the executioner to bring forth the axe, as it were to behead a certaine Captaine, for coming thorow feare too late to the field, and he looking for no other then present death, the said Papirus having thus terrified him, said to the

[14] As White asks in a study of medieval annals, 'What would a nonnarrative representation of historical reality look like?' (*The Content of the Form: Narrative Discourse and Historical Representation* (Baltimore: Johns Hopkins University Press, 1987), 4).

[15] Paul Ricoeur, *Memory, History, Forgetting*, tr. Kathleen Blamey and David Pellauer (Chicago: University of Chicago Press, 2004). For a new historicist understanding of 'the real' constituted by anecdotes see Conclusion.

[16] *Writing from History*, 26. I owe my 'problem of metonymy' formulation to this definition. On the use of anecdotes in another judicial domain—as 'a fundamental epistemological and affective unit of natural history' persisting from the eighteenth century to Victorian science—see Melissa Sodeman, 'Gilbert White, Anecdote, and Natural History.' *Studies in English Literature* 60, no. 3 (2020): 508.

[17] Haydon, *Trve Pictvre and Relation*, 26.

[18] On table-talk promoting 'an effective discourse about the world' see Jeanneret, *Feast of Words*, 259–83.

executioner; Cutt up this roote, that it may not hinder our walking, and so laying a fine on the Captaine, dismissed him.[19]

Henry inverted the lesson's object from himself to his tutor: 'As Papirus was not so terrible as hee threatened,' he replied, 'so will you not likewise be in keeping me all afternoone at my booke, as you have threatned to doe.'[20]

I take this anecdote from one of the early biographies of Henry, William Haydon's *Trve Pictvre and Relation of Prince Henry* (after 1625; printed 1634). Haydon takes pains to reinforce the trustworthiness of his biography of this private and unknown subject. He trades on his familiarity with, and access to, the Prince as senior groom of Henry's bedchamber, claiming that most of his material is 'drawne out of mine own experience' and evidently studious observation.[21] He then compounds the evidence of Henry's qualities with second-hand reports, which display his resourceful labour of compilation.

Haydon tells this story for two reasons: to describe a typical lesson in Henry's '*Courtly College*, or . . . *Collegiate Court*' established by his father;[22] and to emphasize Henry's unsuitability to the schoolroom, his impatience to ride horses instead of recounting Roman histories after lunch. A more speculative interpretation would be that Henry chafed under this pedagogical yoke, and sought instead the cut and thrust of public action.[23] That is the insinuation of another widely circulated anecdote, in which James threatened to withhold Henry's crown unless he followed his brother Charles's studious example. 'I know what becomes a Prince,' came Henry's reply. 'It is not necessary for me to be a professor, but a soldier and a man of the world.'[24]

It is a sententious answer, and feels rehearsed. How much stock can we put in anecdotes that feel so suited to memory, yet whose reciters claim to reveal something true about the past? Both of the anecdotes I have cited are rhetorically mediated, appearing in biographies like Haydon's that recirculate stories that are explicitly exemplary. Indeed Haydon's biography is entirely comprised of disjointed anecdotes, loosely organized by the abstract qualities he wants them to reveal: valour, piety, fortitude, justice, and so on. When Haydon claims, for instance, that Henry 'in divers particular actions did testifie both his great charitie and liberalitie,' he supports this assertion with a series of anecdotes illustrating his

---

[19] Haydon, *Trve Pictvre and Relation*, 26. See Pollnitz, *Princely Education*, 326–7 and 345–7 on Newton's appointment and influence over Henry.

[20] Haydon, *Trve Pictvre and Relation*, 26.   [21] Haydon, *Trve Pictvre and Relation*, 29.

[22] Thomas Chaloner, cit. Parry, *Culture of the Stuart Court*, 69–70. See 'The Education of a Stuart Prince' in Chapter 3.

[23] See Pollnitz, *Princely Education*, 347–8 on Henry's resistance of academic expectations.

[24] Ashton, *James I by his Contemporaries*, 96. Henry then derisively proposed to make Charles Archbishop of Canterbury. Among other sources, see *CSPV 1603–1607*, 739; William Lily, *Monarchy or No Monarchy* (1651), sig. L2r; Peter Heylin, *Life and Reign of King Charles* (1658), 10; and Richard Perrinchief, *Royal Martyr* (1676), sigs. B2v–B3r.

generosity to a stranger, to a poet, and to members of his household.[25] Others concern Henry's chivalric exercises, which Haydon describes with evident regret as the 'seeds and buddes of Princely vertues.' Similarly Haydon describes the Prince's various 'merrie and notable speeches,' like this irreverent response to his tutor, as 'infallible and certaine tokens' of his qualities.[26]

Haydon has transparent rhetorical motives in this biography, which openly selects, interprets, and applies the evidence necessary to make a case about his subject. He wants to create the impression that Henry's preference for soldiering over studying was typical. He gathers and retells stories illustrating Henry's preference for physical over mental exercises, as if they signal his eagerness to lead the nation from Jacobean pacifism to a new militancy under Henry IX's banner. That was already a false promise when Haydon wrote this biography under Charles, after the deaths of both Henry and James. But Haydon's motives and the safety of historical distance mean only that he inflected the truth, not distorted it—as corroborating accounts imply. In 1607 the Venetian Ambassador Nicolo Molin described Henry as reading only under duress: 'He studies, but not with much delight, and chiefly under his father's spur, not of his own desire, and for this he is often admonished and set down.'[27] Haydon's depiction is selective, then, but likely not wrong. Henry's interpretation of his tutor's anecdote about Papirus Cursor does suggest that he was impatient to leave the cloistered school-room; whether it was to engage in public service or in self-serving recreation is speculative.

Throughout *The Trve Pictvre and Relation*, Haydon offers what his subtitle calls 'Certaine Observations and Proofes of his towardly and notable Inclination to Vertue.' Two recurring descriptors for his anecdotes are 'token' and 'testimony,' and their cognates, whose usage and *OED* definitions associate them with distinguishing marks and with evidence of a claim or fact (respectively).[28] Other contemporaneous biographies like Greville's of Sidney (1610/12; printed 1651) also use these terms for this purpose. As evidence or 'proof' of Sidney's attributes, Greville writes, 'I will pass from the testimony of brave men's words to his own deeds.'[29] Like Haydon, Greville uses anecdotes as testimony of his subject's

---

[25] Haydon, *Trve Pictvre and Relation*, 7; for the anecdotes see 8–9.

[26] Haydon, *Trve Pictvre and Relation*, 5, 2.

[27] *CSPV 1603–1607*, 12:513. See further Ashton, *James I by his Contemporaries*, 95–7.

[28] Haydon, *Trve Pictvre and Relation*, 19, 11. For a discussion of anecdotes in historiography, see Patterson, *Holinshed's Chronicles* and Patterson, 'Power of Anecdote'.

[29] Greville, *Dedication*, 25, ll. 17–18. For original, see Fulke Greville, *Life Of the Renowned Sr Philip Sidney* (1651), 48. See also Peter Herman, '"Bastard Children of Tyranny": The Ancient Constitution and Fulke Greville's "A Dedication to Sir Philip Sidney".' *Renaissance Quarterly* 55, no. 3 (2002): 969–1004; and G. A. Wilkes, '"Left...to play the ill poet in my own part": The Literary Relationship of Sidney and Fulke Greville.' *The Review of English Studies* 57, no. 230 (2006): 291–309. The association of testimony with words is attested by the 1670 edition of Izaak Walton's lives of John Donne, Henry Wotton, Richard Hooker, and George Herbert, in which the word appears forty times—often to introduce the verbal evidence of letters written by and about the qualities of Walton's subjects.

properties, to build an overtly rhetorical case from the evidence of Sidney's words and actions.

Anecdotes are forms of testimony, adaptable to a range of rhetorical arguments. Testimonies are the persuasive citations of various authorities (proverbial, sententious, historical, legal, or otherwise) 'brought to confirme anye thyng,' to amplify and support an argument.[30] Their use is an intrinsic component of 'the literature of argument,' which Richard Serjeantson delimits as any 'writing, usually in prose, in which an author is arguing in praise or defence of something or for a particular course of action or for the truth of an opinion or event.'[31] Peacham in *The Garden of Eloqvence* (1593) sets out four categories of testimony for arguments that 'confirm or confute': citing eyewitnesses or first-hand experience; common knowledge or experience; 'some saying or sentence of another worthy of remembrance and observation'; or instead of one worthy of infamy and refutation.[32] The orator's argument precedes and refracts the testimony that serves it. Aristotle and Quintilian classify testimony among the 'artless' proofs because it requires no skill to discover or invent: orators draw testimonies from the common stock of '"topics" or "common-places" (*loci communes*) of argumentative invention' shared by orators and auditors alike.[33] Their 'art' then consists of positioning and interpreting them to readily support the orator's claims.

In judicial rhetoric, anecdotes are descriptive; they help to praise or defend someone. In deliberative rhetoric, examples are prescriptive; they help to exhort or dissuade someone. Lionel Gossman claims that "the anecdote depends on, epitomizes, and confirms generally accepted views of the world, human nature, and the human condition."[34] Yet the anecdote ostensibly has no intrinsic rhetorical motives, no ambition to influence or persuade readers, because as an anecdote it has no readers; its Greek root ἀνέκδοτος (*anekdotos*) means 'something unpublished.' Its exemplary function depends on its publication and reception. This shift from private to public knowledge began, in recorded history, with the Byzantine historian Procopius's *Anecdota or Secret History* (c.550 CE), a disparaging tell-all account by a court historian of the emperor Justinian, his general Belisarius, and their wives. Procopius writes that his motive is to offer a counterweight to his more obsequious, commissioned nine-volume *History of the Wars of Justinian*, to

---

[30] Thomas Wilson, *Rule of Reason* (1551), cit. Richard Serjeantson, 'Testimony: The Artless Proof.' In *Renaissance Figures of Speech*, ed. Sylvia Adamson, Gavin Alexander, and Katrin Ettenhuber (Cambridge: Cambridge University Press, 2007), 180, 186.

[31] Serjeantson, 'Testimony,' 181.

[32] Henry Peacham, *Garden of Eloqvence* (1593), 279; cit. Serjeantson, 'Testimony,' 188.

[33] Serjeantson, 'Testimony,' 184, 182.

[34] Lionel Gossman, "Anecdote and History." *History and Theory: Studies in the Philosophy of History* 42 (2003): 143–168; 167. He qualifies this claim: '[A]s an unpublished, often secret record of events excluded from the official record, anecdotes may challenge the historian to expand and revise established or authorized views of a historical situation, event, or personality or of human behavior generally" and "provoke a reconsideration of what we believe we know about history and society and lead us to consider previously unobserved aspects of the past" (168).

prevent any imitation of Justinian and others with the threat of similar notoriety. Although 'it will be most advantageous that the blackest deeds shall if possible be unknown to later times,' he writes, the advantage will fall to readers who see 'that their own actions and characters will likewise be on record for future time.'[35]

So from their first coinage, anecdotes serve the rhetoric of exemplarity. Titling your book 'something unpublished' clearly draws attention to its revelatory purpose, and can convey a sense of urgency, of uncovering knowledge that powerful forces would keep secret. After the anonymous English translation of Procopius's *Anecdota* in 1674, it 'quickly provided a popular model for the disclosure of state secrets.'[36] The translator's preface makes a clear distinction between this and other histories: '[T]he Historian considers almost ever Men in Publick, whereas the Anecdoto-grapher [*sic*] only examines 'em in private.'[37] Since 1674, 'anecdote' has retained its Procopian meaning of a narrative previously unknown but now published.

Early modern biographies show that this translation satisfied the lack only of a word, not of an idea. They also show that private knowledge, like exemplarity, is morally neutral; it can just as easily serve eulogistic purposes like Haydon's or Greville's. The former is a counterweight to, say, the *Secret History of the Court of King James the First* (1811) compiled by Walter Scott. Haydon offers insights into his subject that will surprise most readers who know only the Prince's public persona: his private conversations, principled actions, and arguments with tutors. But Haydon departs from the Procopian model of a secret history by recounting praiseworthy rather than salacious incidents.

I called the story of Papirus Cursor an anecdote about anecdotes, but that formulation is perhaps too simple: it is also an anecdote about examples, because the tutor Newton uses the story for a prescriptive, deliberative purpose, which aims to provoke change. Newton wants to teach Henry the value of unpredictability, of clemency when circumstances or principles demand it. The biographer Haydon uses the story of Henry's reply for a descriptive, judicial purpose, which aims to reveal knowledge. Judicial rhetoricians repudiate the deliberative rhetoricians' unconcern for truth. Hence their preference for unguarded episodes: unlike the Roman commander's magnanimity when all eyes are upon him, the Prince's fidgeting is meant to reveal his 'true' character, to exemplify only something in the past. The power of Newton's example depends on his audience responding appropriately, registering both its familiarity and its

[35] Procopius, *The Anecdota or Secret History*, tr. H. B. Dewing (Cambridge: Harvard University Press, 1935), 5–7.

[36] McKeon, *Secret History of Domesticity*, 471. Most of the disclosures related to England, France, Poland, and Italy, appearing in some seventeen books titled 'secret history' between 1686 and 1725. On the French, see Robert Darnton, *The Devil in the Holy Water, or the Art of Slander from Louis XIV to Napoleon* (Philadelphia: University of Pennsylvania Press, 2009).

[37] Anon., *Secret History* (1674), cit. McKeon, *Secret History of Domesticity*, 470.

efficacy. When Henry does not, the tutor's prescriptive example shifts into the biographer's descriptive anecdote.

Haydon turns the story of Henry's response to his tutor into an anecdote—a testimony, corroborated by many others, of his praiseworthy irreverence and preference for physical over verbal exercises. As this incident reveals—as does its persistence as an 'incident' to 'reveal' anything—even an unpremeditated desire to escape outdoors one afternoon can become the subject of observation, reportage, and interpretation. Haydon, as a judicial rhetorician, is therefore susceptible to the problem of metonymy—or more precisely, the problem of conflicting testimony.

All testimonies are metonymic. As partial evidence, testimony is always susceptible to the objection that this part does an injustice to the other, contrary parts that are ignored, lost, or yet unknown. The parts of stories, lives, and experiences that examples and anecdotes relate are intended to represent other, unseen parts of those narratives. Differences between them are supposed to be incidental at most. Yet even within Haydon's biography there are inconsistencies. We read that at one moment the Prince defied the 'rules of Physicke' (that is, of a doctor) advising him how to ride his horse, but that on another hunt he proposed taking an attendant physician.[38] Such inconsistencies beset any effort to fashion a consistent character from variable, lived experiences, as Montaigne has reminded us.[39] They are problematic only if they forget these contingencies.

Testimony like the Papirus Cursor anecdote makes judicial suggestions, but it cannot prove them. When rhetoricians make inferences from corroborating anecdotes, they falsely assume that each reveals part of a consistent character. But assumptions can easily be wrong. The same story of Henry's prowess with a lance could be used to praise his maturity and martial readiness, or to critique his militarism and anti-intellectualism. Even the degree of conflict with his father that these qualities may have provoked was cause for debate.[40] In one account Henry is precocious, in the next immature; in one he opposes James, in the next his qualities complement his father's. When the Marquis de Saint-Germain asks whether Henry would rather be hunting than reading, we hear the Prince reply that 'he might well resolue that doubt himselfe: for he had once been of his age.'[41] If that attitude was appropriate to his age, other observers (especially foreigners) were impressed by qualities uncharacteristic of Henry's youth. Scorning 'childish

---

[38] Haydon, *Trve Pictvre and Relation*, 20, 18.

[39] See 'Varieties of Decorum' in the Introduction.

[40] The alleged conflict between Henry's active and James's contemplative 'natures' is too frequently overstated. Even if Henry truly disdained contemplation, James fuelled this attitude in the dedication to Henry of his *Basilicon Doron*, favouring the 'practicke' above the 'theoricke' of kingship, unlike the 'simple schoole-man, that onely knowes matters of kingdomes by contemplation' (*Basilicon Doron*, 10). James underscores his authority to offer Henry concrete lessons in princely conduct based on his own experience ruling Scotland.

[41] Haydon, *Trve Pictvre and Relation*, 25.

toyes' to prepare for his future reign,[42] it was said that 'none of his pleasures savour the least of a child.'[43] 'His countenance and aspect inclining, in those his young years, to gravity and shew of majesty,'[44] Henry presents 'a gravity most certainly beyond his years,' even if he 'studies, but not with much delight.'[45] Thus are judicial rhetoricians misled by a desire for consistency.

Deliberative rhetoricians also confront the problem of metonymy. Recall Hampton's 'discrete metonymically related segments or moments' that constitute every exemplary biography. The division of a life into segments capable of inspiring imitation in the present necessarily misrepresents that life's meaning. These segments cannot be 'true' representations of the exemplar's experience, despite claims of metonymy; they can only manifest its 'value for the present' with an image designed and distorted for the effects one hopes to realize in that present.[46] Hampton is careful to point out that this move is necessary to turn contingent past experiences into 'universal' lessons—in other words, lessons that can affect contingent present experiences. And yet an idealized, exemplary biography will always be more purposeful than the experience of its quotidian readers. In Montaigne's *Essais*, the contemporary text wherein we find the most sceptical judgements of rhetorical examples, the example 'posits a failed representation; it shows the distance between paradigms of ideal behaviour and actual norms of conduct.'[47] The friction between this promise (of a future narrative) and this reality (of that narrative's distance from paradigmatic ideals) owes to the example's unreality, its neglect of externalities like luck or collaboration in its focus on the exemplar's singular self-determination.

The next section of this argument will move into a more expansive treatment of Henry's posthumous biographies. But it will blur the distinction I have posited thus far between judicial biographers and deliberative tutors, because (as I have just shown) even the most principled, judicial biographer makes choices of characteristics that have a deliberative effect—to follow or to avoid a given example of impatience, maturity, or what you will. By examining both the self-descriptions and the methods of these biographies, we will see that their writers are susceptible to deliberative circumstances. They tell versions of Henry's life that attempt to do justice to his experience, in the first instance, and to start a new exemplary cycle for his brother Charles, in the second.

---

[42] Alexander, *Paraenesis*, sig. B1r.   [43] Birch, *Life of Henry*, 75, sig. F6r.
[44] Cornwallis, *Discourse of Prince Henry*, 528.
[45] Letter by Nicolo Molin, Venetian Ambassador, in 1607 (*CSPV 1603–1607*, 12:513).
[46] Hampton, *Writing from History*, 26, 11.
[47] Stephen Nichols, 'Example versus Historia: Montaigne, Eriugena, and Dante.' In *Unruly Examples: On the Rhetoric of Exemplarity*, ed. Alexander Gelley (Stanford: Stanford University Press, 1995), 54–5. Nichols focuses on disjunctions between the orator's words and conduct, as mitigated by poetry, but his argument on Montaigne's critique of *historia* in 'De la cholère' (Of anger) is relevant here. Further discussions of Montaigne's irreverent enthusiasm for examples appear in Jeanneret, 'Vagaries,' 573–8; and Jeanneret, *A Feast of Words*, 275–83.

The Book of Henry

When the time came to write Henry's life, its writers betrayed a sense of the distance between his idealized, aspirational book and the inadequate, actual books that they offered with mock reluctance. Yet they judiciously avoided directly accusing Henry of supplying inadequate material for that book; instead, as I show, they assumed this blame themselves. In this section on those biographies, I examine how their authors described and conceived the lives of princes in textual terms, both of Henry and of his brother and arch-reader, Charles, Duke of York.

Return now to Haydon's *Trve Pictvre and Relation of Prince Henry* (after 1625; printed 1634), the source of my postprandial Papirus Cursor anecdote. That moment is typical of Haydon's disjointed compilation of episodes. He offers the book, in his prefatory epistle, as a collection of undigested material that 'shall serue for an abridgment of his life, untill such time as some other shall write and set downe the same more amply.' Until then, the biography is limited by Haydon's desire 'to eschew prolixity' lest the portrait swell to even more unmanageable proportions.[48]

We have seen this word 'abridgement' before, applied to Henry: in the blithe lifetime tributes of Drayton (1604) and Davison (1611) that cast him as the epitome of his exemplars.[49] Yet in the same discussion, we witnessed how abridgement's other, more menacing meaning of a premature and unexpected end to a story was Henry's actual fate. Henry's posthumous biographers use the same term in their efforts to reconcile his negative experience with his positive exemplarity. They do so in two ways: occluding the negativity of Henry's short life by focusing on its encapsulated positive features, and suggesting that any of its failings or insufficiencies are not his fault, but theirs. When Haydon describes his biography as an abridgement, he does so to invite 'some other' with more skill to amplify 'the same' subject. But he is also inadvertently revealing his compositional method. Haydon's 11,000-word biography occasionally repeats verbatim passages from an earlier 19,000-word epistolary life of the Prince by John Hawkins, *The Life and Death of . . . Henry Prince of Wales* (1613; printed 1641).[50]

If Haydon hopes that someone, someday, will write Henry's unabridged biography, Hawkins less concretely hopes that readers confronted with his inadequacies will meditate on this ideal text. He offers the same caveat as Haydon, but his apology is proverbial: '*In magnis voluisse sat est,*' or 'In great enterprises the intention is sufficient.'[51] 'Rather then it should not be done at all,' Hawkins asks

---

[48] Haydon, *Trve Pictvre and Relation*, 2, 30.

[49] See 'The Education of a Stuart Prince' in Chapter 3.

[50] My word counts are approximate, and use the ABYY FineReader 8.x Engine (for OCR) and the Text Creation Partnership (for transcriptions).

[51] George Herbert offers this conventional disclaimer from Sextus Propertius, *Elegies* (2.10.5) in *Witts Recreations* (1640) (sig. E2v).

the reader to 'only use the same as a Ladder to mount up your thoughts to a far more excellent meditation of his vertues.'[52] For Hawkins, this abridgement is a foreshortening, a 'bridge' or ladder across the gap of time between now and then, real and imaginary. He gestures not toward a greater writer but more abstractly toward a greater conception of Henry's virtues. Henry's admirers must conceive it, entirely or largely, in their own minds. Both Haydon and Hawkins bemoan not only their limited abilities but also the equally conventional inexpressibility of their subject's virtues, and the need for readers to complete their 'great enterprises'—both rhetorically, by meditating on and imitating Henry's virtues; and descriptively, by augmenting Henry's story. Even if the Prince's death made more extensive biographies difficult, the exemplary programme informing his life encouraged admirers like Haydon and Hawkins to describe his life as a commensurate epitome of those exemplars.

Other biographers of Henry incline toward the other meaning of abridgement, directly citing the brevity of his eighteen years. Charles Cornwallis was one who demurred to write more than a brief Life for a brief eighteen-year life. His *Discourse of the most Illustrious Prince Henry* (1626, printed 1641) was just 5,600 words long because anything longer would be 'unproportionable to so short a life.'[53] Like Bacon, whose 700-word elogium *In Henricum Principem Walliae* (?1613) remained in manuscript until the nineteenth century,[54] Cornwallis offers Henry a short collection of observations and reflections, although '*I wish it were in my power to raise such a monument unto his fame, as might eternise it unto all posterities.*'[55] Both Cornwallis and Bacon lament the brevity of Henry's short life, and both are too decorous to speculate on what it might have become.

In Cornwallis's case, that reticence is because of his scruples: he declines to include any material in his biography 'received by tradition from others' in lieu of 'verities knowne to my self.'[56] On the title page of Cornwallis's second edition of 1644, the printer Nathaniel Butter endorses his authority by insisting that he was 'a man very intimate with him in the whole course of his life, and at his death.'[57] It is tempting to argue that Cornwallis distinguished between report and observation in response to Haydon and Hawkins's indecorous inclusions of second-hand material. Of the two, only Haydon meets Cornwallis's criterion of first-hand access; he was in Henry's service longer than Cornwallis, who served for only two years (as treasurer). Both men probably would have known Henry more intimately than Hawkins did, as his master of weapons and infantry formations. So we can imagine Cornwallis's displeasure when in 1641 Butter attributed

---

[52] Hawkins, *Life and Death*, 3, 4; sigs. A4r, A4v.
[53] Cornwallis, *Discourse of Prince Henry*, 25; sig. E1r.   [54] Bacon, *In Henricum Principem*.
[55] Cornwallis, *Discourse of Prince Henry*, 29; sig. E3r.
[56] Cornwallis, *Discourse of Prince Henry*, 4; sig. B2v.
[57] John Hawkins [attrib. Charles Cornwallis], *Short Life and Much Lamented Death* (1644).

Hawkins's *Life and Death* to Cornwallis himself.[58] (Indeed we can only imagine it; Cornwallis died in 1629.) It may have been an honest mistake: a copy of the epistle was among his papers, writes Butter, who 'could not passe by it, as I did the rest.'[59] But it is more likely that Butter could not resist the attribution, because John Benson had printed Cornwallis's actual *Discourse* the same year. As for Haydon's life of Henry, we can only speculate whether or not Cornwallis read it; on the evidence of its prayer for the royal family, it was composed after Charles I's accession (1625) and perhaps after the births of Princes Charles (1630) and James (1633).

Their intended readers were, naturally, not other biographers but new audiences. In 1641 both Benson and Butter were focused on Charles, Prince of Wales (1630–85), Henry's nephew and the future Charles II; they used his dead uncle's Protestantism, for instance, to counterbalance his mother Henrietta Maria's perceived Catholic influence. Benson cited his own 'particular zeale' for publishing Cornwallis's life of Henry, dedicating it to the young Prince Charles as 'the true inheritour of your Noble Uncles vertues.'[60] Butter, who also dedicated Hawkins's 1613 life of Henry to Prince Charles in 1641, drew a more explicit parallel between the two princes. He described Henry as

> *so rare a* Prince, *as it may seeme worthy Your Highnes perusall: In reading Him You may read Your self. His Titles of Honour were the same with Yours: Your titles of Vertues the same with His: He was, as You are the Mirror of the Age.*[61]

Charles's prerogative ('*Titles of Honour*') and innate qualities ('*titles of Vertues*') combine to make him, like his late uncle, '*the Mirror of the Age.*' Their consanguinity makes Charles's reading of his late uncle's life an act of both self-examination and self-actualization.

Benson and Butter followed the long-standing precedent of conflating Henry's lived experience with the textual biography that describes it. As Butter advised Charles in 1641 that his uncle was '*worthy*' of '*perusall*,' so Marcelline in 1610 had used textual metaphors to praise Henry as 'The *Index, Abstract, or Compendium* of the very greatest Princes whatsoever.'[62] Attentive readers will recall myriad instances of writers, from Webster to Drummond to Chapman, describing Henry (alive or dead) in textual terms whenever they underscore his receptivity to exemplary influence or readiness to offer his own example. In 1613,

---

[58] Roy Strong corrects the attribution in *Henry, Prince of Wales*, 227. This is based on its source, BL. Add. MS 30075; a copy (Add. MS 11532) is dated 1613. A third MS, Folger V. a. 486(1), is very similar to Butter's printed edition, and might have served as its copy-text.

[59] Hawkins, *Life and Death*, sig. A2r.   [60] Cornwallis, *Discourse of Prince Henry*, sig. A3r.

[61] Hawkins, *Life and Death*, sig. A2r. His subtitle addresses this biography's motive: '*A Prince (for Valour and Vertue) fit to be Imitated in Succeeding Times.*' Butter (bap. 1583, d. 1664) had also published Chapman's translations of Homer, including the *Iliad* (1611) dedicated to Henry.

[62] Marcelline, *Triumphs of King James*, sig. A2r.

after Henry's death advanced Charles Duke of York in the royal succession, two particular texts represented the transfer of scrutiny and expectations: James's *Basilicon Doron* and Francesco Guicciardini's *Aphorismes Civill and Militarie*, the latter partially translated by Robert Dallington.[63] In 1609 Dallington had presented this book of aphorisms and anecdotes to Henry in manuscript. In 1613, his dedicatory epistle to Charles recalls the spectacle of Charles following his brother's funeral chariot as chief mourner in December 1612. Charles's presence and position in this ceremony reinforce its triumph over death through the succession, a process offering the most literal transfer of Henry's virtues:

> All eyes are vpon you. Those your sweete graces of nature, and ingenuous dispositions to goodnes, makes men looke vpon your worthy Brother in your princely selfe; holding you the true inheritor of his vertues as of his fortunes, and making full account that he had no oddes of you but in yeares. If you wil not haue them fall short in their reckoning, this *Imprimis* of your hopefull beginnings, must be continued with many *Items* of vertuous proceedings, and closed vp with a *Summa-totalis* of all princely worthinesse.[64]

Dallington uses the image of Charles's life as a book, beginning with an itemized table of his 'vertuous proceedings' and ending with a '*Summa-totalis*' or index of his worthiness. Henry represents an account-book, a list of items to fulfil in order to 'perfect the account you are to make, to your King and to your countrey.'[65] It was the second time Dallington had approached a patron to suggest his inheritance of another man's legacy. In 1592 he offered Essex a flattering comparison to Sidney when dedicating to Essex *The Strife of Love*, an incomplete translation of Francesco Colonna's *Hypnerotomachia Poliphili* (1499).[66]

A far more obvious book to rededicate to Charles was the one that initiated his brother's public image as an object of influence; *Basilicon Doron* was a ready and easy way to shuttle between the two sons of a scholarly father.[67] Dallington's next sentence after his injunction to Charles to perfect his account to his father and to his country, 'like a great and high Steward (as you are),' contrasts James's contemplation with Henry's action:

---

[63] Dallington (1561–1636x8) also wrote surveys of France and Tuscany based on his travels in the late 1590s while acting as tutor to the brothers Roger and Francis Manners (successively the 5th and 6th Earls of Rutland). By 1605 he was in the service of Henry, and was confirmed as a Gentleman of the Privy Chamber in Ordinary in 1610. He then served the same office in Charles's household before becoming master of Charterhouse School. For Dallington, see the *Oxford Dictionary of National Biography*; also K. J. Höltgen, 'Sir Robert Dallington (1561–1637).' *Huntington Library Quarterly* 54 (1984): 147–77; Edward Chaney, 'Robert Dallington's *Survey of Tuscany* (1605): A British View of Medicean Florence.' In *The Evolution of the Grand Tour*, ed. Edward Chaney (London: Frank Cass, 1998), 143–60.

[64] Robert Dallington, *Aphorismes* (1613), sig. A3r.   [65] Dallington, *Aphorismes*, sig. A3r.

[66] Strong, *Henry, Prince of Wales*, 16–17.

[67] See 'The Education of a Stuart Prince' in Chapter 3.

Hereunto Example and Precept will enable you. Examples you may haue in your owne family, and (which few Princes haue had) in your owne time. Your matchlesse Brother for these seuen yeares to come, may take you by the hand, and leade you in the faire apprentisage of all honour and vertue: and then your royall Father may for many and many yeares (wee hope and pray) be a liuing and liuely Mirrour vnto you of Pietie, Wisedome, Iustice, Clemencie, and all other regall endowments fit for the high calling to which you are borne.[68]

While James furnishes Charles with 'other regall endowments,' his dead brother is his guide to 'honour and vertue.' Charles bears the responsibility of a 'high calling,' and must be open to both 'Example and Precept' and the 'liuing and liuely Mirrour' of those surrounding, preceding, and prefiguring him. (This praise is conventional; Erasmus addressed the future Habsburg Emperor Charles V in very similar terms at the opening of his *Education of a Christian Prince*.[69]) If this all seems rather oblique, there were more explicit and direct references to James's book of advice transferring to Charles. Wither praises *Basilicon Doron* as a formative text for James's first son: '*Thy Kingly Guift* so well preuail'd to make him | Fit for a Crowne of endles happines.'[70] He then claims that Henry embodied this text so effectively that he became, for Charles, 'himselfe a booke for Kings to pore on: | And might haue been thy ΒΑΣΙΛΙΚΟΝ ΔΟΡΟΝ [*Basilicon Doron*].' And so other poets draw the irresistible connection, urging Charles to read the very text that had so influenced Henry. William Basse encourages James 'to yeeld the same | Divine examples vnto Charles that made | Henry so noble, and so great in Fame.'[71] Thomas Campion similarly uses an architectural metaphor to charge James with the responsibility of 'framing' his second son, as he did Henry:

> And that same Royall workeman who could frame
> A Prince so worthy of immortall fame;
> Liues, and long may hee liue, to forme the other
> His exprest image, and grace of his brother.[72]

---

[68] Dallington, *Aphorismes*, sigs. A3r–A3v. The Stuart/Steward homonym was common in addresses to the family before and after 1612; see e.g. Thomas Dekker's 'Prayer for the Prince of Wales' (and his siblings): 'that they may bee good Stewards ouer this great houshold of the now-firmlie united Families, and co-vnited kingdomes' (*Foure Birds of Noahs*, 15, sig. E5v). Dallington's reference to 'seven yeares' likely refers to the time when Charles will surpass Henry's lifespan. This dedication was reprinted without alterations, despite its specific date-references, in the book's second edition of 1629. In 1641, Benson redacted it (without attribution) when dedicating Cornwallis's *Discourse* to the younger Charles, discussed above: 'If you shall be pleased to adde these examples and precepts to those of your Royall Father [Charles I] taking them hand in hand, they will lead you in your tender yeares, in the faire continuance of Honour and Vertue; and then his Majesty your Royall Father may for many yeares (for whiche we hope and pray) be a living Mirrour vnto you of Piety, VVisedome, and Iustice, and all other Regall Indowments fit for so great a Dignity, to which you are borne' (sig. A3v).

[69] Erasmus, *Education of a Christian Prince*, 3.   [70] Wither, *Prince Henries Obseqvies*, sig. B1r.

[71] William Basse, *Great Brittaines Svnnes-Set* (1613), sig. B2r.

[72] Coperario, *Songs of Mourning*, sig. B1r. The quotation is from 'An Elegie vpon the vntimely death of Prince *Henry*,' preceding Campion's songs addressed to individual members of Henry's family (sigs. A2r–B1r).

It is unclear whether these endorsements are in Charles's best interests, but that is not necessarily their motive; they serve to praise James's influence on his first son.

You would think that the mournful lesson of Henry's premature death would be an opportunity to correct the overly optimistic tone of his education, but optimism was standard practice for poets like Wither, Basse, and Campion. Some were motivated by a desire to serve their own interest in finding a new patron. Like Dallington and a host of other writers, Hayward approached Charles after losing Henry's patronage on his death. His dedication to Charles of his *Lives of the III. Normans, Kings of England*, a history written under Henry's patronage mere weeks before his death, uses the language of '*glory and fame*' to emphasize what writers can supply. Hayward describes Henry to Charles as one '*who was most dearely esteemed by you; who may be iustly proposed, as an example of vertue, as a guide to glory and fame.*'[73]

This self-serving optimism sounds familiar. So too does the obverse pessimism of Henry's chaplains and elegists, who advised Charles to discriminate between his brother's positive and negative legacies. Chaplains, including the familiar figures of Wilkinson and Price, cited Henry's death as the latest in a series, each an instance of the same doctrine. Elegists, including Augustine Taylor and Thomas Campion, echoed the chaplains' division between Henry's 'fame' (or 'fortunes') and his 'fate,' his high station and ignominious death—though they could not agree whether Charles could inherit the former without the latter.

Chaplains teach by admonition rather than by flattery, as we have seen, praising patrons only for their willingness to hear the truth.[74] Wilkinson, who had once preached Henry's 'Sermon of *Mortification*, or Preparation' before his fatal illness, now sought to give Charles the same knowledge of his impending death—knowledge that Henry had gained too late.[75] While it may be indecorous to bring 'Death *into the Court, which is welcome no where*,' Wilkinson feels that Charles must be mindful of it. He characterizes the enthusiastic predictions of Charles's inheritance as misleading: '*Euery man tels you, that whatsoeuer was your Brothers, is now by deuolution yours: giue me leaue also to tel you, that as his fortunes, so his fate also shall one day be yours.*'[76] That proviso, '*one day*,' is essential: Henry's death may have been premature, but Charles's eventual death is inevitable. Price delivered the identical message in *Prince Henry his Second Anniversary*, dedicating the volume to Charles, because 'your *Princely spirit* dare looke *death* in the face, and can be content to hear, that as your

---

[73] Hayward, *Lives of the III. Normans*, sig. A4r. See 'The Education of a Stuart Prince' in Chapter 3.
[74] See 'Warnings' in Chapter 4.   [75] Hawkins, *Life and Death*, 36, sig. C4v.
[76] Wilkinson, *Paire of Sermons*, sig. A3r. Wilkinson's full title elaborates on the occasions and purposes of each sermon, designed to 'set before you life and death' (in the epigram from Deut. 30: 15): *The Former* [sermon] *as an Ante-Fvnerall to the late Prince Henry, Anno Dom. 1612. October 25. The first day of his last and fatall sicknesse. The Latter Preacht this present yeere 1614. Ianuar. 16. To the now liuing Prince Charles, as a preseruer of his life, and life to his Soule.*

renowmed [*sic*] brother's *fortunes*, so his *fate* also shall one day be yours.' Price's familiarity with Wilkinson's sermon is evident in this reiteration to Charles, and to former members of Henry's household, whom he urges to look death in the face, whether or not they are 'content' to do so.[77] This reframing of Henry's experience for Charles's benefit had begun at the close of Henry's funeral. At the end of Archbishop Abbott's funeral sermon, there was a joint prayer or 'comprecation' for Charles to outlive Henry. First, writes Isaac Wake, those who carried the banners of Henry's titles offered them to Charles:

> There after ye sermon was ended all yt caried ye great banners offered them up to ye prince yt liveth who receaued them at ye Communion table & left them to ye church. Then did ye king of Heralds proclaime ye title of him yt was dead, & at ye end used a short comprecation to Prince Charles wishing him longer dayes then his brother.[78]

The herald's comprecation is conventional, but poets extended its wishful thinking into advice for Charles to distinguish between his brother's fame and his fate, to inherit a selective and self-serving legacy.

The elegists Campion and Taylor deny the universality of Henry's death, to distinguish his desirable from his undesirable elements. Addressing Charles in his *Songs of Mourning*, a set of consolatory poems '*Bevvailing the vntimely death of Prince Henry*' to each member of the royal family, Campion echoes Wilkinson's distinction between fame and fate:

> Follow, O follow yet thy Brothers fame,
> But not his fate, lets onely change the name,
>   And finde his worth presented
>   In thee, by him preuented:
> Or past example of the dead be great,
>   Out of thy selfe begin thy storie.[79]

Henry's fame, or his intrinsic worth, was 'preuented' from reaching its potential by his adverse fate, or his premature death; Campion hopes to convince Charles

---

[77] Price, *Second Anniversary*, n.p., sig. *2r. Price follows this dire warning with an equally conventional envoy: 'Many, and happy be your *Highnesse* daies, that you may so long *continue* in the *world*, as the *world* shall *continue*.' He is also addressing a wider audience of men who neglect their spiritual duties.

[78] National Archives SP 14/71/68. Wake's letter is dated 19 December 1612. A comprecation is 'A praying together, joint supplication' (*OED*, misattributing its first usage to 1635).

[79] Coperario, *Songs of Mourning*, sig. C2r. Remorse is absent from Campion's memory of Henry, closing the same verse: 'on his [Charles's] honoured head let all the blessings light | Which to his brothers life men wish't, and wisht them right.' The seven songs, set to music by John Cooper (alias Giovanni Coprario), are addressed, in turn, to James, to Anne, to Charles, to Elizabeth, to her husband Frederick, to Great Britain, and to the World at large.

that he can divide one from the other. Though 'past example of the dead be great' and highly influential, Charles must now begin his own story 'Out of thy selfe.' His own potential far exceeds Henry's accomplishments, but Charles's own story must be unique if he is to avoid Henry's fate. If Campion is guilty of wishful thinking, Taylor commits a greater transgression by recasting the fall of Troy, in a poem addressed to Queen Anne:

> Long remaine
> Blest mother; to another, *Charlemaigne.*
> And I shall liue to see the thame inioy
> Another *Illion* in another Troy.
> So Noble spirits set her breast vpon
> As were the grand sonnes of *Laomedon,*
> And much more happy.[80]

Taylor displays a rare gift for understatement when this final line withholds the negative implications of this rebuilt Troy-on-Thames ('thame'), its namesake destroyed by the Greeks; Laomedon's grandsons, Priam's nineteen sons, were noble, but ultimately far from 'happy.'[81] Both Taylor and Campion emphasize fame, without dwelling on the morbid particulars of fate. For Charles to begin the narrative or 'storie' of his own future, he must revive 'Noble spirits' and past exemplars while remaining unburdened by their fates.

I need hardly tell the reader that Charles would violate receptive decorum by suffering a fate worse than his brother's, in his trial and execution in 1649. In a morbid sense he upheld the elegists' injunctions to avoid Henry's fate, while ignoring the chaplains' advice to fear death from any quarter. Yet a more fundamental truth was that no exemplar can be simultaneously hortatory and cautionary; Charles could not select his brother's admirable features while disregarding his vulnerability. Such promises motivate rhetoricians, but prove unfeasible in practice.

---

[80] Taylor, *Encomiasticke Elogies*, sig. A7r.
[81] For Trojan precedents of Henry's death see Ullyot, 'Fall of Troynovant'.

Conclusion

Exemplary Criticism

Although replicating an ethical exemplar is impossible, it is easy to see the imaginative appeal of hortatory examples. I first noticed this appeal in Chapman's 1611 dedication of the *Iliad* to Henry, the first primary source quoted in my Introduction. Read Homer to learn how to live, Chapman writes to the Prince. The Prince might well reply to the poet, read Homer to learn how to write. Each relies on the other to propagate the exemplary cycle through which they both flourish. Chapman directly urges Henry to master his own 'affections' and self-government 'by Princely presidents. | Which here, in all kinds, my true zeale presents | To furnish your youth's groundworke and first State.'[1] But Chapman is imprecise ('in all kinds') about just which ethical exemplars Homer offers Henry; immediately before invoking Alexander he gestures toward 'All sorts of worthiest men, to be contrived | In your worth onely.'[2] Both uses of 'all' suggest that Chapman knows Henry is more enthusiastic than studious, and expects him not to investigate these claims with exactitude. It seems unlikely that Henry read past the dedication and learned from the intemperate Achilles to govern himself, or from the vulnerable Hector to be a good mortal. Both warriors could be positive or cautionary—particularly Hector, whose death made him a frequent comparison for Henry's elegists. ('New Troy her Prince, James wayles his Hector heire,' wrote Gorges in a typical analogy.[3]) Amid such interpretive nuances it was sufficient for Chapman's dedication merely to gesture toward Homer's 'firme Truth':

> ... lawes, religions, all
> Offerd to Change and greedie Funerall,
> Yet still your Homer lasting, living, raigning,
> And proves how firme Truth builds in Poet's faining.[4]

Exemplary rhetoric relies on a poet's feigning, on gestures toward an ethical authority that scrutiny would unveil as unstable—most acutely when Chapman's

---

[1] Chapman, *Iliad*, 3, ll. 6, 15–17.   [2] Chapman, *Iliad*, 3, ll. 19–20.
[3] Gorges, *Olympian Catastrophe*, 176, l. 1039; for other poets see Ullyot, 'Fall of Troynovant,' 270, 281–2.
[4] Chapman, *Iliad*, 4, ll. 58–61.

The Rhetoric of Exemplarity in Early Modern England. Michael Ullyot, Oxford University Press. © Michael Ullyot 2022.
DOI: 10.1093/oso/9780192849335.003.0007

patron succumbed to 'Change and greedie Funerall' the following year. But Chapman's aim was not to name particular Homeric heroes as unmitigated ethical authorities; rather, his aim was to secure patronage by comparing Henry to Alexander, and himself to Homer. Create the ethos of trustworthiness, and let the details take care of themselves. To cavil over Hector's fate or Achilles' temper is to miss the point of exemplary exhortations: yes, they suffer from the problems of metonymy and of reproducibility, but their purpose is more imaginative than real. Their purpose is to perpetuate themselves through a 'Poet's faining,' to propagate what Shakespeare called a virtuous lie.

My own purpose in this Conclusion is to return to the grounds of my argument for scepticism about hortative exemplarity, and to ask if cautionary rhetoric is any more trustworthy. Then I turn to my own judicial rhetoric to ask if critics are more trustworthy than the tutors or biographers I have addressed—less susceptible, that is, to metonymic fallacies or contingent evidence.[5] I began this study by declaring that I would use judicial rhetoric to make arguments about deliberative rhetoric. Here I qualify those arguments by identifying what qualities they draw from Aristotle's third category, the epideictic or ceremonial. Its aim is to praise or blame, as in a funeral oration, but 'with the intent of celebrating timeless virtues and inculcating them as models for the future.'[6] That sounds very much like exemplary rhetoric, which borrows features from all three branches—and as I will show, so too does my own literary-critical rhetoric.

But first, if historicizing hortatory rhetoric reveals that it is untenable, the question remains whether cautionary rhetoric is therefore tenable or even necessary. A dogmatic historicist would say that, since every moment in time is intrinsically distinct, no exemplar can ever be replicated—and therefore cautionary rhetoric is tautological. Even if you tried, perversely, to imitate a negative exemplar you would fail. If Charles, for instance, learned about Henry's preference for soldiering over studying in a cautionary vein, denigrating his exercises and privations as excessive and foolish, the vices that caused one man's premature death might easily lengthen another's life, owing to the vagaries to chance and circumstance. Contingencies separating the two brothers—one susceptible to disease, the other to insurrection—might even turn blame into praise.[7] Yet there is still a value to avoiding past errors, when those errors are more ethical than circumstantial; only fools and tyrants dismiss cautionary advice on the grounds that now is circumstantially different from then.

---

[5] For tutors and biographers, respectively, see 'Papirus Cursor' and 'The Book of Henry' in Chapter 5.

[6] Aristotle, *On Rhetoric*, 48 n. 79.

[7] It is difficult to imagine Henry IX ceding his generalship to Prince Rupert and losing the decisive 1644 battle at Marston Moor, but that is as far as I will take this particular parlour game. William Hunt attributes Charles's overthrow to 'Henry's shadow regime': 'Charles's worst enemy, after himself, was his brother's ghost' ('Legitimation Crisis,' 327).

A second implicit assumption that demands sceptical inquiry is that my own literary-critical rhetoric is immune to the problems I identify in exemplary rhetoric. Although exemplary rhetoric is prescriptive and therefore deliberative, it is founded on descriptive, judicial assessments of the virtues or vices of its past subjects; those assessments make it susceptible to metonymic error. Rather than imagining Aristotle's three branches (deliberative, judicial, and epideictic) as mutually exclusive domains, making discrete arguments for discrete audiences about discrete time-periods, recall what Lanham calls 'the sponginess of this distinction.' Consider a hypothetical epideictic orator who uses all three time-periods, recalling the past and predicting the future in a present ceremony.[8] There is an epideictic quality to a rhetorician's ethos of trustworthiness, from the tutor's recitation of just the right ethical example to the biographer's indispensable familiarity with their subject. Even if those two rhetoricians are (respectively) deliberative and judicial, they are also in part epideictic—if only as a means to an end.

So too are literary critics like me, who aspire to more than paraphrase of texts. We use the rhetoric of exemplarity; we excise parts of those texts and exposit them as representative of broader categories, of ideas and images conveyed by other parts.[9] From the moment that I quoted Chapman and Drummond in the Introduction, my choice of evidence throughout this study has recurrently, and silently, excluded other evidence that did not serve the various turns of my argument. This applies as much to my choices of words from texts as to my choices of texts from the archives. And so my exemplary rhetoric is susceptible to the problem of metonymy—the threat of possible conflicts between exemplary evidence that happens to have been brought forward, and that which remains (as yet) obscure.[10]

My exemplary rhetoric of citations is overtly judicial and implicitly epideictic. It is judicial because I make judgements about broad cultural phenomena in a historical period based on its texts; and it is epideictic because I make choices about which texts to excerpt and interpret in which order. Readers judge if my selections are credible rather than arbitrary or tendentious, but they are necessary to judicial argumentation. The rhetoric of argumentation gives meaning to archival evidence, disputable as such persuasions may be. Its judgements can be persuasive, but only provisionally so: indeed disputations among interpreters, sceptical of any judgement that claims to be irrefutable and permanent, are the

---

[8] Lanham, *Handlist of Rhetorical Terms*, 165. The other two divisions of arguments and audiences are, respectively: political/legislative, forensic, and ceremonial; and law-makers, law-interpreters, and spectators. See Aristotle, *On Rhetoric*, 47–8.

[9] Lyons, *Exemplum*, 3–4. For a synoptic account of the practice see Ruth Finnegan, *Why do we Quote? The Culture and History of Quotation* (Cambridge: Open Book, 2011).

[10] For my discussion of how progress in archival fields depends on previously obscure knowledge, see Ullyot, 'Augmented Criticism, Extensible Archives, and the Progress of Renaissance Studies.' *Renaissance and Reformation/Renaissance et Réforme* 37, no. 4 (2014): 185.

very purpose of literary criticism. I return to disputations at the end of this Conclusion, but first I address the methods of my epideictic choices and what they owe the rhetoric of exemplarity. Then I describe the methods of new historicist literary criticism, which I have used throughout this study to persuade you (perhaps) as an exemplary rhetorician persuades their audience: that the rhetorician's judgement is trustworthy because it is based on valid evidence, not fanciful argumentation. I compare the critic's use of anecdotes to both the tutor's and the biographer's, recalling Henry's Papirus Cursor episode. Finally I conclude with an ethical exhortation of my own.

The Archive Strikes Back

This study began, like any work of historicist criticism, in an archive: the Huntington Library, where I had travelled to present a paper on Spenser's readers in *The Faerie Queene*. (That was the germ of Chapter 2.) I was researching Thomas Heywood, so I called up the Huntington's copies of his books. After some puzzling over his synoptic verse history *Troia Britannica* (1609), I turned to his elegy for Henry, Prince of Wales. That led to further explorations in the Huntington's rich collections of Henry's elegies; I compiled a list of every one and began reading through the corpus. Joshua Sylvester's *Lachrimae Lachrimarvm* (1613), shown in Figure 4, typifies the genre with its solid-black mourning pages and woodcut borders of skeletons.[11]

What followed was my systematic comparative study of the literary and other textual remains of Prince Henry's life and death: from baptismal entertainments to the *Basilicon Doron*, royal entries to masques, dedications to elegies. (Those, in turn, were the bases of Chapters 3 to 5.) I treated archival sources without categorical distinctions of literary or extra-literary texts, of canonical status, of genre or form; my only criterion was their value to understanding the personage they were constructing and describing. Even authorial attributions were subservient to this topicality; whether a panegyric was by Drayton or Alexander mattered less than the terms of its descriptions of the Prince. This led to my extended studies of rhetorical techniques, as you have read, like their treatment of the Prince as an 'abridgement' of exemplary sources. References in this rhetoric to Sidney, Henry's exemplary predecessor, led me to his legacy, and most directly to Essex whose disgrace rendered him virtually unmentionable after 1601.

The method I followed in reconstructing these and other lines of influence was initially broadly historicist, in the tradition of historical ethnography. Its apotheosis is the Oxford historian Keith Thomas, who has described it as a catholic

---

[11] Compare Figure 3 in Chapter 4.

compilation of evidence on topics (including 'such diverse topics as literacy, numeracy, gestures, jokes, sexual morality, personal cleanliness or the treatment of animals') from a vast range of documents, in the tradition of Thomas's tutor Christopher Hill.[12] This method bears a resemblance to Stephen Greenblatt's definition of new historicist literary criticism, which self-consciously blurs 'the boundaries...between cultural practices understood to be art forms and other, contiguous, forms of expression.'[13] This methodology, which takes Hayden White's treatment of 'the historical text as a literary artifact' and adds the obverse (the historical artifact as literary text), also attempts to mitigate any retrograde great-man or singular-genius tendencies remaining from the vestiges of 'old' historicism.[14] Greenblatt undertakes the 'study of the collective making of distinct cultural practices and inquiry into the relations among these practices,' including inquiry into 'how collective beliefs and experiences were shaped, moved from one medium to another, concentrated in manageable aesthetic form, [and] offered for consumption.'[15] This emphasis on 'collective' aspects of meaning-making and shaping encourages a habit of deliberate indistinction among new historicists, as I alluded to in my choice of panegyrics: a habit of taking up all the written records that critics formerly classified as ephemera, or left to the historians. Arguments like mine combine evidence from a range of archival sources, agnostic about their literary or extra-literary categories: epics, dedications, elegies, sermons, eyewitness accounts, letters, and biographies. My practice owes to the new historicists' expansion of critics' range of texts qualifying for study beyond Shakespeare's plays to legal records, plague pamphlets, broadside ballads, coterie manuscripts, and any other form or medium representing early modern beliefs and experiences.

But this expansion introduces a new problem, new to those who suffer information overload as humanists did amid their own expansion due to print technology: the problem of what to read. We suffer this problem because of new technologies of access, and better surrogates for archival texts. Take just the example of early books printed in English. Since 1999, this archive has been transformed by the Text Creation Partnership which has created machine-readable

---

[12] 'Diary.' *London Review of Books* 32, no. 11 (10 June 2010): 36. Eamon Duffy critiques this method (in a 2009 review of Thomas's *The Ends of Life: Roads to Fulfilment in Early Modern England*), whose wide-ranging quotations are 'all presented as equivalent testimony to the mindset of an age,' leaving it vulnerable 'to the charge that it falsifies the material selected by decontextualising it' ('Common Thoughts.' *London Review of Books* 31, no. 14 (23 July 2009): 18). See Ullyot, 'Augmented Criticism,' 179–80, 192–3.

[13] Stephen Greenblatt, *Shakespearean Negotiations: The Circulation of Social Energy in Renaissance England* (Berkeley: University of California Press, 1988), 5.

[14] Hayden White, 'The Historical Text as Literary Artifact.' *Clio* 3, no. 3 (1974): 277–303.

[15] Greenblatt, *Shakespearean Negotiations*, 5. Louis A. Montrose ably summarizes new historicism's core tenets as the historicity of texts (i.e. their 'social embedment'), and the textuality of history (or 'its surviving textual traces' testifying to 'complex and subtle social processes of preservation and effacement') ('Renaissance Literary Studies and the Subject of History.' *English Literary Renaissance* 16, no. 1 (1986): 8).

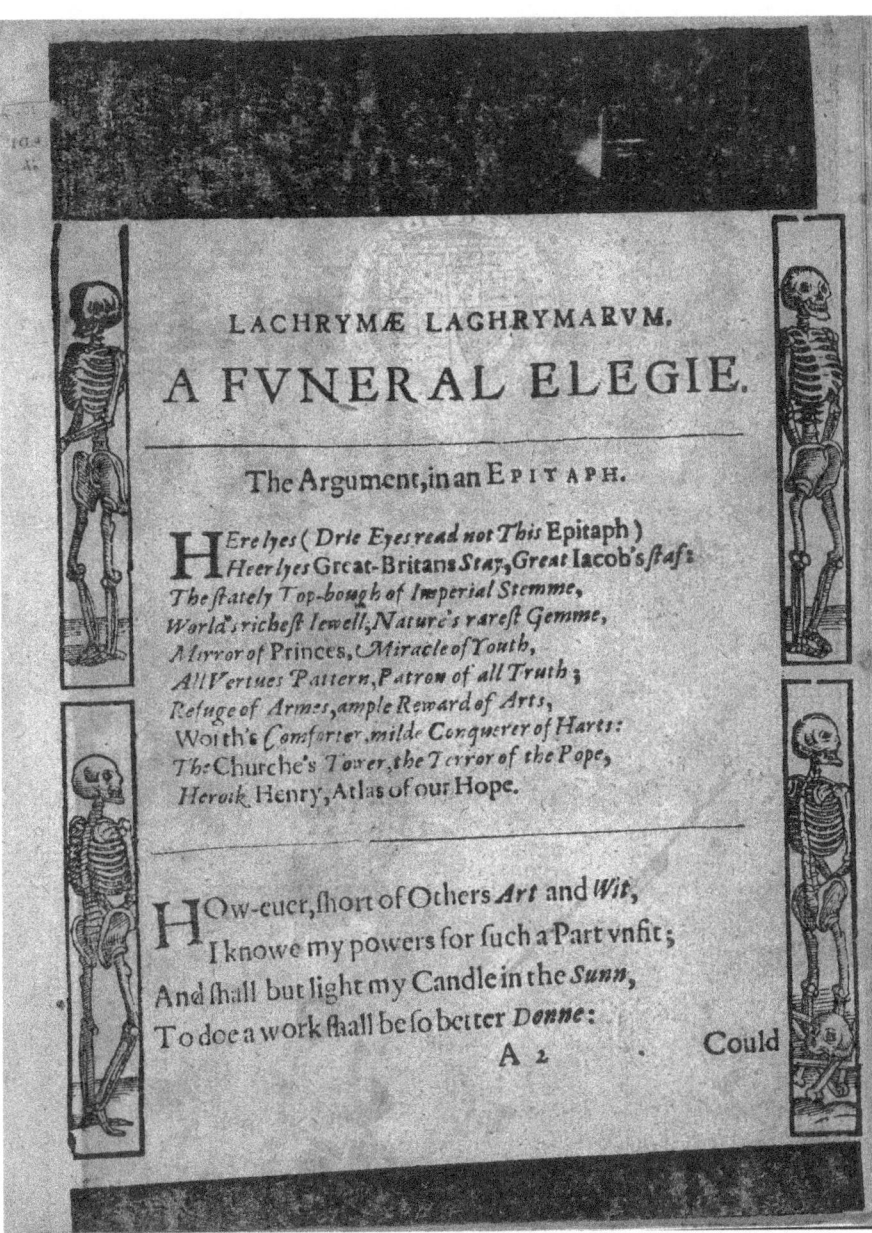

Figure 4. Sylvester's elegy *Lachrimae Lachrimarvm* designates Henry as 'Panaretus' or all-virtuous; these mourning pages, bands, and skeletal sidepieces recur throughout the quarto (sigs. A1v–A2r; RB 381557, The Huntington Library, San Marino, California).

transcriptions of every book in the Early English Books Online database, 70,000 texts printed before 1700. The EEBO-TCP represents the locus of progress in early modern literary studies: the combination of new historicist expansion with emergent technologies of data access and searchability.[16] The algorithmic extension of critics' capabilities to find evidence for our arguments is not my argument here; this expansion of evidence does not obviate the need to make arguments and tell histories based on selected, exemplary pieces of evidence. New historicists are still citing examples of evidence, even if those examples come from a broader array of sources. Even if the outcome of such practices is to substantiate claims with statistical tables and lists of evidence, as my collaborator Adam J. Bradley and I have argued, quantified data will never foreclose qualified criticism.[17] Stephen Ramsay cites a series of misguided claims that these methods will 'support or refute hypotheses or interpretations which have in the past been based on human reading and the somewhat serendipitous noting of interesting features.'[18] This empiricism is misguided, Ramsay argues, because '[l]iterary criticism operates within a hermeneutical framework in which the specifically scientific meaning of fact, metric, verification, and evidence simply do not apply.'[19] Instead, it operates within rhetorical *inventio*: 'the sophistic process of seeking truth through the dialectical interplay of trust, emotion, logic, and tradition.'[20] Empiricism is a persuasive method only for the sciences, in other words; rhetoric is for the humanities, and nowhere is this more overt and more innate than in new historicist criticism. It exercises *inventio* precisely through the epideictic features I cited in my own rhetoric of argumentation: the choices of exemplary evidence to interpret in a deliberate order.

In the remainder of this Conclusion I address the method of new historicist criticism that resembles early modern exemplary rhetoric, its use of anecdotes. In so doing I return to the episode at Henry's court surrounded by concentric rings of rhetoricians: the tutor, Adam Newton, using the Papirus Cursor example deliberately; the biographer, William Haydon, using Henry's sententious misinterpretation

---

[16] I make this argument in Ullyot, 'Augmented Criticism.' The pre-eminent practitioners of the new digital philology are Michael Witmore and Jonathan Hope. One might begin with their coauthored article '"Après le déluge, More Criticism": Philology, Literary History, and Ancestral Reading in the Coming Posttranscription World' (*Renaissance Drama* 40 (2012): 135–150), and follow the footnotes. Writing 'a study on the genres of English prose in the seventeenth century,' Witmore and Hope 'are required not simply to identify a number of exemplary texts but also to take account of all the evidence' (136).

[17] See Michael Ullyot and Adam J. Bradley, 'Past Texts, Present Tools, and Future Critics: Toward Rhetorical Schematics.' In *Shakespeare's Language in Digital Media: Old Words, New Tools*, ed. Janelle Jenstad and Jennifer Roberts-Smith with Mark Kaethler (Abingdon: Routledge, 2017), 144–56; and 'Machines and Humans, Schemes and Tropes.' *Early Modern Literary Studies* 20, no. 2 (2018): n.p.

[18] Susan Hockey, *Electronic Texts in the Humanities* (Oxford: Oxford University Press, 2000), 66, cit. Stephen Ramsay, *Reading Machines: Toward an Algorithmic Criticism* (Urbana: University of Illinois Press, 2011), 4.

[19] Ramsay, *Reading Machines*, 7.   [20] Ramsay, *Reading Machines*, 7.

judicially; and the critic, me, using it to initiate an argument epideictically—but also judicially to describe Haydon's methods.

New historicists frequently begin arguments with anecdotes, for many reasons: because anecdotes compel the reader's interest; because they are plentiful in the archives; because they disrupt the reader's sense of familiarity with known arte-facts and histories; and because they validate the writer's necessity as an indis-pensable interpreter.[21] Anecdotes are the clearest evidence that new historicist criticism, like any criticism, has narrative and rhetorical motivations. Instead of beginning with a familiar text like Shakespeare's *Twelfth Night* and broadening its implications into contiguous texts and documents, new historicists often begin with deliberately jarring or unfamiliar materials which they then reintegrate into the familiar field.[22] *Twelfth Night* and an anecdote from Montaigne's *Essais* about cross-dressing are, in Greenblatt's *Shakespearean Negotiations*, parts of the same network of concepts and beliefs. H. Aram Veeser calls this practice the first of 'five discrete, measured operations' that a 'typical' essay undertakes as it turns 'details' into 'knowledge': 'Each unique detail, episode, or essay comes to represent, duplicate, stand in for much more than its insignificant self.'[23] But this passive construction ('comes to') belies the critic's active rhetorical work: of recognizing the network and assembling the evidence they will make testify on its behalf. That evidence usually begins with an instrumental anecdote, the standard opening of a new historicist argument; Veeser calls it a 'load-bearing prop[] in the argument.' For instance, Greenblatt's seminal 1977 essay 'Marlowe and Renaissance Self-Fashioning' opens with an anecdote compiled by Richard Hakluyt and narrated by the merchant John Sarracoll, who recounts his voyage to Sierra Leone in October 1586.[24] After praising a native village's clean, well-built houses, Sarracoll closes his account with the bland remark that '[o]ur men at their departure set the town on fire.'[25] Greenblatt makes his aims explicit each time he tells this anecdote. In 1977, he writes, it reminds him of the 'casual, unexplained violence' of the English imperial project; and its calm language is evidence of 'the moral blankness that rests like thick snow on Sarracoll's sentences.'[26] In his 1980 reiteration, the same

---

[21] Ullyot, 'Rhetoric of Anecdotes.'

[22] The critique of this method is that it reinscribes the retrograde historicist tendencies to valorize canonical writers (primarily Shakespeare), while merely inverting their trajectory.

[23] Veeser, 'Introduction,' 4.

[24] Stephen Greenblatt, 'Marlowe and Renaissance Self-Fashioning.' In *Two Renaissance Mythmakers, Christopher Marlowe and Ben Jonson*, ed. Alvin B. Kernan (Baltimore: Johns Hopkins University Press, 1977), 41–69. Reprinted as 'Marlowe and the Will to Absolute Play.' In Greenblatt, *Renaissance Self-Fashioning*, 193–221.

[25] For a discussion of this anecdote, Sarracoll's mix of marvel and destruction, and its parallels with another episode in the final chapter of Greenblatt's *Marvelous Possessions: The Wonder of the New World* (Oxford: Clarendon Press, 1991), see Jürgen Pieters, *Moments of Negotiation: The New Historicism of Stephen Greenblatt* (Amsterdam: Amsterdam University Press, 2001), 76–80.

[26] Greenblatt, 'Marlowe and Renaissance Self-Fashioning,' 41–2.

anecdote 'will serve as a convenient bridge' between Greenblatt's chapters.[27] Its function for his immediate argument is to illuminate the restless travels and the violent consumption of experience that characterizes Christopher Marlowe's protagonists.[28]

As I said, one purpose of beginning any argument with an anecdote is to compel the reader's attention. Greenblatt's citation of Sarracoll serves the same function as the *exordium* in classical rhetoric, the 'entrance or beginning' to an argument, wherein 'the will of the standers-by or of the judge is sought for and required to hear the matter.'[29] Using an anecdote for this purpose was a common practice of early modern rhetoric. Consider, for instance, Sidney's opening of his *Defence of Poesy*, in which a horseman's enthusiasm for his vocation exemplifies the poet's for his own. Sidney calls it an 'example' of the kind of vivid 'speech in the praise of his faculty' that he aims to provide in his treatise on poetry.[30] Like all examples it is a provocation, a model for Sidney to imitate. It is also an anecdote in the (auto)biographical sense: it narrates a brief, private experience in the life of the subject, Sidney himself, in this case an encounter that now informs his desire to defend poetry.[31] It certainly did not happen exactly as Sidney recalls or recounts it, or at least as Sidney simplifies its nuances to make it instrumental to his present purpose.

If an opening anecdote is to be compelling, it must be recounted in compelling terms. In a seminal 1986 issue of *English Literary Renaissance* devoted to the new historicist movement, Karen Newman's reading of Shakespeare's *The Taming of the Shrew* opens with a cinematic description of a skimmington, or the humiliating re-enactment of a wife beating and berating her drunken husband: '*Wetherden, Suffolk. Plough Monday, 1604.* A drunken tanner, Nicholas Royser, staggers home from the alehouse.' Like Greenblatt, Newman is overt about her motives for recounting the anecdote: it 'figures the social anxiety about gender and power which characterizes Elizabethan culture.'[32] After reading the anecdote's gender politics, Newman links it to Shakespeare's play. These events 'have an

---

[27] Greenblatt, *Renaissance Self-Fashioning*, 193.

[28] Greenblatt, 'Marlowe and Renaissance Self-Fashioning,' 47.

[29] Wilson, *An English Rhetoric*, 81. This is Wilson's interpretation of Quintilian's *exordium*.

[30] Sidney, *Defence*, 337. Sidney later adds that the poet unites the philosopher's with the historian's strength when he 'coupleth the general notion with the particular example' (351).

[31] On its autobiographical elements, particularly Sidney's compassion for Pugliano, see Christopher Martin, 'Sidney's Exemplary Horse Master and the Disciplines of Discontent.' In *Renaissance Historicisms: Essays in Honor of Arthur F. Kinney*, ed. James M. Dutcher and Anne Lake Prescott (Newark: University of Delaware Press, 2008), 85–102.

[32] Karen Newman, 'Renaissance Family Politics and Shakespeare's *The Taming of the Shrew.*' *English Literary Renaissance* 16, no. 1 (1986): 86. She offers a precedent for this instrumental reading. The anecdote serves the same function as the dream of Simon Forman that Louis Montrose recounts in a 1983 essay, a precedent Newman quotes: 'this incident... "epitomizes the indissolubly political and sexual character of... cultural forms"' ('Family Politics,' 87). The original anecdote is in Montrose, '"Shaping Fantasies": Figurations of Gender and Power in Elizabethan Culture.' *Representations* 2 (1983): 62–4; the quoted text is on 64).

uncanny relation' with *The Taming of the Shrew*, she writes, which 'suggests a tempting homology between history and [such] cultural artifacts,' one that clarifies her aim in the essay: 'to articulate the particular sexual/political fantasy ... that the play projects as an imaginary resolution of contradictions which are never resolved in the Wetherden case.'[33] The effective and pleasing fiction in this transition is that the anecdote spontaneously reminds Newman of Shakespeare's play; the more likely fact is that this 'tempting homology' moves in the opposite direction. Though our rhetoric suggests we are reading Shakespeare through an archival lens, the truth is that we have done the inverse.

Such suggestions give new historicism an epideictic, performative quality: the critic's ability to give anecdotes an unexpected ability to shed light on more familiar artefacts is impressive when it is convincing.[34] Grafting them together requires an air of nonchalance: the critic remarks on how uncannily the anecdote epitomizes certain qualities of the text, and smoothly transitions into an argument about those qualities. These remarks only heighten the sense that this argument depends on the visibly present work of an indispensable navigator. The archive is inauspicious without such interpreters, whose work of selection, placement, and interpretation makes it intelligible. The liveliest anecdote cannot speak for itself, cannot gather itself into a persuasive argument on cultural practices.

I have been calling them anecdotes but, like Newton's story of Papirus Cursor, they are examples: that is, anecdotes rhetorically leveraged to provoke a response in a future they can hardly anticipate. New historicists leverage anecdotes to provoke an ethos of trustworthiness and credibility and to compel readers' attention. The power of their anecdotes resides not only in their networked interconnection with known facts and texts but also in their reliability. This refers not just to their accurate transcription but their freedom from the impurities and distortions of more self-conscious genres, or their comparable proximity to 'the lives real men and women actually live.'[35] That is why both biographers and these critics find testimonies of the past's distance from the present, or more essentially from the present's current misconceptions of that past. The critic extracts anecdotes from the archives that will most convincingly testify to the networks of beliefs and practices they recognize in a given text. They then use those testimonies to reveal new knowledge, to unsettle established thinking and commonplaces, or to make common new knowledge.

Throughout this Conclusion I have demurred to refer to such critical rhetoric in the first person when it feels overly performative and insincere, but the moment has come for me to address the limits of my own methodology more squarely and

---

[33] Newman, 'Family Politics,' 87–9.
[34] '[T]he self-pleasing aspects of rhetorical performance have tended to cluster in this third category' (Lanham, *Handlist of Rhetorical Terms*, 164).
[35] Gallagher and Greenblatt, *Practicing New Historicism*, 21.

concretely. In sum, a trustworthy ethos does not an infallible argument make. My exemplary rhetoric is susceptible to archival disruptions and discoveries, just as Chapman's or Newton's is to lapses of receptive decorum. The difference is that I invite that disruption, because my rhetoric is descriptive rather than prescriptive—and because my discipline is an interpretive community constituted by discourse, with a shared enterprise of weighing and considering common evidence about historical subjects.[36] Because my archival evidence is metonymic, other parts will and should arise to contest my claims about Sidney, Essex, Henry, and the rhetoric of exemplarity encircling them. My arguments are provisional, because all literary-critical arguments are so; if they were definitive they would not invite readers to discourse about these subjects.

Thus for literary criticism, metonymic evidence is not the problem, but the purpose; it provokes the humility necessary to open one's arguments to correction and qualification. One reason that the new historicist method has thrived for so long is because of the methodological openness we see in Greenblatt and Newman, calling attention to their argumentative turns and transitions, their applications of anecdotes to textual problems, and their connections between literary and extra-literary documents. They encourage others to use the same methods on adjacent documents. No, more than encourage—they exhort us in deliberate terms to imitate them. So new historicists are exemplary rhetoricians in both senses of the phrase: epideictically citing and illuminating selective evidence to substantiate judicial arguments that are nonetheless humble and transparent enough to provide models of critical practice. Their imitators' persuasive arguments are results for readers to judge.

---

[36] 'Interpretive communities' is Stanley Fish's coinage in *Is there a Text in This Class?: The Authority of Interpretive Communities* (Cambridge: Harvard University Press, 1980).

Verses on the Death of Prince Henry

This list of elegies and other verses on the death of Henry, Prince of Wales (1594–1612) fulfils G. W. Pigman's appeal in 1985 for a bibliography of these texts (in *Grief and English Renaissance Elegy* (1985), 143 n. 2).

Books and editions are listed by author in chronological order of publication; anonymous works are listed by title. Book titles are transcribed from physical copies, *Short-Title Catalogue* (*STC*) microfilms, or *Early English Books Online* (*EEBO*) images. Titles include every word printed on the title page excepting epigraphs and printer or publisher information; their words are capitalized to follow early print conventions of emphasis (e.g. all-capitalized words) primarily, and modern title-case conventions sparingly. They otherwise ignore variations in typeface (e.g. italics, small capitals, enlarged type), and silently expand contractions. First lines are used when titles of individual poems are absent.

Incomplete lists of these poems appear in Egerton Brydges, *Restituta: or Titles, Extracts, and Characters of Old Books in English Literature, revived* (1814), 4:172; John Nichols, 'Tracts on the Death of Prince Henry' in *The Progresses, Processions, and Magnificent Festivities of King James the First, his Royal Consort, Family, and Court* (1828), 2:504–12; and John Philip Edmond, 'Elegies and Other Tracts Issued on the Death of Henry, Prince of Wales, 1612,' in *Publications of the Edinburgh Bibliographical Society* 6 (1901): 146–7. Edmond claims to add fifteen works not on Nichols's list; the following adds more still. Titles of ballads and of some Latin texts not available in *STC* microfilms or *EEBO* are taken from these sources, as noted.

Although this list excludes multiple editions of individual works, numbers from the *STC* (2nd edition) denote every recorded variant, issue, and edition. This list also excludes memorial sermons; though their printed editions occasionally contain elegies, they are often printed elsewhere, such as in the Oxford and Cambridge anthologies.

1. Single-Author Verses

Alexander, William. *An Elegie on the Death of Prince Henrie. By Sr William Alexander of Menstrie, Gentleman of his Priuie Chamber.* Edinburgh, 1612. [*STC* 339, 340]

Allyne, Robert. *Funerall elegies vpon the most lamentable and vntimely death of the thrice illustrious Prince Henry, Prince of VVales, &c. By R. A.* London, 1613. [*STC* 384]

Aston, Sir Walter. [Poems in Bodley MS. Eng. Poet. c. 37.]

G. B. *'Cestria Lugens': A Collection of epitaphs and elegies on Prince Henry by one 'G.B.', (from Bodley MS Rawl. Poet. 116, fos. 1–16).* 'Appendix A.' In Dennis Kay, *Melodious Tears: The English Funeral Elegy from Spenser to Milton.* (Oxford: Clarendon Press, 1990), 233–50.

Basse, William. *Great Brittaines Svnnes-Set, Bewailed with a Shower of Teares. By William Basse.* Oxford, 1613. [*STC* 1546]

Baudius (Domenicus). *Monumentum consecratum Honori & memoriae Serenissimi Britanniarum Principis Henrici Frederici Authore Dominico Baudio I. C. Historiarum Professore in Academia Leidensi.* Leiden, 1612.

Campion, Thomas. *Songs of Mourning: Bevvailing the vntimely death of Prince Henry. VVorded by Tho. Campion. And set forth to bee sung with one voyce to the Lute, or Violl: By John Coprario.* London, 1613. [*STC* 4546]

Chapman, George. *An Epicede or Funerall Song: On the most disastrous Death, of the High-borne Prince of Men, Henry Prince of Wales, &c. With The Funeralls, and Representation of the Herse of the same High and mighty Prince; Prince of Wales, Duke of Cornewaile and Rothsay, Count Palatine of Chester, Earle of Carick, and late Knight of the most Noble Order of the Garter. Which Noble Prince deceased at St. James, the sixt day of Nouember, 1612. and was most Princely interred the seuenth day of December following, within the Abbey of Westminster, in the Eighteenth yeere of his Age.* London, 1612. [*STC* 4947]

Davies, John, of Hereford. *The Mvses-Teares for the losse of their hope; heroick and ne're-too-mvch praised, Henry, Prince of Wales. &c. Together with Times Sobs for the vntimely death of his Glory in that his Darling: and lastly, his Epitaphs. Consecrated To the high and mighty Prince, Frederick the fift, Count-palatine of Rheyn, &c. Where-vnto is added, Consolatory Straines to wrest Natvre from her bent in immoderate mourning; most loyally, and humbly wisht to the King and Qveenes most exeellent* [sic] *Maiesties. By Iohn Davies of Hereford, their Maiesties poore Beads-man, and Vassall.* London, 1613. [*STC* 6339]

Donne, John. 'Elegie on Prince Henry.' In *Poems, By J. D. VVith Elegies on the Authors Death.* London, 1633. sigs. X1v–X3r; 154–7. [*STC* 7045, 7046, 7047]

Donne, John. 'Elegie On the vntimely Death of the *incomparable Prince,* Henry.' Ed. Gary A. Stringer. Bloomington and Indianapolis: Indiana University Press, 1995. *The Variorum Edition of the Poetry of John Donne.* Gary A. Stringer, gen. ed. 8 vols. to date. 6:160–2.

Drummond, William, of Hawthornden. *Teares on the death of Meliades.* Edinburgh, 1613. [*STC* 7257, 7258, 7259]

Gorges, Sir Arthur. 'The Olympian Catastrophe.' In *The Poems of Sir Arthur Gorges.* Ed. Helen Estabrook Sandison (Oxford: Clarendon Press, 1953), 135–82.

Gordon, Patrick. *Neptvnvs Britannicvs Corydonis. De luctuouso Serenissimi Henrici (æternæ memoriæ) magnæ Britanniæ Principis, &c. obitu. Et felicibus Serenissimi successoris Caroli. F. Ducis Eboracceusis, &c. auspicijs: Queis intermixtus Serenissimi Friderici, Rhenani Principis Electoris, &c. & Serenissimæ Elizabethae magnæ Britanniæ, &c. Infantis Hymenæus.* London, 1613. [*STC* 12068]

Heywood, Thomas. *A Fvnerall Elegie, Vpon the death of the late most hopefull and illustrious Prince, Henry, Prince of Wales. Written by Thomas Heyvvood.* London, 1613. [*STC* 13323, reissued in 24151]

Hume, David, of Godscroft. *Illvstrissimi Principis Henrici Ivsta. Vbi et sponsorvm epithala-mivm; et consolatio; & exhortatio ad principem Carolum ad fratris imitationem.* London, 1613. [*STC* 13952]

Julius, Alexander. *In Henricvm Fridericvm primogenitvm Iacobi Ter maximi Regis magnæ Britanniæ, Galliæ, & Hiberniæ: Serenissimum vero Walliae Principem, morbo de hac vita decedentem Novemb. 1612 Lachrymæ Alexr. Jvlii Scoti, suo & conterraneorum suorum nomine, Namque ab Vno disce omnes.* Edinburgh, 1612. [*STC* 14848]

Juxon, William. [Poems in Bodley MS. Douce f. 5. fol. 34v]

Maxwell, James. *The Laudable Life, And Deplorable Death, of our late peerlesse Prince Henry. Briefly represented. Together, with some other Poemes, in honor both of our most gracious Soueraigne King Iames his auspicious entrie to this Crowne, and also of his most hopefull Children, Prince Charles and Princesse Elizabeths happy entrie into this world. By. I. M. Master of Artes.* London, 1612. [*STC* 17701]

Niccols, Richard. *The Three Sisters Teares. Shed at the Late Solemne Funerals of the Royall deceased Henry, Prince of Wales, &c.* London, 1613. [*STC* 18525]

Peacham, Henry. *The Period of Mourning. Disposed into sixe Visions. In Memorie of the late Prince. Together With Nuptiall Hymnes, in Honour of this Happy Marriage betweene the Great Princes, Frederick Count Palatine of the Rhene, and The Most Excellent, and Aboundant President of all Virtve and Goodnes Elizabeth onely Daughter to oure Soueraigne, his Maiestie. Also the manner of the Solemnization of the Marriage at White-Hall, on the 14. of February, being Sunday, and St. Valentines day. By Henry Peacham, Mr. of Arts.* London, 1613. [*STC* 19513, 19513.5]

Rogers, Thomas, of Tewkesbury. *Gloucesters Myte, Delivered vvith the mournefull Records of Great Britaine, into the Worlds Register. For the inrolement of the euerlasting Fame and perpetuall remembrance of our late most gratious Prince Henrie. With Motiues to Repentance. The materiall points touched, appeare in the next Page.* London, 1612. [*STC* 21241.5]

Sylvester, Joshua. *Lachrimæ Lachrimarvm. or The Distillation of Teares Shede For the vntymely Death of The incomparable Prince Panaretvs. by Iosuah Syluester.* London, 1613. [*STC* 23576, 23577, 23577.5, 23578]

Taylor, Augustine. *Encomiasticke Elogies. Written by Avgvstine Taylor.* London, 1614. [*STC* 23721]

Taylor, John. *Great Britaine, All in Blacke. For The incomparable losse of Henry, our late worthy Prince. By Iohn Taylor.* London, 1612. [*STC* 23760, 23760.5]

Tourneur, Cyril. *A Griefe on the Death of Prince Henrie, Expressed in a broken Elegie, according to the nature of such a sorrow. By Cyril Tourneur.* London, 1613. [*STC* 24148.3, reissued in 24151]

Vicars, John. 'Epig. 102. Vpon the Death of Prince Henry. 1612.' In *Epigrams of That most wittie and worthie Epigrammatist Mr. Iohn Owen, Gentleman. Translated by Iohn Vicars.* London, 1619. sigs. G7r–G7v. [*STC* 18993]

Ward, John. *The First Set of English Madrigals To 3. 4. 5. and 6. parts apt both for Viols and Voyces. With a Mourning Song in memory of Prince Henry. Newly Composed by Iohn Ward.* London, 1613. [*STC* 25023]

Webster, John. *A Monvmental Colvmne, Erected to the liuing Memory of the euer-glorious Henry, late Prince of Wales.* London, 1613. [*STC* 25174, reissued in 24151]

Wedderburn, David. *In Obitv Svmmæ Spei Principis Henrici. Iacobi VI Serenissimi Britanniæ magnæ, Hiberniæ & Galliæ Regis Filii Primogeniti Lessus. Avthore Davide Wedderbvrno Scholæ Abredonensis Moderatore.* Edinburgh, 1612. [*STC* 25188]

Wither, George. *Prince Henries Obseqvies or Movrnefvll Elegies vpon his Death: VVith A supposed Inter-locution betweene the Ghost of Prince Henrie and Great Brittaine. By George Wyther.* London, 1612. [*STC* 25915]

2. Anonymous or Multiple-Author Verses

Printed ballads are given numbers from Nichols's itemized list.

Ballad. 'A Ballad of great Brytayne's greatest comfort or Brytayne's hope for the roiall prynce Charles, Prynce of Great Brytayne and Ireland, Duke of York and Albany.' London, 1612. [Nichols 6]

Ballad. 'A Complaynt againste Death for takinge away the highe and hopeful Prince Henry of Greate Brittayne, with the manner of his funerall.' London, 1612. [Nichols 4]

Ballad. 'Englandes sorrowe for the deathe of the Most Vertuous and pierless Henry Frederick Prince of Wales, eldest son of our Sovereign Lord King James, who deceased the 6th of November 1612, at St. James' House.' London, 1612. [Nichols 3]

Ballad. 'A Farewell to Prince Henry, or his funeral teares shed by his country for his Hynes's deare losse.' London, 1612. [Nichols 2]

Ballad. 'The first and second parte of the Lyfe and deathe of the late noble prince Henry, with the order of his funerall.' London, 1612. [Nichols 5]

Ballad. 'The good shepheards sorrow for the death ef [sic] his beloved sonne.' London, 1612. [STC 13157.5]

Brooke, Christopher, and William Browne. *Two Elegies, Consecrated to the Never-dying Memorie of the most worthily admyred; most hartily loued; and generally bewayled Prince; Henry Prince of Wales.* London, 1613. [STC 3831]

Cambridge University. *Epicedivm Cantabrigiense, In obitum immaturum, semperq; deflendum, Henrici, Illustrissimi Principis Walliae, &c.* Cambridge, 1612. [STC 4481, 4482]

Great Brittans Mourning Garment. Given To all faithfull sorrowfull Subiects at the Funerall Of Prince Henry. London, 1612. [STC 13158]

Magdalen College, Oxford. *Lvctvs Posthvmvs Sive Erga Defvnctvm Illvstrissimvm Henricvm Walliæ Principem, Collegij Beatæ Mariæ Magdalenæ apud Oxonienses Mecænatem longè indulgentissimum, Magdalenensium officiosa Pietas.* Oxford, 1612. [STC 19047]

Mavsolevm or, The Choisest Flowres of the Epitaphs, written on the Death of the neuertoo-much-lamented Prince Henrie. Edinburgh, 1613. [STC 13160]

Oxford University. *Eidyllia In Obitvm Fvlgentissimi Henrici Walliae Principis duodecimi, Romæq; ruentis Terroris maximi.* Oxford, 1612. [STC 19020]

Oxford University. *Ivsta Oxoniensivm.* London, 1612. [STC 19021, 19021.5]

Tourneur, Cyril, John Webster, and Thomas Heywood. *Three Elegies on the most lamented Death of Prince Henrie, the first written by Cyril Tourneur. The second Iohn Webster. The third Tho: Heywood.* London, 1613. [STC 24151]

References

Titles of early printed books (to 1800) are transcribed from physical copies, *Short-Title Catalogue* microfilms, or *Early English Books Online* images; they are capitalized to follow early print conventions of emphasis in the first instance, and modern title-case conventions in the second. Most include the book's principal title only; full titles are transcribed when they address pertinent contexts. Their place of publication is London unless otherwise noted. For full titles of elegies and other verses on the death of Henry, Prince of Wales, see the Appendix.

Alexander, Gavin. *Writing After Sidney: The Literary Response to Sir Philip Sidney, 1586–1640*. Oxford: Clarendon Press, 2006.

Alexander, William, Earl of Stirling. *A Paraenesis to the Prince*. 1604.

Allen, Elizabeth. *False Fables and Exemplary Truth in Later Middle English Literature*. New York: Palgrave Macmillan, 2005.

Allyne, Robert. *Funerall elegies vpon the most lamentable and vntimely death of the thrice illustrious Prince Henry, Prince of VVales, &c.* 1613.

Alpers, Paul. *What is Pastoral?* Chicago and London: University of Chicago Press, 1996.

Altman, Joel B. *The Improbability of Othello: Rhetorical Anthropology and Shakespearean Selfhood*. Chicago: University of Chicago Press, 2010.

Anderson, Randall. 'The Rhetoric of Paratext in Early Printed Books.' In *The Cambridge History of the Book in Britain, 1557–1695*, ed. John Barnard and D. F. McKenzie. (Cambridge: Cambridge University Press, 2002), 636–44.

Anderson, Thomas P. '"We Cannot say Hee's Dead": Writing Royal Effigies in Marvell's Poetry.' *English Literary Renaissance* 35, no. 3 (2005): 507–31. doi:10.1111/j.1475–6757.2005.00069.x.

Anon. *The Life and Death of Iacke Straw, A notable Rebell in England: Who was kild in Smithfield by the Lord Maior of London*. 1593.

Anon. *Great Brittans Mourning Garment. Given to all faithfull sorrowfull Subiects at the Funerall Of Prince Henry*. 1612.

Anon. *Mavsolevm or, The Choisest Flowres of the Epitaphs, written on the Death of the neuer-too-much-lamented Prince Henrie*. 1613.

Anon. *Fvnerals of the High and Mighty Prince Henry, Prince of Wales, Duke of Cornewaile and Rothsay, Count Palatine of Chester, Earle of Carick, and late Knight of the most Noble Order of the Garter. [V]Vhich Noble Prince deceased at S. James, the sixt day of Nouember, 1612. and was most Princely interred the seuenth day of December following, within the Abbey of Westminster, in the Eighteenth yeere of his age.* 1613.

Anon. *The Secret History of the Court Of the Emperor Justinian. Written by Procopius of Cesarea; Faithfully rendred into English.* 1674.

Archer, Harriet and Andrew Hadfield, eds. *'A Mirror for Magistrates' in Context: Literature, History and Politics in Early Modern England*. Cambridge: Cambridge University Press, 2016.

Archer, Harriet. *Unperfect Histories: The Mirror for Magistrates, 1559–1610*. Oxford: Oxford University Press, 2017.

Aristotle. *Rhetorica*, tr. W. Rhys Roberts. Oxford: Clarendon Press, 1924.

Aristotle. *On Rhetoric: A Theory of Civic Discourse*, tr. George A. Kennedy. New York: Oxford University Press, 1991.

Arrian of Nicomedia. *Anabasis*, tr. Aubrey de Sélincourt. London: Penguin, 1971.

Ascham, Roger. *The Scholemaster Or plaine and perfite way of teachyng children, to vnderstand, write, and speake, the Latin tong, but specially purposed for the priuate brynging vp of youth in Ientlemen and Noble mens houses, and commodious also for all such, as haue forgot the Latin tonge, and would, by themselues, without à Scholemaster, in short tyme, and with small paines, recouer à sufficient habilitie, to vnderstand, write, and speake Latin*. 1570.

Ashton, Robert, ed. *James I by his Contemporaries: An Account of his Career and Character as Seen by some of his Contemporaries*, London: Hutchinson, 1969.

Attridge, Derek. *Peculiar Language: Literature as Difference from the Renaissance to James Joyce*. London: Methuen, 1988.

B., G. *'Cestria Lugens': A Collection of Epitaphs and Elegies on Prince Henry by one 'G. B.'*, ed. Dennis Kay. In *Melodious Tears: The English Funeral Elegy from Spenser to Milton* (Oxford: Clarendon Press, 1990), Appendix A. 233–50.

B., I. *An English Expositor: Teaching the interpretation of the hardest words vsed in our Language. With svndry Explications, Descriptions, and Discourses*. 1616.

B., O. *Qvestions of Profitable and Pleasant Concernings*. 1594.

Backus, Irena. *Life Writing in Reformation Europe: Lives of Reformers by Friends, Disciples and Foes*. Aldershot: Ashgate, 2008.

Bacon, Francis. *The VVisedome of the Ancients, written in Latine By the right Honourable Sir Francis Bacon Knight, Baron of Verulam, and Lord Chancelor of England*, tr. Arthur Gorges. 1619.

Bacon, Francis. *In Henricum Principem Walliae Elogium Francisci Bacon*, ed. James Spedding, Robert Leslie Ellis, and Douglas Heath. *The Works of Francis Bacon* (Boston: Brown of Taggard, 1860), 15–22.

Bacon, Francis. *The Essays*, ed. John Pitcher. London: Penguin Books, 1985.

Bacon, Francis. *The Advancement of Learning*, ed. Michael Kiernan. Oxford and New York: Clarendon Press, 2000.

Badenhausen, Richard. 'Disarming the Infant Warrior: Prince Henry, King James, and the Chivalric Revival.' *Papers on Language and Literature* 31, no. 1 (1995): 20–37.

Barbour, Reid. 'Peele, George (bap. 1556, d. 1596).' *Oxford Dictionary of National Biography*. Oxford: Oxford University Press, 2004.

Barroll, J. Leeds. *Anna of Denmark, Queen of England: A Cultural Biography*. Philadelphia: University of Pennsylvania Press, 2001.

Basse, William. *Great Brittaines Svnnes-Set, Bewailed with a Shower of Teares*. 1613.

Bednarz, James. 'Imitations of Spenser in *A Midsummer Night's Dream*.' *Renaissance Drama* 14 (1983): 79–102. doi:10.1086/rd.14.41917202.

Beier, Lucinda McCray. *Sufferers and Healers: The Experience of Illness in Seventeenth-Century England*. London: Routledge, 1987.

Beier, Lucinda McCray. 'The Good Death in Seventeenth-Century England.' In *Death, Ritual, and Bereavement*, ed. Ralph Houlbrooke (London: Routledge, 1989), 43–61.

Berger, Harry, Jr. *Revisionary Play: Studies in the Spenserian Dynamics*. Berkeley: University of California Press, 1988.

Berger, Harry, Jr. 'Narrative as Rhetoric in *The Faerie Queene*.' *English Literary Renaissance* 21, no. 1 (1991): 3–48. doi:10.1111/j.1475-6757.1991.tb01017.x.

Bergeron, David. 'The Emblematic Nature of English Civic Pageantry.' *Renaissance Drama* NS 1 (1968): 167–98. doi:10.1086/rd.1.41917414.

Bergeron, David. 'Symbolic Landscape in English Civic Pageantry.' *Renaissance Quarterly* 22, no. 1 (1969): 32–7. doi:10.2307/2858977.

Bergeron, David. *Shakespeare's Romances and the Royal Family*. Lawrence: University of Kansas Press, 1985.

Bergeron, David. *English Civic Pageantry, 1558–1642*. Tempe: Arizona Center for Medieval and Renaissance Studies, 2003.

Birch, Thomas. *The Life of Henry Prince of Wales, Eldest Son of King James I. Compiled chiefly from his own Papers, and other Manuscripts, never before published*. 1760.

Birrell, T. A. *English Monarchs and their Books: From Henry VII to Charles II*. London: British Library, 1987.

Blaine, Marlin E. 'Drayton's Agincourt in 1606: History, Genre, and National Consciousness.' In *Renaissance Papers*, ed. George Walton Williams and Philip Rollinson (Columbia: Camden House, 1996), 53–65.

Blair, Ann M. *Too Much to Know: Managing Scholarly Information before the Modern Age*. New Haven and London: Yale University Press, 2010.

Blayney, Peter W. M. 'Nothing Succeeds like Succession: The Runaway Bestseller of 1603.' Wahington, DC: Unpublished presentation, Folger Shakespeare Library, 2001.

Bloomer, W. Martin. *Valerius Maximus and the Rhetoric of the New Nobility*. Chapel Hill: University of North Carolina Press, 1992.

Boccaccio, Giovanni. *Genealogy of the Pagan Gods*, ed. Jon Solomon. I Tatti Renaissance Library. Cambridge and London: Harvard University Press, 2011.

Booth, Stephen. *Shakespeare's Sonnets*. New Haven and London: Yale University Press, 1977.

Borris, Kenneth. *Allegory and Epic in English Renaissance Literature*. Cambridge: Cambridge University Press, 2000.

Bos, Sander, Marianne Lange-Meyers, and Jeanine Six. 'Sidney's Funeral Portrayed.' In *Sir Philip Sidney: 1586 and the Creation of a Legend*, ed. Jan van Dorsten, Dominic Baker-Smith, and Arthur F. Kinney (Leiden: Leiden University Press, 1986), 37–67.

Bradford, Alan T. 'Stuart Absolutism and the "Utility" of Tacitus.' *Huntington Library Quarterly* 46 (1983): 127–55. doi:10.2307/3817324.

Brady, Andrea. *English Funerary Elegy in the Seventeenth Century*. New York: Palgrave Macmillan, 2006.

Brathwaite, Richard. *The Schollers Medley, or, An Intermixt Discourse Vpon Historicall and Poeticall Relations*. 1614.

Bright, Timothie. *An Abridgement of the booke of Acts and Monumentes of the Church: Written by that Reuerend Father, Maister Iohn Fox: and now abridged by Timothe Bright, Doctour of Phisicke, for such as either through want of leysure, or abilitie haue not the vse of so necessary an history*. 1589.

Brooke, Christopher, and William Browne. *Two Elegies, Consecrated to the Never-dying Memorie of the most worthily admyred; most hartily loued; and generally bewayled Prince; Henry Prince of Wales*. 1613.

Brown, Rawdon and G. Cavendish Bentinck. eds. *Calendar of State Papers and Manuscripts Relating to English Affairs Existing in the Archives and Collections of Venice*. London: H. M. Stationery Office, 1864–1947.

Brown, Richard Danson. *'The New Poet': Novelty and Tradition in Spenser's Complaints*. Liverpool: Liverpool University Press, 1999.

Browne, Thomas. *Religio Medici*, ed. Geoffrey Keynes. *The Works of Sir Thomas Browne* (London: Faber & Faber, 1964), 1–93.

Browne, William. *Britannia's Pastorals*. 1616.

Bruner, Jerome. 'Narrative and Paradigmatic Modes of Thought.' In *Learning and Teaching: The Ways of Knowing*, ed. Elliot Eisner (Chicago: University of Chicago Press, 1985), 97–115.

Bruni, Leonardo. *The Humanism of Leonardo Bruni: Selected Texts*. Binghampton: Medieval and Renaissance Texts and Studies, 1987.

Brydges, Egerton. *Restituta: or Titles, Extracts, and Characters of Old Books in English Literature, revived*. London: T. Bensley & Son, 1814–16.

Buchtel, John A. 'Book Dedications and the Death of a Patron: The Memorial Engraving in Chapman's Homer.' *Book History* 7 (2004): 1–29. doi:10.1353/bh.2004.0015.

Budra, Paul. *A Mirror for Magistrates and the de Casibus Tradition*. Toronto: University of Toronto Press, 2000.

Burke, Peter. 'Tacitism, Scepticism, and Reason of State.' In *The Cambridge History of Political Thought 1450–1700*, ed. J. H. Burns. (Cambridge: Cambridge University Press, 1991), 479–98.

Burrow, Colin. *Epic Romance: Homer to Milton*. Oxford: Clarendon Press, 1993.

Burrow, Colin. *Imitating Authors: Plato to Futurity*. Oxford: Oxford University Press, 2019.

Burton, Robert. *The Anatomy of Melancholy*, ed. Thomas C. Faulkner, Nicolas K. Kiessling, and Rhonda L. Blair. Oxford and New York: Oxford University Press, 1989.

Bushnell, Rebecca. *A Culture of Teaching: Early Modern Humanism in Theory and Practice*. Ithaca: Cornell University Press, 1996.

Buxton, John. 'Mourning for Sidney.' *Renaissance Studies* 3, no. 1 (1989): 46–56. doi:10.1353/bh.2004.0015.

C., W. *False Complaints. Or The Censure of an vnthankfull mind*. 1605.

Campana, Joseph. 'On Not Defending Poetry: Spenser, Suffering, and the Energy of Affect.' *PMLA: Publications of the Modern Language Association of America* 120, no. 1 (2005): 33–48. doi:10.1632/003081205X36840.

Chaghafi, Elizabeth. *English Literary Afterlives: Greene, Sidney, Donne and the Evolution of Posthumous Fame*. Manchester: Manchester University Press, 2019.

Chaloner, Thomas. 'Letter to Gilbert Talbot, seventh earl of Shrewsbury.' (28 September 1603).

Chaney, Edward. 'Robert Dallington's *Survey of Tuscany* (1605): A British View of Medicean Florence.' In *The Evolution of the Grand Tour*, edited by Edward Chaney. (London: Frank Cass, 1998), 143–60.

Chapman, George. *An Epicede or Funerall Song: On the most disastrous Death, of the High-borne Prince of Men, Henry Prince of Wales, &c. With The Funeralls, and Representation of the Herse of the same High and mighty Prince*. 1613.

Chapman, George. *The Iliad*, ed. Allardyce Nicoll. *Chapman's Homer*. Bollingen Series XLI. Princeton: Princeton University Press, 1956.

Chassanion, Jean de. *The Theatre of Gods Iudgements: Or, a Collection of Histories Out of Sacred, Ecclesiasticall, and prophane Authours, concerning the admirable Iudgements of God vpon the transgressours of his commandements*, trans. Thomas Beard. 1597.

Chetwynd, Edward. *Votiuæ Lachrymæ. A vovv of teares, For the losse of Prince Henry. In a sermon preached in the Citie of Bristol December 7. 1612. being the day of his Funerall*. 1612.

Christian, Margaret. ' "The ground of Storie": Genealogy in *The Faerie Queene*.' In *Spenser Studies: A Renaissance Poetry Annual IX*, ed. Patrick Cullen and Thomas P. Roche Jr (New York: AMS Press, 1991), 61–79.

Cicero, Marcus Tullius. *Pro Archia Poeta. The Speeches*, tr. N. H. Watts. London: Heinemann, 1961.

Cicero, Marcus Tullius. *De inventione*, tr. Harry Mortimer Hubbell. Cambridge: Harvard University Press, 1968.

Clegg, Cyndia Susan. *Press Censorship in Elizabethan England*. Cambridge and New York: Cambridge University Press, 1997.

Clegg, Cyndia Susan. 'Archival Poetics and the Politics of Literature: Essex and Hayward Revisited.' *Studies in the Literary Imagination* 32 (1999): 115–32.

Clegg, Cyndia Susan. *Press Censorship in Jacobean England*. Cambridge and New York: Cambridge University Press, 2001.

Clegg, Cyndia Susan. *Press Censorship in Caroline England*. Cambridge and New York: Cambridge University Press, 2008.

Cleland, James. *Hērō-paideia, or the Institvtion of a Yovng Noble Man*. 1607.

Clode, Charles. *Memorials of the Guild of Merchant Taylors*. London: Harrison & Sons, 1875.

Cohen, Stephen. *Shakespeare and Historical Formalism*. Aldershot: Ashgate, 2007.

Coke, Roger. *A Detection of the Court and State of England during The Four last Reigns, and the Inter-regnum. Consisting of Private Memoirs, &c. With Observations and Reflections*. 1694.

Coke, Roger. *A Detection of the Court and State of England, During the Reigns of K. James I. Charles I. Charles II. and James II. As also the Inter-regnum. Consisting of Private Memoirs, &c. with Observations and Reflections. Wherein are many Secrets never before made publick: As also, a more impartial Account of the Civil Wars in England, than has yet been given*. 1719.

Colonna, Francesco. *Hypnerotomachia. The Strife of Loue in a Dreame*, tr. Robert Dallington. 1592.

Combe, Kirk. 'The New Voice of Political Dissent: The Transition from Complaint to Satire.' In *Theorizing Satire: Essays in Literary Criticism*, ed. Brian A. Connery and Kirk Combe. (New York: St Martin's Press, 1995), 73–94.

Connor, Francis X. "Delivering Forth': Philip Sidney's Idea and the Labor of Writing.' *Sidney Journal* 31, no. 2 (2013): 53–75.

Coperario, John. *Songs of Mourning: Bevvailing the vntimely death of Prince Henry. VVorded by Tho. Campion. And set forth to bee sung with one voyce to the Lute, or Violl: By Iohn Coprario*. (1613).

Cornwallis, Charles. *A Discourse of the most Illustrious Prince, Henry, Late Prince of Wales. Written Anno 1626. by Sir Charles Cornwallis, Knight, sometimes Treasurer of his Highnesse House*. 1641.

Cotgrave, Randle. *A Dictionarie of the French and English Tongves*. 1611.

Craik, Katharine A. 'Spenser's "Complaints" and the New Poet.' *Huntington Library Quarterly* 64, no. 1/2 (2001): 63–79. doi:10.2307/3817877.

Crane, Mary Thomas. *Framing Authority: Sayings, Self, and Society in Sixteenth-Century England*. Princeton: Princeton University Press, 1993.

Cressy, David. *Birth, Marriage, and Death: Ritual, Religion, and the Life-Cycle in Tudor and Stuart England*. Oxford: Oxford University Press, 1997.

Cressy, David. *Bonfires and Bells: National Memory and the Protestant Calendar in Elizabethan and Stuart England*. Stroud: Sutton, 2004.

Cuddy, Neil. 'Reinventing a Monarchy: The Changing Structure and Political Function of the Stuart Court, 1603–88.' In *The Stuart Courts*, ed. Eveline Cruickshanks. (Stroud: Sutton, 2000), 59–85.

Curran, John. 'Despaire and Briton Moniments: Moments of Protestant Clarity in *The Faerie Queene*.' *Reformation* 25, no. 2 (2020): 175–91. doi:10.1080/13574175.2020.1824708.

D'Alton, J. F. *Roman Literary Theory and Criticism: A Study in Tendencies*. London: Longman, 1931.

Dallington, Robert. *Aphorismes Civill and Militarie*. 1613.

Daniel, Samuel. *A Panegyrike Congratvlatorie to the Kings Maiestie*. 1603.

Daniel, Samuel. *Certaine Small Workes heretofore divulged by Samuel Daniell*. 1611.

Darnton, Robert. *The Devil in the Holy Water, or the Art of Slander from Louis XIV to Napoleon*. Philadelphia: University of Pennsylvania Press, 2009.

Davies, John. *The Mvses Sacrifice*. 1612.

Davies, John. *The Mvses-Teares for the losse of their hope; heroick and ne're-too-mvch praised, Henry, Prince of Wales. &c. Together with Times Sobs for the vntimely death of his Glory in that his Darling: and lastly, his Epitaphs. Consecrated To the high and mighty Prince, Frederick the fift, Count-palatine of Rheyn, &c. Where-vnto is added, Consolatory Straines to wrest Natvre from her bent in immoderate mourning; most loyally, and humbly wisht to the King and Qveenes most exeellent* [sic] *Maiesties*. 1613.

Davies, Richard. *A Fvnerall Sermon preached the XXVI. day of November in the yeare of ovr Lord M. D. LXXVI. in the parishe chvrch of Caermerthyn, by the Reverende Father in God, Richard by the permission of God, Bishoppe of Saint Dauys, at the buriall of The Right Honovrable VValter Earle of Essex and Ewe, Earle Marshall of Irelande, Viscovnt Hereforde & Bourgcher, Lord Ferrers of Chartley, Bourgcher & Louein, of the most Noble order of the Garter Knight*. 1577.

Davies, Richard. *Chesters Trivmph in Honor of her Prince*. 1610.

Davis, Natalie Zemon. 'Ghosts, Kin, and Progeny: Some Features of Family Life in Early Modern France.' *Daedalus* 106, no. 2 (1977): 87–114.

Davis, Rebecca A. '"Save man allone": Human Exceptionality in *Piers Plowman* and the Exemplarist Tradition.' In *Medieval Latin and Middle English Literature: Essays in Honour of Jill Mann*, ed. Christopher Cannon and Maura Nolan. (Cambridge: D. S. Brewer, 2011), 41–64.

Davison, Francis. *A Poetical Rapsody Containing, Diuerse Sonnets, Odes, Elegies, Madrigalls, and other Poesies, both in Rime, and Measured Verse*. 1602.

de Man, Paul. *The Rhetoric of Romanticism*. New York: Columbia University Press, 1984.

Dekker, Thomas. *Foure Birds of Noahs Arke: Viz. 1. The Dove. 2. The Eagle. 3. The Pellican. 4. The Phoenix*. 1609.

Dekker, Thomas. *Troia-Noua Triumphans. London Triumphing, or, The Solemne, Magnificent, and Memorable Receiuing of that worthy Gentleman, Sir Iohn Svvinerton Knight, into the Citty of London, after his Returne from taking the Oath of Maioralty at Westminster*. 1612.

Dickinson, Janet. *Court Politics and the Earl of Essex, 1589–1601*. London: Pickering & Chatto, 2012.

Doelman, James. "A King of Thine Own Heart': The English Reception of King James VI and I's *Basilikon Doron*.' *The Seventeenth Century* 9 (1994): 1–9. doi:10.1080/0268117X.1994.10555367.

Doelman, James. *The Daring Muse of the Early Stuart Funeral Elegy*. Manchester: Manchester University Press, 2021.

Dolan, John Carroll. *Poetic Occasion from Milton to Wordsworth*. Basingstoke: Palgrave Macmillan, 2000.

Dolven, Jeff. *Scenes of Instruction in Renaissance Romance*. Chicago: University of Chicago Press, 2007.

Donne, John. *An Anatomy of the World. Wherein, by occasion of the vntimely death of Mistris Elizabeth Drvry the frailty and the decay of this whole world is represented*. 1611.

Donne, John. *The First Anniuersarie. An Anatomie of the VVorld. Wherein, By Occasion Of the vntimely death of Mistris Elizabeth Drvry, the frailtie and the decay of this whole World is represented.* 1612.

Donne, John. *The Poems of John Donne*, ed. Herbert John Clifford Grierson. London: Oxford University Press, 1966.

Dowd, Michelle M., and Julie A. Eckerle. 'Recent Studies in Early Modern English Life Writing.' *English Literary Renaissance* 40, no. 1 (2010): 132–62. doi:10.1111/j.1475–6757.2009.01064.x.

Drayton, Michael. *The Works of Michael Drayton*, ed. J. William Hebel, Kathleen Tillotson, and Bernard H. Newdigate. 5 vols. Oxford: Published for the Shakespeare Head Press by B. Blackwell, 1961.

Drummond, William. *Teares on the Death of Meliades.* 1613.

Dubrow, Heather. 'The Arraignment of Paridell: Tudor Historiography in *The Faerie Queene*, III.ix.' *Studies in Philology* 87, no. 3 (1990): 312–27.

Duchesne, Joseph. *The Sclopotarie of Iosephus Quercetanus, Phisition. Or His booke containing the cure of wounds receiued by shot of Gunne or such like Engines of warre*, trans. John Hester. 1590.

Duffy, Eamon. *The Stripping of the Altars: Traditional Religion in England, c.1400–c.1580.* New Haven: Yale University Press, 2005.

Duffy, Eamon. 'Common Thoughts.' *London Review of Books* 31, no. 14 (23 July 2009): 18–19.

Dugdale, Gilbert. *The Time Triumphant.* 1604.

Duncan-Jones, Katherine. *Sir Philip Sidney: Courtier Poet.* New Haven: Yale University Press, 1991.

Dzelzainis, Martin. 'Shakespeare and Political Thought.' In *A Companion to Shakespeare*, ed. David Scott Kastan (Malden: Blackwell, 1999), 100–16.

Edmond, John Philip. 'Elegies and Other Tracts Issued on the Death of Henry, Prince of Wales, 1612.' *Publications of the Edinburgh Bibliographical Society* 6 (1901–4; published 1906): 141–58.

Eisenstein, Elizabeth L. *The Printing Revolution in Early Modern Europe.* New York: Cambridge University Press, 2012.

Elyot, Thomas. *The Dictionary of Syr Thomas Eliot Knyght.* 1538.

Elyot, Thomas. *A Critical Edition of Sir Thomas Elyot's* The Boke Named The Governour, ed. Donald Warren Rude. New York: Garland, 1992.

Emerton, Ephraim. *Humanism and Tyranny: Studies in the Italian Trecento.* Cambridge: Harvard University Press, 1925.

Engel, William E. *Death and Drama in Renaissance England: Shades of Memory.* Oxford: Oxford University Press, 2002.

Epicedium Cantabrigiense, in Obitum Immaturum, Semperq[ue] Deflendum, Henrici, Illustrissimi Principis Walliae, &c. Cambridge: 1612.

Erasmus, Desiderius. *Copia: Foundations of the Abundant Style [De duplici copia verborum ac rerum commentaris duo]*, tr. Betty I. Knott. Toronto: University of Toronto Press, 1978.

Erasmus, Desiderius. *The Education of a Christian Prince*, tr. Neil M. Cheshire and Michael J. Heath. Cambridge: Cambridge University Press, 1997.

Erasmus, Desiderius. *The Adages of Erasmus*, tr. William Barker. Toronto: University of Toronto Press, 2001.

Ercole, Francesco. *La politica di Machiavelli.* Rome: Anonima Romana Editoriale, 1926.

Escobedo, Andrew. *Nationalism and Historical Loss in Renaissance England: Foxe, Dee, Spenser, Milton.* Ithaca and London: Cornell University Press, 2004.

Falco, Raphael. *Conceived Presences: Literary Genealogy in Renaissance England*. Amherst: University of Massachusetts Press, 1994.

Feingold, Mordechai. 'Scholarship and Politics: Henry Savile's Tacitus and the Essex Connection.' *Review of English Studies* 67, no. 282 (2016): 855–74. doi:10.1093/res/hgw079.

Fennor, William. *Fennors Descriptions, or a Trve Relation of Certaine and diuers speeches, spoken before the King and Queenes most excellent Maiestie, the Prince his highnesse, and the Lady Elizabeth's grace*. 1616.

Ferguson, Arthur. *The Chivalric Tradition in Renaissance England*. London: Associated University Presses, 1986.

Ferguson, Arthur. *Clio Unbound: Perception of the Social and Cultural Past in Renaissance England*. Durham: Duke University Press, 1979.

Fichter, Andrew. *Poets Historical: Dynastic Epic in the Renaissance*. New Haven: Yale University Press, 1982.

Fineman, Joel. 'The History of the Anecdote: Fiction and Fiction.' In *The New Historicism*, ed. H. Aram Veeser (New York: Routledge, 1994), 49–76.

Finnegan, Ruth. *Why do we Quote? The Culture and History of Quotation*. Cambridge: Open Book, 2011.

Fischer, Steven R. *A History of Reading*. London: Reaktion, 2003.

Fish, Stanley Eugene. *Is there a Text in This Class? The Authority of Interpretive Communities*. Cambridge: Harvard University Press, 1980.

Fitzgeffrey, Charles. *Satyres and Satyricall Epigrams*. 1617.

Fletcher, Robert. *The Nine English Worthies: Or, Famous and Worthy Princes of England being all of one name; Beginning with King Henrie the first, and Concluding with Prince Henry, eldest Sonne to our Soueraigne Lord the King*. 1606.

Ford, Emanuel. *Parismus, the Renoumed Prince of Bohemia. His Most Famous, Delectable, and Pleasant Historie*. 1598.

Ford, Emanuel. *The Most Pleasant Historie of Ornatus and Artesia*. 1607.

Fox, Alistair. 'The Complaint of Poetry for the Death of Liberality: The Decline of Literary Patronage in the 1590s.' In *The Reign of Elizabeth I: Court and Culture in the Last Decade*, ed. John Guy (Cambridge: Cambridge University Press, 1995), 229–57.

Foxe, John. *Foxe's Book of Martyrs: Select Narratives*, ed. John N. King. Oxford and New York: Oxford University Press, 2009.

Frazier, Alison K. 'Biography as a Genre of Moral Philosophy.' In *Rethinking Virtue, Reforming Society: New Directions in Renaissance Ethics, c.1350–c.1650*, ed. David A. Lines and Sabrina Ebbersmeyer (Turnhout: Brepols, 2013), 215–40.

Freedman, Aviva, and Peter Medway. *Genre and the New Rhetoric*. London: Taylor & Francis, 1994.

Frye, Northrop. *Anatomy of Criticism: Four Essays*. Princeton: Princeton University Press, 1957.

Gajda, Alexandra. *The Earl of Essex and Late Elizabethan Political Culture*. Oxford: Oxford University Press, 2012.

Galbraith, David. *Architectonics of Imitation in Spenser, Daniel, and Drayton*. Toronto: University of Toronto Press, 2000.

Gallagher, Catherine, and Stephen Greenblatt. *Practicing New Historicism*. Chicago: University of Chicago Press, 2000.

Garbero, Maria Del Sapio, ed. *Identity, Otherness and Empire in Shakespeare's Rome*. Farnham: Ashgate, 2009.

Gazzard, Hugh. 'The Patronage of Robert Devereux, Second Earl of Essex, c.1577–1696.' Diss., University of Oxford, 2000.

Gelley, Alexander, ed. *Unruly Examples: On the Rhetoric of Exemplarity*. Stanford: Stanford University Press, 1995.

Genette, Gérard. 'Introduction to the Paratext.' *New Literary History* 22, no. 2 (1991): 261–72. doi:10.2307/469037.

Gibson, John. *The Sacred Shield of Al Trve Christian Sovldiers*. 1599.

Gibson, Jonathan. 'Sir Arthur Gorges (1557–1625) and the Patronage System.' Diss., University of London, 1998.

Gittings, C. 'Sacred and Secular: 1558–1660.' In *Death in England: An Illustrated History*, (Manchester: Manchester University Press, 2000), 147–73.

Glaisyer, Natasha, and Sara. Pennell. *Didactic Literature in England, 1500–1800: Expertise Constructed*. Aldershot and Burlington: Ashgate, 2003.

Goldring, Elizabeth. '"So iust a sorrowe so well expressed": Henry, Prince of Wales and the Art of Commemoration.' In *Prince Henry Revived: Image and Exemplarity in Early Modern England*, ed. Timothy V. Wilks (London: Paul Holberton, 2007), 280–300.

Gorges, Arthur. *The Olympian Catastrophe*, ed. Helen Estabrook Sandison. In *The Poems of Sir Arthur Gorges* (Oxford: Clarendon Press, 1953), 135–82.

Gossman, Lionel. 'Anecdote and History.' *History and Theory: Studies in the Philosophy of History* 42 (2003): 143–168.

Grafton, Anthony. 'Renaissance Readers and Ancient Texts: Comments on Some Commentaries.' *Renaissance Quarterly* 38 (1985): 615–49. doi:10.2307/2861952.

Grafton, Anthony. *Commerce with the Classics: Ancient Books and Renaissance Readers*. Ann Arbor: University of Michigan Press, 1997.

Grafton, Anthony. 'The Humanist as Reader.' In *A History of Reading in the West*, ed. Guglielmo Cavallo and Roger Chartier (Cambridge: Polity Press, 1999), 179–212.

Grafton, Anthony, and Lisa Jardine. *From Humanism to the Humanities: Education and the Liberal Arts in Fifteenth- and Sixteenth-Century Europe*. London: Duckworth, 1986.

Gray, Hanna H. 'Renaissance Humanism: The Pursuit of Eloquence.' *Journal of the History of Ideas* 24 (1963): 497–514. doi:10.2307/2707980.

Greenblatt, Stephen. 'Marlowe and Renaissance Self-Fashioning.' In *Two Renaissance Mythmakers, Christopher Marlowe and Ben Jonson*, ed. Alvin B. Kernan (Baltimore: Johns Hopkins University Press, 1977), 41–69.

Greenblatt, Stephen. *Renaissance Self-Fashioning: From More to Shakespeare*. Chicago: University of Chicago Press, 1980.

Greenblatt, Stephen. *Shakespearean Negotiations: The Circulation of Social Energy in Renaissance England*. Berkeley: University of California Press, 1988.

Greenblatt, Stephen. *Marvelous Possessions: The Wonder of the New World*. Oxford: Clarendon Press, 1991.

Greenblatt, Stephen. 'The Touch of the Real.' *Representations* 59 (1997): 14–29. doi:10.2307/2928812.

Greene, Thomas. 'The Flexibility of the Self in Renaissance Literature.' In *The Disciplines of Criticism: Essays in Literary Theory, Interpretation, and History*, ed. Peter Demetz, Thomas Greene, and Lowry Nelson Jr (New Haven and London: Yale University Press, 1968), 241–64.

Greene, Thomas. 'Erasmus's "Festina lente": Vulnerabilities of the Humanist Text.' In *Mimesis: From Mirror to Method, Augustine to Descartes*, ed. John D. Lyons and Stephen G. Nichols Jr (Hanover: University Press of New England, 1982), 132–48.

Greenfield, Matthew. 'The Cultural Functions of Renaissance Elegy.' *English Literary History* 28, no. 1 (1998): 75–94. doi:10.1111/j.1475–6757.1998.tb01119.x.

Greville, Fulke. *The Life Of the Renowned Sr Philip Sidney. with The true Interest of England as it then stood in relation to all Forrain Princes: And particularly for suppressing the power of Spain Stated by Him. His principall Actions, Counsels, Designes, and Death. Together with a short Account of the Maximes and Policies used by Queen Elizabeth in her Government.* 1651.

Greville, Fulke. *A Dedication to Sir Philip Sidney*, ed. John Gouws. In *The Prose Works of Fulke Greville, Lord Brooke* (Oxford: Clarendon Press, 1986). 3–135.

Griffin, Benjamin. *Playing the Past: Approaches to English Historical Drama, 1385–1600.* Woodbridge: D. S. Brewer, 2001.

Grogan, Jane. *Exemplary Spenser: Visual and Poetic Pedagogy in The Faerie Queene* (Farnham and Burlington: Ashgate, 2009).

Guarino, Battista. *A Program of Teaching and Learning*, ed. Craig W. Kallendorf. *Humanist Educational Treatises* (Cambridge: Harvard University Press, 2002), 260–309.

Guy-Bray, Stephen. *Against Reproduction: Where Renaissance Texts Come From.* Toronto: University of Toronto Press, 2009.

Hager, Alan. 'The Exemplary Mirage: Fabrication of Sir Philip Sidney's Biographical Image and the Sidney Reader.' *English Literary History* 48, no. 1 (1981): 1–16. doi:10.2307/2873009.

Hall, Joseph. *The Works of Ioseph Hall Doctor in Diuinitie, and Deane of Worcester.* 1625.

Halpern, Richard. *The Poetics of Primitive Accumulation: English Renaissance Culture and the Genealogy of Capital.* Ithaca and London: Cornell University Press, 1991.

Hamilton, A. C., Donald Cheney, W. F. Blissett, David A. Richardson, and William W. Barker, eds. *The Spenser Encyclopedia.* Toronto: University of Toronto Press, 1997.

Hammer, Paul E. 'The Earl of Essex, Fulke Greville, and the Employment of Scholars.' *Studies in Philology* 91 (1994): 167–80.

Hammer, Paul E. *The Polarisation of Elizabethan Politics: The Political Career of Robert Devereux, 2nd Earl of Essex, 1585–1597.* Cambridge: Cambridge University Press, 1999.

Hammer, Paul E. 'Devereux, Robert, Second Earl of Essex (1565–1601).' *Oxford Dictionary of National Biography* (Oxford: Oxford University Press, 2004).

Hampton, Timothy. *Writing from History: The Rhetoric of Exemplarity in Renaissance Literature.* Ithaca: Cornell University Press, 1990.

Hampton, Timothy. 'Examples, Stories, and Subjects in *Don Quixote* and the *Heptameron*.' *Journal of the History of Ideas* 59, no. 4 (1998): 597–611. doi:10.1353/jhi.1998.0037.

Hardison, O. B. *The Enduring Monument: A Study of the Idea of Praise in Renaissance Literary Theory and Practice.* Chapel Hill: University of North Carolina Press, 1962.

Harper, Carrie A. *Sources of British Chronicle History in Spenser's* Faerie Queene. Philadelphia: John C. Winston, 1910.

Hawkins, John. *The Life and Death of ovr Late most Incomparable and Heroique Prince, Henry Prince of Wales. A Prince (for Valour and Vertue) fit to be Imitated in Succeeding Times. Written by Sir Charles Cornwallis Knight, Treasurer of his Highnesse Houshold.* 1641.

Hawkins, John [attrib. Charles Cornwallis]. *The Short Life and Much lamented Death of that most magnanimous Prince, Henry, Prince of VVales. Wherein the whole manner of his life, and specially of his sicknesse, and cause of his death, is set forth at large. Written by Sir Charles Cornwallis, Treasurer of his Highnesse Houshold, a man very intimate with him in the whole course of his life, and at his death.* 1644.

Haydon, William. *The Trve Pictvre and Relation of Prince Henry His Noble and Vertuous disposition, containing Certaine Observations and Proofes of his towardly and notable Inclination to Vertue, of the Pregnancie of his Wit, farre above his Age, comprehended in sundry of his witty and pleasant Speaches. By W. H. With the true Relation of the Sicknesse and Death of the same most illustrious Prince, with the opening of his Body. Written by a famous Doctor of Physick in French, and newly translated into English.* 1634.

Hayward, John, Sir. *The first part of the life and raigne of King Henrie the IIII. Extending to the end of the first yeare of his raigne.* 1599.

Hayward, John. *The Lives of the III. Normans, Kings of England: William the first. William the second. Henrie the first.* 1613.

Hayward, John. *The First and Second Parts of John Hayward's The Life and Raigne of King Henrie IIII,* ed. John J. Manning (London: Royal Historical Society, 1991), 264.

Heaton, Gabriel, and James Knowles. ' "Entertainment Perfect": Ben Jonson and Corporate Hospitality.' *Review of English Studies* 54 (2003): 587–600. doi:10.1093/res/54.217.587.

Helfer, Rebeca. 'The Death of the "New Poete": Virgilian Ruin and Ciceronian Recollection in Spenser's "The Shepheardes Calender".' *Renaissance Quarterly* 56, no. 3 (2003): 723–56. doi:10.2307/1261612.

Helfer, Rebeca. 'Remembering Sidney, Remembering Spenser: The Art of Memory and *The Ruines of Time.*' *Spenser Studies: A Renaissance Poetry Annual* 22 (2007): 127–51. doi:10.1086/SPSv22p127.

Herbert, George. *Witts Recreations Selected from the finest Fancies of Moderne Muses. With A Thousand out Landish Proverbs.* 1640.

Herman, Peter. ' "Bastard Children of Tyranny": The Ancient Constitution and Fulke Greville's "A Dedication to Sir Philip Sidney".' *Renaissance Quarterly* 55, no. 3 (2002): 969–1004.

Heylin, Peter. *A Short View of the Life and Reign of King Charles, (The second Monarch of Great Britain) From his Birth to his Burial.* 1658.

Heywood, Thomas. *A Fvnerall Elegie, Vpon the death of the late most hopefull and illustrious Prince, Henry, Prince of Wales.* 1613.

Hobart, Michael E., and Zachary S. Schiffman. *Information Ages.* Baltimore: Johns Hopkins University Press, 2000.

Hockey, Susan. *Electronic Texts in the Humanities.* Oxford: Oxford University Press, 2000.

Höltgen, K. J. 'Sir Robert Dallington (1561–1637).' *Huntington Library Quarterly* 54 (1984): 147–77.

Horowitz, M. C. *Seeds of Virtue and Knowledge.* Princeton: Princeton University Press, 1998.

Hunt, William. 'Spectral Origins of the English Revolution: Legitimation Crisis in Early Stuart England.' In *Reviving the English Revolution: Reflections and Elaborations on the Work of Christopher Hill,* ed. Geoff Eley and William Hunt (London and New York: Verso, 1988), 305–32.

Huntington, John. 'Furious Insolence: The Social Meaning of Poetic Inspiration in the 1590s.' *Modern Philology* 3 (1997): 305–26. doi:10.1086/392404.

James VI and I. *Basilicon Doron,* ed. Johann P. Sommerville. Cambridge Texts in the History of Political Thought (Cambridge: Cambridge University Press, 1994), 1–61.

James, Heather. *Shakespeare's Troy: Drama, Politics, and the Translation of Empire.* Cambridge: Cambridge University Press, 1997.

James, Mervyn. *Society, Politics and Culture: Studies in Early Modern England.* Cambridge: Cambridge University Press, 1986.

Jardine, Lisa, and Anthony Grafton. '"Studied for Action": How Gabriel Harvey Read his Livy.' *Past and Present* 129 (1990): 30–78. doi:10.1093/past/129.1.30.

Jardine, Lisa, and William Sherman. 'Pragmatic Readers: Knowledge Transactions and Scholarly Services in Late Elizabethan England.' In *Religion, Culture and Society in Early Modern Britain: Essays in Honour of Patrick Collinson*, ed. Anthony Fletcher, Peter Roberts, and Patrick Collinson (Cambridge: Cambridge University Press, 1994), 103–24.

Jeanneret, Michel. *A Feast of Words: Banquets and Table Talk in the Renaissance*, tr. Jeremy Whiteley and Emma Hughes. Cambridge: Polity Press, 1991.

Jeanneret, Michel. 'The Vagaries of Exemplarity: Distortion or Dismissal?' *Journal of the History of Ideas* 59, no. 4 (1998): 565–79. doi:10.1353/jhi.1998.0038.

Johnson, Richard. *The second Part of the famous History of the seauen Champions of Christendome*. 1597.

Johnson, Robert. *A Remembrance of the Honors due to the Life and Death of Robert Earle of Salisbury, Lord Treasurer of England, &c.* 1612.

Johnson, Samuel. *The Lives of the English Poets*. 1781.

Jones, Emrys, ed. *The New Oxford Book of Sixteenth Century Verse*. Oxford: Oxford University Press, 1991.

Jonson, Ben. *Ben: Ionson his Volpone or the Foxe*. 1607.

Jonson, Ben. *Ben Jonson's Conversations with William Drummond of Hawthornden*, ed. R. F. Patterson. London: Blackie & Son, 1923, 1–58.

Jonson, Ben. *The Entertainment at Althorp*, ed. C. H. Herford, Percy Simpson, and Evelyn Simpson. Oxford: Clarendon Press, 1941, 7.119–31.

Jonson, Ben. *The Masque of Queens*, ed. C. H. Herford, Percy Simpson, and Evelyn Simpson. Oxford: Clarendon Press, 1941, 7.278–336.

Kahn, Victoria. *Rhetoric, Prudence, and Skepticism in the Renaissance*. Ithaca: Cornell University Press, 1985.

Kahn, Victoria. 'Humanism and the Resistance to Theory.' In *Literary Theory/Renaissance Texts*, ed. Patricia A. Parker and David Quint (Baltimore: Johns Hopkins University Press, 1986), 373–96.

Kallendorf, Craig W., ed. and tr. *Humanist Educational Treatises*. Cambridge: Harvard University Press, 2002.

Kastan, David Scott. 'Little Foxes.' In *John Foxe and his World*, ed. Christopher Highley and John N. King (Aldershot: Ashgate, 2002), 117–29.

Kay, Dennis. *Melodious Tears: The English Funeral Elegy from Spenser to Milton*. Oxford: Clarendon Press, 1990.

Kellwaye, Simon. *A Defensative against the Plague: Contayning two partes or treatises: the first, shewing the meanes how to preserue vs from the dangerous contagion thereof: the second, how to cure those that are infected therewith*. 1593.

Kelsey, Lin, and Richard Peterson. 'Rereading Colin's Broken Pipe: Spenser and the Problem of Patronage.' *Spenser Studies* 14 (2000): 233–72. doi:10.1086/SPSv14p233.

Kempe, William. *The Education of Children in Learning*. 1588.

Kietzman, Mary Jo. '"Means to Mourn Some Newer Way": The Role of the Complaint in Early-Modern Narrative.' Diss., Boston College, 1993.

King, John N. 'Traditions of Complaint and Satire.' In *A Companion to English Renaissance Literature and Culture*, ed. Michael Hattaway (Malden and Oxford: Blackwell, 2003), 367–77.

Kinney, Arthur. *Humanist Poetics: Thought, Rhetoric, and Fiction in Sixteenth-Century England*. Amherst: University of Massachusetts Press, 1986.

Kinney, Arthur. 'Essex and Shakespeare versus Hayward.' *Shakespeare Quarterly* 44, no. 4 (1993): 464–6. doi:10.2307/2871001.

Kristeller, Paul Oskar. *Renaissance Thought and the Arts: Collected Essays*. Princeton: Princeton University Press, 1990.

Kristeller, Paul Oskar. 'Humanism and Moral Philosophy.' In *Renaissance Humanism: Foundations, Forms, and Legacy*, ed. Albert Rabil Jr. (Philadelphia: University of Pennsylvania Press, 1988), 271–309.

Lamb, Julian. 'A Defense of Puttenham's *Arte of English Poesy.*' *English Literary Renaissance* 39, no. 1 (2009): 24–46. doi:10.1111/j.1475–6757.2009.01038.x.

Lanham, Richard. *A Handlist of Rhetorical Terms*. Berkeley and Los Angeles: University of California Press, 1991.

Larkin, James Francis, and Paul L. Hughes. *Stuart Royal Proclamations*. Oxford: Clarendon Press, 1973.

Lawrence, David. *The Complete Soldier: Military Books and Military Culture in Early Stuart England, 1603–1645*. Leiden: Brill, 2009.

Lemnius, Levinus. *The Touchstone of Complexions*. 1576.

Calendar of State Papers Domestic: Edward VI, Mary, Elizabeth, and James I, ed. R. Lemon and M. A. Everett Green. London: H. M. Stationery Office, 1856–72.

Levy, F. J. 'Hayward, Daniel, and the Beginnings of Politic History in England.' *Huntington Library Quarterly* 50, no. 1 (1987): 1–34. doi:10.2307/3817346.

Lezra, Jacques. *Unspeakable Subjects: The Genealogy of the Event in Early Modern Europe*. Stanford: Stanford University Press, 1997.

Lily, William. *Monarchy or No Monarchy in England*. 1651.

Lindsay, Barbara, and J. W. Williamson. 'Myth of the Conqueror: Prince Henry Stuart and Protestant Militancy.' *Journal of Medieval and Renaissance Studies* 5, no. 2 (1975): 203–22.

Litten, Julian. 'The Funeral Effigy: Its Function and Purpose.' In *The Funeral Effigies of Westminster Abbey*, ed. Anthony Harvey and Richard Mortimer (Woodbridge: Boydell Press, 1994), 3–19.

Llewellyn, Nigel. *The Art of Death: Visual Culture in the English Death Ritual, c.1500–c.1800*. London: Reaktion, 1991.

Lorenzo, Javier. 'Modeling the Self: Ontological and Political Uses of Exemplarity in Renaissance Literature.' Diss., Pennsylvania State University, 2000.

Lynch, Kathleen. *Protestant Autobiography in the Seventeenth-Century Anglophone World*. Oxford: Oxford University Press, 2012.

Lyons, John D. *Exemplum: The Rhetoric of Example in Early Modern France and Italy*. Princeton: Princeton University Press, 1989.

Machiavelli, Niccolò. *The Prince: A Revised Translation, Backgrounds, Interpretations, Marginalia*, tr. Robert Martin Adams. New York: Norton, 1992.

Mack, Peter. *Elizabethan Rhetoric: Theory and Practice*. Cambridge: Cambridge University Press, 2002.

Mack, Peter. *Reading and Rhetoric in Montaigne and Shakespeare*. London: Bloomsbury Academic, 2010.

Maclean, Hugh. '"Restlesse anguish and unquiet paine": Spenser and the Complaint, 1579–1590.' In *The Practical Vision: Essays in English Literature in Honour of Flora Roy*, ed. James Doyle, Flora Roy, and Jane Campbell (Waterloo: Wilfrid Laurier University Press, 1978), 29–47.

MacLean, Hugh. 'Complaints: *The Tears of the Muses.*' In *The Spenser Encyclopedia*, ed. A. C. Hamilton. (Toronto: University of Toronto Press, 1990), 182–3.

MacLeod, Catharine, Timothy Wilks, R. Malcolm Smuts, and Rab MacGibbon, eds. *The Lost Prince: The Life and Death of Henry Stuart*. London: National Portrait Gallery, 2012.

Manley, Lawrence. *Literature and Culture in Early Modern London*. Cambridge and New York: Cambridge University Press, 1995.

Mann, Jenny C. *Outlaw Rhetoric: Figuring Vernacular Eloquence in Shakespeare's England*. Ithaca: Cornell University Press, 2012.

Marcelline, George. *The Triumphs of King Iames the First, of Great Brittaine, France, and Ireland, King; Defender of the Faith*. 1610.

Markham, Gervase. *The English Arcadia, Alluding his beginning from Sir Philip Sydneys ending*. 1607.

Marshall, Peter. *Beliefs and the Dead in Reformation England*. Oxford: Oxford University Press, 2002.

Marston, John. *The Poems of John Marston*, ed. Arnold Davenport. Liverpool: Liverpool University Press, 1961.

Martin, Christopher. 'Sidney's Exemplary Horse Master and the Disciplines of Discontent.' In *Renaissance Historicisms: Essays in Honor of Arthur F. Kinney*, ed. James M. Dutcher and Anne Lake Prescott (Newark: University of Delaware Press, 2008), 85–102.

Martin, Jessica. *Walton's Lives: Conformist Commemorations and the Rise of Biography*. Oxford: Oxford University Press, 2001.

Mason, Thomas. *Christs Victorie Over Sathans Tyrannie. Wherein is contained a catalogve of all Christs faithfvll sovldiers that the Divell either by his grand Captaines the Emperovrs, or by his most deerly beloued sonnes and heyres the Popes, haue most cruelly Martyred for the Trvth. . . . Faithfully abstracted out of the Book of Martyrs, and diuers other Books*. 1615.

Matz, Robert. *Defending Literature in Early Modern England: Renaissance Literary Theory in Social Context*. Cambridge: Cambridge University Press, 2000.

Maus, Katharine Eisaman. *Inwardness and Theatre in the English Renaissance*. Chicago: University of Chicago Press, 1995.

Maxwell, James. *The Laudable Life, And Deplorable Death, of our late peerlesse Prince Henry. Briefly represented. Together, with some other Poemes, in honor both of our most gracious Soueraigne King Iames his auspicious entrie to this Crowne, and also of his most hopefull Children, Prince Charles and Princesse Elizabeths happy entrie into this world*. 1612.

Maza, Sarah. 'Stephen Greenblatt, New Historicism, and Cultural History, or, What we Talk about When we Talk about Interdisciplinarity.' *Modern Intellectual History* 1, no. 2 (2004): 249–65. doi:10.1017/S1479244304000149.

McAlindon, T. *Shakespeare and Decorum*. London: Macmillan, 1973.

McCabe, Richard. *The Pillars of Eternity: Time and Providence in* The Faerie Queene. Dublin: Irish Academic Press, 1989.

McCabe, Richard. 'Annotating Anonymity, or Putting a Gloss on *The Shepheardes Calender*.' In *Ma(r)king the Text: The Presentation of Meaning on the Literary Page*, ed. Joe Bray, Miriam Hadley, and Anne C. Henry (Aldershot: Ashgate, 2000), 35–54.

McCabe, Richard. 'Panegyric and its Discontents: The First Stuart Succession.' In *Stuart Succession Literature: Moments and Transformations*, ed. Paulina Kewes and Andrew McRae (Oxford: Oxford University Press, 2019), 19–36.

McClure, Norman Egbert. *The Letters of John Chamberlain*. Philadelphia: American Philosophical Society, 1939.

McCoy, Richard. *The Rites of Knighthood: The Literature and Politics of Elizabethan Chivalry*. Berkeley: University of California Press, 1989.

McCullough, Peter. *Sermons at Court: Politics and Religion in Elizabethan and Jacobean Preaching*. Cambridge: Cambridge University Press, 1998.

McKeon, Michael. *The Secret History of Domesticity: Public, Private, and the Division of Knowledge*. Baltimore: Johns Hopkins University Press, 2005.

McNamara, Gregory. '"A Perfect Diamond Set in Lead": Henry, Prince of Wales and the Performance of Emergent Majesty.' Diss., West Virginia University, 2000.

McNamara, Gregory. '"Grief was as clothes to their backs": Prince Henry's Funeral Viewed from the Wardrobe.' In *Prince Henry Revived: Image and Exemplarity in Early Modern England*, ed. Timothy Wilks (London: Paul Holberton, 2007), 259–79.

Melehy, Hassan. 'Antiquities of Britain: Spenser's *Ruines of Time*.' *Studies in Philology* 102, no. 2 (2005): 159–83. doi:10.1353/sip.2005.0009.

Milton, John. *Complete Poems and Major Prose*, ed. Merritt Y. Hughes. New York: Macmillan, 1957.

Milton, John. *The Complete Poetry and Essential Prose of John Milton*, ed. William Kerrigan, John Peter Rumrich, and Stephen M. Fallon. New York: Modern Library, 2007.

Milton, John. *Paradise Lost*, ed. Gordon Teskey. Norton Critical Editions. 2nd ed. New York: W. W. Norton, 2020.

Mitchell, J. Allan. *Ethics and Exemplary Narrative in Chaucer and Gower*. Cambridge: D. S. Brewer, 2004.

Montaigne, Michel de. *The Complete Essays of Montaigne*, tr. Donald A. Frame. Stanford: Stanford University Press, 1958.

Montaigne, Michel de. *The Complete Essays*, tr. M. A. Screech. London: Penguin, 1991.

Montrose, Louis A. '"Shaping Fantasies": Figurations of Gender and Power in Elizabethan Culture.' *Representations* 2 (1983): 61–94. doi:10.2307/2928384.

Montrose, Louis A. 'Renaissance Literary Studies and the Subject of History.' *English Literary Renaissance* 16, no. 1 (1986): 5–12. doi:10.1111/j.1475-6757.1986.tb00895.x.

Moore, Cornelia Niekus. *Patterned Lives: The Lutheran Funeral Biography in Early Modern Germany*. Wiesbaden: Harrassowitz, 2006.

Moore, Norman. *The History of the Study of Medicine in the British Isles*. Oxford: Clarendon Press, 1908.

More, George. *Principles for yong Princes: Collected out of sundry Authors*. 1611.

Mornay, Philippe de. *The Mysterie of Iniqvitie, That is to say, The Historie of the Papacie. Declaring by what degrees it is now mounted to this height, and what Oppositions the better sort from time to time haue made against it*, trans. Samson Lennard. 1612.

Muir, Edward. *Ritual in Early Modern Europe*. Cambridge: Cambridge University Press, 1997.

Munday, Anthony. *Londons Love, to the Royal Prince Henrie, Meeting him on the River of Thames, at his returne from Richmonde, with a worthie fleete of her Cittizens, on Thursday the last of May, 1610. With a briefe reporte of the water Fight, and Fire workes*. 1610.

Murray, Penelope, ed. *Classical Literary Criticism*. London: Penguin, 2000.

Nance, Brian. *Turquet de Mayerne as Baroque Physician: The Art of Medical Portraiture*. Amsterdam: Rodopi, 2001.

Nauert, Charles G. 'Humanism as Method: Roots of Conflict with the Scholastics.' *The Sixteenth Century Journal* 29 (1998): 427–38. doi:10.2307/2544524.

Neill, Michael. *Issues of Death: Mortality and Identity in English Renaissance Tragedy*. Oxford: Oxford University Press, 1997.

Nelson, William. *Fact or Fiction: The Dilemma of the Renaissance Storyteller*. Cambridge: Harvard University Press, 1973.

Nenna, Giovanni Battista. *Nennio, or A Treatise of Nobility: Wherein is discoursed what true Nobilitie is, with such qualities as are required in a perfect Gentleman*, trans. William Jones. 1595.

Newman, Karen. 'Renaissance Family Politics and Shakespeare's *The Taming of the Shrew*.' *English Literary Renaissance* 16, no. 1 (1986): 86–100. doi:10.1111/j.1475–6757.1986. tb00899.x.

Newstok, Scott L. *Quoting Death in Early Modern England*. New York: Palgrave Macmillan, 2009.

Niccols, Richard. *The Three Sisters Teares. Shed at the late solemne Funerals of the Royall deceased Henry, Prince of Wales, &c.* 1613.

Nichols, John. *The Progresses, Processions, and Magnificent Festivities of King James the First, his Royal Consort, Family, and Court*. London: J. B. Nichols, 1828.

Nichols, Stephen. 'Example Versus Historia: Montaigne, Eriugena, and Dante.' In *Unruly Examples: On the Rhetoric of Exemplarity*, ed. Alexander Gelley (Stanford: Stanford University Press, 1995), 48–85.

Nicholson, R. H. 'State of the Nation: Some Complaint Topics in Late Medieval English Literature.' *Parergon* 23 (1979): 9–28.

O'Callaghan, Michelle. '*Coryats Crudities* (1611) and Travel Writing as the "Eyes" of the Prince.' In *Prince Henry Revived: Image and Exemplarity in Early Modern England*, ed. Timothy Wilks (London: Paul Holberton, 2007), 85–103.

O'Connell, Michael. *Mirror and Veil: The Historical Dimensions of Spenser's* Faerie Queene. Chapel Hill: University of North Carolina Press, 1977.

Ong, Walter J. *Rhetoric, Romance, and Technology: Studies in the Interaction of Expression and Culture*. Ithaca: Cornell University Press, 1971.

Oram, William A. 'Spenser in Search of an Audience: The Kathleen Williams Lecture for 2004.' *Spenser Studies* 20 (2005): 23–47. doi:10.1086/SPSv20p23.

Osborne, Francis. *Historical Memoires on the Reigns of Queen Elizabeth, and King James*. 1658.

Owley, Steven A. 'The Voice of Complaint: A Study in Political and Moral Rhetoric.' Diss., Ohio State University, 1999.

Palmer, Thomas. *An Essay of the Meanes hovv to make our Trauailes, into forraine Countries, the more profitable and honourable*. 1606.

Parry, Graham. *The Golden Age Restor'd: The Culture of the Stuart Court, 1603–42*. Manchester: Manchester University Press, 1981.

Parsons, Leila. 'Prince Henry (1594–1612) as a Patron of Literature.' *Modern Language Review* 47 (1952): 503–7. doi:10.2307/3719700.

Patterson, Annabel. *Reading Holinshed's Chronicles*. Chicago: University of Chicago Press, 1994.

Patterson, Annabel. *Censorship and Interpretation: The Conditions of Writing and Reading in Early Modern England*. Madison: University of Wisconsin Press, 1984.

Patterson, Annabel. 'Foul, his Wife, the Mayor, and Foul's Mare: The Power of Anecdote in Tudor Historiography.' In *The Historical Imagination in Early Modern Britain: History, Rhetoric, and Fiction, 1500–1800*, ed. Donald R. Kelley and David Harris Sacks (Cambridge: Cambridge University Press, 1997), 159–78.

Peacham, Henry. *The Garden of Eloqvence*. 1593.

Peacham, Henry. *The Period of Mourning. Disposed into six Visions. In Memorie of the late Prince. Together With Nuptiall Hymnes, in Honour of this Happy Marriage betweene the*

Great Princes, Frederick Count Palatine of the Rhene, and The Most Excellent, and Aboundant President of all Virtve and Goodnes Elizabeth onely Daughter to our Soueraigne, his Maiestie. Also the manner of the Solemnization of the Marriage at White-Hall, on the 14. of February, being Sunday, and St. Valentines day. 1613.

Peacham, Henry. Prince Henrie revived. or A Poeme vpon the Birth, and In Honor of the Hopefull yong Prince Henrie Frederick, First Sonne and Heire apparant to the most Excellent Princes, Frederick Count Palatine of the Rhine, And the Mirrour of Ladies, Princesse Elizabeth, his Wife, only daughter to our Soueraigne Iames King of Great Brittaine, &c. 1615.

Peacham, Henry, and Walter Dight. Minerva Britanna or a Garden of Heroical Deuises, furnished, and adorned with Emblemes and Impresa's of sundry natures. 1612.

Peele, George. An Eglogve Gratvlatorie. Entituled: To the right honorable, and renowmed Shepheard of Albions Arcadia: Robert Earle of Essex and Ewe, for his vvelcome into England from Portugall. 1589.

Peele, George. Polyhymnia Describing, the honourable Triumph at Tylt, before her Maiestie, on the 17. of Nouember, last past, being the first day of the three and thirtith yeare of her Highnesse raigne. 1590.

Perrinchief, Richard. The Royal Martyr, or, the History of the Life and Death of King Charles I. 1676.

Peter, John. Complaint and Satire in Early English Literature. Oxford: Clarendon Press, 1956.

Petrarch, Francesco. Sonnets, tr. R. M. Durling. Cambridge: Harvard University Press, 1976.

Pett, Phineas, and William Gordon Perrin. The Autobiography of Phineas Pett. London: Navy Records Society, 1918.

Phillip, John. The Life and Death of Sir Phillip Sidney, late Lord gouernour of Flushing: His funerals Solemnized in Paules Churche where he lyeth interred; with the whole order of the mournfull shewe, as they marched thorowe the citie of London, on Thursday the 16 of February, 1587. 1587.

Piccolomini, Aeneas Silvius. The Education of Boys, ed. Craig W. Kallendorf. In Humanist Educational Treatises (Cambridge: Harvard University Press, 2002), 126–259.

Pieters, Jürgen. Moments of Negotiation: The New Historicism of Stephen Greenblatt. Amsterdam: Amsterdam University Press, 2001.

Pigman, G. W. Grief and English Renaissance Elegy. Cambridge: Cambridge University Press, 1985.

Pitcher, John. Samuel Daniel: The Brotherton Manuscript: A Study in Authorship. Leeds: University of Leeds School of English, 1981.

Plato. Gorgias, tr. W. C. Helmbold. Indianapolis: Library of Liberal Arts, 1952.

Plutarch. The Age of Alexander, tr. Ian Scott-Kilvert. London: Penguin, 1973.

Pollnitz, Aysha. Princely Education in Early Modern Britain. Cambridge and New York: Cambridge University Press, 2015.

Porter, Roy. The Greatest Benefit to Mankind: A Medical History of Humanity. New York: W. W. Norton, 1997.

Prendergast, Thomas A. 'Spenser's Phantastic History, The Ruines of Time, and the Invention of Medievalism.' Journal of Medieval and Early Modern Studies 38 (2008): 175–96. doi:10.1215/10829636-2007-023.

Price, Daniel. Recvsants Conversion: A Sermon Preached at St. James, Before the Prince on the 25. Of Februarie. 1608. By Daniell Price Master of Arts, of Exeter Colledge in Oxford. 1608.

Price, Daniel. *The Creation of the Prince. A Sermon Preached in the Colledge of VVestminster, on Trinity Sunday, the day before the Creation of the most Illustrious Prince of Wales.* 1610.

Price, Daniel. *David his Oath of Allegeance to Iervsalem. The sermon preached on Act Sunday last in the morning, in St. Maries in Oxford. By Daniel Price Doctor in Divinity.* 1613.

Price, Daniel. *Lamentations for the death of the late Illustrious Prince Henry: and the dissolution of his religious Familie. Two Sermons: Preached in his Highnesse Chappell at Saint Iames, on the 10. and 15. day of Nouember, being the first Tuesday and Sunday after his decease.* 1613.

Price, Daniel. *Spiritvall Odovrs to the Memory of Prince Henry in fovre of the last sermons preached in St. Iames after his Highnesse death, the last being the Sermon before the bodie, the day before the Funerall. By Daniel Price then Chaplaine in Attendance.* 1613.

Price, Daniel. *Prince Henry his Second Anniversary.* 1614.

Pritchard, Allan. *English Biography in the Seventeenth Century: A Critical Survey.* Toronto: University of Toronto Press, 2005.

Procopius. *The Anecdota or Secret History*, tr. H. B. Dewing. Cambridge: Harvard University Press, 1935.

Puttenham, George. *The Arte of English Poesie. Contriued into Three Bookes: The First of Poets and Poesie, the Second of Proportion, the Third of Ornament.* 1589.

Puttenham, George. *The Art of English Poesy.* ed. Frank Whigham and Wayne A. Rebhorn. Ithaca: Cornell University Press, 2007.

Quilligan, Maureen. *Milton's Spenser: The Politics of Reading.* Ithaca: Cornell University Press, 1983.

Quintilian. *Institutio Oratoria*, tr. Harold Edgeworth Butler. Cambridge: Harvard University Press, 1969.

Rainolde, Richard. *A Book Called the Foundacion of Rhetorike.* 1563.

Rainolds, John, Lancelot Andrewes, Edward Lively, John Harding, Miles Smith, Thomas Bilson, Cornelius Bol, John. More, John Speed, and Francis Fry. *The Holy Bible, Conteyning the Old Testament, and the New: Newly Translated out of the Originall Tongues: & with the former Translations diligently compared and reuised, by his Majesties speciall Co[m]mandement. Appointed to be Read in Churches.* 1611.

Rambuss, Richard. *Spenser's Secret Career.* Cambridge and New York: Cambridge University Press, 1993.

Ramsay, Stephen. *Reading Machines: Toward an Algorithmic Criticism.* Urbana: University of Illinois Press, 2011.

Rankin, Mark. 'Henry VIII, Shakespeare, and the Jacobean Royal Court.' *Studies in English Literature* 51, no. 2 (2011): 349–66. doi:10.1353/sel.2011.0018.

Rasmussen, Carl J. ' "How Weak Be the Passions of Woefulness": Spenser's *Ruines of Time*.' *Spenser Studies* 2 (1981): 159–81. doi:10.1086/SPSv2p159.

Rebhorn, Wayne A. 'Outlandish Fears: Defining Decorum in Renaissance Rhetoric.' *Intertexts* 4, no. 1 (2000): 3–24.

Riche, Barnabe. *The Frvites of long Experience. A pleasing view for Peace. A Looking-Glasse for Warre. Or, Call it what you list.* 1604.

Rickard, Jane. *Authorship and Authority: The Writings of James VI and I.* Manchester: Manchester University Press, 2007.

Ricoeur, Paul. *Memory, History, Forgetting*, tr. Kathleen Blamey and David Pellauer. Chicago: University of Chicago Press, 2004.

Rigolot, Francois. 'The Renaissance Crisis of Exemplarity.' *Journal of the History of Ideas* 59, no. 4 (1998): 557–63. doi:10.1353/jhi.1998.0042.

Rigolot, Francois. 'Problematizing Renaissance Exemplarity: The Inward Turn of Dialogue from Petrarch to Montaigne.' In *Printed Voices: The Renaissance Culture of Dialogue*, ed. Dorothea Heitsch (Toronto: University of Toronto Press, 2004), 3–24.

Roberts, Henry. *A Defiance to Fortune.* 1590.

Roche, Thomas P. *The Kindly Flame: A Study of the Third and Fourth Books of Spenser's Faerie Queene.* Princeton: Princeton University Press, 1964.

Rodney, Joel Morris. 'Henry Frederick, Prince of Wales, and his Circle.' Diss., Cornell University, 1965.

Rogers, Thomas. *Anglorum Lacrimae: In a sad passion complayning the death of our late Soueraigne Lady Queene Elizabeth: Yet comforted againe by the vertuous hopes of our most Royall and Renowned King Iames: whose Maiestie God long continue.* 1603.

Rosenfeld, Colleen Ruth. *Indecorous Thinking: Figures of Speech in Early Modern Poetics.* New York: Fordham University Press, 2018.

Rundle, David. '"Not so much praise as precept": Erasmus, Panegyric, and the Renaissance Art of Teaching Princes.' In *Pedagogy and Power: Rhetorics of Classical Learning*, ed. Yun Lee Too and Niall Livingstone (Cambridge and New York: Cambridge University Press, 1998): 148–169.

Runia, Eelco. 'Burying the Dead, Creating the Past.' *History and Theory: Studies in the Philosophy of History* 46 (2007): 313–25. doi:10.1111/j.1468–2303.2007.00412.x.

Runia, Eelco. *Moved by the Past: Discontinuity and Historical Mutation.* New York: Columbia University Press, 2014.

Russell, Daniel C. *Practical Intelligence and the Virtues.* Oxford and New York: Oxford University Press, 2009.

Saenger, Michael. *The Commodification of Textual Engagements in the English Renaissance.* Aldershot: Ashgate, 2006.

Salmon, J. H. M. 'Stoicism and Roman Example: Seneca and Tacitus in Jacobean England.' *Journal of the History of Ideas* 50 (1989): 199–222. doi:10.2307/2709732.

Sanok, Catherine. *Her Life Historical: Exemplarity and Female Saints' Lives in Late Medieval England.* Philadelphia: University of Pennsylvania Press, 2007.

Scanlon, Larry. *Narrative, Authority, and Power: The Medieval Exemplum and the Chaucerian Tradition.* Cambridge: Cambridge University Press, 1994.

Scott-Warren, Jason. *Sir John Harington and the Book as Gift.* Oxford: Oxford University Press, 2001.

Scott, Walter. *Secret History of the Court of James the First.* Edinburgh: James Ballantyne, 1811.

Seigel, Jerrold E. *Rhetoric and Philosophy in Renaissance Humanism: The Union of Eloquence and Wisdom, Petrarch to Valla.* Princeton: Princeton University Press, 1968.

Serjeantson, Richard. 'Testimony: The Artless Proof.' In *Renaissance Figures of Speech*, ed. Sylvia Adamson, Gavin Alexander, and Katrin Ettenhuber (Cambridge: Cambridge University Press, 2007), 181–94.

Sessions, William A. *Henry Howard, the Poet Earl of Surrey: A Life.* Oxford and New York: Oxford University Press, 1999.

Shakespeare, William. *The Plays of William Shakespeare: in Ten Volumes*, ed. Samuel Johnson and George Steevens. 1773.

Shakespeare, William. *A Midsummer Night's Dream*, ed. Peter Holland. The Oxford Shakespeare. Oxford: Oxford University Press, 1994.

Shakespeare, William. *King Henry V*, ed. T. W. Craik. The Arden Shakespeare, 3rd Series. London: Routledge, 1995.

Shakespeare, William. *Shakespeare's Sonnets*, ed. Katherine Duncan-Jones. The Arden Shakespeare, 3rd Series. Walton-on-Thames: Thomas Nelson, 1997.

Shakespeare, William. *The Arden Shakespeare Complete Works*, ed. Richard Proudfoot, Ann Thompson, and David Scott Kastan. Walton-on-Thames: Nelson, 1998.

Shakespeare, William. *The Complete Sonnets and Poems*, ed. Colin Burrow. The Oxford Shakespeare. Oxford: Oxford University Press, 2002.

Shakespeare, William. *The Sonnets and A Lover's Complaint*, ed. John Kerrigan. London: Penguin, 2005.

Shakespeare, William. *As You Like It*, ed. Juliet Dusinberre. The Arden Shakespeare, 3rd Series. London: Thomson Learning, 2006.

Shakespeare, William. *Hamlet*, ed. Neil Taylor and Ann Thompson. The Arden Shakespeare, 3rd Series. London: Bloomsbury, 2006.

Shakespeare, William. *A Midsummer Night's Dream*, ed. Stephen Greenblatt. The Norton Shakespeare. New York: W. W. Norton, 2008.

Sharpe, Kevin, and Steven N. Zwicker, eds. *Writing Lives: Biography and Textuality, Identity and Representation in Early Modern England*. Oxford: Oxford University Press, 2008.

Shaw, David. *Elegy and Silence: The Romantic Legacy*. Lethbridge: University of Lethbridge Press, 1992.

Sherlock, Peter. *Monuments and Memory in Early Modern England*. Aldershot: Ashgate, 2008.

Sherman, Anita Gilman. *Skepticism and Memory in Shakespeare and Donne*. New York: Palgrave Macmillan, 2007.

Sidney, Philip. *The Covntesse of Pembrokes Arcadia*. 1593.

Sidney, Philip. *The Poems of Sir Philip Sidney*, ed. William A. Ringler. Oxford: Clarendon Press, 1962.

Sidney, Philip. *A Defense of Poetry*, ed. Katherine Duncan-Jones and Jan van Dorsten. *Miscellaneous Prose of Sir Philip Sidney* (Oxford: Clarendon Press, 1973), 73–121.

Sidney, Philip. *A Defence of Poetry* (1595), ed. Brian Vickers. *English Renaissance Literary Criticism* (Oxford: Clarendon Press, 1999), 336–91.

Sidney, Philip. *An Apology for Poetry or The Defence of Poesy*, ed. Geoffrey Shepherd and R. W. Maslen. Manchester and New York: Manchester University Press, 2002.

Sidney, Philip. *The Defense of Poesy*, ed. Gavin Alexander. *Sidney's 'The Defence of Poesy' and Selected Renaissance Literary Criticism*. London: Penguin, 2004.

Silius Italicus, Tiberius Catius. *Punica*. Cambridge: Harvard University Press, 1934.

Silver, George. *Paradoxes of Defence*. 1599.

Smith, G. Gregory, ed. *Elizabethan Critical Essays*. Oxford: Clarendon Press, 1904.

Smith, Sarah. 'An Unyielding Past: Holy Wells and Historical Narrative in *The Faerie Queene 1–2*.' *Studies in Philology* 118, no. 2 (2021): 284–307. doi:10.1353/sip.2021.0010.

Smuts, R. Malcolm. 'Public Ceremony and Royal Charisma: The English Royal Entry in London, 1485–1642.' In *The First Modern Society: Essays in English History in Honour of Lawrence Stone*, ed. A. L. Beier, David Cannadine, and James M. Rosenheim. (Cambridge: Cambridge University Press, 1989), 65–93.

Smyth, Adam. *Autobiography in Early Modern England*. Cambridge: Cambridge University Press, 2010.

Snare, Gerald. 'The Muses on Poetry: Spenser's *The Teares of the Muses*.' *Tulane University Studies in English* 17 (1969): 31–52.

Sodeman, Melissa. 'Gilbert White, Anecdote, and Natural History.' *Studies in English Literature* 60, no. 3 (2020): 507–28. doi:10.1353/sel.2020.0021.

Soellner, Rolf. 'Chapman's Caesar and Pompey and the Fortunes of Prince Henry.' *Medieval and Renaissance Drama in England* 2 (1985): 135–51.

Spenser, Edmund. *The Yale Edition of the Shorter Poems of Edmund Spenser,* ed. William A. Oram et al. New Haven: Yale University Press, 1989.

Spenser, Edmund. *The Shorter Poems,* ed. Richard McCabe. London: Penguin, 1999.

Spenser, Edmund. *The Faerie Queene,* ed. A. C. Hamilton, Hiroshi Yamashita, and Toshiyuki Suzuki. 2nd edn. London: Pearson Education, 2001.

Staines, John D. 'Elizabeth, Mercilla, and the Rhetoric of Propaganda in Spenser's *Faerie Queene.' Journal of Medieval and Early Modern Studies* 31, no. 2 (2001): 283–312. doi:10.1215/10829636-31-2-283.

Stewart, Alan. *Close Readers: Humanism and Sodomy in Early Modern England.* Princeton: Princeton University Press, 1997.

Stewart, Alan. *Philip Sidney: A Double Life.* London: Pimlico, 2001.

Stewart, Alan. *The Cradle King: The Life of James VI & I, the First Monarch of a United Great Britain.* New York: St Martin's Press, 2003.

Stierle, Karlheinz. 'Story as Exemplum–Exemplum as Story: On the Pragmatics and Poetics of Narrative Texts.' In *New Perspectives in German Literary Criticism,* ed. Richard E. Amacher and Victor Lange (Princeton: Princeton University Press, 1979), 389–417.

Streete, Adrian. 'Elegy, Prophecy, and Politics: Literary Responses to the Death of Prince Henry Stuart, 1612–1614.' *Renaissance Studies* 31, no. 1 (2015): 87–106. doi:10.1111/rest.12197.

Strong, Roy. *The Cult of Elizabeth: Elizabethan Portraiture and Pageantry.* Berkeley and Los Angeles: University of California Press, 1977.

Strong, Roy. *Henry, Prince of Wales, and England's Lost Renaissance.* London: Pimlico, 1986.

Stuart, Henry, Prince of Wales. '*Oratio serenissimi principis ad regem.*' 1 January 1609.

Sugano, Marian Zwerling. *The Poetics of the Occasion: Mallarmé and the Poetry of Circumstance.* Stanford: Stanford University Press, 1992.

Summit, Jennifer. *Memory's Library: Medieval Books in Early Modern England.* Chicago: University of Chicago Press, 2008.

Sutcliffe, Matthew. *The Practice, Proceedings, and Lawes of armes, described out of the doings of most valiant and expert Captaines, and confirmed both by ancient, and moderne examples, and præcedents.* 1593.

Sutcliffe, Matthew. *An Abridgement or Svrvey of Poperie.* 1606.

Sylvester, Joshua. *Lachrimæ Lachrimarvm. or The Distillation of Teares Shede For the vntymely Death of The incomparable Prince Panaretvs.* 1612.

Tacitus, Cornelius. *The Annales of Cornelivs Tacitvs. The Description of Germanie,* tr. Richard Grenewey. 1598.

Taylor, Augustine. *Encomiasticke Elogies.* 1614.

Tennenhouse, Leonard. 'Sir Walter Ralegh and the Literature of Clientage.' In *Patronage in the Renaissance,* ed. Guy Fitch-Lytle and Stephen Orgel (Princeton: Princeton University Press, 1981), 235–60.

Tenney, Mary F. 'Tacitus in the Politics of Early Stuart England.' *Classical Journal* 37 (1941): 151–63.

Thomas, Keith. *The Ends of Life: Roads to Fulfilment in Early Modern England.* Oxford: Oxford University Press, 2009.

Thomas, Keith. 'Diary.' *London Review of Books* 32, no. 11 (10 June 2010): 36–7.

Thomas, Thomas. *Dictionarivm Lingvae Latinae et Anglicanae. In hoc opere quid sit praestitum, & ad superiores lexikographos adiectum, docebit epistola ad Lectorem.* 1587.

Tipton, Alzada. '"Lively Patterns . . . for Affayers of State": Sir John Hayward's *The Life and Reign of King Henrie IIII* and the Earl of Essex.' *Sixteenth Century Journal* 33 (2002): 769–94. doi:10.2307/4144023.

Tipton, Alzada. 'The Transformation of the Earl of Essex: Post-Execution Ballads and "The Phoenix and the Turtle".' *Studies in Philology* 99, no. 1 (2002): 57–80.

Tourneur, Cyril. *A Griefe on the Death of Prince Henrie, Expressed in a broken Elegie, according to the nature of such a sorrow.* 1613.

Trevor-Roper, Hugh. *Europe's Physician: The Various Life of Sir Theodore de Mayerne.* New Haven: Yale University Press, 2006.

Tuve, Rosemond. *Elizabethan and Metaphysical Imagery: Renaissance Poetic and Twentieth-Century Critics.* Chicago: University of Chicago Press, 1947.

Tylus, Jane. *Writing and Vulnerability in the Late Renaissance.* Stanford: Stanford University Press, 1993.

Ullman, B. L. *The Humanism of Coluccio Salutati.* Padua: Antenore, 1963.

Ullyot, Michael. 'The Fall of Troynovant: Exemplarity After the Death of Henry, Prince of Wales.' In *Fantasies of Troy: Classical Tales and the Social Imaginary in Medieval and Early Modern Europe*, ed. Stephen Powell and Alan Shepard (Toronto: Centre for Reformation and Renaissance Studies, 2004), 269–90.

Ullyot, Michael. 'James's Reception and Henry's Receptivity: Reading *Basilicon Doron* after 1603.' In *Prince Henry Revived: Image and Exemplarity in Early Modern England*, ed. Timothy V. Wilks (London: Paul Holberton, 2007): 65–84.

Ullyot, Michael. 'The Rhetoric of Anecdotes in New Historicism.' *Clio: A Journal of Literature, History, and the Philosophy of History* 40, no. 3 (2011): 307–29.

Ullyot, Michael. 'Spenser and the Matter of Poetry.' *Spenser Studies* 27 (2012): 77–96. doi:10.7756/spst.027.004.77-96.

Ullyot, Michael. 'Augmented Criticism, Extensible Archives, and the Progress of Renaissance Studies.' *Renaissance and Reformation/Renaissance et Réforme* 37, no. 4 (2014): 179–93. doi:10.33137/rr.v37i4.22646.

Ullyot, Michael, and Adam J. Bradley. 'Past Texts, Present Tools, and Future Critics: Toward Rhetorical Schematics.' In *Shakespeare's Language in Digital Media: Old Words, New Tools*, ed. Janelle Jenstad and Jennifer Roberts-Smith with Mark Kaethler (Abingdon: Routledge, 2017), 144–56.

Ullyot, Michael, and Adam J. Bradley. 'Machines and Humans, Schemes and Tropes.' *Early Modern Literary Studies* 20, no. 2 (2018): n.p.

Valerius Maximus. *Memorable Deeds and Sayings*, tr. David Wardle. Oxford: Clarendon Press, 1998.

van Es, Bart. *Spenser's Forms of History.* Oxford and New York: Oxford University Press, 2002.

Veeser, H. Aram. 'Introduction.' In *The New Historicism Reader*, ed. H. Aram Veeser (New York: Routledge, 1994), ix–xvi.

Vergerio, Pier Paolo. *The Character and Studies Befitting a Free-Born Youth*, ed. Craig W. Kallendorf. In *Humanist Educational Treatises* (Cambridge: Harvard University Press, 2002), 1–45.

Vickers, Brian. *Francis Bacon and Renaissance Prose.* Cambridge: Cambridge University Press, 1968.

Vickers, Brian. '"The Power of Persuasion": Images of the Orator, Elyot to Shakespeare.' In *Renaissance Eloquence: Studies in the Theory and Practice of Renaissance Rhetoric*, ed. James J. Murphy (Berkeley: University of California Press, 1983), 411–35.

Vickers, Brian. *In Defence of Rhetoric.* Oxford: Clarendon Press, 1988.

Virgil. *The Aeneid*, tr. Robert Fagles. New York: Viking, 2006.

Wake, Isaac. National Archives, State Papers 14/71/68, 1612.

Wallace, Andrew. 'Reading the 1590 *Faerie Queene* with Thomas Nashe.' *Studies in the Literary Imagination* 38, no. 2 (2005): 35–49.

Wayland, Scott. 'Religious Change and the Renaissance Elegy.' *English Literary Renaissance* 39, no. 3 (2009): 429–59. doi:10.1111/j.1475–6757.2009.01053.x.

Webster, John. *A Monvmental Colvmne, Erected to the liuing Memory of the euer-glorious Henry, late Prince of Wales.* 1613.

Weever, John. *Ancient Fvnerall Monvments with in the vnited Monarchie of Great Britaine, Ireland, and the Ilands adiacent; with the dissolued Monasteries therein contained; their Founders, and what eminent persons haue beene in the same interred.* 1631.

Werner, Hans. 'The Hector of Germanie, or The Palsgrave, Prime Elector and Anglo-German Relations of Early Stuart England: The View from the Popular Stage.' In *The Stuart Court and Europe: Essays in Politics and Political Culture*, ed. R. Malcolm Smuts (Cambridge: Cambridge University Press, 1996), 113–32.

Wheatley, Chloe. 'Abridging the Antiquitee of Faery Lond: New Paths through Old Matter in *The Faerie Queene.*' *Renaissance Quarterly* 58, no. 3 (Fall 2005): 857–80. doi:10.1353/ren.2008.0881.

Wheatley, Chloe. *Epic, Epitome, and the Early Modern Historical Imagination.* Farnham: Ashgate, 2011.

White, Hayden. 'The Historical Text as Literary Artifact.' *Clio* 3, no. 3 (1974): 277–303.

White, Hayden. *The Content of the Form: Narrative Discourse and Historical Representation.* Baltimore: Johns Hopkins University Press, 1987.

Whitfield, John Humphreys. *Machiavelli.* Oxford: Blackwell, 1947.

Whiting, Mary Bradford. 'Henry, Prince of Wales: "A Scarce Blown Rose".' *Contemporary Review* 137 (1930): 492–500.

Whitney, Isabella, Mary Sidney, and Aemilia Lanyer. *Renaissance Women Poets*, ed. Danielle Clarke. London: Penguin, 2000.

Wilkes, G. A. '"Left … to play the ill poet in my own part": The Literary Relationship of Sidney and Fulke Greville.' *The Review of English Studies* 57, no. 230 (2006): 291-309.

Wilkinson, Robert. *A Paire of Sermons svccessiuely preacht to a paire of Peereles and succeeding Princes. The former as an ante-fvnerall to the late Prince Henry, Anno Dom. 1612. October 25. The first day of his last and fatall sicknesse. The latter preacht this present yeere 1614. Ianuar. 16. To the now liuing Prince Charles, as a preseruer of his life, and life to his Soule.* 1614.

Wilks, Timothy. 'The Court Culture of Prince Henry and his Circle 1603–1613.' Diss., University of Oxford, 1987.

Wilks, Timothy, ed. *Prince Henry Revived: Image and Exemplarity in Early Modern England.* London: Paul Holberton, 2007.

Wilks, Timothy. 'The Pike Charged: Henry as Militant Prince.' In *Prince Henry Revived: Image and Exemplarity in Early Modern England*, ed. Timothy Wilks (London: Paul Holberton, 2007), 180–211.

Willet, Andrew. *An Harmonie vpon the First Booke of Samvel.* 1607.

Williams, Ethel. *Anne of Denmark: Wife of James VI of Scotland, James I of England.* London: Longman, 1970.

Williams, Franklin Burleigh. *Index of Dedications and Commendatory Verses in English Books Before 1641.* London: Bibliographical Society, 1962.

Williamson, J. W. *The Myth of the Conqueror: Prince Henry Stuart, a Study in Seventeenth Century Personation.* New York: AMS Press, 1978.

Willymat, William. *A Princes Looking Glasse, or a Princes Direction, very requisite and necessarie for a Christian Prince, to view and behold himselfe in, containing sundrie, wise, learned, godly, and Princely precepts and instructions, excerpted and chosen out of that most Christian, and vertuous ΒΑΣΙΛΙΚΟΝ ΔΩΡΟΝ, or his Maiesties instructions to his dearest sonne Henrie the Prince, and translated into Latin and English Verse (his Maiesties consent and approbation beeing first had and obtained thereunto) for the more delight and pleasure of the said Prince now in his young yeares.* 1603.

Wilson, Elkin Calhoun. *Prince Henry and English Literature.* Ithaca: Cornell University Press, 1946.

Wilson, Thomas. *The Rule of Reason, Conteinyng the Arte of Logique, Set Forth in Englishe.* 1551.

Wilson, Thomas. *An English Rhetoric (1560),* ed. Brian Vickers. *English Renaissance Literary Criticism* (Oxford: Clarendon Press, 1999), 73–124.

Windhauser, Kevin. '"This steady counsel": Fulke Greville's Transformation of Sidney in *A Dedication.*' *Studies in Philology* 118, no. 1 (2021): 97–119. doi:10.1353/sip.2021.0004.

Wither, George. *Prince Henries Obseqvies or Movrnefvll Elegies vpon his Death.* 1612.

Witmore, Michael and Jonathan Hope. '"Après le déluge, More Criticism": Philology, Literary History, and Ancestral Reading in the Coming Posttranscription World.' *Renaissance Drama* 40 (2012): 135–150. doi:10.1353/rnd.2012.0009.

Woodcock, Matthew. '"The Breviarie of Soldiers": Julius Caesar's Commentaries and the Fashioning of Early Modern Military Identity.' In *Early Modern Military Identities, 1560–1639: Reality and Representation,* ed. Matthew Woodcock and Cian O'Mahony (Woodbridge: Boydell & Brewer, 2019), 56–78.

Woodward, Jennifer. *The Theatre of Death: The Ritual Management of Royal Funerals in Renaissance England, 1570–1625.* Woodbridge: Boydell Press, 1997.

Woolf, Daniel R. 'Genre into Artifact: The Decline of the English Chronicle in the Sixteenth Century.' *Sixteenth Century Journal* 19 (1988): 321–54. doi:10.2307/2540467.

Woolf, Daniel R. *The Social Circulation of the Past: English Historical Culture 1500–1730.* Oxford: Oxford University Press, 2003.

Worden, Blair. *The Sound of Virtue: Philip Sidney's Arcadia and Elizabethan Politics.* New Haven: Yale University Press, 1996.

Wormald, Jenny. 'James VI and I, *Basilikon Doron* and *The Trew Law of Free Monarchies*: The Scottish Context and the English Translation.' In *The Mental World of the Jacobean Court,* ed. Linda Levy Peck (Cambridge: Cambridge University Press, 2005), 36–54.

Zurcher, Amelia. 'Untimely Monuments: Stoicism, History, and the Problem of Utility in *The Winter's Tale* and *Pericles.*' *English Literary History* 70 (2003): 903–27. doi:10.1353/elh.2004.0011.

Index